Irreconcilable
Differences

Irreconcilable Differences

Ross Perot versus General Motors

By Doron P. Levin

LITTLE, BROWN AND COMPANY   BOSTON/TORONTO/LONDON

FIRST EDITION

LIBRARY OF CONGRESS CATALOG CARD NUMBER 89-30354

10 9 8 7 6 5 4 3 2 1

DESIGNED BY JEANNE ABBOUD

MV PA

*Published simultaneously in Canada
by Little, Brown & Company (Canada) Limited*

PRINTED IN THE UNITED STATES OF AMERICA

This book is dedicated to my parents,

Ruth and Basil Levin

Contents

Acknowledgments

Many people generously contributed their time and effort as sources of information so that this book could be written. I would like to acknowledge all by name, but rather than name some and not others, I've chosen to thank everyone, including assistants and clerical helpers, collectively: I owe you all a great deal and I'm forever in your debt. Whatever good comes from this book is due largely to you. I, of course, accept responsibility for any errors.

I must, however, formally thank Roger Donald, Jennifer Josephy, Kristen Hatch, and Peggy Freudenthal of Little, Brown and Company for their unfailing assistance, editorial guidance, and doses of good cheer.

My literary agent, Jane Gelfman, was always available to lend steadfast support and to offer expert advice. She also is a fine friend. I'm lucky to be associated with her.

Because I mostly wrote this book at home, my family had to contend with a great deal of inconvenience and turmoil. Nevertheless, my parents, children, and sisters were always a source of inspiration and encouragement. I truly couldn't have persevered without them.

Finally, I have to say that this book belongs as much to my wife as it does to me. I wouldn't have attempted it — and couldn't have finished it — without her unflagging belief that it was the right thing to do. Thank you, Adina.

Author's Note

This book is an outgrowth of my reporting and writing on the automobile industry and Electronic Data Systems Corporation for the *Wall Street Journal* during the period September 1984–June 1987.

The American industry must upgrade its automation in order to compete in world markets, but ten thousand new robots will not save Detroit. Nor will more computers and laser beams, nor Japanese-style "just-in-time" inventory control. Massive wage concessions by the labor unions are not the key to salvation. Neither is the answer more modern American factories, which are already collectively equal to any in the world. The industry will not be saved by front-wheel drive, a fresh generation of small cars, or imaginative advertising and marketing campaigns. While all this can contribute to greater industrial health, there is but one true lever to prosperity for Detroit and America: new corporate leaders of sophistication and strength.

> —Brock Yates
> *The Decline and Fall of the American Automobile Industry*

PART I

Ross Perot's World

ONE

An Offer to Buy

O N the morning of April 2, 1984, Ross Perot turned left off the broad avenue and steered his car through the opening in the high steel fence at 7171 Forest Lane. A fine morning dew kissed the vast green expanse surrounding the headquarters of Electronic Data Systems Corporation.

It was a crisp spring day in Texas. Dallas was awake, traffic streaming along the broad cement expressways. The gleaming modern glass office towers, filling rapidly with the city's work force, broadcast the morning light in every direction.

The uniformed guard, a polished chrome .38 Smith and Wesson revolver resting on his hip, straightened, recognizing Perot's gray Oldsmobile. Perot smiled and waved, acknowledging one of the 13,000 employees in his company.

Perot accelerated his car down the long, curving service drive through what had once been a north Dallas golf club. A row of flagpoles along the drive lent a governmental air to the property, an impression enhanced by the architecture of the building itself: a tall, sleek modern box, set in the middle of a big enough expanse of manicured lawn to suggest great importance, a department of state or an intelligence agency.

Perot's parking spot next to the loading dock at EDS headquarters building was unmarked. It wasn't necessary; everyone at EDS knew it belonged to the chairman. He entered the back door, near the mailroom, rode the elevator to the seventh floor, and marched through the double glass doors of his two-room office suite.

The decor of Perot's office described the man: a lover of family, country, history — and EDS. A copy of Frederic Remington's *Bronco Buster* sat on a credenza carved in early American style, *The Spirit of '76*, Archibald M. Willard's original oil painting of the Yankee Doodle dandies, hung behind his desk. There were paintings by Norman Rockwell: a marine returning home with a Japanese flag, and *Breaking Home Ties*, a young man bound for college, his dog's head buried in his lap. A framed canceled $1,000 check, initial capitalization for EDS in 1962, was displayed near his desk.

Abundant photographs of his wife, Margot, son, and four daughters adorned his office. In one, Ross junior, dressed in a flight suit, shook his father's hand before circling the globe in a record-setting helicopter flight.

One didn't have to probe to discover what Perot believed in. He had absorbed the basic values of duty, honor, country many years ago, as a Boy Scout and from his parents. As a boy he had delivered papers, earned merit badges, and minded his parents. He came from a warm, happy, God-fearing family in Texarkana, Texas, attended Bible class every week at the Methodist church, won Eagle Scout in record time, and went to sea for his country.

Perot was sentimental. He wanted to preserve the notions of good from his past. His ideas of virtue and morality were under siege, and he was defending them. The paintings and sculptures were a reminder; so was his unfashionably short haircut.

Prosperity had brought him a more precious asset: the power of influence and the opportunity to change events. He didn't enjoy politics, but he knew how to make his presence felt. Of late, his musings on modern problems had narrowed to a particular issue, something that troubled him greatly. The sorry state of public education in Texas was much on his mind. He had read news about declining educational achievement for the past decade. Now he was told by education experts, though he had trouble accepting it, that many of the students leaving Texas high schools could barely read or write, never mind total a column of numbers.

Drugs were a big part of the problem; he knew about that from supervising Texas's War on Drugs a few years earlier. Many students had a better chance of getting hooked on cocaine than of getting hooked on Dickens. Tougher law enforcement had alleviated, but not stanched, the flow of narcotics into Texas.

Perot began reading about contemporary education. He was astonished to learn that some of Texas's schoolteachers weren't much better educated than their pupils. And he wasn't the only one who was troubled. Many in Texas felt the same way. Yet no one could seem to put together a plan of action — until the spring of 1983.

Texas politicians frequently came knocking on his door with causes for Perot to embrace. Perot, they knew, had little regard for personal popularity and social status; he was the sort who didn't mind standing up for a cause he believed in, no matter who was offended. He took calls, he listened. Then Governor Mark White came to him with a proposal.

A Democrat, White had just flubbed an effort to enact a routine pay increase for teachers through the Texas legislature. Legislators, under pressure from taxpayers, finally had balked at adding money to what was generally acknowledged to be a second-rate school system. Fix the schools, they said, then we'll talk about a pay increase. White was genuinely interested in reform and getting salaries raised, but Perot was interested in something far more ambitious: top-to-bottom overhaul of the primary and secondary education system. White agreed: OK, no holds barred, he told Perot. You lead the commission, figure out what's wrong, and tell us how to fix it. We'll pass the laws and get the money to pay for it.

Perot loved the idea of a frontal assault on Texas's education problem. Big organizations, especially government, rarely worked this way. Committees met, passed resolutions, and recommended nostrums.

This time the state was committed to direct action, and that appealed to Perot. Although Perot had contributed to politicians on both sides of the aisle and was an independent, his instincts as a successful businessman drew him to the GOP. A former Republican governor of Texas, Bill Clements, served as a director of Perot's company.

But education hardly qualified as an issue that should divide Republicans and Democrats. So Perot agreed to accept the appointment from White as chairman of the Select Committee on Public Education.

Almost immediately, the Perot-led commission ignited a furious statewide controversy by proposing that high school students who failed more than one subject be barred for six weeks from extracurricular activities. The proposal put everyone on notice that the education commission wasn't another blue-ribbon, do-nothing forum.

The idea of deemphasizing extracurricular activities played poorly in sports-crazy towns like Odessa and Ft. Worth. High school coaches and administrators argued that nonacademic pursuits kept marginal pupils in school, kids who might otherwise turn to the streets. Of course, there was more than a little self-interest involved, too. By suggesting that football play a diminished role in high schools, the commission was suggesting, by implication, that high school coaches and band directors should exert less influence on the system.

Undaunted and uncompromising, Perot took to the stump, criticizing the high schools as huge football machines interested in winning games instead of winning the hearts and minds of future generations. Although Perot's commission proposed several sweeping reforms, including higher starting pay for teachers, the "no pass, no play" provision attracted banner headlines and strident opposition.

By attacking a sacred Texas ritual like high school football, Perot reaped a tornado of opposition. Coaches inveighed against him. Cars sported bumper stickers reading "I Don't Brake for Ross Perot."

The vituperation fired him up, for he loved debate. Perot sharpened his rhetoric. His specialty was the good-natured zinger, delivered with a grin.

"I thought I was living pretty well," the billionaire told a group of teachers in Austin, "until I found a school system that had towel warmers and electric cleat cleaners for the football team." He loved to remind audiences that education revenue doesn't belong in the pockets of Astroturf salesmen.

Texas liberals were confused. For years they had neatly pigeonholed Perot as a slightly nutty, right-wing flagwaver and enemy of taxation. Lo and behold, here he was in the center of the education debate, making noises like a bleeding-heart advocate of good government. And, like some New Deal Democrat, he was actually supporting additional taxation to improve the schools.

Authentic educational reform wasn't a job for the faint-hearted, and it wouldn't be cheap because it meant, quite simply, putting a whole lot more money into poor school districts.

The massive size of many Texas high schools wasn't efficient, Perot pointed out; it reflected the desire "to assemble a critical mass of guys who weigh 240 pounds or more to go rolling around out there on a field Friday night. It has nothing to do with education."

Overemphasis on football wasn't the only problem. He excoriated schools that handed out credits for motorcycle riding and that sponsored traveling exhibitions of prize chickens.

And he didn't give a damn if Hispanic leaders got their noses out of joint about his criticisms of bilingual education. Immigrants and their children should learn English, not demand instruction in their native tongue. School boards shouldn't be so quick to offer vocational skills as an alternative to reading and writing.

The outcry against Perot was shrill. He was warned his ideas would inflame some powerful educational constituencies. So be it. He had learned long ago that one rarely accomplished anything by trying to make everyone happy.

Finally his commission came up with a set of reforms. Now they were working on legislative passage of a $4.8 billion tax increase to pay for them.

He walked to the huge picture window in his office. As his eyes scanned the green expanse in front of Electronic Data Systems headquarters, he fretted about people who couldn't read or write — and the long-term implications for companies like EDS.

The world today really is a more complicated place than the world of his childhood, he thought. Children today have to learn to compete internationally. They don't have a choice. The steel industry, automobile industry, and much of the electronics industry were losing the battle. Hundreds of thousands of jobs held by U.S. workers already are gone.

Japan's education system has helped make that country the most productive on earth. Russian kids go to school 240 days a year, eight hours a day. Ours go about 180 days a year, six hours a day. And half the time is wasted on band practice, drama practice, and pep rallies!

The signs of decline were all too apparent in the American business world, he thought. Hostile takeovers and greenmail dominated the financial landscape. Once-proud companies like Gulf Oil and Republic Steel were no more. What was the takeover phenomenon really, except uncompetitive public companies struggling to avoid extinction? How had these enterprises become so weak?

He had some suspicions. The stock of these companies wouldn't have become so cheap and so vulnerable to the raiders if the companies had brought to market top-quality products at competitive prices. The so-called leaders and managers of these companies never looked any further than ninety days into the future, to the next quarterly earnings report and their own bonuses.

Football and baseball are fine games, he thought, but the country has to win the really important contests being fought in factories, laboratories, and computer rooms.

Perot's reverie was broken by the voice of Sally Bell, his secretary, on the office intercom.

"Mr. Perot. John Gutfreund for you on the line."

The cigar-puffing chairman of Salomon Brothers, a major New York City investment bank, was one of Wall Street's certifiable titans. Perot had met him once, but EDS had done little business with Salomon over the years.

A call out of the blue from Gutfreund was unusual. If the investment bank just was hustling some business, Gutfreund wouldn't make a pitch to him, and certainly not by telephone. Could it be a social call? More likely a charity request.

"Hello, Ross. I need to speak to you about something of great importance. Would you mind if I came down to Dallas to see you?" Gutfreund said.

"Sure, that would be fine," Perot said. "What would you like to see me about?"

Gutfreund paused momentarily: "I'd rather not say right now, if that's all right with you, Ross. This really is quite sensitive. Would it be all right if I came down tomorrow morning? I should be there before noon."

"Sure, John," Perot said. "See you then."

Why couldn't Gutfreund say what he wanted to talk about? Rather than puzzle through the possibilities alone, Perot dialed Mort Meyerson, EDS's president, who sat in an office just down the hall.

Meyerson entered his boss's office a few moments later. Meyerson had worked for EDS for nearly twenty years and for most of that time had been part of Perot's inner circle of advisers.

In 1971 Perot chose Meyerson to lead the biggest business project he had ever attempted, an ill-fated venture on Wall Street that turned into an embarrassing debacle. Afterward, Perot had shouldered the blame. Nevertheless, Meyerson returned from New York somewhat shaken, determined to prove he still was worthy of the post of Perot's top lieutenant.

From the looks of EDS at that moment, Meyerson had proven his point splendidly. He had regained his old confidence and his standing with Perot. Five years ago, Perot had named Meyerson president and handed day-to-day management of EDS to him.

The two men, although they were fundamentally different types of personalities and had different tastes in many things, had remained close throughout EDS's happy and tough times. Perot, a man of no small ego, cheerfully told everyone that Meyerson was the smartest businessman he had ever met.

Turning over daily operations to Meyerson softened Perot's personal imprint on EDS. It afforded Perot the freedom to spend more time with his family and to dabble in public issues such as the education of Texas schoolchildren.

But EDS was, and always would be, Perot's. He remained highly visible, working on projects public and private from his top-floor suite, running board meetings, delivering pep talks to workers, troubleshooting and gladhanding clients. After all, his personal fortune was his stake in EDS and he meant to protect it: on the day of Gutfreund's phone call, Perot directly owned or controlled through family trusts 26,539,350 shares of EDS, or 44.9 percent of the outstanding shares of the common stock. The stock closed that day at $27½, making his share of the company worth about $729 million.

Perot tracked down another of his close advisers, Tom Walter, at a meeting at Auburn University, his alma mater. Walter was EDS's chief financial officer; he had been with Perot since the early days of EDS, serving as a link to Wall Street security analysts. Unfortunately, Walter couldn't shed any light on Gutfreund's phone call. Perot next would have called Tom Luce, his attorney, but Luce was in Austin, working on education reform; Perot decided it wasn't worth disturbing Luce's work.

Turning to Meyerson, he asked: "What do you make of it, Mort?" Meyerson, who knew Gutfreund from his and Perot's venture ten years earlier on Wall Street, was as aware as Perot that Gutfreund had earned a reputation at Salomon Brothers as a forceful, vindictive man.

Meyerson thought for a moment. Like Perot, he knew it was unusual that Gutfreund had insisted on coming to Dallas immediately. "I think it's pretty clear Gutfreund either has found a company he wants EDS to buy or a company that wants to buy EDS," Meyerson said.

Perot swayed slowly in his rocking chair. He had come to the same conclusion.

The next morning, April 3, John Gutfreund embarked on an eight o'clock flight from LaGuardia. With the time change, he arrived in Dallas–Ft. Worth well before noon and headed immediately east to the Park Central section of the city.

Two nights before, Gutfreund had dined with Roger Smith, the chairman of General Motors Corporation, in Smith's suite at the Ritz-Carlton Hotel in Manhattan. The food was lousy, and the room was crowded with lawyers and bankers. Smith's subordinates, as well as some of Gutfreund's partners at Salomon Brothers, were in attendance. Smith's dinner message to Gutfreund was simple and direct: We want EDS, we want all of it, but we'll only go after it in a friendly transaction.

Now, as Gutfreund walked into EDS headquarters, he hoped the Texan's reaction would be positive.

Frequently, when an investment banker arrives at a company with an unsolicited acquisition offer, the target company's lawyers are summoned into the room immediately. Or, worse still, the investment banker is ushered straight into the general counsel's offices, signaling the first shots in a hostile acquisition. Gutfreund feared this might happen to him at EDS, for he had advised some of his own clients to take exactly such action if approached.

To forestall conflict, Gutfreund had to present his position as unthreatening. He shook Perot's hand, noting the Americana displayed around the office. Then he shook Meyerson's hand. Gutfreund believed in paying attention to small details, which he knew could make a big difference in sensitive negotiations.

Choosing his words so as not to seem too aggressive, Gutfreund said: "I'm on a mission, Ross. I've been charged with asking you if you would be interested in a friendly deal to sell your company."

If Perot was going to call the lawyers, this was the moment.

"Our client is General Motors," Gutfreund said. The name was like a hand grenade, whose explosive charge took a moment or two to affect Meyerson and Perot. General Electric they might have expected. AT&T or IBM would have made sense to them. But General Motors? EDS had worked with and for a great number of blue-chip industrial companies, but it had never considered GM, or any carmaker for that matter, a potential partner.

Gutfreund read the surprise on their faces.

"As you know, GM hasn't made a major acquisition since the 1920s. Roger Smith is in the midst of a strategic undertaking to shape GM's business for the future. I think GM is serious. There's no doubt it's affluent. And I think you'll both find Roger Smith an interesting person," he said.

Gutfreund reviewed the reasons for GM's interest, stressing how much Smith was attracted to EDS's work force and, especially, to EDS's leaders.

"Roger realizes the sensitivity regarding your people, and that without you and your people being happy, you couldn't do a deal like this one," he said. Gutfreund was, in effect, promising to keep the negotiations friendly; if the people of EDS didn't want this acquisition, GM wasn't going to force it.

From the first moment, Perot and Meyerson understood that a company the size of GM wasn't primarily interested in EDS's profits, which were a hundredth the size of GM's. Meyerson quickly reviewed in his mind what EDS could add to an industrial giant like GM. Gutfreund guessed much of what Meyerson was thinking, having been briefed about EDS's capabilities as a provider of computer services and integrator of computer systems. As they chatted, Gutfreund could see that Perot and Meyerson were enthusiastic salesmen of EDS's services. They both had dozens of questions.

Perot appeared to Gutfreund to be pensive. Gutfreund presumed Perot was dreaming of how much money he could make by selling his stock to GM. Perot's stake in EDS had only a theoretical worth based on the current market price. But GM was prepared to pay cash immediately for all of Perot's shares at a premium over the market price. Overnight, Perot — who already possessed cash resources of more than $100 million — would possess an immense liquid fortune, bestowing on him unimaginable financial flexibility. Gutfreund, a New York money man, assumed this must be very attractive.

"Well, we'll talk about this and get back to you," Perot said.

Gutfreund's first meeting was a four-star success. No lawyers. And the target hadn't said no.

"What do you know about General Motors?" Perot asked Meyerson a few moments after Gutfreund departed.

"Not very much, Ross," he said, "except that they make more cars and trucks than anyone in the world. And that means they probably use tons of computing power."

Neither man was trying to imagine what EDS might look like as a subsidiary of GM or what they might have to do as vassals of a huge manufacturing empire. It was inconceivable, too foreign to their daydreams or goals. But the prospect of snaring a customer like GM, with billions to spend on computer services, made their mouths water.

EDS was growing its revenue and its profit at a rate of 20 percent a year, a mighty clip for a company its size. Each year, however, the 20 percent growth rate became more difficult to maintain because the dollar targets grew geometrically larger and the number of potential clients able to spend vast amounts on computing grew smaller. Contracts worth $10 million weren't enough; EDS needed $100-million-a-year contracts to maintain growth. Soon, that wouldn't be enough either.

Perot dialed Tom Luce in Austin. "Tom," Perot said to his lawyer, "I just had a very interesting visit. John Gutfreund of Salomon Brothers came down here representing GM and said they want to buy us. It's strictly a friendly offer."

"Are you interested, Ross?" Luce had never heard Perot talk about selling EDS and couldn't imagine him doing so.

"Oh, I don't think anything is going to come of this, but it might be a good opportunity to get some business from GM. At the scale on which GM probably operates, they could be a huge customer for EDS," Perot said.

From the way Perot described the meeting, Gutfreund hadn't yet discussed price or terms specifically, so GM's approach hadn't constituted a bona fide offer to acquire EDS. Under federal securities laws, EDS would have been required to disclose an acquisition offer to its shareholders. What Gutfreund had done qualified only as flirting.

"Don't get diverted by this GM business," he told Luce. "The main thing now is to keep focused on getting the education bill passed. I'll let you know what happens with this."

One of Perot's strengths, perhaps his greatest strength, was concentration; he didn't like scattering his attention on too many subjects at once. Education was what he liked to call a gut issue. He had sent Luce to hire the best lobbyists in Austin to help him and then hire some of the other good ones so they wouldn't be available for the opposition.

Perot asked his secretary, Sally Bell, to get Ken Langone on the line. Langone, an independent investment banker and trader, operated a small Park Avenue brokerage. He and Perot had been friends for more than fifteen years, ever since Langone had underwritten the first public offering of EDS stock.

Langone's affection for Perot was based on deep admiration. A former GI, Langone years earlier had helped Perot raise money and supplies for U.S. prisoners of war in Vietnam.

"I'm not shocked, Ross," Langone said of Gutfreund's visit. "I know you're going to think about this like you'd think about selling one of your children. But just don't say no right away. Listen to what GM has to say. If you can get $45 or $50 a share and invest it at 10 percent for ten years, you'll be worth more than EDS," he said. Langone had managed investments for Perot and wanted his client to consider the financial benefits of selling.

Perot trusted Langone's advice. He would think about GM.

A week later, the second week in April, Perot called Gutfreund and suggested that he and Meyerson visit Detroit to get a feel for General Motors and Roger Smith.

Gutfreund wasn't raising his hopes yet. An experienced mergermaker, he knew that for every potential marriage of the magnitude of GM and EDS, another hundred are proposed and never go anywhere. The price isn't right, or the chief executives don't like each other, or the government objects. The list of potential deal-killers is endless.

If this merger was to succeed, Gutfreund knew, confidentiality was vital. The moment a rumor about GM and EDS began circulating on trading floors, the price of EDS shares would quickly rise, and Roger Smith could lose his appetite. Or another company, represented by — God forbid! — a rival investment bank, might crash the party.

Salomon needed to provide a cover story in case Perot or Smith had to explain to anyone why they were meeting in Detroit. Perot and Meyerson had told Gutfreund EDS could do a lot for GM. What better cover story, Gutfreund thought, than to make it look as though EDS were soliciting a major computer-systems contract from GM?

Wasn't the point of buying EDS, in fact, to buy the biggest computing contract of all time? It was beautiful, Gutfreund thought. A marriage made in heaven.

TWO

———————— ⟫ ⟪ ————————

Getting Started

TEXARKANA, Texas, Ross Perot's birthplace, lies directly on the border of Texas and Arkansas, as its name suggests, 179 miles northeast of Dallas, about halfway to Little Rock. The last census arrived at a population of just over 52,000, a number that has remained roughly constant since World War II. In some respects, Texarkana really is two towns, Texarkana, Texas, and Texarkana, Arkansas, each with its own fire and police departments, and with separate policies regarding the consumption of liquor. (You can buy booze on the Arkansas side; the Texas side is dry.) It is a quiet, well-manicured, somewhat remote place.

The area surrounding Texarkana was nicknamed the piney woods of east Texas for its evergreen forests and rich soil. King Cotton dominated the economy of east Texas for the first half of the century, until artificial fibers were invented and grew popular. Throughout that time, the livelihood of most Texarkana families depended in some way on the system that grew, processed, and transported raw cotton.

In the 1920s, Texarkana became an important transportation center. Eventually four railroad trunk lines — Texas and Pacific, Missouri Pacific, Kansas City Southern, and St. Louis Southwestern — laid their tracks through the town. The U.S. government built a mail center and a penitentiary, and it became a central destination from which cotton farmers sold their crop and shipped the fiber to textile mills across the South.

In economic terms, Texarkana's best days probably lie behind it. Today, the Hotel Grim sits nearly abandoned, its picture windows lacking glass panes, weeds growing crazily through the stone facade. The federal cotton compress, the U.S. mail center, many of the lumber mills — all lie in ruins. For years, the majority of Texarkana's sons and daughters have left town to seek their futures elsewhere.

The campus of Texarkana College, which started as a junior college, is modern and unassuming. A Sheraton and the usual assortment of fast-food dens line the commercial strip near the interstate. Texarkana, Texas, has a small black ghetto named Newtown, as black ghettos are named in so many southern towns. Newtown is shabby but clean. The prettiest building in town by far is the Perot Theatre, at 219 Main Street. Ross Perot restored the theatre in 1981 at a cost of $2 million as a memorial to his mother.

Gabriel Ross Perot, Henry Ross Perot's father, was born in New Boston, Texas, a village about twenty miles west of Texarkana. Gabriel Ross's father had been a cotton broker and operated a general merchandise store. He died when Gabriel Ross was fourteen years old, having taught his son as much as he knew of the merchant's trade.

Young Gabriel Ross Perot moved from New Boston to Texarkana after his father's death in 1917 and opened a cotton brokerage on State Line Avenue. He was known around town as Ross Perot, a portly, playful man with a generous nature when someone needed help. Unlike his French forebears, he pronounced his family name PEA-row. (Years later, his son Ross corrected teachers who used the French pronunciation by suggesting they associate his name with "a plain old row of peas." At the Naval Academy he finally gave up correcting everyone who called him pe-ROW.)

Lulu May Ray, Henry Ross Perot's mother, was born in Atlanta, Texas, about thirty miles south of Texarkana. Her family was Methodist and deeply religious. Lulu May's brother won local notoriety by building and flying his own airplane. Young Lulu May attended business classes and took a job as a secretary for a Texarkana lumber company. From her second-story office window she could watch the cotton brokers and the farmers' wagons on State Line Avenue, and it was from that aerie she first laid eyes on Gabriel Ross Perot.

As Perot family legend has it, Gabriel Ross and Lulu May attended a town dance — each accompanied by a date. Both loved the waltz and the fox-trot. The up-and-coming cotton broker watched his dainty future wife dancing with someone else and asked her for a turn, and they fell in love. Although Gabriel Ross had attended Catholic church with his father, his mother was Methodist, and he had never formally been confirmed as a Catholic. The couple was married at the Methodist church on February 25, 1923.

In 1925 the Perots spent $4,400 building a three-bedroom brick home at 2901 Olive, just north of the city limit. Their first child, Gabriel Ross Perot, Jr., died of meningitis at the age of three. On February 24, 1928, Lulu May gave birth to a daughter, Margaret Elizabeth, whom they called Bette. Eighteen months later, on June 27, 1930, Henry Ross Perot was born.

The Depression enveloped Texarkana as fiercely as it had the rest of the nation. Men sold apples and pencils on street corners. Women took in washing and sewing to supplement the household budget with nickels and dimes. Church groups and the Salvation Army fed the hungry. The well-to-do shared with the down-and-out.

Ross and Bette Perot were hardly old enough to understand what had befallen the country, though signs of bad times appeared on their doorstep. Hobos rode the country's rails, and because so many trains stopped in Texarkana, mendicants in search of food roamed the city's streets. Lulu May Perot distributed plenty of warm meals from her back door. She was a soft touch — the hobos marked the curb next to the house — but she didn't mind. The Perots certainly never went hungry, and Lulu May was happy to share her family's portion with those who were.

During the Depression's leanest years, the elder Ross Perot was able, by dint of his skills as a merchant, to provide comfortable surroundings for his young family. Bette and Ross weren't lavished with gifts, but they had swings and a sand pile. They played Flinch with a deck of cards and Monopoly and attended the picture shows with their parents. Just around the corner, the Morriss family opened their backyard tennis court to the Perot children.

Young Ross, or "Brother" as he was called by his family, learned how to ride a horse at the age of six. His father was permitted to keep horses across the street in a barn he built on land owned by the Rochelle family. Ross's first horse was a mare named Bee, and later on he rode Bee's colt, Candy.

A short, stout man, the elder Ross Perot was an enthusiastic horse breeder and trainer. In spite of his wife's objections, he delighted in lifting his young son onto the backs of untamed horses and teaching him how to break the animals for riding. Young Ross was smaller than his peers, but he was game. He tamed his share of horses, and he suffered his share of bruises and bloody noses.

Mrs. Perot, by all accounts, was a sweet, strong, spiritual woman, although she didn't wear her religion on her sleeve. Under her direction the Perots repeated the same prayer before each meal: "Gracious Father, make us thankful for all these blessings we humbly ask, for Christ's sake, Amen." She read the Bible each morning and insisted on honesty, uprightness, and perfect manners from her children — as well as clean nails and tidy hair. She had piercing blue eyes, from which she projected a tough, deep gentleness. If her children misbehaved, she lectured them at length. Whipping wasn't her style. Under the influence of his mother, Ross grew a deep sense of self-respect. He wanted to please his mother, but more important, he heeded her encouragement to set high standards and to judge himself rigorously without waiting for others to judge him.

Lulu May's philosophy of discipline and education had a profound effect on her offspring. The Perot children dreaded disappointing their mother. Indeed, they wondered at times whether a swift kick in the pants wouldn't have been preferable to one of her intense, disapproving stares. Mrs. Perot took charge of Ross's formal schooling. She enrolled him in the private Patty Hill School through the fifth grade, because she believed he would benefit from the individual attention, and she drove him there each day in the family car. Afterward, he attended the public Highland Park School, Texarkana Junior High, and Texas High School.

During most of his secondary schooling, Perot belonged to a tight group of friends that included Bill Wright, Ed Overholzer, Paul Young, Jimmy Morriss, and Richard Russell. The pals usually met on Friday evenings and Saturdays and during the week at Boy Scouts. They rode bicycles, played football and baseball, went on Scout campouts, and told each other stories. In an age when church and parents had an ineffable influence over children's lives, the boys in this group avoided alcohol and cigarettes and gave voice to only the tamest schoolyard vulgarities. Ross's father specifically asked his son never to drink, a request he decided to honor for life.

The friends competed fiercely, in class and out. Bill Wright played tailback for the Texas High Tigers football team, and Ross Perot starred on the debate team. One afternoon, Ross challenged Wright to a tennis match. Wright, a demonstrably superior athlete, accepted the offer without hesitation.

"We might as well make it interesting," Perot said, sensing his friend's confidence. "How much money do you have on you?"

Wright, not realizing how much time Perot spent on the Morriss's tennis court, accepted the bet, agreeing to treat Perot at the drugstore soda fountain if he lost. The con worked. Perot bested his friend, and afterward he devoured 78 cents' worth of ice cream at the drugstore.

Ross was quick, pint-sized, and, his friends noticed, fanatically determined to succeed at anything he tried. One summer he decided to learn a back flip from the high diving board at Texarkana Country Club. Ed Overholzer watched in amazement as Ross spent hours perfecting his technique. Over and over he plunged into the water, wearing a T-shirt to protect his back against the water's sting.

From an early age, Ross exhibited a fascination for his father's work. He tagged along while his father "visited" with cotton planters around Texarkana. The elder Perot used his charm to cement friendly relations with the farmers. He relied on that bond during the late summer harvest when competing brokers crowded the stalls near the federal compress where the raw cotton was baled. Before making a deal, brokers first tested the cotton, plunging their knives straight into the bales to extract samples. Depending on the quality of the fiber, they offered a price, usually for the farmer's entire crop. The best bid often determined which broker bought the crop, but price wasn't the only factor. A cozy relationship between buyer and seller definitely helped. All transactions were sealed on a handshake, thus men needed to know and trust one another implicitly.

The art of brokering demanded a certain gregariousness, an ability to tell a joke, a willingness to knock on farmhouse doors, the confidence to ask for orders. A broker had to understand price and value, and to live by the results of a transaction, even when they weren't especially favorable. The elder Perot was a shrewd trader of cotton and horses. A farmer might travel twenty-five miles, knock on the Perots' door, and say:

"I've got that horse you wanted."

Perot's reply, whether he had asked to see the horse or not, would always be the same: "What horse?"

The farmer would tell Perot about the horse and the $300 price tag.

"Don't believe I want *that* horse," he'd reply.

"Well, aren't you going to look at him?" the farmer would demand.

They would walk outside, and Perot would politely praise the animal, never saying he was interested in buying. A few days later they would settle on a price well south of $300.

The younger Perot, literally having studied the process at his father's knee, grew to love buying and selling and especially the subtle give and take leading to a transaction. At first his products were War Bonds, garden seeds, subscriptions to the *Saturday Evening Post*, and Christmas cards.

For many years, Perot's boyhood business ventures interested him far more than his schoolwork, a fact that troubled his teachers. He couldn't grasp why reading another English classic or proving two triangles were congruent would help his fledgling enterprises. His marks weren't awful, but they were beneath his capabilities. Mrs. Grady Duck, Ross Perot's eleventh-grade English teacher, understood how to motivate a competitive underachiever: by dangling a challenge in front of him. It's just too bad you're not as smart as your friends, she told him. When Perot disagreed with her appraisal, she offered their superior grades as evidence. Once he had a challenge in front of him, his grades quickly improved.

Ross Perot, it seemed, needed only to decide a task was worth carrying out, then would fix his attention on it, map out a plan, and charge forward. Texarkana elders marveled at the grit and ingenuity of someone so young, and the early signs of an unusually strong ability to concentrate, all characteristics that marked his later life.

His intensity first was evidenced in the Boy Scouts. The Morrisses, Perot's neighbors with the tennis court, sponsored Texarkana's Troop 18 through the family insurance company. Josh Morriss, Jr., already was an Eagle Scout and a high school hero-athlete at about the time Perot was old enough to advance from the Cub Scouts to the Boy Scouts. Josh Morriss also was reserved and polite, exactly the kind of boy Lulu May Perot thoroughly approved of. Five years Perot's senior, Morriss barely noticed the diminutive new member of Troop 18. For years Perot admired his older neighbor from a distance. In Perot's imagination, nothing could be as wonderful as becoming an Eagle Scout like Josh Morriss. And having decided that, he pursued the Eagle Scout rank relentlessly.

With Lulu May's moral training and Gabriel Ross's guidance in matters of commerce and corral, Ross Perot couldn't have been better prepared to excel in an activity that rewarded Sunday school values and outdoor skills.

The Eagle Scout award ceremony culminates a superior scouting career. Less than one percent of Boy Scouts achieve the rank. A boy must earn twenty-one merit badges and five ranks prior to Eagle, carry out service projects for the community, serve in leadership posts in his troop, and satisfy the adult advisers and the troop leaders that he is worthy of high honor. The aspiring Eagle generally spends three to six years completing the requirements. As a practical matter, the journey to Eagle Scout is helped immensely if the scout has a warm, cooperative relationship with his Scoutmaster. Time runs out at the age of eighteen, when the Scout is too old to belong to the troop.

Sam Schuman, the man hired by the Morrisses to lead Troop 18, probably had encountered few youngsters with Perot's drive. Perot won his Tenderfoot award, Boy Scouting's lowest rank, in June 1942 at the age of eleven; it came during his first month as a Scout. Only fifteen months later, at the age of thirteen, he had zipped through the four remaining ranks and earned the twenty-one merit badges required for Eagle. Scoutmaster Schuman undoubtedly spent much time encouraging scouts to tackle the tough requirements for Eagle Scout, but he barely could keep up with the overachieving young leader of the Flaming Arrow Patrol. One day in town he mentioned his problem to Mrs. Perot.

She didn't give him a sympathetic hearing.

"Is Ross misbehaving?" she wanted to know.

Springing to her son's defense, she said she wasn't about to ask him to slow down for his Scoutmaster's sake. Ross had followed the rules, worked hard, and earned his badges fairly. Receiving his Eagle Scout award was the finest moment of Perot's childhood. In achieving Eagle Scout rank so quickly, Perot learned the value of establishing a goal.

His experiences as a newspaper delivery boy reinforced the lessons he was learning at Scouts. When he had applied to the *Texarkana Gazette* for the job, nothing was available except an unattractive delivery route in the town's black ghetto. However, the newspaper's circulation manager agreed to pay Perot twice the normal commission if he would take it. Rising early, he rode to a filling station to pick up his newspapers, then pitched them from horseback onto the porches of the wood and tarpaper homes along West 23rd, Mill, and Spruce streets. The literacy rate in Texarkana's black community probably wasn't high in those days, but the newspaper sold well among the poor. Newsprint was valued as fuel and insulation as well as reading matter. No sooner had Perot's delivery route begun to yield hefty revenues than the circulation manager ordered his commission halved to the normal rate. The man wouldn't budge and neither would the youngster.

Perot then marched in to the publisher, C. E. Palmer.

"We agreed on the commission, and I think we should stick to it," he said.

If he had merely complained, Perot might have found himself delivering newspapers at the standard rate. Instead, he took his case straight to the person who made decisions at the *Texarkana Gazette* and stated his position unambiguously. The Boy Scout Handbook hadn't addressed this type of problem specifically. Yet Perot's approach to the publisher was Boy Scout honest, upfront, and backed by a solid principle: living by an agreement. The tactic worked, renewing his boy's faith that people, in most cases, will do the right thing when given a chance.

Ross Perot respected adults, but he wasn't overly awed by their status or authority. As president of the student council at Texarkana Junior College, he was appalled by the plan to expand the school at its present site, next door to Texas High. It seemed clear that the school needed more room if it was to grow and prosper. Besides, he and other junior college students wanted their own campus and environment, well separated from the adjacent high school. Ross Perot's speech and debate teacher, Claude O. Pinkerton, listened to his pupil's critique of the expansion plans and wasn't surprised. Pinkerton had taught Perot Bible stories at the Methodist church and marveled at his poise and self-confidence. Once, after listening to classmates criticize a speech, Perot turned to his teacher, in front of the rest of the class, and asked him:

"What do *you* think, Mr. Pinkerton?"

Pinkerton had to laugh. Perot wasn't being disrespectful, but he had been the only one in class with enough nerve to ask the teacher for a direct evaluation.

Opposing the expansion of Texarkana Junior College, Pinkerton knew, wasn't going to win Perot friends on the school board. More likely, they would tell him to mind his own business and then laugh him out of the room. Many of the college's teachers supported the idea of a new campus but were afraid to stick their necks out in front of the school board. Perot visited the superintendent of schools, Dr. H. W. Stilwell. He was convinced, he told the administrator, that the student body would grow 5 to 10 percent a year on a new, bigger campus. He brought along a detailed study of how many students chose to leave Texarkana after high school.

"You're barking at a tree that doesn't have a possum in it," Dr. Stilwell laughed. But he was impressed with Perot's preparation and tenacity and offered to let him present his ideas in front of the school board. A few weeks later Pinkerton received a phone call from a board member: "The little booger has us about convinced to buy forty acres on the other side of town."

Perot had presented his facts courteously, eloquently, and punctuated with good humor. He convinced the board, which bought the land Perot had suggested.

Texarkana wasn't enough of a town to contain Perot's energy or curiosity. By age eighteen he had seen little of the world and wanted to see more. What he really wanted was to follow Josh Morriss's path of glory, which led from Troop 18 to the U.S. Naval Academy. Perot had sent letters to his congressmen inquiring about an appointment and hadn't received a shred of encouragement.

One day during his second year at junior college, the letter Ross had been waiting for arrived. A retiring Texas senator was entitled to appoint someone to a service academy. The boy who had never seen an ocean was on his way to Annapolis. He was sworn in on June 27, 1949, his nineteenth birthday.

Until recently, many future midshipmen attended a year or two of college preparatory classes before attempting the Naval Academy's rigorous engineering program. Josh Morriss enrolled at Texas A&M, where the science and mathematics course requirements were perfectly suited to prepare a student for the academy's discipline. At Texarkana Junior College, Perot had chosen a prelaw curriculum.

Perot's academic career at the Naval Academy was respectable: he finished 454 out of 925. But he exhibited amazing talent for leadership. He was elected class president and head of the honor committee.

He won another prize while at the academy: Margot Birmingham, a student at Goucher College whom he met on a blind date. Attended by his roommate, Lyle Armel, Perot and Margot married in 1956 in Greensburg, Pennsylvania.

Ensign Perot was graduated from the Naval Academy in June 1953. He and his classmates trained as sea warriors while the Korean conflict raged, and now it looked as if they would have a chance to taste battle. The Navy played a supporting role in Korea, shelling positions on shore and blockading enemy ports, a role that carried with it some danger: five Navy ships had been sunk and eighty-two were hit during three years of warfare. The Navy assigned Perot to the destroyer USS *Sigourney*, where he was the assistant fire-control officer. The *Sigourney* set course across the Pacific toward Korea in July 1953. While the ship was tied up at Midway, a truce between Allied and Communist forces was signed. Instead of lobbing shells at the enemy, Perot's ship headed home the long way, stopping at Hong Kong and Ceylon, before sailing through the Suez Canal and docking at several Mediterranean ports. At each port of call, Perot collected a few coins and trinkets as souvenirs while steering clear of the drinking and rowdiness of a typical shore leave.

Perot's second assignment was assistant navigator aboard the aircraft carrier USS *Leyte*. By this time, Perot doubted he was going to remain in the Navy beyond his four-year obligation. He sensed that the Navy was a place that wouldn't satisfy his ambitions to reach the top. From his experience, he could see how the luck of an assignment and the whim of senior officers played a great part in promotions. Unfortunately, the Navy was an organization that sometimes placed more value on personal connections, politics, and blind loyalty to senior officers than on raw ability. He would look for a chance to show what he could do in civilian life, perhaps in a first-class corporation, several of which were blooming in the prosperity following World War II.

As junior officer aboard the *Leyte*, Perot was assigned the duty of escorting visitors aboard ship. On one such visit, he introduced himself to an IBM executive who had come aboard as a guest of the Secretary of the Navy. Knowing little about IBM or what it did beyond the manufacture of typewriters, Perot nonetheless was pleased and flattered that the man suggested he interview with IBM after his discharge. A few months later, he completed his four-year tour of duty, and IBM didn't agonize long over the opportunity to hire a disciplined naval officer, particularly one with sales skills fairly oozing from him. If nothing else, Perot was already accustomed to blue suits, white shirts, and neat grooming, trademarks of the IBM salesman.

With their few possessions packed in the back of a 1952 Plymouth, Ross and Margot bid farewell to the *Leyte*'s home port of Quonset Point, Rhode Island, and set course for Dallas, where IBM agreed to accept Perot as a trainee.

In the late 1950s, IBM workers always were the smartest, exhibited the most energy, and had the most money; or so it seemed to Tom Marquez, a young Notre Dame graduate from Durango, Colorado, who was working his way through Southern Methodist University in Dallas by selling encyclopedias door-to-door.

Trudging through neighborhoods in the midday heat, Marquez quickly noticed that IBM people stood out. They were bright. They had a love of learning and were easily persuaded of the value of the Great Books of the Western World series, which cost $10 down and $14 a month. Jim Campbell, a manager in the local IBM office, was impressed with Marquez when the young man knocked at his door one sweltering Sunday afternoon. He was clean-cut, educated, and outgoing, and he obviously was willing to work hard for what he wanted.

"I'll buy your books," Campbell said, "if you come and interview for a job at IBM."

On Marquez's first day on the job, Campbell introduced him to Ross Perot.

"You watch what Ross does," Campbell told Marques, "and you do it just like him."

Marquez didn't get much of a chance to mimic the office's champion salesman. For one thing, Ross didn't hang around the office. Marquez noticed that while most salesmen spent the first forty-five minutes in the morning having coffee and making plans for the day, Perot already was calling on customers. Perot was all business and no wasted motion. He rarely joined in after-hours socializing, preferring instead to scoot home to his wife. Selling IBM computers proved relatively unchallenging for Perot. He quickly broke into the company's "Hundred Percent Club" for salesmen who achieved their yearly sales quota. To make the task more interesting for himself and earn higher commissions, he asked for a chance to crack some particularly tough accounts such as Blue Cross/Blue Shield and Southwestern Life Insurance, which had been wary of laying out large sums for computers. Perot struck paydirt with a number of resistant customers, improving his income and impressing his managers as someone clearly destined for bigger and better things at IBM.

The more Perot achieved at IBM, the more frustrated he became. IBM wanted to raise sales figures companywide, so it began experimenting with its sales incentives. The changes had a big impact on high-performance individuals like Perot. Sales teams were formed; strong salesmen teamed with the not-so-strong. Territories belonging to successful salesmen were trimmed to encourage more revenue from smaller areas. Compensation was tied to seniority in order to alleviate jealousies that arose when top salesmen's salaries surpassed those of the managers who supervised them. Perot, Marquez, and others sensed IBM was deviating from the principles of rugged individual attainment that had originally attracted them.

In 1961 IBM cut Perot's territory and reduced his quota, which allowed him to reach his annual sales goal by January 19, 1962. It left him with little monetary incentive to work hard, little reason to exercise his natural drive. He was annoyed and frustrated. Now and then he'd go over to the YMCA to swim laps on his lunch hour, making sure to leave his trunks and towel on his desk, before and after his workouts, as a subtle form of protest.

Money wasn't the only irritant. He had tried to interest his supervisors in a new selling concept, based on observations about his customers. He noticed that his customers were more than willing to spend a great deal of money on computers, but all too often they then found themselves unable to use the computers' power fully. So they hired experts and proceeded by trial and error, often spending more to understand how computers could help their business than they had spent to buy the hardware. IBM, meanwhile, had little to offer once the machines were installed; the company only guaranteed that the computers would work as specified.

IBM managers expressed scant interest in Perot's notions. The concept, as far as Perot was concerned, was simple. IBM should start a computer-services division, which would provide complete computerized solutions to business problems, so-called turnkey systems, including skilled workers to run the computers.

IBM regional executives listened to Perot explain his idea, but they weren't interested. The same stifling, thwarted feelings he had experienced in his last year in the Navy seized him at IBM. He had shown initiative and ability, but they weren't appreciated.

Perot realized he belonged to a terrific organization, one of the best around. He was respected, well liked, financially secure. But there was more to life, more for him to do, and he knew the IBM organization was too large, too well established, and too successful to accommodate a dripping-wet upstart from east Texas. The more ideas came to him, the more he felt the urge to speak out and speak up. He did so, and his superiors listened. But beneath their tolerance ran an undercurrent of exasperation. He read in their eyes a wish for him to curb his tongue and not be quite so generous with advice.

Lurking behind Perot's subversive thoughts directed at IBM was the notion of breaking free. He had never been quite as happy at IBM as he had been years earlier in Texarkana, selling seeds and greeting cards and leather bridles. He had inherited the heady joy of personal accomplishment from his father. He could be that happy again selling computer systems. He knew it. It wouldn't take much capital, and he would be limited only by the number of talented people he could find to help him. He was sure the talent existed in practically unlimited quantities.

One day in early 1962 he sat in the barber's chair browsing through *Reader's Digest,* ruminating for the umpteenth time over his vague notions of something new when his eyes fell on a passage from *Walden:*

"The mass of men lead lives of quiet desperation."

It was an electrifying, transcendent moment. Instantly he sensed how Henry David Thoreau's philosophy of American simplicity and individualism, conceived a century earlier in rural Massachusetts, was speaking to him.

Perot's job at IBM, he now knew, had squashed his individuality. It had prevented him from expressing his own concept of work. IBM wasn't evil, but it wasn't the place where he could reach his full potential. He alone could — and must — change that situation. Thoreau would have understood his frustration and, if he had been here, Perot thought, surely would have advised him to stop complaining and change his circumstances. Fighting IBM wasn't productive.

Freshly shorn, Perot emerged from the barber's chair with his thoughts crystallized, determined to shape his destiny. That night at his kitchen table, yellow legal pad in front of him, he sketched the outline for his venture: what he was going to sell, whom he was going to sell to, who was going to help him.

On June 27, 1962, his thirty-second birthday, Perot incorporated Electronic Data Systems Corporation at the Texas secretary of state's office with $1,000 as the company's initial capital. EDS's board of directors consisted of his wife, Margot, his mother, Lulu May, and his sister, Bette.

THREE

———————

Inventing EDS

ELECTRONIC Data Systems Corporation's product, as conceptualized at Ross Perot's kitchen table in 1962, was a simple approach to business computing. Years later, the computer industry gave the product a name: "facilities management."

Ross Perot and EDS told potential customers: Concentrate on what you do best and leave the computing and data processing to us. We'll do it faster and cheaper than you. And we'll tell you in advance how much you'll pay for our services; your costs will be 100 percent predictable during the life of our contract.

Perot modeled EDS's operating style after his former employer IBM, whose success he admired despite the fact that it had squelched him. He aimed to recruit the same type of go-getters as IBM did, dress them in IBM blue and white, and establish the same high business standards. No cheating, no cutting corners, no martini lunches with customers. A lean, serious, tight, focused team. The difference between EDS and IBM, he vowed, would be close attention to the suggestions and ideas of the people who worked with him.

Perot modified the IBM model in one other crucial respect. IBM motivated its salesmen with commissions and bonuses paid as salary. Perot had seen in his own case how cash incentives limited motivation.

And, of course, he didn't have cash anyway. He aimed to motivate EDSers by paying them with stock, a stake in the company's success. After working during the summer of 1962 by himself, assisted by a secretary, Betty Taylor, Perot recruited two former coworkers from the IBM branch in Dallas: Milledge "Mitch" Hart, a boyhood acquaintance from New Boston, Texas, who also had attended the Naval Academy; and Tom Marquez, who had been introduced to IBM while selling encyclopedias. After Betty Taylor, they were EDS's first employees.

When Perot called him, Marquez didn't hesitate for a moment. He was convinced whatever the spunky former IBM salesman decided to do was going to succeed.

"Come with me," Perot said. "If you contribute, I promise you'll be rewarded."

Each day the three men — Perot, Hart, and Marquez — prospected in Dallas's business districts, knocking on the doors of the same places they would have been calling on had they stayed at IBM. After dinner, they met at Perot's house to compare notes and map the next day's sales calls. Initially, few of EDS's sales calls were encouraging. Potential clients were skeptical. EDS, after all, consisted of three salesmen and no orders; its flimsiness was palpable. With only $1,000 of his savings as seed capital, Perot didn't dare try buying a computer. But having sold huge computers for IBM, Perot knew IBM's customers occasionally purchased machines that were larger than they needed at the moment. As the customers grew, they grew into their computers. Eventually they bought larger models; but until they did, they often owned lots of unused computing time.

EDS had to find customers quickly and generate some cash flow if it was to survive beyond infancy. Ross Perot knew that IBM was selling more of its latest model computer, the 7070, than it could build. As a stopgap measure, until the salesmen sold their first facilities-management contract, Perot set out to find someone who needed a 7070 right away. He reasoned that he might be able to sell unused computer time on a 7070 from companies that he knew had excess capacity, such as Southwestern Life Insurance in Dallas.

Armed with a list of 110 users of 7070 computers, Perot scoured the East and West coasts of the country, where the concentration of computers was densest. He turned to the country's midsection next. After seventy-eight dry holes, Perot struck paydirt in Cedar Rapids, Iowa, at a division of Dallas-based Collins Radio. Collins agreed to buy time on Southwestern's computer through EDS. Several months later, EDS attracted a glimmer of interest in a facilities-management contract from legendary potato-chip king Herman Lay. Tom Marquez knocked on Lay's door just as Lay was about to sell a Univac computer and buy an IBM. Ross Perot immediately offered to carry out a "free" study to prove that EDS would do exactly what Lay was planning to do internally, but quicker and for less money.

Herman Lay started his career in Nashville as a traveling snack-food salesman. When rats devoured his inventory, he decided to make his own line of potato chips. A classic entrepreneur, Lay parlayed his success with potato chips into a snack-food empire. Perhaps reminded of his own humble beginnings, Lay was impressed with Perot, Marquez, and EDS, even though they had no track record. So Lay asked Arthur Young and Company to advise him whether to hire EDS. Arthur Young turned thumbs down.

EDS's selling efforts, meanwhile, had attracted the attention of Perot's former supervisors in IBM's Dallas office. Perot wasn't much of a threat to IBM, but the manager of the Dallas office wasn't about to allow such humiliation on his watch. A "Stop EDS" team of five IBM workers shadowed Perot, Hart, and Marquez, reminding whomever they contacted that the EDS group had never sold anything, didn't know what it was doing, was financially untested, and wasn't likely to be around very long.

Herman Lay was intrigued by IBM's tactics. Whatever it was the EDS folks were selling must be pretty good if IBM was trying so hard to thwart them, he reasoned. Lay's Potato Chips was EDS's first facilities-management contract, a five-year pact that yielded $5,500 a month of revenue. And just in case IBM failed to notice that EDS wasn't intimidated by the whispering campaign, Perot promptly hired Jim Cole, a crackerjack systems engineer and member of the "Stop EDS" team.

The next few contracts followed quickly. Mercantile Security Life in Dallas was the first of many insurance companies to hire EDS. Tom Walter, EDS's future chief financial officer, joined EDS and immediately took over supervision of the account. Battling IBM forced tiny EDS to sharpen its business skills and expend twice as much effort as it might have otherwise. Without realizing it, IBM was doing EDS a favor. EDS was a PT boat in an industry of carriers and battleships. And Perot was having the time of his life matching wits with Big Blue and winning an impressive number of contracts. EDS's skirmishes with IBM were instructive, inspirational legends from which Ross Perot could build a folklore.

EDS's early years were lean but filled with promise of future rewards. In fiscal 1964 EDS made a slim $4,100 profit on revenue of $400,000. Ross Perot's decision to award stock options was expedient, since Perot hated borrowing money and EDS possessed very little cash to use as incentive compensation for workers.

Then in 1965 an event occurred in Washington that Perot had neither hoped for nor expected, but that turned into a grand stroke of good fortune. It was the passage of Medicare legislation. Medicare was a major component of Lyndon Johnson's "Great Society." Overnight, some 30 million to 50 million people in America were entitled to some kind of federal health benefits. While everyone debated the massive costs of the programs, no one in Congress or anywhere else had given much thought to the inevitable paperwork crunch. Filling out forms, reimbursing doctors and hospitals, applying for benefits, checking for duplicate benefits — it all spelled bureaucratic delay and a looming rebellion from doctors and hospitals, which were forced to wait long periods of time for payment. Medicare paperwork had been handed to state Blue Cross/Blue Shield agencies and private health insurance carriers for processing. They, in turn, suddenly needed more mainframes, more storage, more programmers, more systems analysts — in short, more of everything EDS and Ross Perot were selling.

By 1968 about a quarter of EDS's revenue came from data processing contracts related to Medicare and Medicaid. EDS's profits soared to a 20 percent after-tax rate compared with a 2 percent after-tax rate four years earlier, thanks in large measure to Medicare-related processing. After developing software for a Medicare program in one state, EDS was able to take virtually the same software program to other states, adapt it slightly, and sell it again. (Medicaid wasn't as profitable, since each state's laws concerning medical benefits for the poor were different.) EDS's development costs for Medicare kept dropping while the demand for services grew rapidly. Thus, EDS was able to maintain high profit margins — and still demonstrate that it was saving customers substantial time and money. Formidable competition was scarce.

Meteoric growth required additional capital, and Ross Perot hated borrowing. It rubbed against the small-town virtues of thrift and financial conservatism he had learned in Texarkana's corrals and at the cotton press. His father wasn't a borrower, even in the worst of times. The profit Perot was plowing back wasn't enough to finance EDS's growth. Perot was recruiting and training his own computer systems engineers, a process that cost about $40,000 an engineer. EDS needed hundreds of them to operate more Medicare contracts and to expand into other industries that needed computing.

Wall Street provided the solution to EDS's capital problem. In 1968 the securities industry was deep in the throes of one of its periodic frenzies of excess. Just about any new technology company was able to raise capital easily. EDS had been awarding stock options to EDS employees as compensation for six years; they wondered what, if anything, the stock was worth. A public market would assign a value to their shares and make them readily convertible to cash. To Wall Streeters, Perot may have appeared to be the naive east Texas bumpkin in 1968, but he was keenly aware that a personal financial payday awaited him and EDS workers if the public was willing to buy EDS stock.

Word of Ross Perot's tentative interest in a public offering spread quickly through investment-banking circles. Wall Street in the late 1960s had no trouble detecting the scent of a new offering from 1,500 miles away. Rampant speculation among small high-technology growth stocks led bankers to pounce on any company that showed potential and plenty that didn't. New issues came to market regularly at a price of 50, 60, and even 100 times earnings, far out of proportion to companies' near-term profit potential. Within a few weeks of Perot's initial inquiry at the Dallas office of Goodbody and Company, seventeen investment banks telephoned EDS for appointments to see Perot.

When word reached Ken Langone in New York that a Texan named Ross Perot was thinking of selling EDS shares publicly, he put his name on the list and hopped a plane for Dallas. Last of the seventeen bankers to visit Perot, Langone was the first to concede that stock prices were a bit loony in 1968. Nevertheless, Langone's firm, Pressprich and Company, earned commission income from investors' willingness to spend those loony sums on the securities Pressprich underwrote. To Langone, EDS looked like the ultimate sure thing. Besides being attracted to EDS's market potential, Langone found Perot engaging. An Italian-American New Yorker, Langone was an outspoken, outgoing family man who, like Perot, had been deeply influenced by his mother. Tall, affable, and straightforward, Langone listened while Perot reviewed the somewhat complicated proposals made by the other sixteen investment banks. "They're making brain surgery out of an ingrown toenail," Langone said. "You've got a terrific company and I believe the market in its current condition will buy EDS for 100 times current earnings."

This was a big gamble for Pressprich, because the brokerage in effect was guaranteeing to pay Perot and EDS an amount based on a 100 times multiple of EDS's earnings. If the market didn't agree with Langone, Pressprich could be stuck with EDS common shares to sell at a loss. Perot liked Langone's simplified approach as much as the premium price he was dangling. Perot identified with the fact that Langone's firm, Pressprich, was a hardworking underdog, just like EDS, competing against some very ritzy investment banks.

"The folks from Dillon Read told us EDS will fetch only about 70 times earnings," Perot told Langone.

"A deal is a deal. If I say 100 times earnings, that's what you'll get paid for your stock," Langone said.

Perot tried to persuade Pressprich to spread the risk by comanaging the offering with another investment bank. Langone declined, telling Perot he would get better service by letting one bank handle the offering. "If that's the way you feel, give someone else the business," Langone said. "It will be better for both of us."

Perot decided on Pressprich. He knew how hungry the small company was for EDS's business. But he couldn't resist playing a prank on the New Yorker. He instructed Mitch Hart, EDS's president, to call Langone and tell him that Pressprich could have won the underwriting if he had just shown more interest. "Ken, I just finished talking with Perot," Hart told him. "He says you're blasé."

Langone's dander rose. He wanted EDS's business and showed his feelings. "I think I have a pretty good knack for expressing myself," Langone said icily. Who the hell did these Texans think they were anyway? Then Langone heard giggling in the background.

Perot took the phone from Hart. "So let's do business," he told Langone, cackling at his own joke.

Langone was selling EDS stock into a market driven by the economics of the Vietnam war. The Paris peace talks hadn't cooled the bulls' ardor. Langone proposed that Perot sell 325,000 of his 9.7 million EDS shares and that EDS issue 325,000 new shares — a total public market of 650,000 shares, and a fairly thin public market by today's standards. The relatively small number of shares in public hands assured the highest possible price when investors were enthusiastic, but it also assured volatility when opinion on EDS softened.

Electronic Data Systems Corporation's initial public offering on September 12, 1968, prompted seen-everything, heard-everything stock traders to sit up straight in their chairs. EDS was offered at $16.50 a share, or 118 times annual earnings of 14 cents a share, and by the end of the day it had closed at $22 a share — nearly a market record. The shares sold out quickly. EDS received $5 million in new capital from the offering, Perot got $5 million in cash, and Pressprich was paid $700,000 in commissions.

Perot welcomed the $5 million cash, of course, but he didn't have a pressing personal hunger for it; he wasn't grasping for a more luxurious lifestyle than he already enjoyed. A four-bedroom house in Dallas's fancy Greenway Parks section, a 1965 Lincoln, a 1968 Plymouth, 1959 Ford station wagon, a lake home with half a dozen boats at the dock, and two big golden retrievers, Amber and Skipper — it was plenty for him.

Perot's big financial prize from the offering was his 9,327,000 remaining shares, an 81 percent stake in EDS. What had been only paper certificates the night before the offering, with no par value, now carried an official market price tag of $154 million. In just six years, at the age of thirty-eight, Perot had parlayed $1,000 and his dissatisfaction with the life of an IBM salesman into a Texas-style fortune.

EDS's stock price, which market skeptics initially scorned as somewhat unconnected with reality, skyrocketed higher through 1969 and 1970, reaching a peak of $160 a share in March 1970. Just two years after EDS's initial public offering, the overnight multimillionaire's stake rose in value to about $1.4 billion.

Ross Perot's relative anonymity was about to end. Until the huge runup in EDS's stock price, he hadn't had much of a public persona outside Dallas, where he had made his biggest impact by contributing $1 million to the Boy Scouts and $2.5 million to the Dallas public schools. Then someone at *Fortune* magazine figured out what Perot's stake in EDS was worth. The night before *Fortune*'s profile appeared, entitled "The Fastest Richest Texan Ever," Perot sat his young children down to explain why their friends soon might be asking them strange questions about the family's money.

There wasn't any way to stay out of the public eye owning a fortune that size. Perot hadn't sought astronomical wealth and wasn't dazzled by it. But he also couldn't try to pretend he was just another member of the middle class. For Perot, the most fascinating aspect of his wealth was his sense that it could increase his effectiveness and his impact on everything he touched. Wealth was a special responsibility, a trust. Yet mastering wealth was difficult. Everyone has an opinion about how it should be used. No matter what you did, someone was bound to be angry. "If you contribute money to the church," he told his friends, "20 percent of the people will be against it."

Still, he wanted to make a difference. Before long he had a chance. It began with a telephone call from Henry Kissinger: Would Ross Perot help wage a public opinion campaign to improve the conditions of U.S. prisoners of war in North Vietnamese jails?

Although the nation was deeply divided over the U.S. war effort, Perot — a Naval Academy graduate with many friends serving in Southeast Asia — formed the "United We Stand" committee, which collected money and bought newspaper ads to pressure the North Vietnamese into improving prison conditions so that more U.S. POWs would survive until the end of the war.

For Perot, support of U.S. fighting men was a deep emotional issue. He had grown up in front of a radio listening to reports of the nation at war and the gallantry of the armed forces in World War II. Contemporaries from Annapolis and the ships he had served on had been killed and wounded in Vietnam. He believed the country had committed a grave error by sending troops overseas without first convincing the nation it was a war worth fighting. However, that didn't change the country's duty to uphold the honor of the military. Agreeing to pull out troops without assuring the health and safety of U.S. prisoners of war was unthinkable.

Nixon wanted the North Vietnamese to provide more information about the 1,400 U.S. prisoners and allow the Red Cross more supervision over their welfare. But North Vietnamese negotiators in Paris, correctly sensing the U.S.'s desire to end the war, made the prisoners' welfare a bargaining chip to be used to speed U.S. withdrawal from the region.

Henry Kissinger, then the secretary of state, called Perot. How can we embarrass the North Vietnamese into treating the POWs better, Kissinger asked Perot, until we're able to turn the war over to the South Vietnamese?

If the government mounted a campaign to improve the welfare of U.S. POWs, the North Vietnamese would portray it as a cynical attempt to gain an advantage at the Paris peace talks. To be effective, the effort had to be private. Any effort on behalf of POWs must be seen as a humanitarian appeal by U.S. citizens, totally separate from the government's efforts. The North Vietnamese might listen to U.S. citizens, Perot believed, and they might understand the horror and loneliness of families who hadn't seen or heard from their sons, husbands, and fathers for months and years.

The concept seemed sound, but how does a computer millionaire establish a dialogue with the Communist leaders of North Vietnam? Perot talked to EDS workers, several of whom had served in Vietnam. He read stacks of Communist literature. The pamphlets stressed that prisoners should be treated well, no matter how reactionary they were. In principle the North Vietnamese accepted humane treatment of prisoners, so they might be susceptible to a public relations campaign. He asked the J. Walter Thompson advertising agency to think of ideas, while staying in touch with the government through an aide to Kissinger, Colonel Alexander Haig.

A week before Christmas 1969, Perot unveiled his plan. As was his nature, he opted for directness and simplicity. Christmas was coming up, so "United We Stand" announced that it was delivering Christmas dinner to the POWs. It was to be a devastatingly simple gesture, an event that focused world attention, if only for a few days, on the POWs.

A squad of EDS managers sprang into action. The group rented two Braniff Boeing 707 cargoliners. Perot contacted people he knew all over the country to help organize food, gifts, and medical supplies for the airlift. The level of thought and detail was amazing. A shipment of hard candies in plastic bags was replaced with hard candies in tin cans instead, because former POWs explained that the cans were needed by prisoners to collect rainwater for drinking. Ken Langone, EDS's investment banker, canvassed pharmaceutical companies for donations and medical supplies.

The press was skeptical, looking for hidden motives and the Nixon administration's role in the operation. No one but Perot expressed much optimism that the North Vietnamese would allow the two planes to land in their country. "I have had no negative comments from the North Vietnamese, and in my mind that is a positive sign," he told reporters.

Three days before Christmas 1969, Perot and one of the two jets — dubbed "Peace on Earth" and loaded with food, gifts, reporters, and a Red Cross team — landed in Hong Kong. Perot hadn't disclosed that the North Vietnamese had informed him specifically, two weeks earlier, that he wasn't going to be allowed in the country.

Perot maintained great faith in the ability of "ordinary folks" to sit down and solve problems with plain talk. If he could just meet face to face with someone in authority in North Vietnam, he knew he could open their minds. The next day, the "Peace on Earth" jet flew to Thailand. In Bangkok, Perot gained permission to fly to Vientiane, Laos, to meet with North Vietnamese diplomats.

The two rented Braniff jets landed in Vientiane on Christmas Eve, and for a short while it looked as if Perot's mission was on the verge of success. He met with a delegation of the Pathet Lao, whose troops were fighting against U.S. soldiers and who reportedly held about 200 U.S.

POWs. Vu Tien, the North Vietnamese chargé d'affaires in Laos, met with Perot for an hour and thirty-five minutes. Perot asked for permission to fly to Hanoi to meet with Pham Van Dong. The North Vietnamese diplomat denied permission.

A wall of suspicion marred the talks, Perot later told reporters. Vu Tien accused Perot of carrying out President Nixon's "aggressive policy" and sabotaging the normal postal channels for sending gifts to POWs. He declined to open POW camps for inspection or provide lists of prisoners being held. When Perot tried to explain his mission as purely humanitarian, reflecting the desires of the American people, Vu suggested he instead take an interest in the suffering of the North Vietnamese people caused by the bombing of hospitals, schools, and other civilian installations. Anxious to seize any opening, Perot immediately offered to rebuild any schools or hospitals bombed by the United States in return for the 1,400 POWs.

Vu didn't respond. He wasn't about to be lured into negotiations with an unofficial freelance diplomat from Dallas, Texas. He reminded Perot once more of the normal postal channels through Moscow for sending gifts but warned that his government wouldn't accept gifts after midnight December 31. Reporters accompanying Perot received a North Vietnamese communiqué describing him as a Nixon supporter who contributed $1 million of his own money "in a propaganda campaign" of support for the President.

Yet the mission had made the North Vietnamese uncomfortable about their inhumane policies toward U.S. prisoners. For the first time they felt compelled to explain themselves. Why, indeed, hadn't the North Vietnamese, who were signatories to the Geneva convention, treated their prisoners correctly? Perot had seized the moral high ground, at least temporarily.

Three days before the New Year's deadline, Perot announced that the mission was bound for Moscow to deliver the thirty tons of dinners and gifts to the POWs for mailing. However, Hanoi declared that all the material must be delivered in parcels weighing no more than seven pounds each. That meant everything had to be repackaged. Perot arranged for more than 1,000 volunteers at an airfield in Anchorage, Alaska, a group that included GIs and hippies, to rewrap all the cargo.

The mission flew from Anchorage to Copenhagen, only to learn from the U.S. ambassador to the Soviet Union that the Russians forbade them to land in Moscow. The North Vietnamese had had enough of Perot's road show. At every juncture, Perot was making them look like heartless ideologues. The North Vietnamese negotiating strategy depended on making America into the heavy. Perot insisted his mission never was intended to bolster U.S. negotiators in Paris.

While some people remained skeptical of Perot's motives, an editorial in the *Chattanooga News–Free Press* suggested that "all patriots should be deeply grateful" for his efforts. Years later many U.S. POWs reported hearing of Perot's mission while being held captive. They said their treatment began to improve, more letters got through, medical treatment was extended to the badly wounded. On January 27, 1973, the United States, South Vietnam, North Vietnam, and the Vietcong signed a cease-fire agreement, providing for return of all prisoners within sixty days. Once the agreement was signed, Perot felt free to disclose that he had been paying cash for almost four years, working through a shadowy world of "intermediaries," for information and pictures of POWs. Men working for Perot, a group that included many EDS employees, met forty-seven times with Pathet Lao, North Vietnamese, and Vietcong representatives around the world.

In April 1973, shortly after the POWs returned, Perot threw a $250,000 weekend bash in San Francisco for a group of former POWs held at the Son Tay camp in North Vietnam and a team of Green Berets who tried unsuccessfully to rescue them in late 1970. The weekend started with a ticker-tape parade and military bands through the center of the city. Luncheons and parties followed. John Wayne, Clint Eastwood, the Andrews Sisters, and other stars appeared to honor the GIs. Perot put up everyone at the Fairmont Hotel.

The Son Tay raid had failed because of bad information. The raiders arrived to find an empty camp; the POWs had been moved to Hanoi. The operation produced a hero, however, Green Beret Colonel Arthur D. Simons, the leader known to his men as "Bull." Perot had met Colonel Simons and his raiders a few years earlier at Ft. Bragg, North Carolina, and assured them that what they had attempted was great. With this party, Perot showed them he had meant it.

Many U.S. soldiers thought to be among the POWs failed to return from Southeast Asia. Perot continued to finance the search for them, later sending Colonel Simons as a private citizen to Laos. Simons came back with pictures and information but no MIAs.

Perot's success at EDS and carefully cultivated contacts in the government created a springboard to carry out a type of private diplomacy that would not have been possible otherwise. Sending private emissaries to negotiate for U.S. POWs seemed from the outside to be skirting formal diplomatic procedures. Reporters quizzed him constantly, as they would years later following other rescues and attempts, as to whether his actions were sanctioned by the government. "We never spell that out," he answered. "We're representing the country's best interests. We made it clear to [government agencies that] if we were into something we shouldn't be in, all they had to do was tap us on the shoulder and we'd stop."

In other words, Perot had acted at the government's request, even though he wasn't supposed to say so specifically.

FOUR

On to Wall Street

O
N the morning of April 22, 1970, as Perot huddled with a client
at EDS's Dallas headquarters, turmoil hit the market for EDS
stock without warning.

At 1:00 P.M., not knowing anything was amiss, Perot emerged from his
meeting and called EDS vice president Tom Marquez for the usual check
on the day's events. Marquez reported very bad news: in the face of heavy
selling, EDS's stock had dropped violently, some fifty or sixty points by
noon. By the close of trading, the rout was devastating: EDS's value was
down by a third. Perot's one-day loss, on paper, totaled $450 million.

To this day no one is sure how or why EDS shares dropped so sharply
and suddenly. The relatively small number of publicly held shares may
have been a factor. EDS's profits had doubled in 1969 and were up 70
percent for the first quarter of 1970. EDS's share price didn't follow the
rest of the market down in 1969 and 1970, so EDS shares may have been
grotesquely vulnerable to a panic selloff. What happened to other stocks
in a year took place in just three hours at EDS.

Reporters who asked Perot on the day following the crash of EDS stock
to describe the horror of his own and EDS's financial loss heard this
instead: "This bothered me less than if one of my children had broken a
finger. It's a non-event."

In his view, nothing important had happened. After the first $100 million or so, the magnitude of his wealth existed for him as an abstraction. He hadn't felt differently having it, therefore he didn't know what it felt like losing it. In any case, Perot's "wealth" wasn't cash. The $160 peak share price had been no more than a manifestation of someone else's wild dreaming. And he'd done nothing to encourage it. Fortunately, Perot hadn't been tempted to borrow huge amounts of cash against the stock's inflated value. EDS's business was healthy and remained rooted firmly on earth: manic investors couldn't sell that short.

Perot's adventures in the magic kingdom of stocks and bonds presented him with the idea of exploiting an obvious market for EDS computer services. The skyrocketing volume of trades was causing the same kinds of backups, mistakes, and delays for brokerages that Medicare and Medicaid legislation had caused for Blue Cross/Blue Shield and the insurers. Untangling Wall Street's paper snarl was a natural opportunity for EDS. A few months after the crash, EDS bought Wall Street Leasing, a computer-services subsidiary of Dupont Glore Forgan, Inc., one of the nation's biggest retail stock brokerages.

Like many brokerages in the early 1970s, Dupont was choking on its own paper, unable to reconcile trades made by its brokers or find securities it was entrusted to safeguard. The deal looked like a good one for EDS. Wall Street Leasing was billing Dupont about $3 million a year for computer services and making about a 10 percent after-tax profit. To unsnarl Dupont's paperwork mess, EDS was going to raise Dupont's outlays for computer services to an average of $8 million a year for the coming eight years. Meanwhile, Perot planned to use Dupont as a laboratory for learning the back-office business of stock brokerages and then selling similar service contracts to other securities firms.

It was a great strategic move for EDS, except for one fact EDS didn't know: Dupont was terminally ill. Like one hundred or so other Wall Street firms that folded or were merged between 1969 and 1971, Dupont had lost vast sums because of its inability to service customers. Slow reconciling of accounts, lost securities, and inadequate computing were only symptoms of Dupont's inability to cope in a fast-changing, competitive industry.

Perot and EDS hadn't a clue how enormous their task was. The more EDSers dug into Dupont's notorious back-office snarls, the more problems they discovered that were not evident at the time of the acquisition. Perot was seeing Wall Street plain. The place suffered from more than mere inefficiency. The Street was slipshod and Perot wasn't shy about saying so. He spoke before investment analysts and at private lunches thrown by stock exchange firms. Spicing his talks with patriotic anecdotes and often accompanied by uniformed veterans, Perot told Wall Streeters that their business practices were substandard. What's more, he suggested, he and EDS might be the antidote to Wall Street's illness. "I feel strongly that everyone ought to make every contribution he can to the country," he proclaimed. "I'm best able to make my contribution in the area of business." He had come to save them.

The brokerage crisis cast a dark cloud over the entire stock market. A crisis committee of the New York Stock Exchange barely prevented the liquidation of venerable Hayden, Stone, Inc., in September 1970 by arranging a merger with another stock exchange firm, Cogan, Berlin, Weill and Levitt, which later evolved into Shearson-Lehman Brothers, a subsidiary of American Express. A liquidation would have left 90,000 brokerage customers high and dry for months and possibly forever. Could companies ever expect to raise capital again on Wall Street if brokerages began stiffing investors?

Led by Felix Rohatyn, a partner in Lazard Freres and Company, and Bernard Lasker, chairman of the exchange, the crisis committee barely had completed rescuing Hayden, Stone when Goodbody and Company, another former powerhouse, lurched into extremis. Lasker approached Donald Regan, Merrill Lynch's chairman, who agreed to take over the dying Goodbody. The New York Stock Exchange promised to indemnify Merrill Lynch for up to $30 million for any losses and litigation resulting from the takeover.

Dupont was a partnership led by scions from one of the nation's most aristocratic industrial families. By the time Perot bought its computer subsidiary, Dupont was on very shaky ground. A year earlier it had acquiesced to a merger with a smaller firm; then Dupont came up $6.8 million short on a capital audit. The partners stalled until a subsequent audit showed a bit more capital. Finally Ross Perot and EDS came aboard to clean up the back-room snarl. As EDS shock troops fanned out to survey the extent of the problem, Dupont seemed to have the capital situation under control.

Rohatyn, however, was worried. He knew any brokerage with a back-office problem couldn't know how much capital it had. It could only guess how much was salvageable. By November 1970, just as the Goodbody crisis was resolved, Edmond Dupont revealed that his partnership needed more capital to survive. Approaching Perot was a logical step for the Duponts: Perot had lots and lots of money, and the liquidation of Dupont and the loss of the Wall Street Leasing data processing account would hurt EDS as well as the Dupont family.

The stock exchange aided the Duponts by bringing President Nixon into the picture. The administration agreed with stock exchange governors that Dupont's collapse might raise the curtain on financial Armageddon. Attorney General John Mitchell and Treasury Secretary John Connally called Perot. Their messages were identical: You'll be saving the securities industry — and performing a great service for the country — by helping Dupont. Meyerson and Hart, meanwhile, flew to New York to check Dupont's finances. They found little prospect of a simple turn-around.

Out loud, Perot mused: "Why not let Dupont fail?"

Apart from the loss of business to EDS, the impact on the country's capital markets would be horrendous, administration officials told him. If disillusioned investors abandoned the stock markets, capital-intensive industries like airlines and utilities might face nationalization. The President's cabinet members assured Perot they wouldn't have approached him unless they thought this was a possibility.

As the Dupont rescue was presented, Ross Perot was being asked, in essence, to preserve the future of capitalism. Despite the ridiculous hyperbole of these arguments, Perot volunteered to help rescue Dupont if others pitched in too.

"Put me down for $5 million and make sure my name's at the bottom of the list," Perot told Rohatyn.

When no one else could be found to help, Perot swallowed hard, and tentatively lent Dupont the $10 million, pending final terms of an agreement under which Dupont was to switch from a partnership, which it had been since 1931, to a corporation. Perot had the right to convert $1.5 million of his loan to 51 percent of the stock of the new corporation. Dupont's 120 general and limited partners were obliged to raise $15 million for the newly organized company. Perot drove a hard bargain for his investment. Or so it seemed at the time. By February, Perot's own audit of Dupont revealed a parade of unpaid obligations dating back years. Dupont needed another $20 million to $30 million to stay in business.

The Duponts screamed that Perot was trying to steal their company. At that point, in early February 1971, Perot was prepared to walk away, possibly losing the $10 million loan and EDS's lucrative data processing contract.

Realizing Perot's serious intent, the Duponts agreed to negotiate. Perot insulated EDS from direct involvement in the Dupont mess. He set up PHMFG Corporation, of which he owned 55 percent and to which he supplied nearly all the money, to dicker with the Duponts. The other owners of PHMFG were Mort Meyerson, 21 percent, Milledge Hart, 15 percent, and 3 percent each to Diane Folzenlogen, EDS's secretary, Bill Gayden, EDS vice president, and Bob Martin, an attorney representing EDS.

The Duponts viewed Perot as a crude arriviste, trying to capitalize on their temporary distress by finagling their company from them with token payment. Who, indeed, was this backwoods upstart, dictating terms to America's most illustrious industrial family? Rohatyn kept reminding the Duponts, sometimes gently and occasionally with the faintest tinge of irony, that without Perot's money the partnership was likely to fail, linking a proud name with a disgraceful fiasco.

Perot was furious. They don't care a fig about what could happen to the stock market if Dupont fails, he thought. Just because they're Duponts they think the rules of the marketplace don't apply to them. They couldn't run a candy store, much less a brokerage.

Then the White House got into the act again. Attorney General Mitchell, Deputy Treasury Secretary Peter Flanigan, and Merrill Lynch chairman Donald Regan confronted the Duponts. They didn't budge.

The next day, Rohatyn suggested a compromise. Why not issue warrants to let the Duponts increase their minority stake to 20 percent at some point in the distant future? Assuming that the brokerage prospered, Perot's 80 percent would still represent a sizable return on his investment. Rohatyn's idea broke the logjam.

Perot wasn't quite finished dictating terms. Meyerson had warned him he might need to spend an additional $40 million to straighten out Dupont. He asked the stock exchange to indemnify him for up to $25 million of his losses; Lasker and Rohatyn agreed to $15 million. Then Perot persuaded the Federal Reserve to bend the margin requirements on EDS stock needed to secure $55 million of bank loans for his investment. Normally the Fed wanted $157 million worth of stock as collateral for a loan that size. Instead, it settled for half as much. The final fly in the ointment was general partner Edmond Dupont's refusal to sign the agreement. He ''retired'' from Dupont on April 27 at the insistence of the other partners. On May 14, 1971, Perot took over the newly incorporated Dupont Glore Forgan, Inc.

For a man supposedly motivated by altruistic patriotism, Perot had gone to some extraordinary lengths to own Dupont Glore Forgan. What started as a $5 million loan turned into a $40 million investment, committing Perot up to his eyes in a business he knew very little about.

Perot, in short order, had become Wall Street's biggest individual investor. It hadn't happened by accident, and he wasn't looking back. He was sure that if he applied the principles he used to make EDS successful — rational, results-oriented management — he could restore the integrity lost to the brokerage community during the past two years of insolvencies and consolidations. Mort Meyerson moved to New York and took over as president of Dupont Glore Forgan. A top EDS vice president, he too was certain that the spirit that built EDS into a firm valued at more than $1 billion could reverse Dupont's fortunes.

Perot and Meyerson's first step was to tighten the slipshod financial controls that first had caused Dupont's accounting problems. Using EDS's computing expertise, Perot ordered accounts reconciled, and cash and securities accounted, each and every night, at every one of the firm's 112 branches nationwide. A profit and loss statement from every branch was to be wired to New York headquarters. Dupont previously had been settling accounts once a month, and in far less detail than Perot demanded.

Meyerson streamlined Dupont's management and sales-reporting system. Previously, all 112 branch managers reported directly to the president. Meyerson divided the country into six regions and appointed a manager for each region. The regional chiefs reported to a head of sales. Perot started a venture-capital unit inside Dupont to invest seed capital in small growth companies.

Perot failed to appreciate the magnitude of differences in attitude and style between the securities industry based in New York and Texas-based EDS. His vocal patriotism didn't play well in the company. New York was an intellectual hotbed, Democratic, hostile to the U.S. war effort. Many brokers and traders at the time favored beards, long hair, bell-bottomed trousers, and Day-glo ties. Marijuana wasn't uncommon on Wall Street and the scent wafted through the air of the financial district during lunch hour.

In Perot's mind, these were symptoms of the slackness that had caused Dupont's monumental losses. Meyerson put the word out: long hair and beards must go. Businesslike dress and professional behavior, EDS style, were the order of the day. An already skeptical work force grew more so. Perot had been able to shape thoroughly the character of EDS's work force by careful selective recruiting; there was no such opportunity at Dupont. However, a new criterion was added to Dupont's recruiting efforts: veterans, especially the gung-ho types who filled EDS's ranks, were welcomed.

Perot attempted to change Wall Street's very parlance. He never liked such terms as "cage," used to describe where back-office workers sat at a brokerage. "How would you like to tell your neighbor you worked in a cage?" was his rhetorical explanation. Henceforth, back-office workers belonged to Dupont's "operations division."

To finance the takeover of Dupont, Perot sold 900,000 of his own EDS shares to the public at $63.50 each, reducing his EDS stake to 63.8 percent from 72 percent. Anyone who doubted the sincerity of Perot's reforms only had to look at the $57.2 million cash raised in the offering. As it turned out, Perot needed every penny of the $57.2 million — and more. As Meyerson dug into Dupont, he discovered more unpaid debts, more unpaid dividends owed to customers, and more evidence that negotiable securities had been stolen or lost. By August, Meyerson had turned up $86 million of discrepancies in customer accounts — surely some kind of record. By summer, Perot had sunk $55 million into Dupont.

The New York Stock Exchange owed a debt of gratitude to Perot, but it wasn't willing to relax the minimum capital rules for him. Whatever discrepancies Meyerson couldn't resolve had to be charged against Dupont's capital, meaning Perot had to replace the bad accounts and losses dollar-for-dollar with new capital. In November, Dupont needed another $19 million to meet the exchange's rules.

Perot considered his investment, now ten times bigger than he had planned and getting more expensive by the day. He wondered if Dupont was a black hole and dismissed the thought. Once committed, he wasn't about to quit.

"My theory is, anything you get ready to do, you ought to be ready to pay for," he told reporters. "I don't ordinarily talk about my personal finances, but let me say I have $55 million cash in hand over and above the $55 million in Dupont. That represents a lot of overkill. We want to be certain we can protect and sustain the firm, and we know we can."

Meyerson's hard work and EDS ingenuity began to pay off at Dupont. From May 1971 to May 1972 Dupont managed to squeeze out a small profit and had no discrepancies in its customer accounts.

As luck would have it, the securities business entered a period of doldrums in the summer of 1972. Brokerage commissions simply were too low to cover expenses. However, once trading volume picked up again, Perot reasoned, Dupont's profit was assured. In 1970, the year Perot made his first loan, Dupont lost more than $17 million from operations, a grim record. By 1975, according to Perot's projections,

Dupont would be earning $20 million a year; at 15 times earnings, the company should be worth $300 million. The other part of the payoff, Perot presumed, was through EDS. While straightening out Dupont, and collecting a nice fee for the work, EDS was learning how to run a nationwide brokerage network.

It was an optimistic scenario. In theory it sounded plausible. So plausible, in fact, that Perot upped his bet in 1973 by investing $10 million in Walston and Company, another retail brokerage with a large network of offices around the country. Walston had hired EDS to organize its accounting, so Perot knew quite well about the firm's recent losses and regulatory problems. In June 1973, Perot exercised his option to buy Walston voting shares and proposed a merger of Dupont and Walston into one holding company. The two brokerages remained separate but shared EDS's accounting services and presumably trimmed operating expenses.

Despite EDS's best efforts, Dupont remained mired in deep financial trouble. The consolidation of Walston's and Dupont's operations was a desperate attempt to use what remained of Walston's strength to prop up Dupont. In the two years Perot and Meyerson controlled Dupont, the brokerage lost $32 million from operations and risked suspension from the stock exchange for violation of the net capital rule.

By the fall of 1973, Perot's investment in the two firms reached a whopping $97 million. A nine-figure loss was enough for any man, even Perot. Perot had been tying rocks together and hoping somehow they might float. His optimism depleted, Perot's psychology turned bearish. He had doubled, tripled, and quadrupled his bet and still faced the need to put up more cash to save Dupont from liquidation. Perhaps through some weird twist of destiny, Perot was being forced to return, from whence it came, the fortune he had made on Wall Street.

In January 1974 the Dupont directors and Meyerson met in New York and decided to dissolve Dupont Walston and Company. Perot's formula for success hadn't worked on Wall Street. EDS had, in fact, cleaned up the operations. Securities no longer vanished. Accounts were settled on time. Dividends were paid to the right customers. But stockbrokers balked at lockstep regimentation and crew-cut discipline. Dupont's entire Decatur, Illinois, office and sales staff walked out in rebellion and joined a rival brokerage. Personnel practices borrowed from EDS, such as making new trainees sign pledges to reimburse the company $12,000 if they left within three years, engendered hostility rather than esprit.

Recruiting ex-military men hadn't worked as well in brokerage sales as it had in EDS's computer operations. A man who thrived on the tight order and teamwork of a combat unit didn't necessarily possess the initiative and interpersonal skills to develop retail brokerage accounts. In retrospect, other Perot tactics to boost revenue appeared uninformed and simplistic. He exhorted salesmen to pursue "elephants," wealthy individuals with large amounts to spend on securities, rather than ordinary wage earners who earned average salaries. In fact, most elephants already belonged to rival brokers and weren't easily stolen. Moreover, heavy trading volume in the stock market was more and more becoming dominated by institutions, pension funds, mutual funds, college endowments, insurance companies.

Ironically, retail customers would return to the market within a few years — but too late for Dupont.

Ross Perot came to save Wall Street, all the while preaching the need to reform sloppy business practices. There was plenty of unkind snickering on trading desks and the exchange floor when Dupont announced it was dissolving operations and selling its offices to other firms. The cocky Texan had ridden down Wall Street with sage advice and was riding home $60 million poorer.

FIVE

The Big Leagues

THE takeover of Dupont, the investment in Walston, the joining of the two companies, the liquidation of Dupont Glore Forgan, and the subsequent Chapter 11 filing of Walston and Company created a decade's worth of legal snarls for Ross Perot.

Nella Walston, widow of Walston and Company's founder, filed suit to undo the merger. Edmond Dupont, Dupont's former chairman, sued Perot, charging misuse of inside information to gain control of the firm. Dupont Walston branch offices were put up for sale. Creditors galore lined up for payment. Perot needed expert legal help fast. On the advice of a Dupont attorney who recommended a law school classmate from Dallas, Perot invited Tom Luce to New York to hear his suggestions for a legal strategy. Luce wasn't inclined to pitch Perot any quick solutions. Perot's problems were enormously complicated. Whoever got the job of coordinating legal strategy had to contend with 300 law firms across the country asserting claims against Perot and EDS.

"I couldn't possibly advise you without spending a month in New York sorting through everything," Luce said.

When Luce agreed to come to New York to formulate Perot's legal strategy, he had been working as a partner in a four-man law firm for just a year. Married at the age of nineteen, Luce was a subdued, softspoken individual who had worked in a Dallas accounting firm by day and attended SMU law school at night. Perot was impressed with his work ethic, straightforward honesty, and down-to-earth business judgment. More important than anything else, Perot sensed he could trust Luce to act in his behalf independently.

As Luce initially suspected, he needed nearly ten years to extinguish the legal firestorm of the Dupont Walston affair. The settlement with the bankruptcy trustee cost Perot and EDS $6.7 million. In the process, Luce won the job as Ross Perot's and EDS's top legal adviser. Luce agreed to serve as general counsel for EDS, gradually adding lawyers to his law firm as he needed them to care for EDS's growing business. Luce's four-member law firm grew to 140 attorneys, one of Dallas's biggest, thanks in large part to Perot and EDS.

Luce felt he best could sum up his relationship with his client by describing him as "legally intensive." Perot felt free to call at any time, at Luce's home if necessary, to confer. Perot sought guidance on any number of business, political, and legal issues. Luce, in turn, had a free hand to hire whatever additional outside talent he needed and submit the bill to Perot. For a lawyer it was the best of both worlds: the franchise of internal general counsel combined with the intellectual and operating freedom of outside counsel. Luce particularly appreciated the way Perot made him feel that he was entrusted to carry the ball and wouldn't be second-guessed — as long as he produced results.

An understanding grew between the two men. They were contemporaries and cherished similar values. They both had left employment in large organizations to build their own. Luce and Perot also were friends, but they seldom found themselves at the same social gatherings in Dallas; and Luce was grateful for the breathing room. Unlike some lawyers who seek to tie themselves inextricably to important clients, socially and otherwise, Luce was comfortable supplying only legal counsel.

Choosing Tom Luce to be EDS's attorney wasn't the safest choice Perot could have made during that black period in New York. Perot never told Luce why he chose him rather than a fancy, established firm. On many issues, Luce learned that an unspoken understanding was best. As Luce came to know and understand his client, he realized it was futile to overtalk, overanalyze, or overintellectualize certain issues. That wasn't Perot's style.

With so much top corporate attention and energy directed toward the Dupont Walston debacle, EDS lost a great deal of sales momentum in the early 1970s. Competitors, meanwhile, had begun selling the same kind of services. Often the competition was willing to perform for lower prices than EDS, which forced EDS to trim its profit margins to win contracts. For the first time in its thirteen-year history, EDS profits dropped in 1975; they continued down the following year. Shaded by the cloud of Dupont Walston, EDS stock dropped to less than $11 a share in late 1974, compared with its $16.50 offering price six years earlier.

In 1975 Mort and Marlene Meyerson gave up their Manhattan apartment and moved back to Dallas. Emotionally, it was a difficult time. Meyerson loved New York and didn't like having to return home with the burden of a failure. Meyerson couldn't be blamed for Dupont's demise, but the episode was something he wanted to wipe out by proving to everyone at EDS that he was still a tough, smart, competent businessman, that he could still hit major-league pitching. On his first day back at Dallas headquarters, Meyerson drove to EDS headquarters in an old, beat-up brown Volkswagen. It was his hair shirt, the badge of his campaign to reestablish himself at EDS. Until he had proven himself again, he wasn't expending an iota of energy on material pleasure.

Sam Meyerson, Mort Meyerson's grandfather, journeyed to Ft. Worth, Texas, from the Lower East Side of Manhattan at the turn of the twentieth century. Mort's grandfather was a tailor in search of opportunity when a cousin from Viluzin, the same Russian village they had both fled from, persuaded Sam to leave Hester Street for the Lone Star State.

Mort Meyerson's father, Brudus, was one of five children and, like Sam Meyerson, harbored few fond feelings toward the old country. He became a thoroughly acculturated American in Ft. Worth, played football in high school, and went to work afterward selling insurance. However, the immigrant creed — my children will have the opportunities I did not — obsessed him. His son, Mort, attended Paschal High School in Ft. Worth and played football. Not one of the Meyersons had attended college yet. Meyerson's father and mother expected their son to be the first.

Meyerson was one of only a handful of Jewish students at Paschal, and though he was conscious of his religion, he rarely noticed any discrimination directed at him. Self-confident and a strong student academically, Meyerson attended the University of Texas, where he was active in student politics, sang in the a cappella choir, and joined the U.S. Army Reserve Officer Training Corps. When Meyerson won his commission, his family was elated. Grandfather Sam hated his Russian birthplace and believed that the members of his family should show their allegiance to the country that gave them refuge and opportunity. The first to attend college also became the first to serve in the armed forces as an officer.

Meyerson's first taste of the army was anything but inspiring. Assigned as aide-de-camp to a colonel at an army base in Indiantown Gap, Pennsylvania, he had little to do but pass the time with handball, bowling, reading, and bridge. Once, at a weekend bridge tournament in Atlantic City, Meyerson was paired with the head of his base's data processing department, who observed that Meyerson's style of play suggested an aptitude for more cerebral pursuits, like computers. Meyerson was transferred to the army's data processing department and attended computer school in Ft. Monmouth, New Jersey, learning the mysteries of the model 650, an IBM workhorse of the 1950s and early 1960s. After his army service, Meyerson returned to Ft. Worth, where he married his college sweetheart, a Galveston girl named Marlene Nathan, and went to work for Bell Helicopter as a programmer. Two years later in 1965, he was about to accept a promotion from Bell's corporate parent, Textron Corporation, when a former colleague at Bell invited him to an interview at EDS.

At EDS he met Milledge "Mitch" Hart, Perot's colleague from IBM, who helped found EDS and later would become president. Hart immediately offered to match Textron's offer. In the long run, he told Meyerson, compensation would be better at EDS than at Textron, because EDS was private, paid according to merit, and planned to distribute stock generously as an incentive for hard work. Hart also claimed that EDS offered opportunity to prove oneself without the tangle of corporate bureaucracy and gamesmanship. Meyerson was tempted by EDS's wide-open playing field. He had one reservation, though: to him, it looked as if nearly everyone at EDS was a Perot clone: white, Protestant, and ex–Naval Academy.

"I only qualify in one of three categories," he told Hart.

Nonsense, Hart insisted. At EDS, the best person gets the job.

Meyerson got a fast start at EDS because his talent caught Ross Perot's attention immediately. With his background in IBM equipment from the army and Bell, Meyerson was able to write some of the first programs EDS used in the health insurance field. Perot liked Meyerson for another reason: he was creative, just a little offbeat, a healthy complement to himself. Perot was straightforward, perhaps a bit narrow; Perot knew he could always count on Mort Meyerson to give him a slightly oblique approach to solving a problem. And Meyerson's ideas worked. Thirteen years after wondering whether a young Jew from Ft. Worth could fit in at

EDS, Meyerson had reached as high as anyone not named Perot was going to at the company.

After running Dupont Walston, Meyerson was returning to EDS in 1975 without a defined role. Perot asked him to find out what was wrong with EDS's faltering Medicare and Medicaid business. He drove across the country and visited all of EDS's accounts. He returned to Dallas and told Perot there was a great deal of business out there, and EDS must build a team that understood the Medicare and Medicaid market and could land some major contracts right away. Taking command of the job, Meyerson asked Ken Riedlinger, then a promising manager in EDS's Columbus, Ohio, office, to be regional manager in charge of selling contracts in the eastern United States.

A Kansan who had gained computer experience in the aerospace industry, Riedlinger was very much the model of a tough, loyal manager who showed initiative and independence supervising the operation of EDS accounts. A former college football player, he was formidable in size and demeanor. He also was idealistic: as a young man he had volunteered to work as a Catholic lay missionary in Central America. Riedlinger joined EDS in 1968, having been attracted to the small, egalitarian, action-oriented team Ross Perot had created. Perot fascinated him. He had never met a person who was capable of such intense concentration. In the early days of his EDS career, he felt that working for Perot was as exciting and perilous as trying to drink from a roaring fire hose.

But by 1975 Riedlinger had spent seven grinding years supervising operations for various EDS clients around the country, during which time he had moved his family four times. He thought EDS wasn't paying him much by industry standards, less than $30,000 for the job of experienced systems operations manager. Worse yet, the first round of EDS stock options, Ross Perot's technique for motivating workers, had, because of the poor performance of the EDS stock price, cost him much of his savings. Just before Meyerson returned, Riedlinger was feeling particularly low, having been passed over for promotion to regional manager.

At a sales meeting in Dallas, Meyerson took Riedlinger aside and told him that he understood his frustration. If Riedlinger helped him sell new Medicare and Medicaid business, together they could write a fresh chapter at EDS and play a big part in its future. Meyerson promised to let Riedlinger pursue new contracts on his own and earn commissions on his sales. More financial rewards awaited beyond that.

"I'll give you $26,000 right now as a draw against what you'll earn in the first year," Meyerson said.

It didn't take Riedlinger long to say yes. Money wasn't the issue. Fundamentally, he still yearned to belong to a group, to have a mission. He enjoyed the spirit of adventure at EDS, the way everyone pulled together toward a common goal, the feeling of camaraderie, and the excitement of success.

Riedlinger saw that Meyerson was trying to turn EDS around. If he succeeded he would be a strong contender someday for the job of Perot's top lieutenant. Besides Les Alberthal and some other vice presidents, Meyerson was the only other candidate to someday succeed Mitch Hart as president. Alberthal was responsible for operating the Medicare and Medicaid contracts that Meyerson sold. Meyerson told Riedlinger he intended to sell so many new contracts that Alberthal wouldn't be able to run them all.

Winning state health-care contracts was as much about politics as it was about aggressive selling. Riedlinger's experience had been mostly managing data processing contracts. His new job took him to state capitals, where he spent much of his time cultivating health-care commissioners and politicians. Riedlinger kept a list of dates when bids were due, and he quickly learned useful tricks: If EDS needed more time, he tried to delay the bid deadlines. If EDS was ready but the competition needed more time, he cajoled health-care commissioners to move the date up. EDS's strength was the ability to amass swiftly a team of committed, zealous workers to carry out studies and write complicated proposals. They swooped into town and rented a "war room" at the local Holiday Inn. The team set up cots, ordered in fast food, and worked day and night analyzing the job. Do we buy a computer or lease time? How will we link the offices? How many people do we need? What's the present cost of data processing? Can we beat the current cost and still make a profit?

More often than not EDS's massive assault worked. The EDS team produced thick, detailed bid proposals fast. The proposals were impressive and they promised substantial savings for the state. How could health-care officials ignore such zealousness? EDS showed how competing data processing methods wasted money. How would it look if politicians and legislators passed up a chance to economize? Without saying so directly, Riedlinger made state government officials understand the possible consequences of denying EDS a contract. EDS performed better, faster, and for less money than anyone in the business. By this logic, EDS was entitled to win the contract. If EDS didn't win,

Riedlinger assumed someone had violated the accepted rules of play, and he could bend the rules when necessary, too.

Riedlinger helped EDS win a political fight for North Carolina's Medicaid contract in 1975. Then Meyerson sent him to Alabama. It was Riedlinger's first experience leading an EDS platoon into battle. Blue Cross/Blue Shield had run Alabama's health-care contracts for years without opposition. Riedlinger hired a group of politically astute Montgomery lawyers to represent EDS. They reviewed the state's bidding laws, carefully finessing the ground rules in EDS's favor. By the time Blue Cross/Blue Shield woke up to EDS's challenge, it was too late to organize an effective bid. Moments before the bid deadline, Riedlinger and Meyerson were camped outside the office of Governor George Wallace, scribbling EDS's final offer for the governor on a yellow legal pad. EDS won by a hair.

Riedlinger's next campaign was Tennessee, where the deck was stacked heavily against EDS. In theory, Tennessee law required competitive bidding for all state contracts. Riedlinger visited the state's human-resources director. When Riedlinger declared that EDS wanted to bid for the state's Medicaid contract, he was told with southern politesse: Forget it; Tennessee doesn't want or need EDS's data processing expertise, thank you. The job's already taken.

Riedlinger dutifully reported the rejection to Meyerson. He was told to hire Frank Gorrell, a lawyer with solid connections to politicians and newspapers in Nashville. Gorrell was friendly and encouraging; he told Riedlinger to sharpen his pencil and make the best bid possible.

If it's the low bid, EDS will get the job, Gorrell told him; the law requires competitive bidding.

Bullshit, Riedlinger thought. He had seen the contemptuous expression on the health commissioner's face. This thing's rigged so Blue Cross will win, Riedlinger realized, but he followed Gorrell's advice.

In the autumn of 1976, EDS submitted a bid for a five-year contract. It was $7 million lower than the bid of the incumbents, Blue Cross/Blue Shield and Equitable Life Assurance Society. A legislative committee recommended that the state award the contract to EDS. Instead, Governor Ray Blanton's cabinet delayed the award.

Riedlinger smelled a rat. Eugene Fowinkle, the state health commissioner, publicly favored awarding Blue Cross/Blue Shield the contract. Blanton, however, was worried about potential fallout from voters displeased with the state's failure to take advantage of $7 million in savings. He delayed his decision and then announced that the delay meant

EDS didn't have enough time to set up operations before the January 1 deadline. Blanton's action was transparently unfair, and Perot flew to Nashville to say so. Fowinkle awarded a one-year "temporary" contract to Blue Cross/Blue Shield and Equitable anyway, citing too many "unknown" factors in EDS's bid.

EDS and Gorrell, backed by the *Nashville Banner*, were pitted against Blanton, Blue Cross/Blue Shield, and the *Nashville Tennessean*. The Blanton administration looked bad. Gorrell and Riedlinger were talking to reporters frequently, driving home the notion that Blanton unfairly favored Blue Cross and Equitable, which was going to cost taxpayers plenty.

A day or so before Christmas, Riedlinger was in his room at the Hyatt in Nashville. He felt temporarily deflated and out of ammunition. He had done everything he could think of and the state seemed bound to keep Blue Cross/Blue Shield anyway. Meyerson finally advised him to give up on Tennessee.

Suddenly, someone shoved an envelope under Riedlinger's door. It contained a request for Ross Perot to meet secretly with Blanton's representatives. They were ready to surrender! It was the break Riedlinger was waiting for. Overjoyed at the good news, Riedlinger called Meyerson, who was staying at Perot's cabin in Vail, Colorado.

"You've got to get Perot and come to Nashville immediately. They're ready to give us the contract," Riedlinger said excitedly.

"No way," Meyerson said. "First of all, Ross has a bad back. He can't travel." But Riedlinger pleaded until Meyerson agreed to call Perot. A chartered Learjet picked up Meyerson at Vail and flew him to Dallas. Because Meyerson had forgotten his housekeys in Colorado, he had to break into his house to get a business suit. He picked up Perot and together they returned to the waiting Lear.

Riedlinger was waiting for them at a private hangar at Nashville airport. Fowinkle, the health commissioner, hadn't arrived yet.

Perot's back was aching, and the only way to relieve the pain was to lie down. Riedlinger couldn't believe his eyes as the founder of EDS stretched out on the floor of the hangar. "Maybe I'll just stay here on the floor and they'll think I'm a kook, like Howard Hughes," Perot joked.

By the time Fowinkle arrived, Perot was on his feet, and he wasn't smiling. "Our position is simple," Perot said, staring at Fowinkle. "The January 1 expiration on the old contract is a few days away. We won this competition fair and square. EDS submitted the low bid and is entitled to the contract. You need to know that we will spare no effort or expense or legal action to make sure we get it.'' The threat was effective.

"I guess we have no choice," Fowinkle said. "You win."

There weren't any negotiations. No new terms or promises. To Riedlinger, it appeared as if Fowinkle just wanted to hear one last time, from Perot himself, that EDS wasn't going to back off. Ever. EDS had defeated an entrenched political alliance. Perot had always said: Just hang in there. If you're right, sooner or later the tide will turn.

And it had in Tennessee.

State officials were tough, but EDS had trouble landing contracts at private companies, too. Internal data processing managers always argued against hiring EDS; they were proud of their work and resented EDS's claims of superior performance. The managers also feared EDS's corporate culture. When EDS took over, the managers knew, Perot insisted that everyone on the job become EDS employees, subject to EDS's code.

If he demanded higher standards of behavior and performance, Perot also believed he was offering data processing workers better career opportunities. Instead of working for a small or medium-size data processing department with limited chance for advancement, data processing workers joined a fast-growing company with scores of career paths and management posts all over the country.

EDS offered greater monetary incentives as well. True, the salaries and benefits weren't lavish. EDS paid entry-level workers the industry average. For top people, however, financial rewards were great. Perot paid cash bonuses and he built longer-term incentives using EDS stock. By encouraging top-performing EDS workers to buy stock at very cheap prices, Perot gave them a stake in EDS's future. The principle, used by thousands of startup companies, was simple: As EDS grew more profitable, the value of the stock increased. Therefore, top EDSers were motivated through self-interest to improve profits by trimming costs and boosting revenue. Lower-level EDSers were motivated to reach the higher levels by watching those above them grow wealthy.

The principle was sound, but EDS's plan required some tinkering. Perot's first attempt to use EDS stock as an incentive was a dud. In EDS's 1968 and 1970 stock-option plans, EDS lent Ken Riedlinger and many other managers money to buy options. The price of the option was equal to the price of the stock at the time of the award. As EDS stock rose in value, or so the theory went, the holder could exercise the option, repay the loan, and pocket the difference.

Unfortunately for Riedlinger and others, EDS's share price plummeted in the mid-1970s because of the Dupont Walston fiasco. Some EDSers who paid $100 a share for options watched in horror as the share price dropped to less than $11 a share. The options expired worthless but the optionholders still were obliged to repay huge loans.

Using a plan developed by Luce's law firm for the Harte Hanks newspaper chain, Perot and Meyerson modified the stock-option plan when EDS's profits resumed growing in 1977. This time, he put aside a million EDS shares to sell to EDS's top 200 employees. But the price was as little as 5 cents a share. Since the shares were worth $18 on the open market, the second stock incentive plan was an immediate, risk-free windfall. Meyerson, for example, paid 20 cents each for 100,000 EDS shares in 1977, a $20,000 price for stock worth just under $2 million. Under the terms of the plan, Meyerson was permitted to sell shares as EDS's stock reached certain price levels over a ten-year period.

The first big break for EDS in the international market was a contract with King Abdulazziz University in Saudi Arabia, followed by a $41 million pact with the Iranian social security system, announced in November 1976. EDS's 1978 upbeat annual report for the fiscal year ended June 30, 1978, which highlighted the contract in Iran, reached shareholders about the same time that the faltering Iranian government stopped paying EDS for its services. Written before the worst trouble broke out, the report rhapsodized about EDS's "exciting role" in bringing computers to the region.

"This challenge, combined with outstanding opportunities for exciting recreation [desert jeep caravans and photography safaris] and economical travel to many of the world's most interesting cities, has made the Middle East a choice assignment for the 200 EDS people from the U.S. and Europe who are working there," the report said. A smiling picture of Paul Chiapparone, EDS's country manager in Iran, greeted shareholders on page thirteen.

By December 1978, EDS's situation in Iran had turned critical. Many of the Iranian officials whom EDS had dealt with in the past were jailed by "revolutionary" officials. EDS hadn't been paid since June, and it notified the government that it was suspending operations. This was no small step. EDS issued all the health-care and social security checks in Iran. No one could guess what further havoc a suspension of payments might cause in the revolution-torn country. The unrest hadn't been aimed directly at EDS, but to be safe, Perot ordered all 80 EDS workers and 150 dependents out of the country. Hopeful that order might be restored, a handful of top officials remained behind.

The arrest of Chiapparone and his assistant Bill Gaylord abruptly ended EDS's innocence. Revolutionary officials, now in debt to EDS for millions of dollars and without computers, were determined to trump up evidence proving that EDS had corruptly diverted millions of dollars from the Iranian treasury. Their evidence was EDS's partnership with an Iranian national, although such partnerships were a requirement for companies wishing to do business in the country. Ross Perot wasn't afraid of playing hardball to win a contract, but he drew the line at breaking the law. (An official in Louisiana once had suggested that EDS could have a major piece of Medicare business if it agreed to a "partnership" with one of the official's friends. "Sorry. That's illegal as hell," Perot told them.) Iran's practices differed from those in the United States. EDS had agreed to a joint venture with an Iranian businessman because that was the only way foreigners were allowed to do business there, but Perot wasn't about to compromise his company by engaging in corrupt practices. He hadn't paid bribes. Other U.S. companies like Lockheed had been sullied by charges of overseas payoffs, and he wasn't going to let it happen to EDS.

Anyone could see that in the midst of revolutionary unrest, random jailings, and executions, EDS wasn't about to receive a fair hearing on its business practices. Law had broken down. The Iranian justice minister tried to confiscate Gaylord and Chiapparone's passports. When that didn't work, he arrested them and set bail at $12 million.

Perot first tried to apply pressure on the Iranian captors through the State Department and through personal contacts with Henry Kissinger. Although Kissinger was no longer in government, many in the State Department remembered that Perot had responded to the government's requests to help the POWs and to prop up Dupont Walston.

Unfortunately, the days of U.S. influence in Tehran were over, and there was little Kissinger or the State Department could do. The country learned a few months later, when its own embassy was captured, what little regard Iran's new rulers had for the United States, let alone the desires of a Texas businessman.

After diplomatic channels proved unnavigable, Perot resorted to direct action. Directness was the style he had been born to, and the one he preferred. Perot believed in experts. He hired people who were the best at what they did, and he happened to know the best in the rescue business: Bull Simons, the man who led the attempted rescue at the Son Tay prison camp in North Vietnam. After meeting Simons at the party he threw for the Son Tay raiders, Perot had employed the ex–Green Beret to search for U.S. soldiers missing in action in Southeast Asia.

In a revolution, nothing goes according to plan. Chance and random events play an extraordinary role in success or failure. Perot was able to survey the chaos and danger for himself when he took the enormous risk of visiting the two jailed executives prior to the rescue. He simply entered the country on his U.S. passport and prayed that airport officials didn't associate him with Chiapparone and Gaylord. The visit convinced him there was no way to get the men out but to rescue them.

In early January 1979, Simons and a small team of EDS executives selected by Perot flew to Tehran to try to break Gaylord and Chiapparone out of Gasr Prison. When they scouted the prison, the task seemed impossible. But incredibly, a young Iranian national who worked for EDS in Tehran organized a mob that broke into Gasr and released all the prisoners. Gaylord and Chiapparone were able literally to walk out of the prison and hitch a ride to the Hyatt Hotel, where they found their rescuers. The most difficult task turned out to be fleeing the country, which the rescue team and hostages accomplished by crossing the Turkish border on foot.

Overjoyed as he was about the rescue, Ross Perot hadn't much enthusiasm for celebration. His eighty-two-year-old mother, Lulu May, was dying of bone cancer. Perot's late father, Gabriel Ross Perot, had taught him how to trade and how to break a wild horse. His mother gave him his moral fiber, his discipline, his iron will, his soul. He had consulted her in 1969 when he was contemplating a trip to Southeast Asia on behalf of the POWs. She had advised him to go. EDS was a tiny, brand-new public company. He would be jeopardizing the stakes of hundreds of investors by exposing himself to danger.

"Those men fought for this country," she said. "Can you compare their sacrifice sitting in jail against someone's financial investment in EDS?" As always, she reduced the situation to its essence. She was right and, as always, he listened to her.

He had asked her advice again before traveling to Iran to visit Chiapparone and Gaylord. They both knew she was dying, and they might never see each other again.

"You sent those men over there. You'd never be able to live with yourself if you didn't help them out."

On April 3, 1979, she died, three months after the rescue.

EDSers proved their ingenuity and courage in Iran. "Don't tell us how to do the job,'' EDS managers often told Perot, ''just tell us what we're trying to accomplish and we'll find a way to do it.'' The Iranian rescue exemplified the very best about the people of EDS, he thought, for it was another example of EDS spirit and the loyalty EDSers had for one other. The escape from Iran was a legend that belonged in the company's official history, right beside the Frito-Lay contract and the skirmishes with IBM. He wanted the story cast in heroic terms; he wanted to give it a larger-than-life flavor. Perot's wife, Margot, suggested the way.

''You should hire the fellow who wrote this,'' Margot Perot told her husband one evening, showing him a copy of *Eye of the Needle*. Perot hadn't heard of Ken Follett, but he called the British author's agent and asked whether his client might be interested in trying his hand at a true-life hostage thriller. As a matter of fact, Follett had begun his career writing nonfiction. Born in Cardiff, Wales, Follett studied philosophy in London and became a newspaper reporter. While working for the *London Evening News* he wrote his first novel and published it under a pen name. It sold poorly. After writing ten more undistinguished novels, he hit the jackpot with *Eye of the Needle*, an international bestseller. *Triple*, *The Key to Rebecca*, and *The Man from St. Petersburg* followed and were all number-one bestsellers.

When Follett's agent delivered Perot's message, the author didn't know what to think. Since his books had become bestsellers he had been averaging about one letter a week suggesting an idea for a book.

Perot's approach, however, piqued Follett's curiosity. The man was a self-made billionaire and certified hero. He seemed nothing like the reclusive, quirky types often associated with great wealth. Follett was between projects in any case, having just finished *The Man from St. Petersburg*, and Perot's adventure in Iran was the most attractive story on Follett's horizon in the summer of 1981. He agreed to fly to Dallas to meet Ross Perot.

Immediately, Follett sensed he was dealing with someone who shaped events to his own specifications. Perot told Follett he wanted veto power over what Follett wrote. Like most writers who had grown up as journalists, Follett was uncomfortable giving up the freedom to portray events as he interpreted them. As he got to know Perot, Follett knew he was dealing with a once-in-a-lifetime character. Small-town roots, east Texas twang, storybook family, world-class fortune and business career: the elements were there for a magnificent story.

Follett was surprised to learn that Perot wasn't too concerned about his own image. But he demanded the right to protect the name and memory of the gruff and profane Bull Simons. Simons had died after a series of heart attacks in May 1979, and Perot wanted him portrayed as sympathetically as possible.

Follett insisted that Perot give him a free hand to write the story as he saw it. So author and billionaire struck a bargain. Follett could drop the book project at any time. Perot also had the right to cancel the book, but in that case he was required to reimburse Follett's publisher, William Morrow and Company, $1 million to cover the author's advance. With that understanding, the two men worked together in reconstructing the tale.

As a former journalist tackling his first work of nonfiction in some time, Follett placed high priority on checking and double-checking facts. As always, Perot loved to spin folksy yarns to illustrate points he wanted to make; the nitty-gritty details and the sequence of events sometimes differed from the tale in minor ways. In Perot's view, the details were beside the point. What mattered was the lesson.

Follett wanted all the facts plain; from them he planned to weave the rescue story. At first Perot bridled. He objected to anyone tinkering with his version of the truth. He was sure the Iranians had merely fabricated charges against his people to evade paying their bills. A major stumbling block emerged in the writing of the book over how Follett was to portray EDS's partner in Iran, the Mahvi group. It was this relationship that was the pretext for the arrest of Chiapparone and Gaylord. In the United States there were words to describe such illegal arrangements between government and business: *bribery*, *kickback*, *corruption*, but in Iran it was legal.

A certain Dr. Towliati, an official of the Iranian Health Ministry, had appeared on EDS's payroll. Understandably, the revolutionary officials who questioned Chiapparone and Gaylord wanted to know if Iran's money was being funneled to friends of the Shah. No, the EDS executives explained. Dr. Towliati was a consultant paid by EDS. The government reimbursed EDS for his salary, so he wasn't really paid by EDS.

In the United States someone might have gone to jail for setting up a business arrangement such as this. In Iran, it was kosher. Perot wanted Follett to write specifically that EDS never paid any bribes. Follett convinced Perot to compromise by letting him describe the situation in a way that wouldn't cast EDS in a bad light.

As portrayed in *On Wings of Eagles*, EDS looked very much the innocent abroad. The revolutionary regime may have had some reason for wondering why so much money landed in the pockets of people close to the Shah.

And a perceptive reader understood that from Follett's description. Perot was satisfied. Follett succeeded in writing the book he wanted to write, and charmed the Perots with his British accent and manners.

Having decided that Mort Meyerson was the smartest businessman he had ever met, Ross Perot chose him to run EDS as its president. Perot had been running the company for two years after Hart resigned in 1977.

A systems engineer, Meyerson enjoyed the technical side of EDS's business. He also liked leading teams on missions, but he wasn't sure about the permanency of being president and whether he was cut out for the job.

More important, Meyerson understood that EDS belonged to Ross Perot and, in a sense, always was going to be his. Perot promised Meyerson a free hand in running the company. But was Perot really willing to deliver true responsibility and freedom to Meyerson? Or was Meyerson setting himself up for a storm of second-guessing and, ultimately, a collision with EDS's founder, a man whom he had enjoyed a remarkably good relationship with until that point?

By making Meyerson president, Perot said he wanted to step back from the company and spend more time with his family and pursuing public issues. Meyerson, like Perot, didn't expend much energy on self-doubt. He believed himself to be the most qualified of anyone at EDS to assume the mantle of chief operating officer, vacant since Mitch Hart's resignation. Either he had to take the job or start working for someone less qualified than himself.

In the summer of 1979, a month after Meyerson took over, he was jolted by his first profit and loss statement, which came in 75 percent below projections. He decided to reorganize EDS, separating the highly profitable health insurance business from every other account and pushing the rest of the company into new fields. Meyerson was confident that EDS's future growth lay in data processing for commercial and industrial enterprises, not just in health care. He needed Ken Riedlinger's high energy level to move EDS in that direction.

"You're needed on the commercial accounts. I want you to get involved in banking, savings and loans, credit unions. We're losing money on the commercial side and it's got to stop," Meyerson said.

EDS had experimented briefly with distribution of consumer electronic products and with the manufacture of minicomputers. Both ventures failed. EDS thus was employing more people than it needed. Some operations needed to be trimmed, others reshuffled. In order to stem losses, it fell to Riedlinger to close offices and terminate the EDSers who were no longer needed.

In the summer of 1980, while Riedlinger was trying to straighten out the banking and savings and loan division, EDS's health insurance subsidiary was blindsided by a stunning setback. The Texas Board of Human Resources voted to award the state's lucrative $2 billion Medicaid contract, which EDS won in 1976 and which provided about 14 percent of EDS's net profit, to rival bidder Bradford National Corporation of New York. Bradford National's proposal was $40 million to $50 million less expensive than EDS's.

To Ross Perot, being beaten in his home state in a crucial contract competition was a humiliating disaster. He cut short a European family holiday and flew to Dallas to survey the damage. He immediately issued a statement saying that the Board of Human Resources staff erred in its evaluation of EDS's bid. Using his considerable political clout, Perot lobbied Governor William Clements, Attorney General Mark White, and the three human-resources commissioners, after which the board decided to reconsider.

State officials granted a reprieve. Now, Perot had to figure a way to get the Medicaid contract back.

"Ken, you and Ron Sperberg are to find out just whatever these guys have done wrong and get the smoking gun, do you understand? This is a gut issue and a gut contract. We are not going to lose this one, understood?" Perot said. "Ken, I'm putting you in charge of the strategy to get this contract back."

Perot told Riedlinger that he was convinced Bradford National was a thieving band that had stolen EDS's Texas Medicaid contract from its rightful owner. Riedlinger loved working with Perot when a battle loomed before them. The consummate field general, he allowed nothing to divert him or intrude on his path. Perot operated on the edge of rage, but a rage he never allowed to explode; it was a laserlike focus on the problem at hand, which in this case was how to grind Bradford National and its winning bid into dust.

With EDS lawyers publicly questioning Bradford National's bid, Riedlinger commanded the underground war. The strategy was to dig up anything that compromised Bradford's reputation and make sure it appeared in the newspapers and on TV. Sperberg leased a private jet and brought a New York state senator to Texas, who spoke to any reporter who would listen about what he claimed was Bradford National's substandard performance on the New York Medicaid contract. Reporters in Austin covering Texas government learned about a two-year-old federal investigation into possible problems with Bradford National's data processing for the U.S. Navy, details provided courtesy of EDS. It was a ruthless campaign, which EDS claimed it was conducting for the public's benefit, to prevent Bradford from seizing the important public trust given to health-care insurers of the poor, blind, and crippled.

Riedlinger dug up a lead to a former New York health-care bureaucrat named Michael Diem, who Riedlinger had heard was supposed to have been offered a $185,000 bribe by a Bradford National executive. Confronted with Riedlinger's suspicions and frightened by the possibility of a jail term, Diem agreed to meet Riedlinger in Dallas, where he promised to confess everything to EDS in return for legal counsel and protection for his family. Diem's statements were sure to be especially damaging on TV or in the hands of the FBI, so Riedlinger invited a TV investigative reporter to film the meeting. Diem also agreed to sign an affidavit about the purported bribe offer, which Riedlinger sent to Dan Dorfman, the financial columnist. Dorfman's story was plastered across the United States in 180 newspapers, including the *Dallas Morning News*.

Bradford's officers gamely denied any wrongdoing in Dorfman's article, but the damage to Bradford's contract in Texas reached critical mass. With skillful political manipulation added to the roar of media gossip against Bradford National, EDS established strong grounds for reconsidering the Texas Medicaid bidding procedure. By the time the Texas Board of Human Resources called for new bids in 1982, Bradford National had lost its stomach for Ross Perot's scorched-earth campaign and dropped out of the Medicaid business altogether. In fact, eighteen months after the original decision, EDS won back a new $2 billion contract without a competing bid. "It would have been a waste of time," the president of Computer Sciences Corporation noted ruefully.

The knockout victory over Bradford National was an emotional event that bound Ken Riedlinger to Perot and EDS. He was needed, and he had delivered. He had been brave under fire and he had been willing to do things he might otherwise have regarded as a bit underhanded, like hounding those poor devils from Bradford National, to enhance the fortunes of EDS. At times, when Riedlinger thought about what he had done, he tried to put the reservations out of his mind. His actions didn't precisely square with the noble ideals of his youth. He hadn't done anything illegal, nor had EDS. But EDS operated in the very real world of business, and, Riedlinger lamented, that world was sometimes a very tough place indeed.

PART II

The Negotiations of Spring
1984

SIX

Gameplan

To Bob Scully, the name General Motors denoted more — much more — than just a big midwestern company selling Chevrolets and Cadillacs. A rising star in the corporate finance department of Salomon Brothers, Inc., Scully viewed GM as a big catfish, a whopper he sorely longed to haul into his boat.

In the world where an investment banker's prestige varies directly with that of his clients, Scully and Salomon Brothers longed to corral big, venerable, and wealthy clients, of which GM was the leading example in late 1983.

Founded in 1910, Salomon had built its reputation as the premier bond-trading and underwriting firm on Wall Street. Salomon, known on The Street by the nickname "Solly," prided itself as the class act when it came to raising large amounts of cash for corporations by selling so-called fixed-income securities or bonds. Solly's traders traditionally were among the keenest judges of worldwide interest-rate trends. Hunched over their green flickering screens, banks of telephones at the ready, they could detect from the changing numbers a hidden pocket of demand for certain kinds of securities, a weakening interest for others.

Educated at Princeton and Harvard Business School, Scully joined Salomon Brothers in 1980 and began his career where all Solly's newcomers begin, in front of a video screen on the trading floor. Salomon traders translated their knowledge of money markets to satisfy their clients' desire for the lowest possible borrowing costs and the best repayment terms. They were experts at shaving a few hundredths of a percentage point from interest rates through deft bidding or the careful timing of a big trade. Such tactics put dollars in their clients' pockets and in the pockets of Salomon's partners.

As merger and acquisition mania grew during the 1970s, the partners who constituted Salomon Brothers' management couldn't help but gaze enviously at many well-heeled bond clients who were forking over hundreds of millions of dollars, some of which Salomon helped raise, to buy major public corporations. In its early days, mergers and acquisitions — "M&A" in the argot of the business — represented an important, lucrative trend in the securities business to which Salomon Brothers had very little access. But since the firm already was raising huge sums of money, Salomon partners figured they should be brokering the purchase of companies — and should be collecting the fabulous seven- and eight-figure fees that resulted from such transactions.

The times they were a-changing, John Gutfreund and his fellow partners decided, and Salomon Brothers must change with them. Thus, Salomon determined to strengthen its capabilities in stock offerings, mergers and acquisitions, and commodities. Doing so placed the firm in direct competition with more experienced bankers from Morgan Stanley, Goldman Sachs, and First Boston. The pie, as it turned out, had grown large enough for everyone. In the mergers arena, Salomon landed Gulf Oil Corporation as a client, helping the energy giant repel the unwanted advances of Boone Pickens, Jr., and Mesa Petroleum Company, and collecting a $28 million fee when Mesa drove Gulf into the arms of Standard Oil Corporation of California.

Salomon's stable of blue-chip investment-banking clients was growing, but it was able to grab only minor tidbits of GM's business, helping GM to raise cash by selling General Motors Acceptance Corporation bonds. GM used the funds raised in GMAC bond offerings to finance the sales of new cars and trucks for retail customers. In a typical GMAC bond offering, Salomon promised to pay GM a certain amount, based on what it judged to be the market price of GMAC bonds. Then Salomon sold the bonds to various institutional customers through a syndicate of investment banks. If Salomon's judgment of the market was correct, it pocketed the difference between the money raised and the amount promised to GM. If the market changed adversely, Salomon stood to lose. The fees in bond offerings were worth pursuing but were far less substantial than fees from a major corporate merger, especially considering that mergers posed little risk, except the risk of wasted time. A blown bond underwriting, on the other hand, could cost millions of dollars in capital.

Nibbling at GM's investment-banking business brought Bob Scully in contact with several members of GM's financial staff from GM's New York headquarters. He struck up a cordial relationship with Courtney Jones, GM's graying but cherubic treasurer. As head of GM's New York financial staff, Jones served as the top contact man between the company and Wall Street. A Detroit native and Wayne State University graduate who worked in a variety of GM finance posts, Jones combined a puckish sense of humor with an astute grasp of numbers. Unlike most of the investment bankers he dealt with, Jones was a midwesterner by upbringing and education. He was reared professionally as an accountant and controller in GM auto plants. But during his years in GM's New York treasurer's office, Jones grew fond of the fast-paced whirl of Manhattan and its dealmakers. Jones and Scully appreciated each other and would kid each other with high praise. Scully lavishly complimented his friend's financial acumen, and Jones, slightly embarrassed by the stroking, kidded Scully about his smooth treatment of customers. Good feelings notwithstanding, GM didn't present an investment-banking prospect for Salomon in 1983. Morgan Stanley and Company for years had handled much of GM's business and, therefore, was presumed by Wall Street to command the inside track on any major financial transactions.

Besides, GM hadn't attempted a sizable corporate merger in more than half a century. It seemed aloof from the feeding frenzy that gripped Wall Street, even though GM probably had more financial wherewithal than any company in America. Times were changing for GM, too. At the very least, GM in 1983 was prepared to listen to investment bankers who suggested that it consider a major acquisition. Scully and Jones dined together several times and had chatted superficially about possibilities for GM, but no specific ideas took root. Scully wasn't impatient. He considered ways to expand Salomon's relationship with GM, always freshening his contacts in the GM treasurer's office, always alert for the signal of an opportunity. Scully had worked at Salomon for three years. His goal, like that of most junior workers at the investment bank, was to be made a partner, which entitled one to share in Salomon's annual distribution of profits. A Salomon employee made partner in the same way an Indian earned the feathers of a brave: by consensus of fellow braves, after a number of conquests, by a record of achievement — and, that most frustrating of ingredients, by the passage of time. Scully had some scalps on his belt but still was waiting. Landing GM as a mergers and acquisitions client would speed the process considerably.

Late in the summer of 1983 he decided to shake things up on the GM account ever so slightly. To initiate a reaction, he knew he first must put ingredients in a beaker and stir. He decided, therefore, to throw a dinner to "celebrate" Salomon's recent handling of a small GM Eurobond offering. The guests of honor at the dinner were Roger Smith, GM chairman, and John Gutfreund, *capo di tutti capi* at Salomon Brothers. The evening of Monday, October 3, 1983, was a festive one. GM traditionally held its board of directors meeting on the first Monday of the month, Scully knew, and it was an event held most months in New York. Hosting GM chairman Roger Smith at dinner demanded a certain diplomatic protocol and a high level of elegance. Gutfreund and Smith, flanked by Scully and Jones, toasted one another in a private room at "21." Henry Kaufman, Salomon's celebrated chief economist and interest-rate forecaster, joined the party, as did half a dozen others from GM and Salomon.

Gutfreund inaugurated the soiree with a short speech.

"We wish to thank you, Roger, for showing your confidence in us, and we hope we may serve GM and serve you in the future," Gutfreund said, holding a glass of wine aloft.

"We've been in the bond business for almost seventy-five years, and think we're pretty good at what we do. But we'd also like to expand our business into areas that aren't strictly . . . transactional," he said, using a euphemism to denote the trading of bonds.

Rising to respond to Gutfreund, Smith spoke of GM's "strategic vision." For three years he had been delivering a great number of speeches around the country about turning GM into a "twenty-first-century" car company and about "leapfrogging" the competition at home and abroad with advanced technology.

"You're awfully bright folks," Smith said, responding to Gutfreund's gentle stroking. When the occasion called for it, Smith's charm and gentleness were unmatched among corporate chief executives.

"As you know, GM is one of the most financially strong companies in the world. We currently have nearly $10 billion in our little green box, and we are always open to good ideas," he said. Smith wasn't indulging in hyperbole. Historically, GM had adopted the stance that no one could teach GM anything about building cars, buses, and trucks. Since taking over as chairman in 1980 Smith had changed that policy. A year earlier,

GM joined in a venture with Fanuc Ltd., a Japanese maker of robots. And earlier in the same year, GM announced a far-reaching reorganization of its carmaking divisions, shuffling the jobs of tens of thousands of engineers. GM based the shuffling on a study by McKinsey and Company management consultants. GM and Toyota also devised a venture to build cars in Fremont, California. GM's change purse, as well as its appetite for new ideas, seemed bottomless.

As Roger Smith spoke to his dinner companions, an imaginary gate swung open before Gutfreund's and Scully's eyes. The new thinking at GM included the idea of a major acquisition. Smith was inviting the investment bankers in; Salomon Brothers was getting a chance to assist GM to make an acquisition!

The evening at "21" ended in a warm glow. The following morning at Salomon Brothers headquarters in lower Manhattan, "a crisp, penetrating discussion," as John Gutfreund later recalled it, was held in Salomon Brothers' mergers and acquisitions department. The M&A department, as well as most other Salomon offices, sits high in one of the island's southernmost office towers, directly overlooking the Staten Island ferry's berth, Governors Island, and the passage to the Atlantic Ocean.

It's an appropriately majestic setting for a financial powerhouse that stamps its mark on so much of what lies below it. Gutfreund and Scully reported to their colleagues in the M&A department about the previous evening's dinner party and the exciting prospect of GM's willingness to launch a multibillion-dollar shopping spree. Jerry Rosenfeld, head of M&A, listened to Gutfreund but didn't immediately light up with the same enthusiasm. In fact, Rosenfeld waxed somewhat skeptical about trying to find merger candidates for a company like GM, which, everyone knew, didn't do mergers. Partners at Salomon could — and did — come into Rosenfeld's office with brilliant merger ideas. Every idea, alas, was only an idea. Before suggesting it to a client, the M&A experts performed detective work and analysis, researching and analyzing financial statements, assessing the value of various assets, examining whether a transaction made financial sense. Very few bright sparks actually turned into suggestions; fewer still turned into mergers. Rosenfeld wanted to channel his department's time and talent into the most promising ideas.

A Ph.D. in mathematics, Rosenfeld was a rather fleet numbers man and stayed abreast of current events. GM had plenty of money and, theoretically at least, was the ultimate M&A candidate. But he hadn't attended the previous night's dinner, and GM hadn't demonstrated any obvious symptoms of merger mania to him.

Permitting himself a touch more vehemence, Gutfreund suggested that the M&A department try developing some merger ideas for GM — right away. Gutfreund was the firm's managing partner, and when Gutfreund commanded M&A — or any other department — to jump, the only questions that remained were how high or from what floor.

When the phone rang at his bedside table, Ken Riedlinger's first thought was: "Who the devil would call me on my honeymoon?"

Ken and Judy, his wife of two weeks, were blissfully hunkered down in early September 1983 at the Hotel du Cap on the French Riviera. The summer, with its crowds, had evaporated; the air remained sultry, yet refreshing, a perfect antidote for the workaday world. That day, tired of playing on the beach, Ken and Judy had rented motorbikes and ridden to Cannes and St.-Tropez, luxuriating in the Riviera's idyllic splendor.

A senior vice president and director of Electronic Data Systems Corporation, Riedlinger had enjoyed precious few stretches of free time such as this — never mind the fabulous scenery — in his fifteen-year career at EDS. His first marriage had broken apart two years earlier, partly from the stress of constant out-of-town trips, late nights, and weekends at the office — all for EDS.

This time around was going to be different. He loved EDS and had to admit he looked forward to returning to Dallas. But he wasn't going to allow his marriage to suffer. He was going to take better care of his life at home, his health, and his wife.

"Hi, Ken," said the voice on the phone. It was Shirley Garren, Ken's secretary, calling from EDS headquarters in Dallas, relaying a message from Mort Meyerson. Meyerson, the president of EDS, was Riedlinger's direct superior and had been his mentor for the past nine years.

Riedlinger was happy working for Meyerson, but it was, from his point of view, becoming a somewhat tense relationship. Although he admired Meyerson and felt Meyerson bestowed on him an extraordinary amount of freedom and responsibility, Riedlinger also felt at times, and much more so recently, as if he were jerked from assignment to assignment, place to place. Meyerson had ordered him to wear a beeper at all times and he had been scolded recently for taking it off at 11:00 P.M. to have dinner with Judy after work. Sometimes he wondered if Meyerson called him late at night just to check if he was wearing the beeper. It seemed there was little lately he did that wasn't affected by some impending competition for a new contract, meaning long hours of labor.

"Ken, Mort wants to know if you could come back a little early to attend a meeting on Monday," his secretary said.

Incredible, he thought. Meyerson must have known about this meeting before he had left for Europe.

"Sure," he said. "What's going on?"

"I have reservations for you to leave on Sunday, rather than Monday. As you know, there's an officers' meeting, followed by a directors' meeting and shareholders' meeting on Tuesday. The next morning I have you scheduled to depart Dallas on a company plane to Beaver Creek, Colorado. Mort wants all the officers to be there."

"No problem," Ken said. He was annoyed. Originally, he had been excused from the meetings. Now Mort would have to pay for the new airline tickets, and he won't be happy about that, Riedlinger mused to himself. Meyerson wasn't exactly a tightwad, but his tightfistedness with EDS's money was legendary.

Reluctantly, Judy and Ken packed their bags a day early.

The EDS shareholders' meeting on Tuesday was a short, placid lovefest, as well it should have been. Ross Perot, owner of 46 percent of EDS's stock, and the other stockholders had every reason to be pleased with their company: profit was up 25 percent for the year to $58.7 million in 1983, revenue was up 28 percent to $651.6 million. The return on average shareholders' equity topped 25 percent, more than double the average for publicly traded companies.

Finances told only part of the story. EDS was humming like a well-oiled machine. EDS's record in signing new contracts was the envy of the data-service industry. The payroll included more than 13,000 highly trained EDSers, an all-time high. In the past four years, productivity, measured as revenue per employee, had shot up 71 percent. And if all that weren't enough, EDS had just won a magnificent day in court against the revolutionary regime in Iran, collecting a $16.5 million judgment. It was an especially sweet legal victory, coming four years after the dramatic rescue.

Perot felt particularly pleased about — and responsible for — the growing number of EDSers and public stockholders who were sharing with him in the company's prosperity. He expressed the feeling in his 1983 report to shareholders: "The people who lead a company have a tremendous responsibility to run it well and to handle it with care."

Following the annual meeting, Riedlinger, Meyerson, and the other EDS officers boarded two Learjets for Beaver Creek, Colorado. In a sense, Mort Meyerson convened the Beaver Creek meeting because he had heeded Ross Perot's message on the annual report. Meyerson, too, felt acutely responsible for EDS and knew it was facing a big problem. It was a "problem" for which other companies would be grateful. Ironically, EDS's past growth curve made future profit and revenue growth a huge, nearly impossible, burden. Investor confidence depended on continued growth at a steady, predictable rate. To maintain a strong growth rate, EDS in recent years had tried entering some new fields, such as minicomputer manufacturing and retail distribution of retail products — and had failed miserably.

Now, as Meyerson saw it, EDS had no choice but to stick to the traditional path of pursuing data processing contracts. Meyerson delivered this message to the officers at the rented mountain home in Beaver Creek. But now, Meyerson said, we've got to shoot for megacontracts. Buffalo and antelope won't cut it anymore, we've got to hunt elephants.

"We can't afford to waste Gary [Fernandes] and Ken [Riedlinger] on Mickey Mouse deals anymore," he said, meaning contracts in the $10 million range. "We've got to dig elephant traps all over the place and get a big one to fall in every year or we'll never be able to maintain our high growth rate.

"Besides government megacontracts, like the one we just signed with the U.S. Army (worth about $1 billion over ten years), we've got to go after Fortune 100 companies, because they're the only ones big enough to spend the money we're looking for," Meyerson said.

The data processing contract EDS was negotiating with AT&T in late 1983 was potentially just such a beast. Having recently divested the Bell operating companies, AT&T was considering hiring EDS to process all the billing for its long-distance telephone service, which could be worth $1 billion a year or more in revenue. If EDS won such a contract, it would mean doubling its work force overnight.

"We may just win the AT&T contract," Meyerson said. "But we've got to look to other big companies, too, like ITT, Bank of America. As officers of EDS, you've got to let your imaginations go."

Letting the imagination soar wasn't difficult at that moment, Riedlinger thought. Meyerson had chosen a perfect setting for the meeting. The aspens had turned color already, tinging the Colorado Rockies in gold. It was still early autumn, but the air was very cold. Flames crackled in the big stone fireplace. Riedlinger peered outside: big clumps of snowflakes drifted from the sky.

"Just about any huge company is a potential customer," Meyerson said.

"There's only one I can think of that's probably too big for us," he said. "General Motors."

As Christmas approached, and with John Gutfreund's marching orders fresh in their minds, Jerry Rosenfeld and his staff at Salomon Brothers put the finishing touches on the shopping list for GM.

From what Roger Smith had indicated, GM loved high technology. Moreover, whatever company GM bought had to fit somehow with its current operations as a vehicle manufacturer. Smith wouldn't be interested in gene splicing or high-tech trash compactors.

Rosenfeld divided GM's list into four main areas: defense electronics, the fastest-growing part of the defense business; financial services, which might blend well with the GMAC automotive-financing subsidiary; general technology, always useful in vehicle manufacturing; and data services, a must for any large, sophisticated user of information.

Salomon Brothers' research department proved very handy for compiling shopping lists. The research analysts suggested some promising acquisition candidates and provided detailed, well-documented reasons for persuading GM as to why Salomon's choices were worth considering. In each of the four categories, Rosenfeld listed the three best companies he could find. Twelve companies in all. They included Hughes Aircraft in the defense electronic group and EG&G, a maker of components for nuclear weapons, in the general technology group.

Steve McClellan, a Salomon Brothers research analyst and Wall Street's leading expert on data-services companies, suggested putting EDS on the list. McClellan had a special interest in EDS. He had followed the company longer than any other and was well acquainted with Perot, Meyerson, and other top EDS officers. Over the years he had nurtured a special affection for the Dallas company, watching it grow from a tiny, agile band of computer commandos, scurrying to pay their bills, to an acknowledged power in the computer industry that had defeated IBM in direct competitions.

"You should put EDS on the list, and if you do, it should be number one," McClellan told Rosenfeld, "but I think you may have a tough time making it happen. Ross Perot isn't likely to sell."

McClellan grew up in the suburbs of Chicago and joined the Navy during the Vietnam war. He served aboard ship in the Atlantic and the Caribbean, nurturing a youthful love of the stock market by reading the *Wall Street Journal* daily in the officers' wardroom. Upon his discharge, McClellan interviewed for a job at Merrill Lynch. He was turned away summarily with the advice to earn a graduate business degree before returning. Undaunted, McClellan enrolled in night classes at George Washington University, working during the night as a computer industry analyst at the U.S. Department of Commerce. Two years later, he landed a job at a small Wall Street firm that seemed more interested in his knowledge of computers than in his MBA. EDS caught McClellan's attention immediately. He recognized, and in some ways was drawn to, what seemed like EDS's unusual spirit and unquenchable desire to succeed.

Every year McClellan journeyed to Dallas faithfully for EDS's annual meeting, one of the few analysts on Wall Street to do so. He met and chatted with Tom Walter, Mort Meyerson, and Perot. To him, they seemed an engaging, action-oriented bunch, unintimidated by bigger rivals. They also were warm and courteous to him personally, perhaps because he was one of the few to pay attention to them. He was invited to the homes of EDS officers, met their families, and listened to their adventures. For a while McClellan was the only Wall Street analyst who formally tracked EDS's progress and wrote research reports. The lack of attention through the 1970s didn't particularly bother EDS. After EDS's successful initial public stock offering in 1968, Ross Perot and his cohorts lost a huge sum in the Dupont Walston fiasco and thus nursed suspicions of Wall Street's motives and practices. Moreover, McClellan believed that Perot's outspoken patriotism, if anything, drew negative attention to EDS stock. The country was smarting from Vietnam and the demise of Richard Nixon's presidency, of which Perot had been an early booster. Investors and analysts couldn't muster much enthusiasm for EDS's apparent regimentation or its close-cropped troops.

By 1980, Perot and Wall Street had relaxed their mutual suspicions a bit. The war was long over. Perot had taught the country a little lesson in the field of hostage rescue. And Meyerson was putting more of his own stamp on EDS. Longer hairstyles and pastel shirts were tolerated. EDS ventured outside its bread-and-butter businesses. EDS started an investor-relations program and renewed its contacts on Wall Street. Salomon Brothers bankers were hired in 1980 to suggest some long-term financial strategies for EDS; ever mindful of the fees Salomon could collect, the bankers' report suggested channeling EDS's wealth to acquire companies or selling out to a bigger company, like IBM or AT&T.

EDS certainly wasn't interested in selling out. McClellan wasn't surprised about that. In his opinion, Perot was Mr. Long-term and hadn't any burning desire to cash in his chips. Without EDS, he was a captain without a ship. Now, three years later, McClellan believed nothing had changed. Perot was — and always would be — Perot.

Courtney Jones sat in his office in the GM Building in New York, listening carefully for two and a half hours to the presentation by Bob Scully, Jerry Rosenfeld, and Dennis Bovin. He promised to take their list of twelve companies home during the Christmas vacation for review.

U.S. car companies traditionally close down between Christmas and New Year, which meant a long winter holiday for GM's New York financial staff. Jones loved the season, for it afforded him the opportunity to retreat to the quiet and solitude of his vacation home in Southampton, Long Island. With the latest reading matter from Salomon Brothers, Jones now possessed a sizable stack of shopping lists from investment banks. As was the practice at GM, he composed a written report on the latest effort by Salomon Brothers for F. Alan Smith, his superior and GM's executive vice president for finance. No relation to Roger Smith, Alan Smith nonetheless was a powerful influence at GM and a very strong candidate to one day become chief executive. He was young, possessed the right credentials as GM's second-highest financial executive, and, most important of all, was being touted by GM insiders who sprinkled such insights among journalists, dealers, financial analysts, and investment bankers.

Shortly after Courtney Jones's return from Christmas vacation in January 1984, just as GM was unveiling its massive reshuffling of tens of thousands of automotive engineers and managers, Jones received an answer from Alan Smith. EDS, of the twelve companies on the list, had captured the chairman's interest: Can we find out more about it?

The treasurer swung into action. The need for secrecy dictated that it was time to move this project out of GM's offices. Roger Smith, first of all, was interested in the merger only if it was friendly. Perot mustn't hear about this one second before GM presented him the idea on a golden platter. And even the most closely guarded secrets had a way of leaking out of offices. Water-fountain talk turns into rumor.

The project needed a hiding place and a code name, Jones decided, so that no one would have to so much as utter a name or word that might be overheard and bring on disaster. The Plaza Hotel, situated across Fifth Avenue on the southeast corner of Central Park, provided a convenient place to meet with Salomon Brothers bankers, away from the eyes and ears of underlings. "Project Plaza" was a perfect code name. The nearby Ritz-Carlton was a backup hiding place.

In early February, Steve McClellan was summoned to meet with Jones at the Ritz-Carlton. Jones indicated from his questions that GM was interested in EDS, but he shared McClellan's initial skepticism about EDS as a merger partner for GM. "Why do you think EDS is acquirable?" he asked McClellan. McClellan wasn't sure EDS was acquirable, but he said there might be some reasons for trying. First of all, he recalled that EDS hadn't rejected the notion out of hand three years ago. Meyerson hadn't been enthusiastic, but he had mentioned that if EDS agreed to merge, it would have to be with a "bluer-than-blue-chip company," like IBM or AT&T. GM certainly fit that description. McClellan also knew that Perot harbored a great dream, that EDS someday might grow into the IBM of its generation. Perot saw EDS one day as a giant employer, as large, as influential, as respected as IBM. If an alliance with GM could hasten that day, he just might go for a merger.

The GM treasurer fired three hours' worth of questions at McClellan and listened carefully to the answers. What was Perot like? What was Meyerson like? Tell me about EDS's contracts, its reputation. McClellan spun a rich tapestry of anecdotes from his decade of visits and meetings in Dallas. By the time his meeting with Jones was over, McClellan was impressed by the great amount of information Jones already knew about EDS. He began to wonder if GM just might make a grab for EDS.

Jones, meanwhile, hadn't heard anything from McClellan he didn't like. Perot surely was a maverick. And EDS people were as tough and aggressive as they come. In his view, they might provide a refreshing change from the plodding, bureaucratic pace at GM that often annoyed him and infuriated his boss, Roger Smith.

Christmas 1983 was a dreary one for Mort Meyerson and Ken Riedlinger. The elephant had slipped out of their trap.

AT&T and the regional Bell companies were spending almost $4 billion annually to process and collect telephone bills. EDS proposed to take over the operation and slash that number drastically. As negotiations proceeded with AT&T, Meyerson ordered Riedlinger to prepare plans for hiring and organizing 10,000 new EDS workers in the first year. On December 16, after strenuous objections from AT&T data processors, EDS learned that AT&T had decided to retain its internal billing operations after all.

Meyerson was crushed. Months of high hopes and expectations disintegrated before his eyes. As had happened so often in the past, EDS, promising greater efficiency, competed against a client's internal data processing department. This time, EDS lost. "Take a couple weeks off," Meyerson told Riedlinger dismally. "We'll talk about what to do next after the New Year."

On January 9, Meyerson told Riedlinger he was transferring him to New Jersey to continue pursuing smaller data processing contracts at AT&T. The huge telephone billing contract wasn't going to come true, but there were plenty of other opportunities at AT&T, and EDS needed more contracts desperately. More business at AT&T was the only way to meet EDS's revenue target for fiscal 1984, which ended in six months.

"Mort, this is a terrible time for me to be moving to New Jersey," Riedlinger said. "Judy has just moved from San Diego to Dallas so we can be together. My kids are here in Dallas."

"Ken, I need you up there as soon as possible. We've got to get these smaller deals signed quickly. You go up to New Jersey and do the job, and I'll make sure you get a $50,000 cash bonus," Meyerson said.

It's a pretty tall assignment, he thought, but $50,000 will soothe the sting of forced separation from Judy.

Still, Riedlinger wasn't thrilled. He had promised to concentrate more on his new marriage, to spend more time at home and with his children. Once again, Mort Meyerson was ordering him to uproot his life. Once again, he was charging into battle.

SEVEN

Mating Dance

B Y the third week in April 1984, two weeks had passed since John
Gutfreund's journey to Texas. The lid stayed on the secret. Only
a few GM and EDS executives and Salomon Brothers investment
bankers knew of the visit.

The more he thought about GM's approach, the more Ross Perot felt
flattered. GM had the prestige and image he felt appropriate for any
company that would presume to merge with EDS. But he didn't believe
GM's interest would blossom into a full-fledged merger offer. Besides,
he remained occupied full-time, as he had been since the previous
summer, working on Texas education reform. That still was his top
priority, not GM. Perot didn't allow his emotions about the offer to
proceed from flattery to excitement.

Mort Meyerson, the man responsible for EDS's operations, regarded
GM's interest as a potentially huge business opportunity. Whether or not
a merger materialized, GM well might be persuaded to sign a juicy data
processing contract, he thought, and might become the elephant that fell
into EDS's trap. This was the strategy he had asked his top executives to
pursue at the Beaver Creek, Colorado, conference a few months earlier in
October. Ironically, he told them that just about any company but GM
could be lured into the trap; and it was GM that came knocking, without
a bit of enticement from EDS.

As a light spring rain fell over Dallas, Ross Perot and Mort Meyerson boarded EDS's Learjet for the flight to Detroit and their first look at General Motors. Two hours later the jet descended to Willow Run Airport, an airfield just west of Detroit that had been used for the ferrying of bombers in World War II. Less congested than Metropolitan Airport, Detroit's main airline terminal, Willow Run is used a great deal by corporate aircraft and is a short distance from one of GM's thirty-six North American vehicle-assembly plants.

Roger Smith, GM's chairman, and F. Alan Smith, GM's chief financial officer, were waiting for the EDS executives at Willow Run with a plush, four-seat GM Sikorsky helicopter. As the chopper thrashed skyward, Perot and Meyerson could see GM's Ypsilanti, Michigan, car-assembly plant, the inside of which was being tooled for manufacture of GM's H-body standard-size sedans, the Buick LeSabre and Oldsmobile Delta 88. The EDS men also could see a GM Hydra-Matic plant, where workers assembled automatic transmissions for various car and truck models. The outline of a GM parts warehouse loomed nearby. Looking down at the H-car plant near the airport, Perot and Meyerson assumed that the Willow Run complex constituted GM's main manufacturing presence in Detroit. It was miscalculation on a giant scale, which became apparent in a few moments. In fact, they were looking at a fraction of a fraction. GM's operations in the Detroit area represented an important, though relatively small, segment of GM's entire U.S. manufacturing empire.

The helicopter flew north for two minutes to Milford and circled the GM test track and proving grounds before flying to a Chevrolet engine plant in Romulus, where it hovered to afford them a view. They proceeded to the Fiero assembly plant a few miles north in Pontiac, one of three major assembly complexes there. Next to the Fiero plant was a huge foundry. Then to the Cadillac plant on Clark Street. A new car-assembly plant, nearing completion, in Hamtramck. A diesel-engine plant in the city limits of Detroit. An axle and steering-gear plant in Detroit. Everywhere they looked, Perot and Meyerson saw GM smokestacks. The scale of GM was huge, overwhelming; every minute in the helicopter reinforced that impression. The EDS executives were sophisticated businessmen and had worked with industrial customers before. They were Texans, too, and thought they understood what was meant by "big." But neither man had realized on just how gigantic a scale GM operated. GM sprawled over enormous acreage. Each parking lot overflowed with thousands of cars, each car representing at least one GM worker.

The helicopter swooped low over the stately fifteen-story GM headquarters building a few miles north of the Detroit River downtown, where
Perot and Meyerson assumed they would be dropped off for lunch and
some meetings. But the helicopter ascended once more, this time turning
north for the short flight to Warren, Michigan, on the northern outskirts
of Detroit.

Within moments, Perot and Meyerson beheld GM's Technical Center,
a surprisingly contemporary 330-acre oasis of twenty-five low-lying
buildings, surrounded by parking lots, avenues, and lawns — all placed
in the center of Warren, Michigan's, industrial sprawl. A rectangular
artificial lake, twenty-two acres in size, lay in the center of the property.

In the 1940s GM hired renowned Finnish architect Eero Saarinen to
design the buildings and property, and they retained a timeless, modern-
istic flair four decades later. Within the property, GM operated a maze of
laboratories, wind tunnels, styling studios, and engineering centers. The
"tech center," as it was nicknamed, also housed many of GM's
computers and the headquarters of General Motors Information Services
and Computer Activity (GMISCA), GM's data processing division. The
tech center, Smith explained to his guests, was the science, engineering,
and design nerve center for the corporation.

At that moment, the tech center was in turmoil. Three months earlier,
Roger Smith had announced a massive corporate reorganization. Instead
of each car division operating its own manufacturing plants, aided by
GM's Fisher Body and General Motors Assembly divisions, all manufacturing was to be consolidated into two manufacturing "supergroups,"
Buick-Oldsmobile-Cadillac and Chevrolet-Pontiac-GM Canada, or BOC
and CPC for short. McKinsey and Company recommended the reorganization after studying GM's management and decisionmaking structure
for more than two years. The new organizational structure tore apart
engineering teams, destroyed decades-old loyalties to car divisions,
precipitated mass relocations of offices, telephones, and computers, and
generally confused many of GM's 750,000 workers. The goal was
efficiency and streamlined decisionmaking. On a human level, the
reorganization brought about tremendous confusion and disorientation.
Informal people networks, which didn't exist on any chart but were vital
for accomplishing critical engineering tasks, disintegrated. Engineers and
managers sometimes found themselves sitting in corridors as they waited
for new assignments, trying to figure out for whom they worked.

As the GM top executives escorted Perot and Meyerson through the
buildings, Meyerson was impressed by the GM managers and executives

to whom he was introduced. True, it was just a fleeting impression based on a few moments of inconsequential patter, but just about every person he met struck him as bright and well-spoken. They described their computer-aided design, computer-aided engineering, and sophisticated computer language protocols and joked gamely about the temporary chaos of reorganization. Although the scientists seemed genuinely proud of the technologies they were describing, it seemed to Meyerson that GM's technological advances, especially in computers, weren't quite as spectacular as he would have expected from the world's biggest auto-maker. Meyerson noticed outdated equipment and saw people applying the computers in ways that struck him as rather quaint, compared with applications by some of EDS's customers.

Most striking of all, GM engineers and designers were using numerous types of computing machines that didn't "talk" to one another, Meyerson noticed. If two sets of engineers wanted to communicate, they would often have to reenter data, a tedious and time-consuming process that defeated the efficiencies of computer technology.

Now Meyerson understood why Roger Smith needed EDS so desperately. Given the personnel reorganization and the hodge-podge of computers, GM needed a company like EDS to modernize GM's systems of doing business.

From the monstrous size and complexity he had encountered in just a few hours in Detroit, Meyerson knew that an accurate assessment of GM wasn't going to be a simple assignment. At lunch in the private dining room in GM's design center, Perot and Meyerson listened to the GM chairman describe his vision of a twenty-first-century car company, the company he wanted EDS to help him build.

It was an awesome vision. The car buyer of the future, Roger Smith explained, will sit down with a dealer at a computer terminal and "build" a car, choosing model, engine size, color, and a range of options. The information will be sent via satellite from the dealership to the assembly plant. The moment the order is received, the tires, raw materials, paint, engine, transmission, upholstery, and other parts will be ordered for that customer's car. GM's suppliers will be connected to this system. By ordering the parts when needed, rather than stocking them in inventory, GM will be able to avoid the cost of inventory and the inevitable delays. Paper shuffling will be minimized. As GM begins to assemble the customer's car, a highly automated assembly process will swing into action, Smith explained. Robotic workstations will perform tasks with great precision. Each station will know precisely which car is being assembled and what the customer ordered. Meanwhile, GM's finance arm, GMAC, can process the customer's loan application. Computers will check credit ratings automatically and evaluate car customers as prospects for mortgages, accident insurance, and a host of other GM financial services. Inside GM, information from the customer's order will be distributed to managers and analysts who need it: marketers who want to know what colors are popular this season, material controllers who need to know how much steel and plastic the company is using, financial specialists who control cash flow and credit.

All this knowledge will be available on GM computer screens, Smith explained, obviating the stultifying blizzard of paper clogging in-baskets throughout the organization.

GM's telephone network, engineering, designing, health insurance, payroll, employee newspaper — all of it will be handled by a huge integrated network of computers that can talk to each other.

Meyerson and Perot listened to Smith warm to this vision of GM's futureworld. Evidently, he found the vision hugely exciting. As he became more and more wrapped up in his descriptions, Smith peppered his speech with expressions drawn from a midwestern crackerbarrel: "Holy Toledo!" and "Gee whiz!" His pale, mottled complexion grew pink, his features brightened, and his already high pitched voice squeaked and cracked as he attempted to amplify his enthusiasm. He was sincere and likable, and he was funny, Perot and Meyerson thought. Smith's blue eyes twinkled and he displayed what seemed to Meyerson to be a good-hearted Irish wit.

"Roger, how much is GM spending today on data processing?" Meyerson asked.

"About $2 billion a year," was the answer. "But we should be spending more, maybe $3 billion, maybe more." (One can only wonder how Smith knew what GM was spending on computing because outlays for items like machine controllers, which were computers, weren't counted.)

For Meyerson, this was a mind-bending number, more than three times the size of EDS's current annual revenue.

Smith continued his pitch, alluding to the "global" and "strategic" nature of a transaction with EDS. He was careful to use the euphemistic word *transaction* when referring to GM's possible business association with EDS rather than to confront the issue of an acquisition head-on. The GM chairman was in a sales mode, but it still was too early to ask for the order: Salomon Brothers had warned him that buying EDS was going to be tricky.

After lunch the foursome piled back into the Sikorsky for the short return flight to Willow Run. Just before boarding the Lear, Meyerson asked Smith: "What, in simple terms, are you trying to accomplish?"

"We've got computer technology inside this company that we can take to the marketplace. GM doesn't have any experience doing that, and EDS does. We have a lot of data processing work we need help with. And we also want to diversify," Smith said.

"What's the order in which you want those things?" Meyerson said.

"One, one, and one," Smith replied, "and I want them as fast as possible."

A week later, Roger Smith and F. Alan Smith paid a reciprocal visit to Dallas to see EDS's dog-and-pony show.

Tom Walter, third in command at EDS, picked up the GM chairman and chief financial officer at Dallas–Ft. Worth Airport. To make sure the GM executives didn't take offense at his choice of cars (and to give them more legroom), Walter left his Porsche at home that day and borrowed a Chevy Suburban wagon. It was a typical bit of smoothness by EDS's chief diplomat.

Since 1979 Tom Walter had supervised EDS's investor relations. In addition to his duties as chief financial officer, that meant arranging meetings with Wall Street research analysts, whose recommendations to investors had an enormous impact on the price of EDS stock. Partly because of Tom Walter's careful tending of investor relations, and because of EDS's sterling financial performance, the analysts showered hosannas on EDS. EDS common shares commanded a premium price-to-earnings multiple compared with similar data-service companies. A high price for the stock was crucially important to maintaining an effective stock incentive program to attract and hold EDS executives.

Tom Walter succumbed to Ross Perot's importunings and joined EDS in 1963 after working a short stint as a systems engineer for IBM in Atlanta. Perot and Walter had been fellow officers on the USS *Sigourney* and they remained friendly throughout their service, meeting each other now and then at Newport, Rhode Island, and Guantanamo Bay. When Perot quit IBM, Tom Walter was one of the first people he wanted to hire. Walter fit comfortably in Perot's tiny new company, beginning as a systems engineer on life insurance accounts and later running EDS's life insurance group. He moved to internal administration in 1977 and became chief financial officer in 1979. A handsome, softspoken man, Tom Walter was extremely well liked and respected within EDS, even in the midst of the natural rivalries that sometimes sprang up.

The presentation Tom Walter developed for potential customers like GM was virtually identical to the presentation shown to Wall Street securities analysts. Once a year, EDS vice presidents stopped what they were doing for a week to write and rehearse an updated sales pitch, which then was used to present to security analysts and later to woo prospective customers. EDS had spent tens of thousands of dollars on slides and visual displays explaining its outstanding computer capabilities, exacting personnel policies, and great financial strength. The chief executive of AT&T had visited EDS headquarters to see the show, as had the U.S. Postmaster General, the head of the U.S. Internal Revenue Service, the chairman of IT&T, many high military officers, and a horde of lesser executives. It was an impressive display, the GM executives commented. When the lights came on, Roger Smith and Alan Smith asked several perceptive questions, Walter thought, which seemed to reflect their favorable impression.

Indeed, Smith had liked what he saw. Salomon Brothers was right. EDS obviously was a class act in the systems-integration field, and the EDS work force knew it. Everyone he met appeared bright-eyed and ready to swing into action at a moment's notice. The EDS offices and computer centers had a clean, modern, professional appearance. And, best of all, it was obvious EDS wasn't hung up on pomp or ceremony or procedures. Everything in the organization happened swiftly, with a minimum of paper shuffling or delay.

Ross Perot had done an impressive job of creating a specialized culture with a unique set of customs and procedures. Roger Smith could see the evidence at every turn. Recruiting, for instance. Instead of harvesting the most highly rated engineering graduates and MBAs from prestigious Ivy League schools, Perot's recruiters scoured Brigham Young, Texas A&M, and other state colleges. Perot disliked privilege. He wanted people who had proved themselves in some field, whether it was music, athletics, or computer science. Perot loved kids who worked their way through school. He looked for people who had been in battle, whether at the state piano-playing contest, the finals of the chess tournament, or in Khe Sanh. He admired toughness born of conflict.

"Find people who love to win," he lectured the recruiters. "If you can't find people who love to win, then find some people who hate to lose."

Personally, Roger Smith found himself attracted to Ross Perot's company immensely. Perot wasn't like any of the business executives who served as GM directors; in fact, he was unlike any corporate chieftain Smith had ever met on the Business Roundtable or in any of the other groups he belonged to; and certainly Perot was stunningly different from anyone at GM. Perot was a real entrepreneur, like Roger Smith's father had been, not a one-minute manager from Harvard Business School or the heir to a family business. In addition to his native business sense, Perot was witty, and he listened intently when Smith talked. Smith was sure he could count on him to inject some spirit and energy into GM.

A few days after Roger Smith's initial visit, Courtney Jones, GM's treasurer, arrived in Dallas with Bob Scully and Jerry Rosenfeld of Salomon Brothers and lawyers from Skadden, Arps, Meagher and Flom. Once again, Tom Walter's Porsche stayed in the garage and the big Chevy wagon was pressed into service. GM's legal due-diligence requirements dictated that before GM and EDS conducted any transaction that might affect shareholders, GM must thoroughly examine EDS's annual reports, filings with the Securities and Exchange Commission, five-year plans, and tax returns. There conceivably might be all kinds of landmines in EDS's financial statements, which EDS might not have disclosed to public shareholders but which GM would want to know about before it made an offer to buy EDS. Due diligence didn't obligate either side to proceed. However, GM's look at the books subtly elevated the seriousness of the negotiations. GM, after its initial interest, now felt the flush of attraction as its treasurer and hired experts pored over EDS's financial documents and discovered that the numbers supported EDS's sterling reputation.

Tom Walter noted that his GM counterpart, F. Alan Smith, wasn't leading the expedition through EDS's documents. Instead, Courtney Jones, the treasurer and Alan Smith's subordinate from the New York office, seemed to be in charge. This must be Roger and Courtney's deal, thought Tom Walter. Alan Smith had been quiet and reserved during the first visit to Dallas. Could he have seen something that caused him to oppose a deal with EDS?

His financial and accounting concerns alleviated after several days of sleuthing, Courtney Jones turned to the basics of EDS's operations. "We know you guys are good. What we want to know is, what can you really do for us, for our business?" Jones asked Tom Walter. He wanted EDS's operations people, its commandos, to evaluate GM's computer systems, as they were operating, in the context of GM's plants and offices.

"No problem," Tom Walter said. "We'll put a team together right away. Is next week too early for you?" All at once Tom Walter found himself back on a faster track than he had wanted. Two years earlier, doctors had discovered a malignant tumor on his jaw. It had been treated successfully. After his treatment he decided to slow down from the usual murderous pace at the office, perhaps take a day off now and then during the week and keep shorter hours. Clearly, until the GM deal was settled he would have to put his slowdown plans aside.

The EDS team, led by Meyerson and consisting of about a dozen or so, including systems engineers and secretaries, arrived in Detroit the following Sunday night and checked into the Westin Hotel in the Renaissance Center downtown. Monday morning, Walter and the engineers fanned out in rented cars to meet with GM systems experts at the tech center and at the Lake Orion Township Buick-Oldsmobile-Cadillac plant. Walter commanded the manufacturing team; another group looked at GM's health-care system. Walter and the others were struck by the dreariness and squalor of downtown Detroit and the irreducible grime on the environs. Only as they headed out of the city did the landscape become a bit more palatable. Whatever happened with GM, Detroit certainly wasn't an attractive place to call home.

For three days, Walter and the other EDS systems specialists listened to GM engineers describe their problems. GM engineers at the tech center bemoaned the terribly slow process of making change orders on the designs of cars in production. If, for example, line workers discovered that bumpers lacked a hole that was designed to fasten a bumper onto a car body, it took twenty-eight days from the moment the engineers learned of the glitch until they could send the design change to the plant where the bumpers were made. Until the change was made, workers might have to use portable drills to put holes in the bumpers, drastically slowing production and often spoiling product quality. The GM engineers appeared desperate for computer expertise to help unsnarl the change-order system. Although he was appalled by the delays and inefficiencies he saw, Tom Walter also was heartened in a sense, for he knew EDS had installed similar systems, and they certainly didn't take twenty-eight days to work.

Walter and the team members collated their findings and transferred them to paper and slides. On Friday, at a dinner at the Renaissance Center for Alan Smith, GM financial vice president Jack Edman, and GM vice chairman Howard Kehrl, EDS presented the results of its quick study. From what the EDS team had seen in just three days, Walter reported, the world's biggest private user of computers needed a massive overhaul of its systems. It was a slick, classic EDS sales presentation, much like the thousands EDS had put on for customers during its twenty-two-year history.

The secrecy so carefully nurtured in April by Courtney Jones at General Motors, by the Salomon Brothers investment bankers, and by Ross Perot and his top officers began to disintegrate in May 1984.

Dan Dorfman, one of New York's best-connected financial journalists, called Mort Meyerson — seemingly out of the blue — to ask him whether EDS was in merger negotiations with anyone. Meyerson had met and gotten to know Dorfman slightly a decade earlier during EDS's fiasco on Wall Street. "No one would want to buy EDS, Dan. You know that. The majority of the stock is tied up by Perot and the rest of the officers. It couldn't happen," Meyerson lied. He didn't like fibbing to Dorfman, but he had to fend him off. Meyerson understood that to disclose anything about the negotiations with GM was a violation of federal security laws — and to confide in Dorfman was tantamount to taking out a newspaper advertisement announcing that GM and EDS were in talks.

"Well, I've been talking to arbs [risk arbitragers], and several people are telling me that EDS is going to be sold. I heard you might be driving a Cadillac pretty soon," Dorfman said.

"That's the craziest thing I've ever heard," Meyerson said. He made a mental note to tell his secretary to put through no more telephone calls from journalists. Meantime, the constant visits to EDS headquarters by Salomon Brothers investment bankers were becoming more and more difficult to explain to EDS employees. If anyone asked why the investment bankers were visiting, Meyerson and the few others who knew the real reason were supposed to say they were helping GM evaluate a potential data processing contract with EDS.

GM pressed forward on an intensive week of discussions and due diligence. Courtney Jones, Jerry Rosenfeld, and Bob Scully of Salomon Brothers stayed at the Lincoln Hotel on the LBJ Expressway. Each morning a Chevrolet van rented by EDS picked them up and brought them and the Skadden Arps lawyers to headquarters; they were waved through the gate without the usual heavy security check by armed guards at the front gate.

Ironically, as head of Salomon Brothers' mergers and acquisitions department, Rosenfeld had conducted a seminar about mergers and acquisitions at EDS a year earlier. At the time, Salomon was trying to convince EDS to use Salomon Brothers' M&A department for acquisitions of their own. Mike Farmer, EDS's treasurer, had arranged the meeting, so when Farmer spotted the investment bankers one day in the building, it occurred to Rosenfeld that Farmer now must be able to guess what was going on.

In the minds of the GM people and the investment bankers, the artifice of a data processing contract and the precautions were a mere prelude to what they saw as an all-out effort for 100 percent purchase of EDS.

But in the minds of Ross Perot, Mort Meyerson, and Tom Walter, the cover story constituted their true version of reality; they understood that GM wanted to acquire EDS, but they believed a giant data processing contract, or perhaps a joint venture, was most desirable for both companies. EDS's independence was crucial to its effectiveness. In countless instances, EDS had been hired to bring forth business solutions for problems that clients failed to solve on their own. Clients thought of EDS as "a computer company" or a "systems integrator," when, in fact, Ross Perot's people saw themselves as efficiency experts of a sort, agents for change, disguised as a computer company. As it was for many management consulting firms, EDS's freedom to say and do difficult things, things that might be unthinkable for company management, was the essence of its power. Quite often EDS was hired by a chief executive who couldn't make his own data processing managers perform as he wanted. When EDS came in, the data processing department was transferred to EDS's authority; they actually became EDS employees, part of a turnkey system operated on the customer's premises; anyone from the old regime who couldn't deal with the new regime was shown the door. Typically, EDS initially was hired to install systems for simple jobs such as automating an order-entry or inventory system; but within a few months, the EDS project manager, who always operated with a great deal of individual authority, often was making important policy decisions.

Thus, the notion of belonging to GM while simultaneously taking over GM's data processing and altering policy to conform with EDS practice didn't quite click for Perot, Meyerson, and Walter. They suspected it couldn't work on that basis.

Ross Perot tried to explain to Roger Smith why acquiring EDS was a self-defeating idea during a series of one-on-one meetings in Dallas. "Roger, our people are extremely independent, and they're given an extraordinary amount of freedom on the job," said Ross Perot. "They can't be under the authority of the people they're trying to help. It won't work."

Smith didn't see this as a problem. Quite the contrary. He told Perot how he'd been preaching to middle-level managers at GM to take more responsibility instead of always looking for direction from above. Rather than make EDS behave more as GM did, he expected EDS to set an example for his managers. EDS would provide positive examples of what he was talking about. This answer, although somewhat encouraging to Perot, didn't quite explain why EDS shouldn't continue as an independent company helping GM as a client.

"How do you compensate your people, Roger?" Perot asked him.

Perot knew that GM hourly workers were represented by a United Auto Workers union contract, and EDS never had been associated with any sort of union. Perot thought they were unnecessary in organizations that treated people with respect. He was concerned about white-collar pay since, presumably, the GM compensation system for managers and executives would apply to EDS. Smith related the details of GM's generous bonus program, which had been in effect since 1918. GM's bonus program heaped cash, a portion of annual profits, on the top five or six thousand managers. The bonus was paid in cash and stock as a supplement to GM's hefty salary and benefits package.

"EDS pays bonuses, too, Roger. Ours are paid on the spot, immediately following an outstanding job such as winning a big contract, while they're still sweating from the effort. When we won the Viable competition [for the U.S. Army data processing contract] against IBM, we paid bonuses to the members of the team the same night we won.

"The big motivator at EDS is stock. A lot of our managers have become wealthy at a relatively young age. Heck, my secretary is wealthy from EDS stock. Getting the price of the stock up is what makes this organization go. As EDS profits go, so goes our people's financial future," Perot said.

Perot and Meyerson knew their top managers wouldn't be thrilled about GM's compensation package. GM common stock was a dog. It hadn't grown significantly since it began trading publicly decades earlier, although it paid a fat dividend. EDS workers tended to care far less about dividend income than the chance to participate directly in the growth that resulted from their efforts. That meant share-price appreciation, something that didn't appear to be in the cards with GM common stock.

Courtney Jones, Roger Smith's representative, and the Salomon Brothers M&A team discussed the various problems raised by Perot among themselves. Compensation was a tough one. Moreover, EDS said it needed independence to work effectively at GM. Yet Smith and Jones weren't at all comfortable with the notion that EDS, as an outside supplier of services, would have access to and control of all of GM's most sensitive information. That was a function that would inextricably tie the two companies; it was a blood bond. The GM executives felt strongly that whoever controlled their computers should be a blood member of the family.

Scully and Rosenfeld, the Salomon Brothers dealmakers, endorsed this line of thought. They realized something else as well: an EDS and GM joint venture or an EDS data processing contract with GM didn't generate the multimillion-dollar fee that would result from the acquisition of EDS.

What once appeared to have made so much sense was becoming obscured in cross-purposes. The negotiations reached an impasse.

Mort Meyerson wasn't discouraged. He had been correct in feeling something big was in the cards for EDS months before GM came knocking. Despite the problems with compensation and independence, he still felt positive; and Meyerson was nothing if not intuitive.

Riedlinger, who by this time was in New Jersey on Meyerson's orders and was drumming up contracts for EDS with AT&T, knew and respected his boss's intuition. If Meyerson said something was going to happen, Riedlinger learned to prepare for it. In late April, as the negotiations with GM centered on issues of compensation and independence, Meyerson flew to New Jersey to meet with Riedlinger to discuss progress at AT&T. In four months, Riedlinger was able to increase EDS sales at AT&T by $1 million a month, adding almost $400,000 monthly in pretax profit to EDS coffers. The annoyance of being forced to move from Dallas had subsided a bit. Riedlinger had found an apartment in Bernardsville, and he was pleased to tell Meyerson how well sales were adding up at AT&T. In fact, he reported to Meyerson at dinner that he was shopping for a new Mercedes, which was to be his company car. He had certainly earned it this year, he thought.

"I think you better forget about the Mercedes and look at the domestics. GM makes some terrific-looking cars," Meyerson said coyly, and then, quite casually, added: "Perot and I were just up in Detroit, and we saw the new GM cars. As a matter of fact, EDS may have a chance to do some great things for GM, so you had better forget about Mercedes."

This is unbelievable, Riedlinger thought. Meyerson was smiling at him like the cat that just swallowed the canary. In a conversation about company cars, Meyerson had just signaled that something big was up between EDS and GM. Riedlinger knew that it must be pretty significant or Meyerson would have just told him what it was. Why was he being cagey? A few days later, while speaking to someone in Dallas, Riedlinger learned that Perot and Meyerson were negotiating with Roger Smith. Regretfully he dropped the Mercedes from his shopping list and tried to recall the location of the nearest Buick dealer.

After several hours of discussions in early May, Roger Smith and Ross Perot emerged from Perot's office. They looked tired, and neither of the men was smiling.

After a month of exploring various options, the two chief executives still hadn't resolved their differences, but they had come up with the germ of an idea. Courtney Jones relayed Roger Smith's report on the meeting with Perot to Salomon Brothers' Bob Scully. Smith and Perot still were seriously at odds over issues of independence and compensation. If the two companies could somehow combine — yet allow EDS to stay independent — then maybe a deal still could be struck. The glue, the solution to the impasse, would have to be "some kind of security or stock that will link the two companies and motivate EDS workers."

Scully's heart sank. So did Jerry Rosenfeld's. It was a very abstract concept. If the two chief executives were dreaming about some weird financial instrument that would solve all their operating concerns, the merger — and Salomon Brothers' fee — was most likely a dead duck. Until this meeting, Scully and Rosenfeld hadn't any reason to be overly pessimistic about the merger, since no serious deal-killing "negatives" had cropped up. As seasoned investment bankers, they knew most merger ideas have a less than 50 percent chance of success, because a killer negative often crops up. The price is too high. The chief executives don't like each other. There are antitrust problems. Or now, in this case, there was the need to invent a new kind of financial instrument that would satisfy both chief executives.

What kind of securities could link the two companies and motivate EDS workers? How could this hypothetical security satisfy GM's requirement to own EDS 100 percent? No one had heard of such an animal.

Scully and Rosenfeld called Salomon chairman John Gutfreund in New York to relate the bad news.

Then the six members of the GM team — Scully, Rosenfeld, Courtney Jones, GM assistant treasurer Stan O'Neal, and the Skadden Arps attorneys — repaired to dinner at Uncle Tai's, a fancy Chinese restaurant in the Galleria shopping complex. As far as Scully and Rosenfeld were concerned, the dinner would be a farewell to Dallas and their hope for a

GM acquisition of EDS. As they munched on an hors d'oeuvre of candied walnuts, the group began analyzing what kind of security Roger Smith was groping for. How the devil could they invent a piece of paper to make this deal work?

The discussion focused on Smith's theoretical security. Perhaps it could be a species of General Motors common stock, created especially for the purpose of joining GM and EDS. The stock would have to allow GM to own EDS. Smith had insisted on that, and Jones understood.

But Perot insisted on independence. What could new common stock represent, if not GM's ownership of EDS? They discussed EDS's future profitability and dividends. Maybe this new stock should be more like a preferred stock, guaranteeing its holder a relatively safe stream of income. But preferred stocks typically don't offer much growth potential. Perot wouldn't buy it.

Maybe it could be a stock whose dividend was tied to the performance of EDS. As EDS's profit grew, dividends would grow. Technically, it would be a class of GM stock, but it wouldn't represent ownership of EDS, but rather ownership of a small part of GM.

Ross Perot and EDS's top management might be willing to accept this type of GM stock as payment for their EDS shares, with the right guarantees. Hence, they'd be motivated to make EDS succeed inside GM. Dividends from the new stock would be tied to the success of EDS.

Smith would be satisfied, Jones reasoned, because GM would own and control 100 percent of EDS. The dinner group permitted a touch of exuberance to creep into the conversation. Maybe the deal wasn't dead after all. The men drew out their pens and yellow legal pads and began to sketch the terms of the stock they had just invented.

By 1:00 A.M. the waiters had removed the remnants of the Chinese dinner and the GM team members returned to their hotel rooms. They had sketched the outline of GM Class E stock. E for EDS. No one had ever offered such a creature for sale on the New York Stock Exchange. In fact, many problems remained to be solved, not the least of which was the New York Stock Exchange's policy of opposing multiple classes of common stock. (The Big Board had aimed its rule at companies trying to protect themselves from hostile shareholders by issuing separate classes of nonvoting stock or stock with expanded voting power.)

Perot was certain to scrutinize GM's new stock idea warily. Before trading his stake in EDS, worth about three-quarters of a billion dollars, Perot would want ironclad guarantees from GM that any Class E shares he accepted would retain their value. The market might simply turn up its nose at a new class of GM stock, and Perot would be left holding worthless, or close to worthless, paper. The tax implications surrounding a new and unusual class of stock were critically important for GM, Perot, and EDS shareholders.

But if all these issues could be resolved, if the new stock worked, surely its invention would be a stroke of originality and genius, a feather in Salomon Brothers' cap.

Despite the late hour, GM treasurer Courtney Jones called Roger Smith at his hotel room to report what the lawyers and bankers had proposed.

The GM chief executive was pleased. He told Jones to keep working. Many details remained to be resolved before GM's E stock brainstorm was ready for Ross Perot's consideration.

EIGHT

The E Stock Solution

S TEVE McClellan knew it was a perfect time to keep his mouth shut.
Standing before McClellan at the speaker's rostrum, EDS president Mort Meyerson rhapsodized about glorious achievements, past and future. It was Tuesday, May 15, 1984 — EDS's annual conference with the security industry analysts, the men and women who monitor computer and software companies for Wall Street brokerages, pension funds, and bank trust departments in order to evaluate their securities as investments. Meyerson was painting the rosiest possible portrait of EDS, but he didn't have to lay it on too thick, because the analysts already were favorably disposed to EDS stock and were recommending it to clients.

Naturally, Meyerson didn't mention GM during his speech. But a few of the analysts at the conference had detected vague hints that EDS was in some sort of merger discussions. They asked Meyerson and others, but everyone in EDS's management denied the stories. Throughout Tuesday's presentations, the security analysts listened and took careful notes; the undercurrent of merger talk continued. McClellan sat attentively, straight-faced. He imagined the pandemonium among his fellow analysts if they knew GM was interested in EDS. For the past day and a half, he had been exchanging winks and smirks with Meyerson and other EDS executives.

As a member of the Salomon Brothers group that initially proposed the merger to GM, McClellan was prohibited ethically and by federal law from using his inside knowledge about the negotiations to trade EDS or GM securities or to convey the information to anyone else. More important, a leak almost certainly would have caused EDS's price to jump in value and bump Perot's asking price higher. GM probably would get cold feet and back out. Security at this point was severe: McClellan's own boss Ed Olsen, the head of Salomon Brothers' equity research, was in the dark about GM and EDS.

If the merger proceeded smoothly to a conclusion, McClellan expected a big payday for himself. On Wall Street success wasn't measured in promotions, titles, or office size, it was measured in dollars. From what he had seen during his seven years at Salomon Brothers, he stood to earn anywhere from 1 percent to 10 percent of Salomon's fee. Normally it would be awarded as a part of the year-end bonus, raising his 1984 salary as much as $100,000 above the $200,000 he had earned the year before. Certainly, he would get $50,000 at a minimum. The top researchers on Wall Street earned $500,000 and more. He was climbing in their direction.

As he gazed at everyone listening intently to Meyerson's speech, McClellan wondered if Scully and Rosenfeld, his compatriots from Salomon Brothers, and Roger Smith and Courtney Jones truly possessed the powers to persuade Perot to give up his child, EDS. Part of him hoped not. McClellan was convinced EDS was destined one day to become the colossus of the data-services industry, the IBM of its time. McClellan had written a book, *The Coming Computer Industry Shakeout,* predicting that EDS would become one of the world's top ten computer companies by 1990. He doubted that that level of greatness was possible for EDS as a GM subsidiary. He had seen too many well-intentioned mergers go sour in his time. EDS's élan and spirit needed special nurturing. McClellan didn't know much about the automobile business; but when a company like GM developed the hunger to acquire and diversify, it often was a danger signal of internal confusion and decline, a fundamental disorientation the acquiring company tries to end by buying and devouring healthy businesses.

Trading in EDS stock since John Gutfreund's visit to Perot in early April remained unremarkable, suggesting that McClellan and the tight circle who knew about the negotiations were keeping their secret well. The price of EDS stock hovered in the range of $28 to $30 a share, while the trading volume remained steady at about 50,000 shares a day. The day following the security analysts meeting at EDS, Wednesday, May 16, the smooth flow of trade in EDS shares was thrown into turmoil.

The *Dallas Morning News* and several other newspapers around the country carried an exclusive story by Dan Dorfman saying EDS was in "exploratory merger talks" that could lead to acquisition of EDS by a "giant U.S. corporation." Dorfman apparently hadn't felt solid enough about the GM rumor when Meyerson declined to confirm the story for him on Tuesday night, but he wasn't timid about printing rumors if he believed they had some chance of being true. The stock market, as they say, liked Dorfman's story. Strong buying pressure for EDS stock drove the price up more than $5 a share on Wednesday. At the closing bell, EDS was selling for $35¾, compared with Tuesday's closing price of $30⅞. The trading volume for the day skyrocketed to 539,000 shares.

By Wednesday afternoon, EDS's switchboard in Dallas was besieged with telephone calls from journalists, stock traders, and customers from all over the world. The crush of rumors grew too heavy to maintain the veil of absolute secrecy. An EDS attorney, Richard Salwen, acknowledged to reporters that "talks" were taking place but tried to minimize their importance.

"EDS will talk to anyone who comes to us with a favorable business deal, but I stress they are just conversations," he said. "There is no deal yet."

McClellan, aware from his newspaper that word of negotiations had leaked out, flew early Wednesday from Dallas to Atlanta to meet important Salomon Brothers clients for a golf outing. As McClellan and his clients drove their golf carts down the seventh fairway of the Peachtree Country Club, they saw the club pro racing toward them in a golf cart. The pro carried an urgent message for McClellan to call Ed Olsen, Salomon Brothers' director of research in New York.

McClellan excused himself and drove back to the pro shop. He didn't like what he was ethically bound to do. Trying to sound surprised and flustered, McClellan dialed Olsen and told him he hadn't any idea EDS was in merger talks, and, no, he couldn't imagine who the talks were with. He could imagine how frustrated Olsen was to hear those words. Salomon Brothers' clients had come to regard McClellan as the leading outside expert on EDS, and rightly so; now those same clients were furious with Salomon Brothers, which was forced to profess ignorance about a crucial development in EDS stock.

Ever the digging journalist, Dorfman kept up his search to discover the identity of EDS's potential buyer. More than anything, Dorfman, a syndicated columnist and TV commentator, loved scooping the *Wall Street Journal,* which had once employed him as writer of the influential "Heard on the Street" column. Now that EDS had confirmed his scoop about merger talks, he was anxious to score again. On Thursday, a Wall Street source told Dorfman the suitor was GM. He prepared to break the news on his broadcast that night on Cable News Network.

Stumping across Texas in behalf of education reform, Ross Perot stayed in close touch with Meyerson as news of the talks with GM spread to the public and through the markets. Perot was disappointed that word was out, for he still wasn't absolutely sure what, if anything, he wanted to do about GM. He *was* sure the fuss over EDS was going to interfere with the campaign to improve Texas schools.

There was nothing to do but keep marching forward, Perot reasoned. On Thursday night he traveled to Lubbock to address a businessmen's group. Waiting for Perot was Jonathan Dahl, a Dallas-based reporter for the *Wall Street Journal.* The story about GM Dorfman was preparing to confirm on cable TV was spreading quickly, prompting Dahl's editors to send him to Lubbock to confront Perot. EDS stock had closed another $2¾ higher in price that day on a volume of nearly one million shares traded.

"When a company the size of GM approaches, you have to consider it," Perot told Dahl, skirting the veil of secrecy. "We were flattered they came to us. In fact, I'm surprised they ever heard of us."

With the cat out of the bag, Mort Meyerson told reporters that negotiations with GM weren't going to drag over a long period of time. There were big problems and differences the two companies hadn't resolved. Neither GM nor EDS could afford for their top executives to spend too much time and attention away from their basic businesses. They were going to make it happen — or not — in the next couple of weeks. In a separate interview with the *Wall Street Journal,* Meyerson cautioned investors not to assume the inevitability of a GM acquisition of EDS. He told reporters that GM and EDS might form a joint venture or work out a data-service contract, with GM taking an equity position in EDS. Whatever happened, he said, it was to be settled soon.

The EDS president wasn't hedging for public relations reasons: Meyerson's caution sprang from some deep, nagging premonitions about GM, which he didn't yet fully understand, nor could he explain. The key, Meyerson knew, was independence. GM had to understand that whatever happened, EDS, in order to succeed, must be free to operate without interference from GM. The EDS style had always been to seize a data processing contract like marines hitting the beach. To achieve their objectives, EDS managers moved aside all obstacles in their path, including recalcitrant employees, outdated equipment, and irrational operating policies. This kind of action required committed and faithful support from top management, not consent of the governed. The transition period sometimes was uncomfortable for the customer and its employees. Explicit in this operating style was the option of EDS or the customer to terminate a relationship, if they agreed it wasn't working or was too painful. That, he knew, would be impossible if GM owned EDS.

Meyerson had explained EDS's style to Roger Smith, to GM president Jim McDonald, and to Courtney Jones, GM treasurer, several times over the past month. They hadn't seemed put off. Roger Smith, particularly, seemed enthusiastic about the idea of bringing a whirlwind organization like EDS into GM. The GM executives' reactions were positive, Meyerson thought. He told the *Wall Street Journal:* "They [GM] said, 'We've studied you from the outside and you seem to have an independent culture. We don't want to absorb you into a large company to become part of the bureaucracy.' "

No one likes change, and no one knew that better in early 1984 than Roger Smith.

Hourly workers on General Motors assembly lines in the early 1980s hadn't liked the fact that competitive labor rates from overseas translated into reduced benefits and lower salary increases in the United States. GM engineers and managers likewise were grumbling about the massive corporate reorganization that severed their affiliation with GM's five car divisions, transferring them to new organizations like the Buick-Oldsmobile-Cadillac (BOC) group or Chevrolet-Pontiac-GM Canada (CPC) group. In some ways, the white-collar bitching and moaning had been more disturbing to top GM management than the complaints from hourly workers. Roger Smith expected GM's salaried work force to understand the need for efficiency, the absolute imperative to rationalize antiquated procedures. How many lectures had he delivered to vice presidents on the need to write fewer reports, to stop holding so many meetings, to cut out repetition and ceremony and to get on with the tasks at hand? Was anyone listening?

It was frustrating. Smith's sermons hadn't budged many of the group he referred to as "the frozen middle," GM's white-collar employees. The frozen middle couldn't move and wouldn't be moved. The endless management seminars didn't inspire them. Buzzwords and slogans didn't help. Roger Smith was dubious about the mission statements and all the rest of the management happytalk being sold by industrial psychologists. The reorganization of the car groups was designed to force change, to shake up the ranks and streamline reporting relationships, to push decisionmaking down through the ranks. The new structure was accomplishing those goals very slowly. Complaints filtering up to Roger Smith from inside GM were long and loud; they dealt with giving up offices and titles, changing telephone numbers, switching computers. No, indeed, change wasn't easy. Everyone at GM loved the snug GM nest, with its cozy salary and benefits package.

Ross Perot never had to confront management inertia at EDS, Roger Smith was certain of that. Perot and his outfit moved fast and knew how to make things happen. An EDS set loose inside GM would teach GM managers the benefits of the can-do spirit, and perhaps it would inspire them a bit. The toughest part of this merger would be transferring EDS spirit into GM intact, Roger Smith thought. How can we attract and motivate people who aren't attracted by cash? We need a way to bind Ross Perot and his troops to us, to give them a stake in our future. The separate class of GM stock might be the answer if we can solve the legal and financial riddles posed by this kind of security. Will investors value these new shares highly enough to cover the cost of the acquisition? Will the New York Stock Exchange exempt GM from the rule against multiple classes of common stock?

Ross Perot and Roger Smith and their aides had been wrestling with these issues for weeks. Now that the merger talks were public, the issues had to be resolved quickly. Roger Smith knew that very little time remained to forge an agreement with EDS. Merger negotiations have a life of their own, and a limited store of enthusiasm and momentum. When the store is depleted, the campaign collapses.

In late May 1984, Mort Meyerson flew to Detroit armed with ideas and proposals about the structure of the merger from Ross Perot. Meyerson was scheduled for a negotiating session at GM headquarters with Roger Smith and GM's executive vice president for finance, Alan Smith.

The fourteenth floor at GM headquarters is a fortresslike affair, with two sets of heavy, bulletproof glass doors controlled by a receptionist who permits entry only to GM's top officers and guests. Arriving on the private express elevator for GM top executives, Meyerson greeted the receptionist, who had seen him on several occasions, and was escorted into Alan Smith's office, where Alan Smith and Roger Smith were waiting. It was an impressive setting and protocol, which bestowed an aura of high importance and secrecy on the top executive offices.

Ross Perot hadn't totally given up trying to sign up GM as a customer. EDS has got to be independent, Meyerson told the men. Ross wants us to be crystal clear on this point. Roger, you and Alan have to understand that the people in EDS don't want to sell the company. The emotional ties to EDS are very strong, and the company has given terrific financial returns. There's a universal feeling inside of EDS that no matter what kind of agreements we reach, we'll lose a great deal of personal freedom as a result of a combination with GM. If the two companies have to combine, Meyerson said, Perot likes the idea of accepting a separate class of GM stock as payment. But there were problems. Was he going to have to pay a huge tax bill, or did the IRS regard this type of exchange as tax-free? Perot has been involved in a number of public-interest issues like education reform, and the war on drugs before that. Will an agreement to form an alliance with GM limit his involvement?

Perot's ideological concerns, as presented by Meyerson, suddenly touched a stream of live current in Roger Smith's psyche. After all this time talking, was Meyerson trying to tell him, the chairman of the world's biggest corporation, that EDS wasn't interested in GM's attentions? What kind of stunt was Perot trying to pull? They'd been over a lot of this ground together; they'd agreed they could work this out.

The rage that overcame Roger Smith at that instant was as irrational as it was complete, for no one was challenging him or arguing with him.

Smith had never displayed publicly the level of anger he showed Meyerson that morning, but all his close associates had seen it before. To Meyerson, it wasn't unlike the tantrum of a spoiled child who, accustomed to receiving whatever he wants, suddenly was deprived of a favorite plaything or morsel of candy. It was the rage of a man who regarded himself as all-powerful in the sphere in which he operates, someone who didn't have to accept arguments or rejection. Such tirades aren't unknown in corporate America; executives who can't allow themselves to be punctured occasionally by subordinates or who aren't capable of self-deprecation now and then are the most vulnerable to utter loss of temper.

As he watched and listened to Smith unravel, Meyerson was awestruck. He had been in lots of delicate corporate negotiating situations, but he had never encountered anything like this. Perot had sent him to Detroit to work on problems, none of which Perot thought were particularly intractable or insoluble. This was to have been an ordinary business meeting to discuss the terms of a deal. Meyerson had no idea what he had said to trigger this reaction.

Smith's display began with some garden-variety shouting. Apparently Alan Smith must have known what was coming, Meyerson thought later, because he sat quietly and appeared uncomfortable but not surprised. The shouts, abuse directed at EDS's negotiating tactics, became more and more high-pitched.

"You don't have to yell to make your point," Meyerson finally said to the GM chairman.

Roger Smith didn't think much of Meyerson's suggestion. Smith's complexion grew florid as a river of invective filled the room. Alan Smith sat silently as his boss ranted.

Meyerson had seen Ross Perot get angry — Perot's left ear grew beet red when he was upset and he could dress down subordinates without mercy — but Meyerson had never seen anything like this in a business setting. Perot got mad, but he didn't bully, he didn't tolerate bullying by EDS managers, and he never lost control in the manner in which Smith had lost control of himself.

"I don't think we have anything further to discuss," Meyerson said, closing his briefcase.

Suddenly Roger Smith grew quiet. Meyerson stood up, shook hands with both men, and left the office. As he headed toward the elevators, Meyerson ducked momentarily into the men's room. When he came out, he saw Roger Smith and Alan Smith in the corridor looking for him.

"Let's talk this thing out," Roger Smith said in a calm voice, perfectly composed, the tirade seemingly forgotten. "It's just not reasonable that things should end this way. Let's really talk things out."

Meyerson returned to Alan Smith's office. The discussion continued without incident or rancor, as if nothing had happened. After the meeting, Meyerson again shook hands and descended to the lobby of GM headquarters. From a payphone he dialed Ross Perot's office at EDS headquarters.

"Ross, something really strange has just happened. I'll be back today and I'll tell you about it," Meyerson said.

On the flight back to Dallas, Meyerson couldn't reconcile what he had just seen with his preconceived notion of the chairman of GM as a wise, powerful, and controlled figure. Something didn't make sense. The man had lost control, totally. A few minutes later he was perfectly calm, even charming. If Smith acted this way now when only negotiating items were at stake, how was he going to deal with the inevitable pressure and upset of EDS exerting its influence inside GM?

The next day in Dallas, Mort Meyerson related his adventure on GM's fourteenth floor to Ross Perot.

Perot didn't like what he heard. He harped constantly on the three things about which EDS never compromised: the quality and price of its services; ethical standards; and the way people in EDS treat each other.

The way Mort described it, Roger Smith had bullied him in an unforgivable manner. Perot knew Meyerson shared his desire to pursue any opportunity for EDS that looked promising for the long term. An alliance with GM could give EDS a way to develop factory-automation computer systems, which EDS knew nothing about, and sell them to every manufacturer in the world. And, of course, EDS would continue to sell health-care, insurance, and banking systems as it always had and improve its penetration into the government and the military data processing fields, fertile areas in which they had already landed some hefty contracts.

"Ross, I've thought about what happened and I'm not sure we should do a deal with GM," Meyerson said. "At the very least, I think we should be very careful. I know we're looking at a big opportunity for growth. What I saw the other day in Roger Smith's office . . ."

"Now, Mort, we've all had bad days," Perot began. "How crazy is this guy? It must have been something off the wall, unusual. Look, GM can double or triple EDS's revenue in a couple of years. GM overnight can at least double the revenue numbers it took us twenty-two years to build."

"I realize that, Ross. A lot of this depends on whether guys like Roger Smith are serious about letting us bring about the vision they told us about," Meyerson said.

"What choice will they have? Our deal with GM will be nailed down sixteen ways from Sunday or we don't do it. A separate class of stock that I own a substantial portion of, plus the merger agreement, forces them, in effect, to do all their data processing business with us at prices we decide for them," Perot said. "And the beautiful part is that GM can't go back on any of it."

"Ross, given what happened with Roger, I think you should have someone else negotiate with GM," Meyerson said.

Ross Perot understood Meyerson's reservations. Mort had always shown uncanny instincts about people and situations. Mort's instincts probably were based on substance, on real problems EDS will have with GM if we don't strike an absolutely bulletproof deal, Perot thought. Perot knew GM couldn't buy EDS without making extraordinary provisions to protect and motivate EDS's work force.

"Mort, I appreciate your concern. If this is what you want, I'll let Bill Gayden take over the negotiations with GM so we can made sure that if we do this deal we'll be protected in every single way we can be protected," Perot said.

Bill Gayden, senior vice president in charge of EDS's international business, was one of Ross Perot's closest associates, a droll man with the negotiating talents of a world-champion poker player. Meyerson agreed to put Gayden on the GM case for the time being. Ross Perot was calling the shots, and he wanted an agreement with GM.

EDS senior vice president Bill Gayden had pranksterism in his blood.

Unlike the typical EDS officer who fit the mold of the earnest Boy Scout, Gayden was the guy who always could be counted on for a cigarette, a drink, and a hilarious story. He had been at EDS since nearly the beginning and had been involved in some of the most unusual data processing contracts anyone had seen, like EDS's first contract in Saudi Arabia, an agreement to install a computer system from scratch within sixty days. Gayden rented a Boeing 707 and filled it with IBM mainframes and all the paraphernalia, down to the air conditioners and special floor panels for the computer room. He supervised the loading of the aircraft and set up the system specified in the contract. After the system was up and running, Gayden returned from the Arabian peninsula with yarns about a primitive, conflicted culture, struggling against itself to join the modern world. Having once gotten himself stuck in a sweltering Saudi Arabian apartment without running water, Gayden told how he bought $40 worth of Perrier from the local supermarket for his bath.

In a way, EDS's hostage rescue in Iran in 1979 was caused by Gayden's optimistic approach to business in the Middle East. When the first stirring of the Iranian revolution surfaced in early 1978, Ross Perot was alarmed. By summer, the Iranian government had suspended payments on EDS's computer contracts with the social security administration. Violence was escalating daily. Perot told Gayden, who was in charge of EDS's international contracts, to evacuate all EDS personnel from the country.

Gayden resisted Perot's instincts. To him, the disorder was temporary.

Once a new government was established, he believed, EDS would continue its work.

"Ross, it's no worse here than downtown Dallas on a Saturday night," Gayden joked once while talking to Perot on the telephone from Tehran. At that moment, gunfire erupted nearby, which Perot could hear over the telephone line back at his office in Dallas.

"Don't worry, Ross," Gayden chortled. "They're shooting in the other direction."

Perot wasn't convinced. By the time the order was given for everyone at EDS to leave Tehran, prosecutors already had arrested EDS managers Bill Gaylord and Paul Chiapparone. Ross Perot was angry at the Iranians and he was angry at himself for not insisting that Gayden evacuate the EDS workers earlier.

After Iran, Gayden remained a key member of Perot's inner circle, the kind of man who could be relied upon to quickly grasp the essential elements of a deal and map out a bargaining position. He was too valuable to banish. So when Meyerson stepped aside as chief negotiator with GM, Perot naturally turned to Gayden.

Gayden immediately immersed himself in the details of the special common stock GM proposed, the operating issues for EDS inside of GM, and Ross Perot's concerns for personal and corporate independence.

The chemistry between Gayden and the GM and Salomon Brothers negotiating team members — Scully, Rosenfeld, Courtney Jones, and the GM lawyers — seemed, initially, quite positive. The group's first formal negotiating session, in late May 1984, was conducted in vintage Gayden style. Bob Scully, Jerry Rosenfeld, and Courtney Jones filed into Gayden's cramped, unassuming office at EDS headquarters. In front of Gayden's desk was a small table, low chairs, and a blackboard. Five or six people could sit, but not without bumping elbows. Gayden asked Courtney Jones to review GM's proposal, which he did during the better part of half an hour.

It was Gayden's turn to respond. Peering at GM treasurer Jones without expression, he didn't object directly to any of GM's proposals specifically. Instead, he aimed his comments at GM's entire initiative.

"I just don't think this can happen," he said, with an air of finality. A silence fell over the room. No one knew what to say, least of all Courtney Jones. Was that Gayden's role? To tell them Ross Perot didn't want to do the deal? After about forty-five uncomfortable seconds had passed, Jones finally opened his briefcase, inserted his papers, thanked Gayden, and turned to leave. The Salomon Brothers bankers, stung with disappointment, got up to leave, too.

"Oh, come on back in here," Gayden said, grinning at their discomfiture. They'd fallen for his joke. Scully, Rosenfeld, and Jones giggled appreciatively. The performance broke the tension of long weeks of haggling, secrecy, and wearying trips between Dallas and New York.

Gayden was the catalyst that drove the reactive flow of the talks. Each side now seemed to accept the other's eccentricities. Gayden's joking was more than matched by Courtney Jones's beverage requirement for negotiations: Tab served warm in the can.

By early June, as issues were settled one after another, Gayden and the GM team felt a growing confidence that they had paved the way for Ross Perot to accept the acquisition of his company by GM.

"If it happens, it's going to happen on June 27," Gayden told the group from GM. "Somehow or other the great events of Ross Perot's life always take place on his birthday."

As his negotiators worked on the deal in Dallas, Roger Smith attempted to build a consensus among members of the GM board of directors for spending several billion dollars to buy EDS.

"If we need EDS's data processing help, why not just hire the company?" asked Ed Pratt, chairman of Pfizer Corporation, and a member of the finance committee of the board. The idea Ross Perot had been pushing was so simple, so obvious, it had immediately occurred to a member of GM's finance committee.

Why not, indeed? Because data processing was like legal or public affairs, Roger Smith explained to the finance committee, too integral to GM's basic lifeblood to trust to outsiders. Moreover, a data processing contract didn't offer the diversification into the nonautomotive business of factory automation that GM wanted. And a data processing agreement alone didn't inject the spirit of Ross Perot and the can-do mentality of EDS's executive corps into GM's lethargic bureaucracy.

Pratt sensed that Roger Smith was in a buying mode, but he asked his question anyway. Pratt didn't like the idea of a merger that brought Ross Perot into GM. Not one bit. He had what he felt was a strong reason. A couple of years earlier he had agreed to serve on a committee of volunteers to establish the memorial for Vietnam veterans in Washington. Ross Perot, a vocal longtime supporter of U.S. fighting men, contributed $160,000 to sponsor a design competition. The winning design, submitted by a young woman from Yale, was controversial. Many Vietnam vets thought her V-shaped design was unbecoming and inappropriate, reminiscent of the peace signs flashed by protestors. Perot spoke up on behalf of veterans who objected to the winning design, Pratt recalled, putting tremendous pressure on the committee members to change it.

Perot hadn't been aware of Pratt, but Pratt remembered the incident vividly. In the end, a compromise was reached. Pratt came away from the episode feeling abused. Perot had been an unchained tiger, he remembered, using his financial support to buttress his arguments, seemingly impervious to reasonable persuasion. Stories had appeared in newspapers suggesting irregularities in the committee's finances, which were later proved unfounded. Pratt suspected the stories were leaked by Perot. The guy was capable of doing anything to get his way.

Pratt told Roger Smith the story of Perot and the Vietnam Memorial following GM's finance committee meeting in early May.

"Perot is a bulldog and has very little restraint," Pratt warned Roger Smith. Like Pfizer, GM was a corporation shaped from a standard mold, where one succeeds, to a certain extent, by going along. There's no way these two cultures are going to coexist peacefully, Pratt thought.

I'm trying to force-feed technology to an organization that doesn't want it, Smith explained to Pratt. I need to blast through the resistance. Unless we buy EDS and bring EDS people in-house, the GM organization will find a million ways to stonewall them.

Like many chief executives, Ed Pratt had served on numerous corporate boards of directors. None of the posts, including his chairmanship of Pfizer, one of the nation's leading pharmaceutical firms, carried as much prestige or clout as his GM director's seat. In Pratt's eyes, GM was an American institution, the country's dominant single business force. Hell, GM was America. For a businessman such as himself, who had started as an IBM salesman just like Ross Perot and worked in big companies his whole life, association with the nation's premier corporation was an immense honor. Wherever Pratt went, people wanted to discuss cars and GM with him; rarely did people want to chat about Ben-Gay, an ointment for sore muscles and one of Pfizer's important products.

When considering matters confronting GM, Pratt attempted to balance his opinions against what he saw as the prerogatives of management. Legally, directors of public companies are voted into office by shareholders, and their duty is to represent the shareholders' financial interests. The laws of corporate governance only require directors to exercise prudent judgment; they're not held responsible for mistakes. Pratt, like most of the business executives who sat on GM's board, regarded his job more in the nature of adviser, consultant, and sounding board to Roger Smith than as shareholder advocate, whose duty it was to oppose something he saw as inimical to shareholder interests.

In the matter of EDS and Ross Perot, Ed Pratt knew he was swimming against the current in the finance committee. Rarely, if ever, did a director vote against the wishes of GM management, and no one was likely to challenge Smith directly on this issue. It simply wasn't done at GM. Directors openly expressed their concerns, but if theirs was a minority view they joined the consensus and went along.

Ed Pratt registered his concern about Ross Perot. He then dutifully joined the majority in favor of allowing Roger Smith to proceed.

On the first Monday in June, the full GM board of directors was scheduled to listen to Roger Smith and to deliberate about the proposal to acquire EDS.

Courtney Jones worked feverishly over the Memorial Day weekend to prepare Roger Smith's slide presentation for the directors. Each time Courtney ran into a question or a problem, he called Tom Walter, EDS's chief financial officer. On that Sunday, Walter was outside socializing at his neighborhood block party in Dallas; each time his beeper went off, he grabbed something to eat or drink and ducked inside to the telephone to help rehearse the EDS slide show with Courtney.

Their consultations helped paint a complete picture for GM's board of directors the next day. Directors couldn't review the price and the terms of the deal because they weren't final, but the full GM board accepted Smith's concept, endorsing the green light the finance committee had given for the acquisition and issuance of the new class of GM stock.

On June 12, Roger Smith sent an agreement in principle by telex for Ross Perot to sign. It was a short, twelve-paragraph document, offering to buy all EDS public shares at $44 cash and create a new class of GM stock to exchange for EDS shares held by Ross Perot and other EDS managers. Under the plan, GM would own 100 percent of EDS; the new stock would represent a proportional claim to the assets of General Motors Corporation and a dividend based on EDS's profits.

The telex message contained a space for Ross Perot's signature.

Ross Perot read Smith's message. The buyer was eager, but Perot wasn't inclined to sign anything — yet. Perot still wondered whether Smith truly grasped the importance — and implications — of EDS's independence, and the importance of allowing EDS to motivate its people and to operate as it always had.

Perot remembered, too, how blasé his father had behaved when someone came to sell him a horse. He had seen that great quality in dealmakers such as Charles Allen, the investment banker who had tried to take EDS public in the early 1960s. It wasn't good to be too eager. This was the most important deal of Ross Perot's life; Roger Smith should hear about his, Ross Perot's, concerns and respond with the proper assurances in his own words. That way the deal would be bonded not only by contract, but by two men who understood each other. It should all be put down clearly in black and white.

Perot had an idea. Normally he would rather speak to someone face to face than exchange memos. This time he thought it was important to write down explicitly what needed to happen in order to make this deal go. He wanted to read that Roger Smith understood and agreed. He would send his questions to Roger personally and ask Smith to write down his answers, to make sure there was no misunderstanding. To speed the process, Perot used a telephone facsimile machine, which transmitted the questions, page by page, directly to Smith's office in Detroit.

June 12, 1984

DEAR ROGER:

I am sending you my thoughts on the transaction. I have broken these down into the following categories:
— Objectives of the transaction
— Attitudes within EDS about the transaction
— Comments on the importance of GM/EDS independence
— Comments on GM/EDS profitability
— Comments on capital
— Perot/Meyerson involvement with GM
— The liquidity of 20 pc stock holdings
— Comments on contracts for EDS key people.

I will send these papers to you as we complete them.

SINCERELY,

ROSS

OBJECTIVES OF THE TRANSACTION

1. Make GM the automobile industry leader in terms of effective, state-of-the-art information systems and communications with the purpose of making GM even more competitive worldwide.

2. Become the world's largest computer service company.

3. Quickly build the world's second largest computer company (second only to IBM) by combining EDS and GM's data processing and communications.

4. Become the dominant supplier of computer services to the following industries: manufacturing, communication, insurance, banking/thrift, credit unions, cad/cam, health care, large-scale systems integration, government systems.

5. Build a state-of-the-art, standard production control system for all GM divisions using Saturn as a model. [The Saturn project was an advanced vehicle and GM car division that would be announced the following January.]

6. Build a state-of-the-art worldwide communication system . . .

7. Administer health insurance for all GM employees worldwide, with an estimated annual savings of over $100 million after one year.

8. Using the communications network, link all GM suppliers on-line to minimize inventory costs and down time due to parts shortages.

9. Build a state of the art, on-line system for GM dealers.

10. Build a nationwide commercial bank using GMAC and the communications network as a nucleus.

In his memo to Roger Smith, Ross Perot emphasized that EDS was "honored and flattered that a company of GM's stature is interested in EDS." He said the two companies together could accomplish the program in five years, rather than the fifteen or twenty it might take to accomplish the goals separately.

EDSers were worried though, and he listed his concerns for Roger Smith to read. He also called Smith to tell him the price was too low; Ross Perot didn't like to leave any money on the table. He thought GM just might be willing to pay another $4 to $6 per EDS share.

The next day, Roger Smith responded with the following note:

June 13, 1984

DEAR ROSS:

I appreciate receiving your thoughts on the proposed venture. There is a remarkable similarity between the way you and I both see the future potential for an alliance between GM and EDS. In an attempt to bring the transaction to a conclusion, I would like to give you my comments on your thoughts as honestly and candidly as I can. I have inserted my comments following each of your thoughts where applicable. I have not commented on the "Objectives of the Transaction" because I agree completely with your thoughts in this area.

SINCERELY,

ROGER B. SMITH
CHAIRMAN

The following questions and answers were transmitted by facsimile machine over a period of three days. They are arranged with Roger Smith's answers following Ross Perot's questions and comments.

PEROT: The people in EDS don't want to sell the company.

SMITH: This is understandable. The people in EDS must decide whether they would be better off "going it alone" or by teaming up with GM. For all the reasons set forth in the "objectives of the transaction" we believe that the truly best future for EDS is with a GM alliance.

PEROT: Over the past five years EDS [stock] has appreciated at a compounded rate of 44 per cent a year. The opportunities for such future appreciation may be lost.

SMITH: Corporate histories tell us that most "new" industries experience a rapid growth in sales and earnings in the early years. This, of course, attracts a multitude of other companies into the field with the end result that while the high growth rate for the industry may continue, the individual company growth rates level off and even decline. . . . While EDS has been highly successful in achieving a remarkable growth rate in the past, it will be extremely difficult to maintain this rate in the future.

To our mind, the best opportunity for EDS to maintain their [sic] high growth rate will be through an alliance with GM.

PEROT: The management team has done a great job in taking EDS from an idea to a substantial company in 22 years, against overwhelming odds. The emotional ties to EDS are very strong because of the level of effort that has been expended. This is a tested, tough, proud team.

SMITH: This is exactly why GM likes the EDS team.

PEROT: To a large extent, the EDS management team created what is now a multi-billion dollar market for computer services.

SMITH: I agree and that very success will attract many other competitors to the field.

PEROT: The people in EDS are all financially successful. They have no desire to get liquid or diversify their holdings.

SMITH: I agree, but prudent estate planning might suggest something different.

PEROT: Many of the families of key people are negative about the sale of EDS. (Perot's family feels it is like selling a member of the family.)

SMITH: Understandable. However, this is a bit like whether you want to send your son off to college or keep him home. . . .

PEROT: Entering into a taxable transaction on the sale of the stock is unattractive.

SMITH: The tax consequences are inevitable, only the timing is optional. . . .

At this point, Ross Perot raised several technical questions about the Class E stock, which Roger Smith answered. Then they continued:

PEROT: The management team is concerned it might be more difficult to sell EDS's services to non-GM prospects.

SMITH: Our experience tells us that EDS will gain many more customers than it would lose. In the U.S. alone, we have 35,000 suppliers, 10,000 dealers and many non-GM related companies that follow our lead. Lack of business will not be a problem. . . .

PEROT: As a part of GM we are concerned that EDS would become a prime target for labor unions.

SMITH: Our salaried workforce is non-union, despite 50 years of union effort.

PEROT: The price offered by GM ($44 a share) does not fairly reflect the value of EDS, based on our ability to sell EDS quickly in the marketplace, by disposing of its systems, computer network, operating divisions and land.

SMITH: Most companies I know are "worth more dead than alive," but this is really a useless valuation unless the only future for the company is liquidation.

PEROT: In order for GM/EDS to retain its multiple [i.e., for its stock to sell at a high price], it should be carefully positioned as an independent company with a clear, independent identity.

SMITH: I agree and this is what we propose.

PEROT: GM/EDS would continue to maintain its headquarters in Dallas.

SMITH: I agree and this is what we propose.

PEROT: GM/EDS financial records, accounting principles and all other elements of its corporate identity would be maintained separately.

SMITH: I agree and this is what we propose.

PEROT: GM/EDS would retain its capital and other assets.

SMITH: I agree and this is what we propose, except to add capital and assets to accomplish objectives.

PEROT: GM/EDS would continue actively marketing to non-GM prospects.

SMITH: I agree and we would expect this portion of the business to expand as new business items are developed through the alliance with GM. (e.g., manufacturing processing)

PEROT: GM/EDS would maintain a separate board of directors, including EDS's management as determined by [Perot] plus GM representatives on the EDS board. The chairman, president of GM and chief financial officer being the three preferred persons.

SMITH: I agree and we would propose that all the members of the GM executive committee would be EDS board members as you suggested.

PEROT: The GM/EDS board will continue to meet quarterly.

SMITH: I agree and meetings should be in Dallas.

PEROT: Ross Perot will continue to serve as chairman and chief executive officer.

SMITH: I agree and this is what we propose.

PEROT: Mort Meyerson will continue to serve as president.

SMITH: I agree and this is what we propose.

PEROT: General Motors will own both EDS and GM. There is no conflict in allowing a fair profit to be earned by EDS for work done within GM.

SMITH: I agree and this is what we propose.

PEROT: The savings and efficiencies GM/EDS generate for GM will create sizable additional profits for GM. That makes the profit paid to EDS for its work insignificant. This will allow GM/EDS to keep a high multiple on its earnings. In considering this issue, it is important to keep in mind that GM/EDS is so small compared to GM, that the profit EDS is paid for its work to GM that allows GM/EDS to keep its high multiple has an insignificant impact on GM profitability.

SMITH: I agree with the expected savings. But a proper and reasonable EDS profit is important to all of us and is not "insignificant."

PEROT: A 30 per cent before-tax profit based on GM/EDS direct costs and overhead will support an earnings growth record that is consistent with EDS's past record of growth.

SMITH: I agree and we would expect GM/EDS to earn a profit of this magnitude. Many of our component divisions earn this and more.

PEROT: There are many ways that GM/EDS work for GM could be priced. The simplest is simply to agree on a pre-tax profit based on direct costs and GM/EDS overhead.

SMITH: This may be the simplest but certainly not the best. Cost-plus and fixed profit rate contracts are notorious for destroying cost control incentives. GM/EDS can become all it wants to be on a commercial pricing basis.

PEROT: In developing prices and plans, GM representatives should keep in mind that a dollar of profit from GM automobile earnings carries a multiple of four. On the other hand, a dollar of profit for EDS earnings carries a multiple of thirty. In other words, $1 of GM profit converts to a stockholder value of $4, while $1 of EDS profit converts to a stockholder value of $30. (Assuming a 20 per cent dilution since GM owns 80 percent of (new) EDS shares, the value becomes $24.)

SMITH: We are very aware of this and this is part of our logic behind the issuance of GM/EDS shares.

PEROT: The GM bonus and incentive plans for its divisions could create a negative attitude toward allowing GM/EDS to make a profit. This concern should be addressed.

SMITH: Not so. EDS profits will be included in overall GM bonus calculation. This is not a problem. . . .

PEROT: Perot will become a member of the GM board, serving on the ——— committee. [This was left blank for Smith to fill in.]

SMITH: We would hope that Ross would agree to serve on the GM board. I have discussed this informally with the members of the nominating committee who are in agreement.

PEROT: Perot intends to become a substantial stockholder of GM, as long as GM management has no objection.

SMITH: No objection. This should be a personal decision of Ross.

PEROT: Perot will be available to assist GM in any of the areas we have discussed, plus other areas that may arise in the future.

SMITH: We believe Ross could help in several key areas.

PEROT: Perot would prefer that all of his compensation for GM activities be in GM stock options.

SMITH: No problem.

PEROT: Mort Meyerson will become a group vice president of GM, in addition to becoming president and director of GM/EDS. As a group vice president, he will be responsible for GM/EDS and communications worldwide. As a group vice president, Mort will report directly to the president of GM.

It is anticipated that GMAC will report to Meyerson, but this responsibility will be delayed until the transition has been completed.

Meyerson would prefer to be compensated with GM options for his duties as GM group vice president.

SMITH: We would be delighted to elect Mort as a vice president of General Motors (we have no title of group vice president). We believe this would aid significantly in Mort's relationship with the GM organization. As president of GM/EDS he would, of course, have responsibility for all of the current EDS plus such activities as transferred to GM/EDS from GM. As vice president of GM, he would be responsible for whatever [GM data processing] facilities it was decided to leave with GM.

GM/EDS and Mort should not report to the president. This would be counter-productive to the independent status necessary to the success of the alliance. The president is the chief operating officer of GM and manages the operating division. The vice chairman is in charge of staff activities. EDS should not report to either of these two. Instead, the closest parallel of an independent company with its own board is GMAC and this is where EDS belongs.

With respect to GMAC, its revenues are $7 billion and its net income $1 billion. Therefore, it is a major segment of GM's business. We believe that Mort has the potential to oversee this company but there are considerations. First, we believe that doubling or tripling EDS will require Mort's full attention for some time. Second, to take on GMAC, Mort could not do that and also be president of GM/EDS. Someone else would have to do that. Third, and perhaps minor, Mort would have to move to Detroit.

All in all it seems best to let this develop over time.

PEROT: All EDS compensation decisions and employee benefits will continue to be made by Perot and Meyerson.

SMITH: I agree.

There were some additional Ross Perot comments, followed by responses from Roger Smith, relating to the payout schedule on contingent notes from GM guaranteeing 16 percent compounded price appreciation of the new stock over seven years. Finally, Roger Smith told Perot that GM wasn't sweetening the deal any more and it was time for Perot to decide.

June 13, 1984

Ross,

I believe we have come to the point of decision. As you know, we feel strongly that the proposed alliance would be good for all concerned for all the reasons we have discussed.

I know and appreciate the value you place in your holdings of EDS. However, the price to the public of $44 is overly generous in relation to the market price of the stock, which, in reality, is the only measure that can be used for the publicly held stock. For your holdings it seems to me you have to look to the future of GM/EDS and what we can make of it working together. In the final analysis, however, the decision must be yours. We have gone to the top limit of our Finance Committee and board approval.

Please let me know your decision.

ROGER

But Ross Perot wasn't finished haggling. The next day, via fax, he sent Roger Smith the following letter and a list of issues for Smith's response.

June 14, 1984

ROGER:

I received your reply to my comments.

It is a pleasure to do business with you. I admire and appreciate your directness.

Bear with me while we continue to try to sweep out the various issues that are of concern to us.

I believe the questions and comments listed below will be my last.

After receiving your response, you and I need to have a face-to-face meeting. I am still swimming in alligators on the education issue in Austin. Unfortunately, the special session is underway and I cannot hand this project over to anyone else.

I will make time for the two of us to meet at your earliest convenience, after I receive your response to the items listed below.

SINCERELY,

ROSS

PEROT: It is my understanding if an employee participating in [the contingent notes guaranteeing the stock price] should leave voluntarily, he would be paid off according to the schedule at the time he leaves. Again, because of the magnitude of my situation I would be unwilling to have the plan capped in the event that I was terminated. Is this acceptable? The problem here is that future management of GM might conclude that it would serve GM's financial interest to terminate me.

SMITH: No one here in GM can imagine EDS without Ross Perot. Moreover, we believe that your personal dedication to EDS transcends termination provisions and we would be happy to stipulate that the full seven year plan will apply to your shares, regardless of your employment status.

PEROT: EDS has little experience in naming companies, products, etc. GM has a great deal. It is my impression that GM has historically kept the names of its car companies. For example, Chevrolet is the dominant name, not GM on the Chevrolet line. In my opinion, we should carefully consider the name of the new corporation to take advantage of EDS's good name in the computer service industry and the marketplace [and] to take advantage of GM's world class status and reputation.

This comment is triggered by our mutual reference to the new company as GM/EDS. This would be comparable to naming cars GM/CHEVROLET, GM/BUICK etc. We should carefully think through a proper name to maximize the advantages that both corporations bring.

SMITH: As you have suggested, GM has been included in the new company name to add further global recognition and financial credibility to your already strong EDS systems reputation. Just as importantly, the linkage of GM's name with EDS should give another dimension to GM's rapidly developing high technology product and manufacturing process profile. Additionally, I think the ability of EDS to do business with GM business units around the world will be helped by this increased recognition factor. Finally, the association with GM Class stock should be strengthened by including GM in the formal company name.

Actually, the decision to exclude GM from our divisional product nameplates represents a conscious give-up in return for increased diversity in the market presence.

Having said all this, we have no "hang-up" on the name and can see some advantage to simply carrying on the EDS name.

PEROT: We need to have a clear understanding that while I will be very active in the affairs of both EDS and GM, I would want to retain the personal freedom to involve myself in issues as I have in the past. If there is going to be a problem regarding controlling my time or independence, we should clear that up now. I propose that I be held accountable for results and not for hours worked. This is the way I have always operated and so far it has worked out well.

SMITH: We had not planned to put a timeclock in your office.

I tried in a previous note to address this issue and perhaps I should elaborate a little more to clear up any concerns you might have. Both GM and EDS have high moral and ethical standards and this is very important in our minds. If this were not the case we could not make our alliance work. There are many companies in the U.S. where the ethical standards are such that we could not work with them as we plan to work with you. (We discussed one with you the other day.) So, basically we propose that you continue just as you are doing. This includes the good work that you do outside EDS. General Motors also tries to do its thing in the "outside world" and many of our executives serve on hospital boards, etc. Unfortunately, the pressures of our industry have been such that we have not been able to do as many things as we would like, but what we do, we do well. (I wish you could have attended the GM Cancer Research Foundation dinner in Washington last Wednesday.)

In the final analysis it is the results that count and certainly EDS has not suffered due to a lack of effort on your part.

Several of Ross Perot's final questions for Roger Smith centered on capital, asset valuation, and accounting issues, such as the type of depreciation accounting GM planned to use for EDS assets. Perot again raised concern about his potentially huge tax liability; he asked GM to indemnify him against the possibility.

Roger Smith turned down Perot, suggesting they "work carefully together to make sure [tax liability] isn't a problem."

Ross

I hope our "exchanges" have been helpful in sorting things out. While I would be happy to meet with you anytime, I believe that you need to think this through carefully in your own mind. It is a big and important step for you and for EDS. I know you will make the right decision.

ROGER

As the pages of Roger Smith's responses had rolled slowly out of the fax machine in Tom Walter's office at EDS during the preceding three days of negotiations, Ross Perot and Tom Walter noticed something strange: the price of EDS stock began to behave erratically. They could see big price changes flashing on the Quotron machine.

Perot couldn't believe his eyes: each time Smith sent him positive and encouraging responses, it seemed that the price of EDS stock got stronger. Each time Smith showed the slightest hint of exasperation or balked at a Perot negotiating tactic, like the suggestion that GM pay the income-tax bill on the transaction, the price of EDS shares weakened. On June 13, the day Roger Smith declined to pay more than $44 a share, EDS closed down $2 at $34¼.

Were they imagining this? Was it a coincidence? Possibly, but Ross Perot didn't think so. Every time they had a good meeting, the stock price went up. Every time he and Smith disagreed on something, the price of EDS stock went down. It looked to him as if persons who were privy to the negotiations — lawyers, investment bankers, principals, or somebody — were trading on inside information.

After one negotiating session in early June, Perot sent two EDS security men with walkie-talkies to follow the GM negotiators back to the Lincoln Hotel. The security men were instructed to radio back to EDS headquarters as soon as the men entered the hotel. Sure enough, a few minutes after the signal that the negotiators had entered the hotel, EDS's stock price began to move sharply.

Perot telephoned the hotel and immediately assembled the GM team, including Rosenfeld, Scully, and the Skadden Arps lawyers, at EDS headquarters.

"Now this has got to stop," Perot said, relating what he and Walter suspected. "I don't know who's doing it, but it's got to stop. Every time we have a good meeting, EDS stock gets strong, and every time we run into problems, someone starts selling. Our people have been on notice for some time not to trade the stock, and I won't have this kind of behavior. It's blatantly illegal and immoral."

Scully and Rosenfeld were mortified. Why was Ross Perot singling them out for this speech? Did he actually believe they were involved in such a thing? Perot had been careful not to say directly that he thought the GM team was trading EDS stock illegally. After all, his own advisers could have been the culprits. But the implication was there.

Embarrassed and angry, Scully and Rosenfeld telephoned John Gutfreund in New York and vented their rage to him. If Ross Perot was accusing them of criminal behavior, they told him, they would just as soon drop what they were doing and come back to New York.

"Don't worry about it," Gutfreund soothed his young subordinates. They were close now, very close. The last thing Gutfreund wanted was a blowup over charges of insider trading. It certainly would kill the merger and possibly stain Salomon Brothers. "You two are too big and too professional to let this bother you. Just keep going and finish your work and forget about Ross Perot's ridiculous suspicions."

Inwardly, Gutfreund seethed. How dare Perot impugn Salomon Brothers? It wouldn't stop the deal, though; no, nothing would stop it now.

PART III

Roger Smith's World

NINE

***

A Proud Tradition

CCORDING to tradition, the job of GM chief executive was to guide the corporation, trim GM's sails, find the heading of the wind, and let the great clipper ship surge powerfully in the direction of greater prosperity. GM's chief executive was expected to be officer of the watch more than captain, to preserve the concept of the corporation more than create it.

Smith's election as chief executive in 1980 at the age of fifty-five presented him with nearly a decade before retirement to accomplish his goal of completely reordering GM. He had no intention of being a caretaker. He believed that he needed every moment of his tenure to bring about historic change. Not since GM chairman Frederic Donner ruled for nearly a decade starting in the 1950s had any chief executive received as grand an opportunity to leave his mark. Only the great Alfred Sloan had been in control longer, fourteen years as president and nearly twenty more as chairman.

When Smith retired in 1990, everything in sight would carry his stamp. His mentors and peers would be gone. The next generation of leaders, he was convinced, must inherit a different and improved GM. The massive job of reshaping the corporation, in order for GM to contend with new economic realities, stood before him. It was a task that held vital significance for the U.S. economy and for the lives of millions of working people.

On February 16, 1981, less than two months after taking over as chairman, Smith delivered his inaugural address to the company's 500 top executives and managers at the yearly management conference. What he had to tell GM's ruling class that day was bound to be a bucket of cold water in their faces.

Once-mighty GM had turned into a drowsy, corpulent giant at a time when the market demanded agility and speed. Sloan's principles of decentralized operations, which forced lower-level managers to make critical decisions about their business, were rusty from disuse. Instead of seizing initiative, GM managers were prodigiously writing reports and generating snarls of paper at a time when GM desperately needed action.

Foreign competition was gaining on many fronts, the new GM chairman told the group. Capital had to be conserved for massive investment in new plants and processes through the 1980s. The shift from rear-wheel-drive to front-wheel-drive cars and factories wasn't half complete. GM no longer could afford to carry unproductive assets. What couldn't make money would be shut down or sold.

In his most recent job as executive vice president of finance, Smith proved he could make the tough decisions. He had divested Frigidaire, the venerable maker of refrigerators, and Terex, the earthmoving equipment company. The economy wasn't sympathetic to underachievers and neither was he.

"It's a rude shock laying off people, as has been done at Terex and Frigidaire," he told GM managers in his inaugural. "It teaches the importance of what I like to call the three R's: responsibility, risk, and reward. If we are to achieve true decentralization, which is important to keeping GM profitable, then we must review the three R's and practice them every day."

Frigidaire had been carrying about twice as many people on the payroll as necessary. When White Consolidated Industries, Inc., bought Frigidaire from GM, it immediately cut the staff in half.

A West German concern that bought Terex laid off 750 workers immediately; Terex's costs and payroll had been way too bloated.

"The man in charge of the firm that bought Terex has given the people there the responsibility to run their business," Smith said. "Responsibility. The first R. He's also made it clear that his management team must produce results or else it will be changed promptly. That's risk, the second R. And, finally, he's put in an aggressive stock-option plan that turns profits into a handsome reward for management."

This wunderkind asked to see only one piece of paper from his companies each month, Smith gushed to his managers. All he wanted was the profit and loss statement! Horst-Dieter Esch's managers have the responsibility, they take the risk, and the rewards are waiting for them.

If only bureaucracy-bound GM could be more like Esch's company, IBH Holding AG. Smith thought wistfully: If only I had his freedom!

It wasn't the first time — or the last — that Roger Smith was to be impressed by a magnetic, freewheeling entrepreneur of one stripe or another.

The most important entrepreneur in his life and the man he credited for having the greatest influence on his career was his father. The son of a Chicago doctor, Emmet Quimby Smith returned to the United States from Europe after service in World War I and took a job in banking in Columbus, Ohio. Since no bank in town was able to exchange his French francs for local currency, he hit upon the idea of opening a foreign-currency window. The young banker married Belle Obetz, assistant superintendent of Columbus schools. Roger, the third of the couple's four children, was born on July 12, 1925.

Quimby Smith's mindset was that of creator and innovator, not pencil-pushing clerk. In less than a decade he was president of his own bank in Columbus. When the Depression wiped out the bank, Smith moved his young family to Detroit to start over. He took a job as controller, helping to organize Bundy Tubing Corporation. In addition to his bookkeeping responsibilities, Smith had a creative side; he loved inventing new tools and tinkering with manufacturing processes.

The Smith family's circumstances hardly were desperate. They lived in a mansion formerly owned by a governor of Michigan in the Indian Village section of the city. The Smiths belonged to the Detroit Boat Club, wintered in Florida, and owned a second home in northern Michigan. As the economy improved, they became more comfortable. Quimby Smith was promoted to vice president of Bundy and started his own manufacturing company on the side. Young Roger was enrolled in the private University School.

Smith, his two brothers, and his sister were reared to behave in keeping with the family's economic circumstances and social standing. His father, the children were told, traced his lineage to a member of the British aristocracy and signator to the Magna Carta. His mother's forebears came over on the *Mayflower*. In matters pecuniary, Smith's father didn't spoil his children. He insisted they work for their spending money. Roger and his brother delivered newspapers. He rode his bicycle, often in the dark, hurling the Wall Street edition of the *Detroit News* onto the porches of subscribers. With the liquidity his paper route brought him, Roger showed an early facility for financial matters; he lent his siblings money from his earnings and charged them interest.

Quimby Smith understood that the world was far more hospitable to the well educated. He rewarded his children with nickels and dimes for their good grades. Involving himself in their intellectual development, he asked them riddles, led field trips, stimulated creative thinking, and introduced Roger and his siblings to the breadth of the universe beyond their experience.

The Smiths employed a nanny to take care of the children. But the youngsters were expected to perform household chores and to wash the dishes. They all learned musical instruments. Roger chose the drums. A lefty and not a particularly gifted athlete, he learned to hunt, fish, and sail instead of pursuing team sports.

In 1942, at the age of seventeen, Smith enrolled at the University of Michigan with a major in business administration. Numbers were his forte. He specialized in accounting, taking differential equations and other math courses to keep his grade point average high. By all accounts he was well liked by his brothers at the Phi Delta Gamma house. They recalled Smith as an unremarkable, studious, red-haired collegian who mixed well into the group and enjoyed a beer and a good laugh at the Pretzel Bell in downtown Ann Arbor.

Smith enlisted in the Navy two years into his college career and was posted as a radioman aboard the USS *Montpelier*. Two years later he returned to campus to finish his undergraduate and master's degrees in business. By then, he was afire to absorb as much as possible about numbers and accounting. He particularly loved the courses of Professor William Paton, who had tutored a string of bright numbers men serving in high posts at GM. Albert Bradley, Richard Gerstenberg, and Frederic Donner all had studied with Paton and had been graduated from Michigan business school. All became chairmen of GM.

Degree in hand, Smith in 1949 set his sights on California and the burgeoning aerospace industry. His father stopped him. In Quimby Smith's opinion, the best-managed company in the world was in Smith's own backyard. GM in the 1940s had transformed itself almost overnight from a vehiclemaker into an armaments manufacturer. Now it was back to making cars and trucks again, in greater volume than ever amid the booming postwar economy. Smith agreed at least to inspect what GM had to offer.

Legend has it that Smith parked in front of the GM building in front of a thirty-minute meter. He had made an appointment for a job interview in the accounting department but didn't expect to get an offer. When he came out he had a job as a general accounting clerk and a $2 parking ticket.

One of Smith's first duties was tracking complex overseas consolidation accounting. For six months he struggled to keep his head above water, working harder to master the numbers than he had ever worked in his life. He telephoned Professor Paton to find out why, in light of his success as a student, he was having so much trouble at work. Paton reassured him that his university courses had been elementary compared to what he was facing on the job. The professor recommended some books to read. In a short time, Smith mastered the puzzles of international accounting.

When Smith's coworkers reminisce about him, the word that keeps coming up is *industrious*. The man, they say, was a veritable beaver in human form, diving with gusto into whatever task was available, especially projects involving fact gathering, number-crunching, and report producing. For example, a study was needed on Opel, GM's West German subsidiary. Legend records that Smith quickly produced a hundred-page horse-choker for his astonished supervisors.

Smith met his future wife at the Grosse Pointe Hunt Club in 1953. Barbara Ann Rasch was a comely clerk in GM's public relations department. Within a year they married and began building their nest in the northern Detroit suburbs. Like his father, Smith devoted himself, despite the long hours at GM, to making an impact on his children's educational and social development. He took them hunting with him for deer and wild turkey and fishing for Atlantic salmon. (As he climbed the executive ranks, he often ordered the GM plane back to Detroit late at night rather than spend the night out of town, so that he could spend a short time with his children.)

Eager and confident, Smith lugged his overstuffed leather briefcase into the GM building early each morning and out late each night, toiling far more hours than was usual or expected. His zeal was noticed. Smith's comfort with numerical concepts, and the skill and energy with which he applied them, led to the first big break of his career. Tom Murphy, a financial analyst ten years his senior, was preparing the facts and figures for critical antitrust hearings in Washington. Smith was asked to help.

The mid-1950s was a period when many in government believed GM had grown so large that it monopolized the automotive market and inhibited competition. Members of Congress called for the government to break GM into several smaller companies, as had been done to Standard Oil earlier in the century. Smith, Tom Murphy, and others prepared numerous careful studies, filled with persuasive facts and figures illustrating GM's positive effect on the nation's employment and on the gross national product. Alfred Sloan, GM chairman at the time, noticed the work of the junior finance men with favor. The aged founder of the modern GM used their briefing papers for his testimony, struggling all the while to hear the senators' questions through his balky, oversized hearing aid.

Smith's work also attracted the approving attention of Fred Donner. The cold, authoritarian finance chief had assumed the mantle of chairman and chief executive in 1958, heralding an era of hardheaded numbers-oriented management at GM. Donner's ascendancy immediately boosted the careers of the bright, financially minded GM youngsters. Smith admired Donner and recognized in him a sensitive, sympathetic side that others didn't see.

In 1963 Smith's promising career was interrupted briefly by a frightening bout with cancer. Doctors diagnosed a strange-looking growth on his skin as malignant melanoma. Happily, early detection and excellent treatment at Sloan-Kettering Memorial Institute cured his disease. But he learned he must be especially careful for the rest of his life to protect his pale, sensitive skin from sunlight. (The brush with cancer also helped inspire his later involvement with the GM Cancer Research Foundation, which contributed several million dollars to research during his service as chairman.)

By 1970, as Murphy inched closer to the chairman's seat, Smith was promoted to treasurer, a key position of power at GM. For lesser men, this might have constituted the pinnacle of a career. Yet Smith was only forty-five years of age, had been in GM for twenty-one years, and hadn't lost any energy or enthusiasm for work. The office of treasurer was a showcase and a springboard. It brought his meticulous staff reports to the constant attention of top management and the directors. No matter how difficult or time-consuming the project at hand, he never flinched or dodged. He was so eager and dogged about the work it was almost amusing. Murphy and the directors used to laugh that "if you asked Roger to move the GM Building across the street, he'd ask what direction you wanted it to face."

At this stage in his career, Smith had trained himself to focus his bottomless energy on planning and analysis. When looking at a business problem, he disciplined himself to peer down every alley, to explore every option and alternative, to make sure his plans encompassed every contingency. In presenting his work, he knew how to choose the relevant facts carefully, using only those with the keenest edge.

To prevail in discussion or debate, Smith was forced to rely on substance, not style. He wasn't blessed with the physical presence, oratorical skills, or smooth charm of some of his peers. His voice was too high pitched and nasal. He was short and unprepossessing, and his skin became blotched and mottled when he was tense.

In 1974 Tom Murphy was anointed GM's ninth chairman; Smith, not yet fifty years old, became executive vice president of finance and a director. By this time it already was obvious that Smith was the solid, perhaps even likely, candidate to succeed Murphy. Six years later, the board of directors' nominating committee considered Jim McDonald, a manufacturing engineer with experience running the Pontiac and Chevrolet car divisions, and Howard Kehrl, a scientist and engineer, before deciding that Smith was the best choice to lead GM through the eighties. (McDonald became president; Kehrl became vice chairman; both reported to Smith.)

His willingness to tackle any task, his prodigious, detailed planning, grasp of financial concepts, and aggressiveness — and, of course, Murphy's endorsement — won the day with the nominating committee.

Smith had served only a short stint in charge of GM's diversified operations, his only operating role. He had no experience as a carmaker. It didn't matter to the GM board. Neither had Murphy. As far as the directors were concerned, the mundane tasks of building and designing cars were of secondary importance to Smith's work as a financial thinker and planner; in the minds of the directors, McDonald and Kehrl could easily handle the operations of the business.

Donner, Gerstenberg, and Murphy had always expected Roger Smith, their apprentice financial whiz, to run GM one day. He hadn't disappointed them.

Smith charted his actions as GM chairman in a fashion that laid to rest all the jokes about dull, plodding accountants.

Three years before taking office, he set up GM's first office of strategic planning, labeled it with an innocuous title to protect it from corporate controversy, and put a young Englishman named Michael Naylor in charge. Naylor kept Smith briefed about advancing trends in computing and manufacturing technology. Together they began to search for ways to decentralize GM's decisionmaking.

When Smith took the reins from Murphy in 1980, GM was coming off its first unprofitable year since the 1920s. The numbers proved GM was vulnerable to the rising tide of imports and the mushrooming cost of its operations. So Smith first determined to slash costs and return GM to profitability.

He first attempted to wrench pay and benefits concessions from UAW workers by promising to pass savings in labor costs to car buyers. The heavy-handed tactic blew up in his face. Sales dried up as buyers waited for a new labor contract. In the end GM accepted a concessionary pact patterned on a similar agreement at Ford. To make concessions more palatable to the workers, Smith had promised equality of pay sacrifice all the way to the top of the executive ladder. His share, he announced, was $131 a month, prompting hoots of derision from UAW headquarters.

Compounding the damage to Smith's credibility among hourly workers, GM executives unveiled a lucrative new executive bonus program on the same day the workers signed the lean contract.

Barely a year into his term of office, the new GM chairman had displayed a clumsy, ham-fisted public relations technique and an incredible insensitivity to hourly workers. Forty-five years of bitter feeling dating from the 1937 sit-down strikes in Flint had bubbled to the surface again.

Strained labor relations and organizational turmoil also were evinced by the demonstrably mediocre cars GM was putting on the road. GM's new line of front-wheel-drive small cars (the Pontiac Sunbird, Chevy Cavalier, Cadillac Cimarron, and others) received disappointing marks from reviewers and were priced too high. Their introduction, a period that should have been full of hoopla and brisk sales, was one of the more embarrassing sales duds in modern GM history.

Radical action was needed. Smith gave the go-ahead for a crash program, code-named Saturn, to reinvent the process of building small cars in the United States. Saturn was to test completely new assumptions about manufacturing methods and labor relations. Smith also sent Jack Smith, a bright protégé from the GM finance department, to Japan to forge a joint venture with Toyota Motor Corporation. GM desperately needed to understand the details and methods of how Toyota produced such high-quality vehicles. Smith also approved enormous expenditures to buy or invest in every new piece of high-tech manufacturing technology that might be relevant in GM's current plants; this meant more robots, more vision sensors, more computers, and expanded use of artificial intelligence.

This was his vision of the twenty-first century. GM had to leapfrog beyond today by reinventing itself. Solving today's problems incrementally was a losing strategy. On paper the fully robotized factory looked feasible. GM possessed the financial muscle to search for the technologies it needed and to buy them. Michael Naylor, his strategist, and other advisers assured Smith that the cybernetic factory of the future, which could operate with far fewer workers, was a valid concept.

The biggest unknown was whether the salaried and the hourly workers, the engineers and riveters, the accountants and the advertising executives, had the stamina to run by Smith's side during this long and arduous race for the future.

Horst-Dieter Esch, Smith's model of the modern entrepreneur, was awash in journalistic adulation when Tom Murphy first spotted a story about him in a news magazine in 1979. By taking over a string of floundering construction-equipment companies with borrowed money, the young German had managed to build a worldwide organization that had the support of major West German banks. Although he knew very little about Esch, Roger Smith immediately envied and admired him. Unlike Smith, Esch wasn't buried in reports or in meetings. He jetted to and fro, decided his moves instantaneously, and carried everything he needed in his vest pocket. He made things happen quickly.

To Murphy, Esch looked like the perfect person on whom GM could unload Terex, GM's troubled construction-equipment subsidiary.

Smith liked Murphy's idea as much as he liked Esch. After he and the West German businessman dined at the Bloomfield Hills Country Club in the spring of 1980, they came up with a clever financial plan that suited both their needs.

Esch, for reasons that would become apparent a few years later, didn't have any cash. So GM agreed to sell Terex to Esch in return for a promissory note. GM also agreed to invest in Esch's company, IBH Holding. IBH would owe GM the money for Terex and pay it back over time from the money GM had "invested." That way, Terex was off GM's books; and if IBH Holding succeeded, GM owned a stake in Esch's success. The cash GM put into IBH Holding would come back as loan payments. Financially, the maneuver was tricky. But for Smith, it was a snap. It had, in dealmakers' parlance, lots of "upside."

Legally, the deal was highly questionable. GM's lawyers in West Germany warned Smith that the proposed transaction appeared to violate German law. That law differentiated between was what true investment of capital and what was, in essence, a phony investment disguising under-the-table "roundtripping" of GM funds, in this case, repayment of the GM loan. In other words, German business law forbade investors from putting in capital with one hand and withdrawing it with the other.

Smith was risking legal trouble in West Germany, but he had been thoroughly smitten by Esch's entrepreneurial bias for bold action and had declared his zest for this sort of fellow in the address to the GM managers. The lawyers' warnings didn't worry him too much. In case of legal trouble, Smith assumed GM was powerful enough, influential enough — and rich enough — to extricate itself.

Unbeknownst to Smith, Esch and IBH were sinking fast in 1979. Quarter by quarter IBH's losses in the early 1980s mounted; and there was no improvement in sight for the depressed construction-equipment business. GM, which had already "invested" $23 million in IBH, tossed $13 million more in the pot in 1981. The following year Smith agreed to put up another $8 million. The terms were spelled out in a letter Esch had requested from Smith. The wily Esch then used Smith's letter to entice Saudi millionaire Sheikh Saleh Kamel to invest $37 million cash in IBH. Unfortunately for Sheikh Saleh, his money wasn't flowing back under the table, as was GM's.

Meanwhile, GM's legal staff in Detroit grew alarmed and warned Smith about Esch using GM's participation to deceive Sheikh Saleh. It was certainly improper and possibly illegal. Again, Smith stubbornly ignored the warning.

IBH filed for bankruptcy in November 1983. The bankruptcy set off tremors in the West German financial community, nearly sinking the Schroeder Muenchmeyer bank, which had exceeded its lending limit to Esch. During the untangling of IBH's finances, Esch was charged with financial fraud and later was convicted and jailed. The bankruptcy trustee then sued GM, and so did Sheikh Saleh.

After it became apparent that Esch couldn't have stayed afloat as long as he did without GM's help, a West German prosecutor opened a criminal investigation of Roger Smith for alleged violations of the statute governing capital investment.

Ultimately, the prosecutor decided against filing formal charges against Smith, and within a few years the IBH affair was quietly settled by GM's restitution to the bankruptcy receiver; the prosecutor dropped the criminal investigation. The cost to GM: $40 million and some mild embarrassment for Smith and the company.

The episode, however, was revealing. It is not every day the chairman of the world's largest corporation finds himself the target of a criminal prosecutor. Why had the debacle occurred? First and most important, Esch was able to bamboozle GM because of Smith's fascination with entrepreneurial style, which overcame his better instincts as a seasoned financial executive. Esch was precisely the sort of man Smith wished to have working with GM and inside GM. Smith had been impulsive. He had grabbed for a quick fix as soon as the apparently perfect solution to Terex presented itself. In retrospect, the risk was unacceptable. Another couple of months spent investigating Esch and IBH and a dash of caution wouldn't have hurt anything and well might have prevented the transaction. Smith had been impatient, and it showed.

Third, Smith had turned stubborn when his lawyers warned him. As chief executive he felt he was entitled to pursue any strategic action he deemed necessary. (He actually started dealing with IBH when he was executive vice president and continued the relationship as chairman.) He received two warnings: one from GM's lawyers in West Germany; the second from GM's own legal staff.

Yet Smith had refused to change course. Action-oriented businessmen don't like to listen to lawyers because they are always turning thumbs down on projects and ideas. In this case, heeding legal advice might have saved GM from a nasty black eye.

Smith's desire to push power and responsibility lower on the GM management ladder was, in a sense, inherently contradictory, for the effort itself required him to seize a great deal of central control and micromanagement of details.

Nevertheless, Smith said clearly that he wanted fresh, nonbureaucratic thinking and fresh approaches to business. GM executives and managers weren't as responsive as he wished them to be. They had grown up in a system far more consensus-oriented and committee-oriented than the one he was building. In GM, managers avoided personal responsibility. Every decision was spread over as big a group as possible so no individual could be held accountable.

Smith loved to recite the parable of a GM manager clinging to a tree stump, refusing to swim across the fast-moving river. His job was to convince the manager to let go, to swim hard, because he surely was going to reach the other side — perhaps at a different spot from the one that he envisioned. The tree stump in his allegory was the old way of doing things, the river was the fast-moving marketplace, the spot on the other shore was GM in the twenty-first century.

In Smith's judgment, no amount of gentle persuasion could loose the grip of GM workers. The only way was to blast them loose from the stump with explosions like Saturn, like robotics, like the joint venture with Toyota.

These changes were numerous, they were difficult to adjust to, they followed one after another with great speed; hence, they presented great difficulties for lesser mortals than he.

When Smith met Ross Perot in early 1984, he believed Perot could be another essential element for GM, a way to blast GM managers away from the tree stump. Perot was an entrepreneur who made things happen quickly and had little tolerance for bureaucratic dithering. Perot's people were relentless.

Roger Smith was convinced it would take a company like the one Perot had built — and a man like Perot — to loosen GM's grip on outmoded computing practices.

TEN

GM's Travails

AMERICANS of Roger Smith's and Ross Perot's generation grew up associating the nameplates of General Motors cars with affluence. Perot remembered vividly from his childhood in Texarkana that GM cars, especially Cadillacs, Buicks, and Oldsmobiles, were driven by the wealthiest, toniest people in town: the doctors, the lawyers, the president of the bank.

As Perot and EDS executives became financially comfortable through the 1960s and 1970s, they tended to buy the quintessential symbols of success, new Cadillacs and Buicks. As times and fashions changed, they traded their GM cars for Mercedes, BMWs, Audis, Hondas, and other fashionable automobiles that are prominent on Dallas roadways. For security reasons, Perot for years stuck with a bulletproof Chevrolet. Besides, he wasn't a fancy person. He wasn't preoccupied with tastes and styles, and he didn't waste time wondering why the glitzy folks in Dallas seemed to be buying so many foreign cars.

When Roger Smith came courting in 1984, Perot had traded up to an Oldsmobile 98 and was satisfied with it. Perot's wife, Margot, on the other hand, loved the beautiful and exotic and chose an expensive European roadster for herself.

Had Perot studied the shifting demographics and trends of the U.S.

automotive market in early 1984, he would have discovered a sea change engulfing GM. By the time Perot contemplated joining forces with GM, the insurgence of Japanese cars and trucks was old news. Far more insidious was the erosion of GM's position in the luxury car market, once a Cadillac bastion, by foreign carmakers. The auto industry in Detroit had been acutely aware of the implications of Cadillac's decline and its impact on all of GM's sales, but they weren't immediately apparent to Ross Perot.

There was a time, not too many years in the past, when thunder from Chevrolet 454-cubic-inch engines and squeals from tires of Pontiac GTOs resounded through high school parking lots across the land. Sleek Oldsmobile Cutlasses, elegant Buick LeSabres, and glittering Cadillac Sedans de Ville glided along the boulevards, rolling manifestations of affluence and privilege.

Such were the buying tastes of the typical General Motors family, as originally conceived by Alfred P. Sloan, Jr. The legendary chairman of General Motors Corporation and his cohorts devised a pricing system in 1921 to snatch the young male head of a household, sell him a Chevrolet, and then sell his family ever more expensive GM cars as he grew older and more affluent: Pontiac, followed by Oldsmobile, Buick, and, finally, Cadillac. GM's ingenious marketing strategy reached the greatest number of potential car buyers and minimized competition among GM car divisions. The strategy worked well because GM arranged its car lines so that they offered a competitively priced vehicle for every budget. As soon as a buyer's taste or pocketbook outgrew one car line, Chevrolet, for example, a Pontiac dealer was waiting to show him an array of distinctive (and more expensive) cars. As far as the customer was concerned, ''GM'' denoted nothing more than a vague corporate entity to which several car brands belonged.

Sloan understood how to captivate the psyche of car buyers who wanted more than mere conveyance. Businessman though he was, Sloan was living through the Jazz Age; he perceived a budding national appetite for style and elegance, color and comfort. For Americans, the family automobile was becoming an emblem and a badge, like a silk top hat, a way to broadcast status to friends, neighbors, and relatives.

Sloan's insight was especially timely in light of GM's most formidable competitor, Ford Motor Company. Henry Ford viewed the automobile as a strictly utilitarian instrument. He insisted that cars and luxury mustn't have anything to do with one another. Cars were to be sold cheaply and plainly, Ford thought, so that as many people as possible could own them. By the time executives at Ford Motor Company convinced Ford of his folly, GM was able to exploit the mistake and take a dramatic lead in bringing automobiles into the world of fashion and fantasy. In 1927, while Henry Ford wisecracked that his Model T came in any color "as long as it's black," Sloan hired Harley Earl, who was building custom automobiles for Hollywood movie stars, and presented him with a mandate to expand the notion of automotive beauty. The son of a coachbuilder, Earl had been toiling in the employ of a Cadillac dealer in Los Angeles when GM found him. Sloan was so impressed with Earl's work that he opened an "Art and Color Section" at GM headquarters in Detroit and put Earl in charge. Earl's flights of imagination profoundly affected automotive style. His first glimpse of the P-38 fighter plane, for example, inspired him to design the first automobile fins, which appeared on the 1948 Cadillac.

Sloan's greatest legacy to the automobile business, however, wasn't in the field of styling or market planning. In fact, his most important contribution transcended the automobile business altogether: while guiding GM's growth during his forty-year career, Sloan and his colleagues practically invented a management system for the large, modern corporation and defined the role of the professional manager.

The son of a coffee and tea merchant, Sloan earned an electrical engineering degree at M.I.T. He commenced his business career producing roller bearings for the infant automobile industry. A slim, almost gaunt figure, Sloan had a longish face and pronounced ears, cheeks, and chin, topped with reddish hair. He rarely smiled in published pictures. Although he was an imperious, commanding personality, given now and then to violent temper tantrums, he wasn't dictatorial and became known for his unusual commitment to building consensus among his associates.

Sloan came to GM in a roundabout manner. In 1916 William C. Durant, the celebrated founder of General Motors Corporation, asked Sloan to sell his company, Hyatt Roller Bearing Company, to GM. Sloan agreed to trade his stake in Hyatt, which was based in Newark, New Jersey, for shares in a components company that would soon become a part of GM. Durant had incorporated General Motors Company, the forerunner of General Motors Corporation, in 1908. Starting with his own stake in Buick Motor Company of Flint, Michigan, Durant assembled GM by acquiring a disparate array of motor builders, carriagemakers, and parts suppliers, of which Hyatt was one. In many instances, the major stockholders of the companies GM acquired accepted GM stock instead of cash. The owners often continued, as executives and managers of GM, to run their operations as part of a larger, integrated vehicle company.

In this way, Sloan, in 1918, became GM's vice president of parts and accessories, a GM director, and a significant owner of GM shares. Sloan's outlook and mentality remained those of an owner and entrepreneur, as he had been at Hyatt Roller Bearing. He dealt with a broad range of basic issues, such as sales, quality, productivity, and financial performance. Sloan couldn't afford to narrow his vision to issues relating to components. His entire investment had been converted to GM stock, the value of which depended on the success of GM. As it turned out, the infant enterprise needed all the managerial depth and breadth Sloan could muster. GM's early history was characterized by disorganized operations and haphazard financial planning. The automotive market was chaotic because the youthful auto industry knew little about its customers or what they would buy. Worse still, the tinkerer-engineers who were able to invent and build horseless buggies often didn't possess the management skills to run a large, fast-growing manufacturing enterprise.

A rational, practical businessman, Sloan discovered that GM had little reliable information with which to tackle basic questions, such as how much capital to spend on each division or how to manage the incoming flow of cash. He was alarmed at a decisionmaking process that seemed to consist of divisional managers battling among themselves for scarce resources. "Management by crony," as he called it, rewarded the most influential executives, not the executives who presented the most rational plan. Durant, in Sloan's view, decided important questions far too casually and without consulting his colleagues, which caused delays followed by necessarily impulsive actions.

Because Sloan had more automotive experience than his peers, who mostly were financial men from E. I. Dupont Nemours and Company, which owned 36 percent of GM, GM's executive committee appointed Sloan president and chief executive in 1923. He likely was selected as president as much for his breadth of view — his ability to see GM in perspective against the backdrop of an expanding, vibrant new automotive society — as for his native, almost instinctive, grasp of how to organize and motivate people and operations. Under Sloan's leadership during the next quarter century, GM turned into an industrial monolith surpassing anything the world had seen.

Sloan and Company based GM's organizational structure on a limited form of decentralized operations under central control, analogous to the Federalist compromise between states' rights and central government power that preceded the U.S. Constitution. Some issues at GM were settled by operating divisions and some dealt with by central management. Dupont had been struggling to reduce centralized power and give more responsibility to its divisions. GM's problem was the opposite: to form a central, coordinated policy for a number of conflicting, independent divisions.

In the early 1920s, GM created the product policy that aimed five different automotive divisions at five different groups of buyers. Previously, several of the divisions competed against each other, selling similarly priced cars to the same customer groups. It also made sense, in Sloan's mind, for GM central research and development laboratories to tackle engineering problems and to develop product innovations, such as new paints, that could be used by all the divisions. Divisional operations managers, by contrast, were given a fairly free hand to design, build, and distribute GM cars and trucks in their own way.

From a totally decentralized company with very little financial information or control, GM under Sloan's guidance evolved through the 1920s and 1930s into a balanced system of decentralized operating units coordinated by a central management. Using financial methods developed by Donaldson Brown, recruited from Dupont where he had served as treasurer, GM executives finally were able to measure the performance of the operating units. Examining GM's operating units with these so-called yardsticks of measurement was no hollow exercise, for GM's executives effectively represented the Duponts, Sloan, and the others whose fortunes were invested in GM stock. Brown later recruited Albert Bradley, a statistician teaching at the University of Michigan, to develop economic models correlating automotive demand with the rise and fall of gross national product and personal income. For the first time, GM could predict the size of the overall U.S. car market with some degree of accuracy.

Sloan also used his yardsticks to measure GM's managers. A vice president or general manager always knew how well he was doing by looking at the financial performance of his operations. Sloan strove to eliminate subjective factors, such as his personal like or dislike of an executive. Promotions were rewards for improved productivity or market penetration. The only limitation on Sloan's method of evaluating people and performance was the information on which the judgments were based. Thus, he harped constantly on the need for collecting more accurate, relevant data and developing it quicker. (One can only imagine how Sloan might have rejoiced had he lived to see the power of modern computers!)

A balanced, decentralized meritocracy helped GM score smashing gains over Ford, its chief rival, a company dominated by the whims of its founder and lacking a coordinated, rational operating system. GM's manufacturing empire spread over the continent and then the globe. GM acquired European car- and truckmakers Vauxhall Motors Ltd. of Great Britain in 1925 and Adam Opel AG of Germany in 1929. GM expanded its huge parts and components business that supplied itself and competing carmakers; it moved into related lines, such as railroad locomotives, household appliances, earthmoving equipment, and aircraft engines. Further stimulated by its role in making armaments in World War II, GM — along with U.S. Steel, General Electric, and other industrial giants — grew to great size and influence as employers and fundamental economic components of U.S. society. The success of these enterprises raised logical questions about the dimensions and scope of their role in U.S. society.

Peter Drucker, a young Bennington College professor, wrote a book in the early 1940s entitled *The Future of Industrial Man*. Examining the rise of huge business enterprises in the United States, Drucker concluded that Americans increasingly would rely on big companies as much more than the source of their paychecks. Americans increasingly expected these huge companies, their employers, to define their purpose as workers in society, their rank, and the rules and customs by which they lived.

Naturally, Drucker was curious to know precisely how large business enterprises worked. By narrowing his focus to a single corporation, he hoped to examine customs and institutions and then report on their vitality and contribution to society at large. One after another, the large corporations declined Drucker's request to study them. GM, however, was as interested as Drucker in reflecting upon the nature of its practices and policies. GM's interest in a study was different from Drucker's. As World War II drew to a close, a new generation of GM managers was about to take over. (Sloan had postponed his retirement as GM chief executive because of the war.)

Sloan's colleagues were eager to document GM's management system rather than leave to chance its comprehension by succeeding generations. GM had grown quickly into a powerful economic force, but no one at the company really was able to explain how or why. In 1943 GM vice chairman Donaldson Brown invited Drucker to wander about GM for two years, interviewing whom he pleased, after which he was free to publish his findings. Brown agreed to match Drucker's academic salary and promised not to interfere with his writing.

Brown hoped Drucker would codify the GM formula for success, a project that, in Sloan's opinion, was pointless. To Sloan, what GM had accomplished was perfectly self-evident and didn't require professorial analysis. In their first meeting, the GM chief executive told Drucker he had opposed letting him into GM but had been "overruled" by his associates. However, precisely because Sloan had been against the idea of letting Drucker in, he also felt it was his duty to make sure the young professor received cooperation. Under Sloan's code of corporate governance, sabotaging a project that a consensus of GM executives supported would have been unthinkable. Sloan was a model of cooperation, encouraging Drucker to attend meetings of top executives to see how the company approached problems and made decisions. Sloan and Drucker often met afterward to discuss the meetings.

Viewed forty years later, Sloan's treatment of Drucker was as revealing an insight into GM's top management style as anything Drucker found in his two years inside the company. It showed how deeply Sloan valued opinions from his inner circle, and how those opinions signified much more than political expediency or lip service. Obviously, Sloan didn't want yes-men; he wanted informed back talk, and he wanted the "right" decision, even if he didn't agree with it. Once a decision had been made, Sloan was prepared to subordinate his status as chief executive to the weight of informed consensus.

Sloan altered any preconceived notions Drucker may have harbored about the activities of one of the world's most powerful chief executives. Drucker was astonished by the detailed, seemingly interminable discussions Sloan held about filling personnel vacancies. For Sloan, nothing was more important than selecting the right managers, and doing it correctly required time. "The decision about people is the only truly crucial one," Sloan told Drucker. "You think, and everybody thinks, that a company can have 'better' people; that's horse's apples [his favorite expression]. All it can do is place people right — and then it'll have performance."

Evidence of Sloan's diligence was manifest at all levels of GM management. Drucker discovered an intricate, collegial hierarchy of executives supervising divisions, which themselves were run by hierarchies of executives and managers. Numerous policy and administrative committees passed information up and down the network, all the while encouraging debate and criticism. Twice a year, Sloan conducted so-called Sloan meetings in Detroit for the top few hundred senior executives and managers, who relayed wisdom to lower-ranking managers at divisional meetings.

Unfortunately, GM's effective, harmonious management structure contrasted sharply with its miserable relations with factory workers. In 1937 a series of violent sit-down strikes racked GM and helped the United Auto Workers become the bargaining agent for GM's hourly workers. The strikes were a symptom of years of conflict, caused by GM's failure to provide adequate pay, benefits, and humane working conditions to hourly workers. Instead of improving conditions in the face of complaints, GM managers hired spies and detectives to head off an uprising. The strategy backfired. GM's heavy-handed dampening of free expression only helped win converts to the union cause. After hourly workers thoroughly defeated management in 1937 and demonstrated that they could shut down the company, GM executives were doubly frightened, embittered, and spoiling for revenge. The tone for the next forty years was set.

In a way, GM's labor relations on the factory floor echoed the struggles of a class society. GM workers, by and large, were southern blacks, first- and second-generation European immigrants, and recent arrivals from the mid-South hill country. GM managers, on the other hand, belonged to predominantly "older" families from small midwestern towns. Class division within the company, in Drucker's view, was one of GM's biggest failings and augured badly for the future.

Four decades before Japanese-style teamwork became the holy grail for U.S. industry, Drucker urged GM to find a way to integrate its factory workers into the life of the large corporation. He suggested better educational opportunities, a profit-sharing plan, imaginative mass-production techniques — ideas that GM had considered and eventually would adopt in one form or another. At the time, Drucker believed that GM was doomed to fail as an important institution in society unless it provided avenues for career advancement and a creative, fulfilling working atmosphere. Years later, a far more compelling reason for better labor relations would emerge: the need to compete more effectively against low-cost, high-quality imports.

After World War II, booming demand for cars and trucks simply was too ripe a business opportunity for labor and management to waste time arguing over compensation and working conditions. After a strike in 1948, UAW leaders and GM management forged a practical but cynical dance routine, the choreography of which was repeated each time the two sides negotiated. UAW president Walter Reuther and his heirs always demanded far more than they expected to win; GM always offered a stingier package than it ultimately granted. In the end, union workers got their raise, while a corresponding increase was parceled out to managers. Hence, the cost of labor peace really was borne by U.S. customers. GM built its added labor and management costs into the price of its vehicles. It could afford to do this, of course, since it dominated the U.S. automotive market and set the pricing structure. GM's competition was minimal, consisting of Ford and a number of smaller companies that divided the half of the market GM didn't own.

Labor relations became largely an exercise in posturing and politics. True and meaningful membership in factory society, as defined by Drucker, remained theoretical. Anything management granted, it granted in the most grudging, cynical manner possible. Charles E. Wilson, GM president from 1941 to 1953, told Drucker he favored the idea of paying supplemental unemployment benefits (SUB) to laid-off auto workers but wouldn't grant SUB until the UAW fought hard to win it. The UAW leadership would never accept SUB, he argued, if GM proposed it publicly. The same belief applied to pensions. Wilson long favored a formula using GM profits to establish an employee pension fund, but he waited until the UAW proposed it in 1950 before endorsing the idea.

Dishonesty and distrust characterized the bargaining ritual, but Wilson defended it. The proof of GM's approach to labor relations, as far as Wilson was concerned, was in high wages, high productivity, and the relatively few days lost to strikes and layoffs.

"A union is a political organization and needs adversary relations and victorious battles. And a company is an economic organization and needs productivity and discipline. At GM we get both — and to get both we need the union relations we have," Wilson told Drucker.

Still, Drucker argued that GM workers considered their jobs much more than the means to a paycheck. If Drucker was right, it meant GM was badly neglecting its work force. Wilson was skeptical, but to test Drucker's assertions, he held an essay contest entitled "My Job and Why I Like It," for which the company offered small prizes. About two-thirds of GM's 200,000 hourly workers entered, and their essays proved Drucker correct. The entries showed that workers valued job satisfaction highly. Workers wished to respect the company and their supervisors. (The UAW, alarmed by the contest's popularity, made its abolition a condition for a new contract in 1948.)

Wilson left GM in 1953 to become Eisenhower's Secretary of Defense and was replaced by one of the great GM salesmen of all time, Harlow W. "Red" Curtice. Curtice, an accountant from Eaton Rapids, Michigan, who had run GM's Buick division, loved big, flashy cars and ever-growing ten-day sales reports. He was fascinated less by technology than by the decorative glitz and chrome doodads used to catch a buyer's attention and make car models distinctive. At Buick he invented the "ventaport," decorative holes on a Buick's hood that became the division's hallmark.

While some corners of the automotive world were calling for development of small, economical cars in the 1950s, Curtice ordered ever-more-powerful engines to drive the expanding array of profit-boosting options, such as air conditioning, which was first offered on the 1953 Cadillac. In their more candid moments, GM executives confided that it cost them almost as much to produce small cars as large cars, although the profit potential in large cars was far greater. Besides, their countrymen desired big, flashy symbols of affluence. To them, the Volkswagen Beetle, which first made its appearance in the United States in the 1950s, was a car for the lunatic fringe, not for real Americans.

GM's expansive sales in that era certainly suggested that America accepted GM's logic. The U.S. government, however, was a different problem. During the Roosevelt and Truman years, GM had tempered its appetite for ever-higher revenues with a healthy respect for antitrust laws. If GM grew to control more than half the market, its executives feared that the company might fall victim to a regulatory attack. Red Curtice, on the other hand, regarded Ike's election and the appointment of a Republican Justice Department as a green light to chase higher revenue with bare-fanged rapaciousness. GM's share of the new-car market, which had hovered around 45 percent under Charlie Wilson, grew to more than 50 percent in 1954. GM's clout spread to other sectors of the economy. Its advertising budget, already the biggest in the country, topped $100 million. General Motors Acceptance Corporation grabbed ever-larger chunks of the automotive lending business, despite government opposition.

Curtice's style of governing GM differed greatly from that of Alfred Sloan, who finally stepped down from active management. Curtice didn't build consensus or encourage debate before making decisions. For him, opportunity loomed too ripe and compelling. He preferred to deliberate quickly and decide major issues on his own, bragging to *Time* magazine that the best committee is a "committee of one." GM's unbridled growth, coupled with Curtice's devil-may-care attitude toward antitrust regulators and his fellow executives, projected an image that seemed to say: "Behold, ours is the most important company in this country's most important industry. We shall dictate the pattern of society's fabric. No one knows GM's business better than we do. And by God, if GM doesn't know what it's doing — then we're all in trouble.''

The generation of owner-executives like Sloan, Charles Stewart Mott, and Charles F. Kettering — powerful men who directly owned much of the company and controlled it from their seats on the board — passed into history in the 1950s. Their stakes in GM fragmented as their GM shares passed to heirs or were sold to pay taxes. The U.S. Supreme Court shattered the biggest controlling block of GM shares when it ordered Dupont to divest its 23 percent of GM to satisfy antitrust law. Overnight, the control of GM flowed to the thousands and thousands of shareholders and professional managers of trust accounts, pension funds, and portfolios, which are represented by the directors they elect.

Such, at any rate, is the theory of broadly held stock ownership and shareholder democracy. In reality, big public companies like GM came to be controlled by a small number of top managers backed by handpicked directors. The chief executive often decided major issues by himself, including selection of directors. Authority at GM shifted in the 1960s from Dupont and the small group of GM founders to a single man, GM's chief executive.

Sloan and his retiring colleagues on GM's board of directors appointed the first of these truly all-powerful GM chief executives, Frederic Donner, to succeed Harlow Curtice as chief executive in 1958. Donner, a small-town midwestern accountant who had taken his business degree at the University of Michigan, was known as a cold, brusque man and had inched his way up the ladder through GM's financial ranks. Donner, like Robert McNamara and J. Edward Lundy at Ford Motor Company, Lynn Townsend at Chrysler Corporation, and a whole generation of finance men in the automobile business, viewed the car business largely from the perspective of cash flow, revenue, profits, investment credits, and tax-loss carryforwards. His work was management of these flows — investing in a new midsize sedan here, writing off an obsolete stamping plant there — in the name of maximizing profits and return on equity.

Indeed, the size and sophistication of multibillion-dollar corporations like Ford and GM demanded specialists like Donner, who spent their entire professional lives mastering the numerous branches of finance, pricing theory, tax strategy, and international economics. The single-minded focus on finance limited their appreciation of engineering, styling, marketing, and other automotive disciplines. Talented automotive engineers abounded, but their projects and ideas frequently were canceled or ignored in the name of financial prudence. In some respects, the financial executives were correct, given what was known then about the market. Automotive demand truly seemed limitless, and no companies but GM, Ford, and Chrysler could produce for the U.S. market in any quantity. Auto executives in the mold of Alfred Sloan, who could extemporize about double-entry accounting and air-cooled engines with equal skill, were rare indeed.

In the late 1950s and early 1960s, European carmakers built a beachhead in the U.S. market with small, fuel-efficient cars like the Volkswagen Beetle and Renault Dauphine. Detroit automakers first rejected them as unworthy of the small number of college professors and other spoilsports who bought them.

In fact, the market Sloan had neatly segmented and defined was changing rapidly. A growing and significant number of buyers were looking for smaller and more efficient cars, more economical and stylistically understated cars, safer cars.

Responding to these trends, GM finally introduced the Chevrolet Corvair in 1960. What should have been a triumph was, in fact, a sad chapter for the automaker. The Corvair actually sold quite respectably, considering the volume of bad publicity it earned after early versions of the car proved unstable. Ed Cole, Corvair's chief engineer and a future GM president, wanted to add a $15 stabilizing bar and better tires on the car to improve its handling. The financial brass, who ascended to power when Donner took over, vetoed his suggestions. Numerous Corvair accident victims subsequently sued GM for negligence in putting an unsafe car on the road. GM insisted, indeed continues to insist, that only the "early" Corvair models had problems, which were corrected. In fact, GM won two major Corvair lawsuits, and a U.S. Department of Transportation study maintained that GM's design of the Corvair wasn't faulty.

GM's arguments may have been true, but they proved irrelevant. The first Corvair didn't handle as well as it should have, and GM knew it. Refusing to add the stabilizing bar and better tires suggested that short-term financial gain took precedence over safety. The episode gave GM a public-be-damned image in the eyes of safety advocates, particularly a young Harvard Law graduate named Ralph Nader. When Nader brought GM's penny-pinching attitudes into center spotlight with publication of *Unsafe at Any Speed,* GM reacted as it had when threatened by labor organizers: it hired spies. Using spurious evidence, GM vilified Nader as a troublemaker who didn't even know how to drive a car. GM's harassment of Nader was a glimpse into the company's soul and further evidence that GM shirked its public responsibility to promote safety.

As industry leader, GM had been slow to install safety features on its cars; it first offered seat belts as an option nine years after they were first offered at Ford and Chrysler. GM executives countered repeatedly that when its customers "demanded" seat belts, GM would offer them. It was another way of saying that when customers were willing to pay for safety as an option, GM would sell it. (Sloan held the same attitude toward safety glass, withholding it until he believed customers would pay the price.) But society had changed since Sloan's day. By capturing more than half of the booming automotive market and growing into a multibillion-dollar behemoth, GM outgrew its role as simply the largest of several large car companies. Drucker's prophesies were coming true. The company had failed to appreciate its impact on, and its duties to, society. Instead of perceiving Nader's activism as a symbolic warning to heed public sensibilities, GM was confident he was an isolated nuisance. GM clung to the outdated notion that it was powerful enough to create its own social and economic landscape.

Donner and James Roche, GM's grandfatherly president, couldn't blow off Senator Abraham Ribicoff's auto-safety investigation as easily as GM executives had done the majority of antitrust investigators in the 1950s. Ribicoff's feisty sidekick, Senator Robert Kennedy, peppered the executives with prosecutorial zingers, so badly flustering Donner that the punctilious accountant could barely remember during his testimony how much profit GM had made in the previous year. GM was anything but a criminal gang — it had every reason for pride in its automotive accomplishments, in its role as a defense contractor during World War II — yet the Nader episode and GM's attitude toward safety made it look venal and shabby.

Roche finally apologized publicly to Nader, although the apology hardly heralded a new age of enlightened thinking. GM top management remained convinced that no one ought to be telling it how to run its business. Inherent in GM's pride was a near-aboriginal suspicion of ideas and concepts originating outside the palace walls. The so-called Not Invented Here syndrome was devastating in GM factories, where foremen and plant managers decided how to organize work and, for the most part, cared little for the opinions of hourly employees.

GM's proud nature also expressed itself in its devotion to the concept of white-collar loyalty. Fresh young GM engineers and finance men quickly learned the concept of the pecking order and the importance of making the boss look good by letting him make as many decisions as possible. An engineer who started his career in Buick's assembly plant in Flint, Michigan, explained it this way:

Let's say you're designing a particular station on the assembly line and a vendor has a new machine he wants to sell you. The machine has all the technology and is priced right. You think: OK, let's buy it. But you wouldn't dare invite the vendor in to talk with you — not even for a first meeting — without including your boss. And your boss wouldn't dare express an opinion about the machine unless his boss and his boss's boss "buy in." Believe me, we're not talking about consensus. We're talking about spreading a decision over the greatest number of people so no one really has any responsibility for it. If the machine screws up, no one has made a mistake because it's impossible to figure out who really made the decision.

Making the boss look good delayed decisions and drove them higher on the organizational ladder. Young managers learned to avoid responsibility because decisionmaking held within it the possibility of career-ending mistakes. "GM is rich and successful and will be that way for a long, long time," GM veterans counseled their protégés. "Let our competitors take chances and make mistakes. We're in front and must avoid being knocked off track."

GM reinforced these notions, as well as the hierarchy of the organizational ladder, with Prussian-style regimentation. Employees learned never to talk back and never to cross the boss. Subordinates proved their loyalty to this code by silently enduring an occasional tongue-lashing or reprimand.

A successful East Coast GM dealer tells of arriving early one morning a few years ago for a breakfast meeting with an assistant Chevrolet zone sales manager. The bleary-eyed GM man yawned through the entire meal. When the dealer inquired about his breakfast partner's fatigue, the GM man explained that he was required to rise at 5:30 each morning and drive forty miles to a nearby town to pick up a copy of a newspaper for his superior, the Chevrolet zone manager.

"Doesn't it bother you to have to perform such menial chores?" the dealer asked. "Sure it's a pain," the GM man confided, "but someday I'll be zone manager, and I'll be in charge of someone who will fetch the newspaper for me!"

GM white-collar workers weren't humiliated by the system. On the contrary, they were proud of their company, the most successful in history, and knew that obeying its rules held rewards in the form of pay, perquisites, and promotion. The assistant Chevrolet manager had learned the GM system well. Had he ever questioned whether driving forty miles each day was an efficient use of his time or talents, alarm bells would have sounded; his supervisor would have regarded the question as a warning sign of breakaway, disloyal, non–team thinking. GM tried to bar such thinkers from the system and wasn't shy about expelling them if they somehow sneaked in.

John Zachary DeLorean, of gullwing-roadster and felony-narcotics-indictment fame, probably rose higher and faster in the GM hierarchy than any breakaway, non–team thinker before or since. DeLorean, by most accounts, was a gifted engineer who possessed charisma and flair in abundance. However, he outraged straitlaced team thinkers with a combative arrogance and defiance of corporate customs. (DeLorean's tank tops, dyed hair, Hollywood starlets, and gold chains didn't win him any points, either.) DeLorean's story, *On a Clear Day You Can See General Motors*, by former *Business Week* correspondent Patrick Wright, struck a responsive chord among the scattered critics within GM's white-collar ranks. DeLorean had been erratic — capable of abandoning company cars on public thoroughfares and picking ridiculous, unprovoked fights with colleagues — but DeLorean inveighed against systemic evils the critics recognized, evils that, starting in the 1960s and 1970s, fostered mediocrity from GM's work force in the name of teamwork.

Donner, followed by every GM chief executive after him, slavishly treated GM as a business institution with a permanent, divinely granted franchise to supply at least half the nation's vehicles. It was almost as if GM had turned into the U.S. Department of Personal Transportation. From management's perspective, the expense of improving and differentiating car models could be justified only if it improved volume and profits.

Foreign competition wasn't an issue because Detroit's small cars — the Corvairs, Chevy IIs, and Ford Falcons — had succeeded in blunting, at least temporarily, the imports' growth in market share. Under GM's financial approach to business, bigger profits and improved returns on shareholder investment resulted from squeezing costs out of the system and improving productivity — not just from boosting revenue. Engineers and product designers attempted to ''sell'' expensive improvements and new car models to the all-powerful finance men. But unless the designers could assure a quick payoff on the bottom line, they weren't likely to succeed. Why offer seat belts or four-wheel drive if there wasn't a profit to be made?

Customers might buy a new design feature, the finance men pointed out, but that didn't bring in additional profit if the new sales ''cannibalized'' sales of existing GM cars. It was much easier for GM to add a $20 piece of chrome or a $5 sports stripe and call the car a ''new model'' than to take a chance with costly new technologies, such as antilock brakes or multivalve engines. Donner also cut costs by tinkering with Sloan's tenets of decentralization. He merged the coachbuilding and assembly plants of all the car divisions except Cadillac into one assembly division. And he ordered that standard parts be used on as many car models as possible, which made manufacturing more flexible and saved development costs. Cost-cutting on the manufacturing side of the business had the effect of boosting profits, but it robbed power from the designers and engineers and permitted them less creativity. The car divisions were encouraged to utilize basic designs and common parts from other divisions in developing their own cars. Pontiac executives, for example, wished at one time to use their LeMans chassis to produce a lower-priced car called the Ventura; however, corporate executives compelled them to take the Chevy Nova chassis from the Chevrolet division to better utilize the plant where the Novas were built.

In a market where buyers for GM cars always were plentiful, producing the cars on time assumed paramount importance. GM plant managers earned their stripes by delivering the number of cars scheduled for assembly each day. That meant they had to keep assembly lines moving at all costs, even when the quality wasn't topnotch. Better to repair a car at the end of the line, the finance men lectured, than to stop a machine and lose production that never could be made up. Plant managers and foremen didn't want to hear about delays caused by substandard quality. And, in fairness to the plant managers, the only irate calls they received were from zone managers demanding more cars, not zone managers complaining about quality. Except for Volkswagen and the expensive exotic cars, the U.S. car-buying public in the early 1970s didn't yet know much about imports. The cars that arrived from Japan in the early 1970s weren't impressive. The Honda 600 and Subaru 360 looked comical by U.S. styling standards and were woefully underpowered for U.S. highways. Toyota and Nissan (then known as Datsun) offered decent designs and more power but failed to comprehend fundamental marketing truths, such as the fact that few Americans would buy a turquoise car, no matter the price or quality. In all, the imports hovered at a measly fifteen percent of the U.S. market.

Perhaps with some reason, GM sales and financial executives openly sneered at the cheap little ''shitboxes'' from Japan and the Volkswagens from West Germany. Apart from the Vega, an ill-conceived and poorly manufactured GM economy car that was rejected utterly by the buying public, GM had made few serious efforts to create a small-car contender to the imports. If the imports wanted that end of the market, reasoned GM strategists, let 'em have it; we'll make our money where we always have, from big luxury cars, family cars, station wagons. Although Donner retired as chief executive in 1967, he remained a powerful director until 1974, using his influence to make sure finance men like himself would run GM in the future. As Richard Gerstenberg, a self-described "book-keeper," was taking over as vice chairman in 1970, Donner engineered the promotion of Thomas A. Murphy, then treasurer, to vice president of cars and trucks. Those who read the tea leaves recognized that Murphy was in line to succeed Gerstenberg eventually, which he did in 1974.

GM continued to resist what it regarded as government intrusion in the areas of safety and the environment. By the 1970s, however, the nation's growing and vocal concerns for clean air and an end to highway carnage emboldened Congress to pass into law stiff regulations requiring all cars to be fitted with antipollution devices on engines and safety features such as fortified bumpers, shoulder harnesses, and anticollision beams for doors.

An environmentally clean engine delivered less power, forcing auto-makers to switch to lighter materials in order to maintain adequate power and acceleration. Protruding bumpers looked clunky, requiring expensive and sometimes awkward-looking body designs. Safer, cleaner cars would cost GM, Ford, Chrysler, and AMC untold hundreds of millions of dollars, only some of which they could recover through higher car prices.

Government-mandated regulations were pinpricks to the auto industry compared with events that began to unfold on the first Saturday of October 1973 at the Suez Canal. The Yom Kippur War brought about sweeping, grotesque changes to the economic landscape, forever altering the ground rules for carmakers. The Arab oil embargo against the West sent the price of gasoline soaring. Overnight, U.S. car buyers awakened to the importance of fuel economy. (Japanese and European drivers always had paid much more than American drivers for gasoline; they were accustomed to energy conservation, and their cars reflected it.) The lighter, smaller, less expensive, and fuel-efficient imports, the "shit-boxes," suddenly were selling like Popsicles at the beach. Federal regulators, seeing that saving fuel was desirable and possible, passed laws requiring car companies to improve fuel economy.

The second oil shock following the Iranian revolution of 1978 ushered in hyperinflation and a major U.S. economic recession. Since 1973 the

U.S. automakers had been scrambling to adjust to the new rules of the marketplace. Who from the Big Three ever would have dreamed that car ads would brag about a car model's "range," that is, how far it could travel on a full tank of gas? After Iran, sales of domestic cars again plunged while the imports doubled their share of the U.S. market. Chrysler flirted with bankruptcy. Ford's financial predicament was almost as scary as Chrysler's, though far less publicized. Both companies cut deeply into overloaded management ranks and operating budgets in a desperate race to trim costs and rationalize operations before their cash and credit gave out.

In the midst of recession, GM's vaunted financial strength served it well. The historic parsimony of Frederic Donner and his heirs created a fat cushion. GM had lots of cash and very little debt. The company's U.S. car and truck sales dropped 26 percent in 1980, contributing to a loss of more than three quarters of a billion dollars. Still, GM managed to pay more than $861 million in dividends to shareholders the same year. If GM executives were worried, they weren't showing it. The dividend was small change compared to the $40 billion GM was preparing to spend through the 1980s to build new factories and switch its entire car lineup to more fuel-efficient front-wheel drive from rear-wheel drive.

Large though it was, GM's capital budget wasn't large enough — and could never be large enough by itself — to bring to market the high-quality, well-performing vehicles the company needed to fight import competition. By the late 1970s, the imports had made tremendous improvements in quality while domestic automotive engineers had been concentrating on fuel efficiency and clean-air and safety standards.

GM didn't sneer at imports any longer. Alex Mair, a GM vice president in charge of technical staffs who had come up through the ranks at Chevrolet, Pontiac, and the GM Truck and Bus Group, revived a program in the late 1970s to tear apart every competitive car in the world for analysis. He was astonished to discover that Honda, which only a few years earlier had blundered into the U.S market with a tinny jokemobile, had gone back to the drawing board and returned with the Accord, a nifty little car whose manufacturing precision surpassed that of GM. Buyers liked the imports' efficiency and price advantage, their quality, comfort, and improved reliability. Especially alarming was consumer research proving import buyers to be highly educated and quite affluent, not the bohemians and subversives Detroit had imagined. Mair invited GM brass, including future GM president F. James McDonald, to GM's sprawling technical center to inspect the chilling evidence. McDonald, according to people who attended the inspection of the dissected competitors, dismissed Honda's accomplishments as inconsequential. He wasn't alone. Many GM executives believed the Japanese had "brainwashed" the U.S. public into buying their vehicles; they cited instances of poor Japanese quality, such as a rust problem on Hondas, or safety statistics suggesting that imports weren't as safe as GM cars (attributable mostly to the Japanese cars' smaller size), as proof that Japanese cars weren't as good as Chevrolets.

A minority of GM engineers and product men, tinkerers and designers such as Mair, realized that GM was steaming straight for an iceberg. They could see that Honda, Toyota, Nissan, and other import competitors had accomplished far greater manufacturing discipline and precision in their plants. Their engineering designs weren't necessarily better, but all the parts were built much more accurately.

The hubris of GM's top executives was impenetrable and massively defended. They would have no truck with poor mouths who weren't grateful for membership on the world's greatest automotive team. GM financial managers paid designers and engineers to improve returns on investment, not to fumble about tearing apart Japanese cars. Besides, executives believed GM's coming generation of front-wheel-drive cars would defeat the imports. Unfortunately, the first members of this generation, the 1979 X-body cars (Chevrolet Citation, Buick Skylark, et al.) and the 1982 J-body cars (Chevrolet Cavalier, Pontiac Sunbird, Buick Skyhawk, et al.), greatly disappointed the automotive world, especially the so-called car-buff magazines such as *Car and Driver, Road & Track, Motor Trend,* and *Auto World.* GM's engineering and design skills simply didn't match those of the best Japanese competition.

(Impressing automotive reviewers is critically important to the success of new car models, because hundreds of thousands of enthusiasts pay heed to their reports. The effect of their reviews ripples through the marketplace; enthusiast-magazine readers often serve as "experts," upon whom nonenthusiasts rely when choosing a new car.)

In stinging articles, car reviewers in the 1970s commenced warning domestic car companies that their cars weren't up to worldwide standards. The imports had skipped the decorative gimmicks and frou-frou that had been Detroit's hallmark and in their place delivered imaginative features like interior trunk and gas-cap releases, little touches that made life easier. The body designs of the imports were balanced, harmonious; the paint was rich and brilliant; and all the panels and parts fit together with exquisite precision. Reviewers particularly savaged GM, as industry leader, for its delinquency in failing to keep up with Japanese and European competitors. This wasn't historical inevitability, they said, it was a giant managerial and engineering screwup.

Perhaps no one targeted blame on GM's leadership with more wit or bite than Brock Yates, a columnist at *Car and Driver* and one of the nation's most authoritative and best-known automotive journalists. Yates, in a trenchant essay, "The Detroit Mind," portrayed the stereotypical GM executive: a small-town midwestern WASP with narrow tastes and only a dim grasp of current trends and styles on either U.S. coast. Yates excoriated these executives for cowering "in magnificent isolation" in their Bloomfield Hills, Michigan, mansions while the public's automotive desires changed. Rather than recognize the changes and build automobiles that reflected them, GM and, even to a greater extent, its domestic competitors insisted on clinging to outmoded tufted-brocade upholstery, garish chrome trim, unresponsive power trains, and ungainly, awkward-looking body designs.

In early 1981 Yates and a group of automotive journalists gathered at a press briefing in Tempe, Arizona, near GM's proving grounds, for the introduction of GM's highly touted import fighter, the J car, a project that GM president F. James McDonald called a $5 billion "roll of the dice." An undistinguished, disappointing imitation of the Japanese subcompacts was paraded before Yates and his colleagues, although GM's brass enthused unabashedly over the car's fine qualities and features. To save money, GM's cost-conscious engineers had borrowed the basic transmission design from the much-heavier X car and put it in the J car. GM engineers modified and shrank a twenty-five-year-old Chevrolet pushrod engine design and came up with a feckless, noisy power plant. Hence, the J car that would sell as the Chevrolet Cavalier was disappointingly sluggish. (GM did put a peppier Opel engine in some other J-car configurations, such as the Pontiac Sunbird.)

GM had set about to destroy the myth of Japanese automotive superiority and come up short. It was as if, in Yates's description, GM had sent a children's crusade to drive the infidels from the holy land. The GM parade of disappointments that started with the Chevy Vega in 1970 continued with the X cars and finally the J cars. These weren't bad cars, they simply were mediocre. More to the point, GM's competitors were constantly raising consumer expectations.

Interestingly, the perpetually optimistic GM executives gave no sign that they regarded the Xs and Js (or the midsize A platforms that followed in 1982) as anything but smashing successes. Their evidence: the millions of units sold. "The real index of quality is what the customers say, and we've sold a million and a half [X cars] — all we could make," GM vice chairman Howard Kehrl told the *New York Times* in 1981. "I don't understand what this flap is all about."

In fact, the raw, seemingly huge sales numbers belied an insidious weakness in GM's market position. The million to two million cars of each platform design were sold under four or five different nameplates from different GM divisions. True, the luxury subcompact J car, the Cadillac Cimarron, sold a few hundred thousand units, compared to half that for BMW. But the whole luxury segment was growing and Cadillac was getting a smaller proportion, creating opportunities for import models such as the Audi 5000S, Acura Legend, and Mercedes Benz 190 series.

Moreover, relentless cost-cutting and parts standardization at GM contributed to an unmistakable lookalike syndrome among cars from the same platform group. It became transparently obvious to buyers by the mid-1980s that a midsize Buick Century, for example, was little more than a higher-priced Chevrolet Celebrity. Lest anyone fail to notice GM's lookalike trend, Ford sponsored a television commercial for its Lincoln Town Car highlighting the confusion in a parking lot as a frustrated attendant tried to differentiate among the Cadillac DeVille, Buick Park Avenue, and Oldsmobile 98.

Ford's TV commercial was harmless from a sales standpoint, but it showed in startling fashion how vulnerable GM had become in its own backyard. In years gone by, a swipe at GM by a smaller competitor would have been unthinkable. No Detroit auto man in his right mind would have risked insulting GM. Besides GM's role as a major supplier of parts and components for competing auto companies, including Ford and Chrysler, GM's clout among suppliers was supreme. Vindictive GM managers could make life very unpleasant for suppliers, consultants, or law firms who had offended them. Apparently, Ford no longer feared GM.

But as the auto industry recovered its financial strength during the 1980s, Chrysler and Ford executives cautioned one another against overconfidence. They were concerned that a rejuvenated and revived GM might arise to dominate the car business again. When that happened, GM surely would settle accounts with those who had bet against Number One. For the moment, GM was an institution in retreat, temporarily blinded and disoriented by forces it didn't completely understand and wasn't prepared to deal with.

The world outside of Detroit, places like New York and Dallas, hadn't much reason before 1984 to worry seriously about GM's health. Despite the intrusion of imports onto GM's turf, the company bounced back from a financial loss in 1980 to three straight years in the black, capped by a record $3.7 billion profit in 1984. Even more encouraging, Roger Smith seemed to be taking bold, innovative action to catch up with the product quality of the imports. GM had launched a joint venture with Toyota Motor Corporation of Japan to build cars at a GM plant in Fremont, California, and its multibillion-dollar Saturn project to revolutionize the way cars are designed, built, and marketed in the United States. And GM seized the lead in the field of factory automation, buying thousands of robots, computers, and other high-technology machines, in an effort to bring manufacturing precision up to the highest standards.

Ross Perot and Mort Meyerson saw the evidence of Roger Smith's drive to transform GM into a twenty-first-century car company on their tour of the technical center. Saturn, the robots, the Toyota venture — Smith's moves were dazzling, impressive. He was just the rare sort of farsighted executive GM needed.

It wasn't easy for GM to overcome all those years of success, Peter Drucker liked to quip. But EDS executives believed that GM and its chairman were well on their way to recapturing lost glory.

PART IV

The Brass Ring

ELEVEN

———⟹ ⟸———

Decision Time

T<small>OM</small> Luce felt an ever-so-slight wave of misgiving creep over him. On June 2, 1984, Luce and Ross Perot, his longtime client, were flying together on the EDS Learjet to Austin in preparation for a special session of the Texas legislature, called to consider the sweeping education reform proposed by Perot's committee. Time had run out on the legislature's regular session and controversies still loomed: merit pay for teachers, competency testing, equalization of funding for poor and rich school districts, no football or extracurricular activities for students with poor grades, and perhaps the toughest task of all, passage of a $4.3 billion tax bill to pay for the reforms.

Perot briefed Luce about the GM deal, the money, the new GM Class E stock, and the guarantees. Because he had been working on educational reform for Perot full-time, Luce didn't know much about the negotiations, even though his firm was preparing the legal documents.

From the way Perot described the negotiations, Luce understood that Perot was favorably disposed to a deal with GM. As Perot's lawyer, Luce had stood up for his client during the retreat from Dupont Walston, the rescue of EDS executives from Iran, and countless other adventures and business deals.

But as chairman of what would become a GM subsidiary, Perot wasn't going to have the same freedom. Luce worried that Perot didn't realize how much independence he was giving up by selling EDS.

"Tom, I'm impressed with Roger," Perot said. "He's determined to make GM over into a supermodern automotive company. Highly automated. Lots of computer power. With EDS as an ally, he'll accomplish his goal a whole lot quicker than without us. And with GM, we'll be able to make EDS the biggest computer-integration and -services company in the world.

"I can't think of a better way to spend the rest of my business career than to help make GM the number-one car company in the world," Perot said.

Far be it from Perot to try something modest, Luce thought wryly.

"What guarantees do you have that GM's going to do everything Roger says it will do?" Luce asked. Luce, forty-three, had seen more than his share of business agreements that started harmoniously on the day they were signed and ended with lawsuits and rancor.

"Gayden's been working on it. Roger has agreed to just about everything we could think of that's good for us. We'll be running EDS, not GM. I have his personal word on everything, written down in black and white. I'll show it to you," Perot said.

Writing down his questions for Roger Smith and sending them to Detroit on the fax machine had relieved Perot enormously. Smith's answers showed that he had paid attention to Perot and truly grasped the need to give EDS a free hand and continue to let Perot and Meyerson run the company.

"The way it's set up, I'll be working with Roger directly. No one at GM has any direct authority over anyone at EDS. Mort will be a GM vice president, but he'll report to me," Perot said. "GM promises to do all its data processing through EDS and we can charge GM commercial rates. The new GM Class E stock will pay a dividend based on those profits, and I'm free to compensate EDS people as I want to. If there's ever any kind of problem, I'm going to know about it immediately since I'll be a GM director.

"If we've missed anything," Perot said, "I don't know what it is."

When he heard Perot was going to join the GM board of directors, Luce was heartened. A board seat proved Roger Smith's high regard for Ross Perot. And a board seat was, at the very least, an important listening post and a place to be heard. If tensions do arise, they won't get out of hand without Perot knowing about it, Luce thought.

*   *   *

True to Bill Gayden's prediction to the GM negotiators, Ross Perot signed a memorandum of understanding to merge EDS with GM on June 27, 1984, Perot's fifty-fourth birthday.

First, Perot had called a meeting of EDS's twenty-eight officers and directors. "This is the deal," he explained to them, outlining the details of the financial package, GM's guarantees, and EDS's role in the future of the car company. "I will do what you guys want to do."

While Perot's statement may have been technically true, no one in the room dreamed of opposing what clearly was Perot's wish, to sell his company to GM.

Then Perot left the meeting and Meyerson took over. Most of EDS's directors were senior vice presidents, such as Ken Riedlinger, Les Alberthal, Tom Walter, Jeff Heller, and Gary Fernandes. A few outsiders sat on the board as well: former astronaut and Eastern Airlines chief Frank Borman, Lazard Freres partner Felix Rohatyn, former Texas governor William P. Clements, Jr., and Dr. Harold Urschel, Jr., a neighbor and close friend of Perot's.

All twenty-eight men heard Perot's enthusiastic description of an offer he regarded as a tremendous opportunity for the company he had founded and built. The deal also was a gilt-edged, guaranteed payday for every one of the officers. Along the way they had been hearing bits and snatches of the negotiations and what changes were coming to EDS. Perot's protests to Smith that his top people didn't want to merge with GM had been more or less a negotiating tactic to influence Smith to sweeten the pot.

Meyerson asked the men at the table if they wanted to go with GM. He heard no nays.

Under the terms of the financial arrangement with GM, holders of EDS shares were entitled to exchange each of their shares for $44 cash or $35.20 cash and one-fifth of a share of new GM Class E shares. In addition, GM promised to issue notes attached to the new Class E shares guaranteeing that each share was to be worth at least $125 at the end of seven years or GM would pay the difference. In other words, for every one hundred EDS shares that were worth $28 a share, or $2,800, when John Gutfreund came calling in early April, GM was agreeing to pay $3,520 plus stock guaranteed to be worth $2,500 in seven years. Moreover, GM promised to trade new GM Class E stock with $125 contingent note guarantees, share for share, for all the unvested EDS shares held in stock incentive plans by key EDS employees. If the Internal Revenue Service taxed the transaction at the higher ordinary-income rate, GM also agreed to pay Perot and EDS employees additional amounts to approximate what they would have received under lower capital-gains rates.

For his 45 percent stake in EDS, Perot was to be paid more than $930 million cash and 5.5 million GM Class E shares with a guaranteed worth of nearly $700 million in seven years.

It wasn't any wonder that EDS's top officers approved the merger without hesitation. GM's largesse was an unbelievable windfall for them. Mort Meyerson, for example, owned 628,718 EDS shares at the time of the proposal, a one percent stake in EDS worth, at a minimum, $22.1 million cash plus 125,743 GM Class E shares, which were backed by GM notes with a guaranteed minimum value in seven years of $15.7 million. Meyerson also was entitled to receive another 180,000 unvested EDS shares, worth a minimum of $22.5 million in seven years. It was the chance of a lifetime for EDS's people to liquefy their holdings.

All told, GM was paying $2.55 billion in cash and stock to Perot and the public holders of stock to buy EDS. As Salomon Brothers and GM financial experts figured it, the price was a bargain. GM was keeping 75 percent of the Class E shares for itself. They'd be worth a fortune once the stock started trading. U.S. tax law allowed GM to perform a few neat, perfectly legal maneuvers in revaluing EDS's assets. In addition to the expected efficiencies of computer integration, the $2.55 billion transaction might pay for itself in as little as six months. Six months! Payback in a year was awesome, Bob Scully of Salomon Brothers had told GM treasurer Courtney Jones. But six months? Unbelievable.

The key to GM's tax strategy was the millions upon millions of lines of EDS computer code. Over the years, EDS had spent anywhere from $10 to $250 a line to develop code that made up the computer programs that ran its massive systems. For tax purposes, the code was carried on EDS's books at no value. Deloitte Haskins and Sells, GM's auditor, reported to Courtney Jones that GM was entitled to revalue EDS's software at $2 billion following the merger. The code was fully depreciable under IRS rules. That meant $1 billion in tax benefits to GM. Courtney Jones was impressed with the auditor's report; from a financial point of view, it made the EDS acquisition a near no-brainer. Sure, Perot and his people were going to get rich on GM money. But their wealth wasn't going to cost GM much at all.

Ross Perot and Roger Smith held press conferences on Thursday, June 28, 1984, each expressing — in the most glowing terms — their admiration for EDS, GM, and for one another.

To Smith, bringing Ross Perot and EDS into his company was the crowning achievement of his term as chief executive. This was his move to unfreeze GM's organizational inertia. If nothing else about the merger succeeded, he told his investment bankers and lawyers, at least the EDS culture would be inside GM.

Perot saw the merger as the opportunity to go straight from Little League to the majors, to make his company into a worldwide force. Several issues remained to be negotiated, but both men expected a definitive merger agreement to be worked out before summer's end.

The press release distributed the following day was worded carefully to highlight the principles and goals each partner sought in the combination of the two companies — while reassuring EDS that this wasn't a simple case of paying money and collecting the goods.

"We know EDS is the one company capable of successfully addressing GM's systems development needs while enhancing its current business directions and not disturbing established customer relationships," Roger Smith's prepared statement said. He was saying to Perot, We recognize EDS as unique and won't do anything to jeopardize what it has achieved.

Security analysts and other professional watchers of the two companies already were raising logical questions about how a nimble, flexible outfit like EDS might be slowed down or encumbered as a member of the GM family.

Roger Smith brushed aside those fears. EDS was free — no, EDS was encouraged! — to operate autonomously with Ross Perot at the helm. GM wasn't going to interfere or try to impress its corporate culture on EDS.

"Anyone showing up at EDS with a GM procedures manual in his hands will be shot on sight," Smith proclaimed with an air of biblical certitude. He was rewarded with an appreciative chuckle from reporters.

On Saturday morning, June 30, forty-eight hours after Smith and Perot signed the memorandum of understanding, Mort Meyerson met with EDS's top officers to reorganize the company.

In classic EDS style, Meyerson wasn't wasting a moment assembling the vanguard to tackle "the GM account." He had seen GM's gargantuan size and scope and well understood that $2 billion a year worth of new data processing far outstripped the ability of EDS's organization. He realized that EDS must quickly expand in size to take over GM's computers, while making sure the company wasn't too thinly stretched to shepherd its other clients.

Commanding the long table in EDS's fifth-floor conference room,

Meyerson explained his general strategy: EDS would send a cadre of top officers to Detroit but retain EDS's executive branch in Dallas. His idea was to keep EDS's headquarters as far removed as possible from GM, which was to be treated as just another, albeit huge, customer. To carry out the job in Detroit, EDS would immediately launch a national recruiting drive to bring thousands of new workers to GM.

The main topic on the officers' minds was: Who is going to Detroit and who is staying in Dallas? Most of the men in the room had spent years moving to strange cities on short notice to do EDS's bidding. It wasn't going to be anything new. But moving to Detroit was a grim prospect for most of them. Tom Walter and his team had seen the poverty and squalor surrounding the downtown business district in April, the grime on the buildings, the harsh, lingering winter. Perot and Meyerson had chosen and promoted them for their toughness. Any one of them would have accepted an assignment in Detroit without complaint if Perot asked it, but few relished the prospect.

"You're staying in Dallas," Meyerson said to chief financial officer Tom Walter, with a downward motion of his index finger.

"You're going," to Jeff Heller. A pause. "Stay," to Les Alberthal. Alberthal was needed to run the rest of EDS's health-care businesses. "Go," to Kenn Hill, who had just moved to Washington. When Meyerson reached Kenneth Riedlinger, he expanded his remarks only slightly.

"You're coming with me to Detroit. You'll be directly in charge of the GM account, reporting to me," Meyerson said.

Riedlinger closed his eyes and a small wave of joy coursed through him. He had been silently wishing to be chosen, while considering how to handle the disappointment if Meyerson chose Alberthal or Fernandes instead of him. He had just spent nine grueling months in New Jersey scratching for small pieces of business at AT&T after the disappointment of losing the multibillion-dollar telephone billing megacontract. GM represented the biggest event in EDS's history by far, and now it was his to run. By itself the GM account was three times larger than all of EDS's other contracts.

For the moment, Riedlinger wasn't thinking about his honeymoon resolution at Cap d'Antibes, in which he had promised himself to stop allowing EDS to intrude so deeply on his marriage, his health, and his personal life. Fourteen years of EDS campaigns, battles with legislators and bureaucrats, late nights, and long trips out of town had worn him down emotionally and physically. Because of EDS, he had missed

Ross Perot in Texarkana.

Perot, flanked by his parents and sister, at his graduation from the Naval Academy.

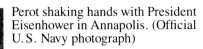
Perot shaking hands with President Eisenhower in Annapolis. (Official U.S. Navy photograph)

Perot (center), a major investor in Dupont Glore Forgan, at the New York Stock Exchange in 1971.

Ross Perot and Bull Simons upon return from rescue of EDS officials in Iran.

Roger B. Smith, chairman and chief
executive of General Motors Corporation.
(Courtesy General Motors)

John Gutfreund, chairman of Salomon
Brothers, Inc. (Courtesy Salomon Brothers)

Courtney Jones, former treasurer of General
Motors Corporation. (Courtesy General Motors)

F. Alan Smith, General Motors executive vice president and chief financial officer. (Courtesy General Motors)

Elmer Johnson, former Kirkland and Ellis managing partner and General Motors executive vice president. (Courtesy Kirkland and Ellis)

Ira Millstein, senior partner of Weil Gotshal and Manges, counsel to General Motors oversight committee. (Bonnie Geller, courtesy Weil Gotshal and Manges)

Prince Charles awarding Ross Perot the Winston Churchill medal in 1985.
(David Woo)

Perot and Smith at the Economic Club of Detroit luncheon, one week after General Motors' buyout of Ross Perot in December 1986. (Peter Yates, courtesy *The New York Times*)

Perot's farewell speech to Detroit at the Economic Club. (Peter Yates, courtesy *The New York Times*)

wedding anniversaries, holidays, and most of the birthday celebrations of his three sons. Two years ago, worn out from a murderous schedule, he had almost died after a bout of blood poisoning. (Perot had sent an EDS jet to bring him home; he had made sure Riedlinger got only the best medical care. Afterward, EDS paid for his recuperation at the Pritikin Longevity Center in Santa Monica.)

As he sat listening to Meyerson reshuffle EDS's corporate staff, Riedlinger recalled that he had tickets to attend *Brighton Beach Memoirs* with his wife, Judy, that very evening in Manhattan. He would have to cancel. Running the GM account was going to dominate his life completely for the foreseeable future. He wasn't going to have much time for Broadway shows.

His wife's reaction was quite different. Judy Riedlinger had been working as a marketer for EDS when she met Ken. Later she moved to a bigger job at IBM in Dallas. She had been there for three months when Ken told her the GM deal was likely to happen. Just as both their lives and their jobs appeared set and stable, she understood that the deal now was likely to upset everything. This was confirmed in a telephone call from Ken right after Meyerson appointed him head of the GM account.

"Well, the good news is they've decided to keep EDS headquarters in Dallas," Riedlinger told his wife. For days they had been talking about what GM's merger with EDS might mean to both of them.

She was momentarily relieved.

"I've been given GM," he said. "I'm going to Detroit. You can come if you want to." Riedlinger was so energized with the honor and responsibility of being given GM to run, he didn't want to acknowledge that the job might disrupt his marriage. So he didn't allow the possibility of turning the job down to enter the conversation.

His wife felt dizzy, as if she had been knocked on the head. She wasn't able to understand why he had spoken so insensitively to her. Did he want her to come or not? Was this his macho defense mechanism against her probable and reasonable reservations about chucking her job to follow him?

Judy Riedlinger sat down in her darkened house. She wasn't wild about the idea, but what choice did she have?

On to Detroit, she thought grimly.

GM's $2.55 billion acquisition of EDS raised many more questions for the million or so employees of GM than it answered.

GM workers, from powerful executive to assembly-line riveter, first read the news in the newspapers on June 29. Because the deal had been kept within a tight circle of people around Roger Smith, few at GM realized that a plan hadn't yet been formed for merging GM's computing activities with EDS. Part of the reason there was no plan was that there hadn't been any time to think of one. More important, the concept of integrated computer operations was a vague one in Roger Smith's mind, and he had never consulted about EDS with GM's in-house data processing experts. Was EDS going to install new computers and systems? Was EDS going to own the equipment? Were GM workers going to work for EDS, or would EDS workers become GM employees? Was EDS going to take over just the health-care and business applications, or was EDS going to get involved in computer-intensive factory automation projects? (*And what did these Medicare specialists from Texas know about factory automation anyway?*)

On the weekend of June 29, 1984, the EDS acquisition appeared only as a further troubling complication for GM engineers and managers already disspirited and confused by the six-month-old realignment of car manufacturing divisions into the Buick-Olds-Cadillac (BOC) and Chevrolet-Pontiac-GM Canada (CPC) groups.

To Alex Mair, GM vice president and group executive of technical staffs, the reorganization had been an unfortunate attempt by Roger Smith and GM's financial executives, guided by independent management consultants, to boost efficiency and managerial effectiveness. Not that Al Mair was against efficiency. But in his view, GM was too large for McKinsey and Company consultants to reorganize. It should have been done internally by him and the other top executives. A lifelong GM engineer, Mair desired that GM always remain the proud, flexible, and nimble company that had geared up in a matter of months to help the country win World War II, in which he had served fighting the Japanese. Mair was a tinkerer and fixer, an engineer's engineer. After earning an engineer's degree at General Motors Institute, Mair had started as a draftsman, progressed to service engineer, then worked on Chevrolet engines and GM aircraft engines. He had served a stint designing GM truck chassis and was GM's chief truck engineer before becoming director of all Chevrolet engineering. His skill and varied experience led to his appointment first as GM vice president in charge of all truck and bus operations and then as head of the Pontiac division. In his latest executive post, Mair headed the technical center and all the central GM scientific, engineering, and design staffs.

Since the late 1970s, Alex Mair's voice had belonged to a tiny chorus at GM pleading for more attention to quality and better design of cars and trucks. Mair had seen the competition as few GM executives had, splayed into hundreds of thousands of disassembled pieces on the massive floors of GM laboratories. Roger Smith's answer to GM's competitive disadvantage was a multibillion-dollar modernization program, with heavy emphasis on computers and robots, to automate GM assembly lines. GM planned to remove many traditional hourly workers from the plant floor and eventually to replace many of them with computer technicians and highly complex automation.

An engineer with intimate knowledge of machines, Mair was convinced that automation technology wasn't advanced enough to take over assembly-line jobs as quickly as Smith wanted. Sure, if GM threw enough time and money at the problem, scientists could equip a robot with vision and program its computer controller to insert bolts into a car body and tighten them. But in the daily reality of the assembly line, hundreds of problems can occur at any moment, from a software glitch to a drop of oil on a camera lens. If the robot isn't working, the line shuts down. It's no major hassle if a computer goes down for a short time in an insurance office or accounting firm; but on a complex manufacturing line, computer glitches may shut down operations for hours or days, meaning lost, and often unrecoverable, production. GM blue-collar workers weren't trained to improvise solutions, therefore new production technology only confused and alienated them.

Like many others at GM — and despite his high executive rank — Mair learned about the EDS negotiations by reading the newspaper. As he pondered EDS's desire to be the biggest computer-service company in the world, he also thought about GM's enormous health-care operations, accounting operations, GMAC vehicle financing, parts and services operations — all with huge computer systems. It makes sense, he thought. EDS must get involved somehow in those operations. Mair and other GM executives had discussed repeatedly the need to improve GM's computer capabilities, especially in data processing. The newspaper articles said EDS one day would sell computer-aided design and computer-aided manufacturing systems, too. Mair guessed EDS would be learning the automation business from GM engineers and then selling systems to outside clients. He correctly presumed that EDS didn't currently know anything about factory automation, nor was it big enough to handle GM's enormous size immediately.

In truth, GM at that moment possessed very little in the way of factory automation in any condition to sell to outside clients. Hundreds of automation projects were under way at various GM plants in fields as diverse as painting, parts recognition, and installation of major components such as windshields. Very few of the automation projects were working properly yet, a not unexpected development, since these applications of computers and machines had never been tried before. GM's newest and most highly automatic assembly plant, on the border of Detroit and Hamtramck, Michigan, was nearing completion. Computer specialists and engineers at Poletown (so nicknamed for the thousands of Polish-Americans who lived near the plant) were working around the clock, without much success, to de-bug the balky automation gear and make it operate according to specifications.

Several days after the announcement of the EDS acquisition, Mair was walking into the lobby of his office building when a research-laboratory manager stopped him.

"Mr. Mair, some people from EDS are here and they said they've come to take inventory. They want to put EDS property tags on all the equipment," the manager said.

At first puzzled, Mair grew angry. No one had briefed him about EDS.

"No one from EDS is going into the computer room, and no one will put EDS property tags on anything," he declared.

So it's come to this, Mair thought. Roger doesn't tell us anything about a deal with EDS; no one briefs us about what we're supposed to do; and then people from EDS just show up and start taking over.

Mair went to the research labs and shooed the EDS workers out of the building. He hadn't much power compared to Roger Smith and the financial men, but he would use every bit of it to stop EDS from trampling his domain.

TWELVE

Knocking Heads

D ESPITE the sizable and complicated task before him, Riedlinger
was seized by a rush of excitement and exhilaration. He immediately began sorting mentally through the details of the mission.
He would have to put his and Judy's house in Dallas on the market.
Someone must be hired to pack up his things at the apartment in
Bernardsville, New Jersey, while Judy started looking for a place in
Detroit. He wasn't abandoning his promise to devote more time to his
marriage and to his life; he simply was putting the promise on hold until
the GM account was rolling.

He didn't dwell much on the personal financial terms of the merger.
Yet they transformed Riedlinger's situation from one of comfort to
potential life-changing wealth. The cash and stock he would receive for
his EDS shares amounted to $1,527,644 plus 8,679 Class E shares (worth
another $1,084,875 in seven years). The big payoff was his unvested
EDS incentive shares, which GM promised to trade one-for-one for Class
E shares. Those 115,000 Class E incentive shares would be worth a
minimum of $14,375,000 in seven years. Assuming he sold half the
shares to pay his taxes (and assuming he stayed with EDS), he would
have another $7 million or $8 million waiting for him — more than
enough money for the rest of his life.

Strangely, the millions in stock meant less to him than the $50,000 cash bonus that Meyerson had promised him for drumming up AT&T contracts during the past six months. Stock was only paper, it always was cancelable or changeable. He had learned that once the hard way in EDS's early years.

"Mort, the stock transfers are going to take a while and I can use my bonus money now. Do you think we could take care of that?" Riedlinger said.

"Forget about the bonus, Ken. It's small potatoes compared to the opportunity we're giving you in Detroit," Meyerson replied. He said it in a tone of finality that Riedlinger recognized.

Riedlinger was momentarily angry, but he decided not to challenge his boss. Damn him! Riedlinger thought. He knows he can get away with reneging on his promise because he knows how eager I am to run the GM account. And he's right. I'm not going to make an issue out of this because GM is too important to kick away. He's manipulating me, and I'm making it easy for him.

Monday morning, in line with the GM chairman's orders to start moving immediately, Meyerson boarded an EDS Learjet to Detroit for his first operational meeting with F. Alan Smith, GM executive vice president of finance. Riedlinger flew in from New Jersey.

General Motors Information Services and Computer Activity (GMISCA), GM's data processing arm, reported to Alan Smith. Smith invited all of GM's top data processing managers, a group of fifty or so, including the heads of data processing for the car groups, components operations, and the research labs, to meet the EDS executives.

Meyerson and Riedlinger had attended countless gatherings like this before, on a much smaller scale. This was the meeting when the chief executive of the new EDS client, having just turned over data processing to Ross Perot and his troops, tells his own data processing workers: "You all now work for EDS." It was more effective for a top executive of the client and the EDS account manager to deliver the news together, in support of one another, so that the data processing department understood that EDS was backed by the very highest authority.

This time, circumstances were different. This time GM was buying EDS, as well as conferring upon EDS authority over its computers. In Meyerson's mind, however, the operating principle remained the same: GM was EDS's client, therefore EDS now took over the ultimate responsibility and the ultimate authority over computing at GM.

"As you know — from reading the newspapers — General Motors has bought EDS for $2.5 billion," Alan Smith told the group seated before him at the design center auditorium.

"These two gentlemen, Mort Meyerson, EDS president, and Ken Riedlinger, EDS senior vice president, will be responsible for the GM portion of EDS's business, and I'm sure you'll give them your full attention and cooperation as they outline for you the challenges that lie ahead."

Concise corporate boilerplate, Meyerson thought. No long-winded definitions. No limitations. The road is wide open for us. Good. We'll be able to do what we must and to execute in our own style.

"And now, since I'm running late for another meeting," Alan Smith said, "I'm going to turn the meeting over to Mort Meyerson. Mort?" The GM executive turned and walked directly out of the room.

Meyerson and Riedlinger were floored. Smith is leaving? Now? Can he possibly be too busy to attend the critical organizational meeting? GM just spent $2.5 billion to buy EDS, its biggest acquisition ever, and Alan Smith intends merely to introduce Meyerson and Riedlinger and tell everyone at GM to follow their directions? Smith barely had explained to his key data processing managers what the merger meant. And now he was off to another meeting! It was almost as if he were washing his hands of the EDS merger as quickly as possible, Riedlinger thought, as if he didn't want to touch it. Alan Smith not only didn't know what was in this mystery box Roger Smith had bought, he didn't appear too eager to find out.

Momentarily nonplussed by Smith's abrupt departure, Meyerson nonetheless stood up to address the GM data processing managers. This is one strange place, he thought. First, Roger blows his stack like some kind of lunatic; he throws $2.5 billion on the table to buy a company he barely understands; and now Alan Smith, who ought to care as much about this as anyone, walks out of the first operating meeting of the biggest merger GM has ever undertaken.

"General Motors and EDS, through their association, indeed have tremendous opportunities before them," Meyerson said, laying down some corporate babble of his own while mentally scrambling to shake off his surprise and catch up with his thoughts. He quickly recovered his balance, delineating the points Smith and Perot had agreed upon concerning EDS's responsibilities at GM, and explaining how EDS aimed to take over and eventually coordinate GM's $3 billion a year or more in computing activities.

As Meyerson spoke, the GM data processing managers sitting in the audience whispered and buzzed among themselves. It was a worried buzz. They had had little warning of how their lives were going to be changed by the merger. Meyerson's speech gave them some idea, and it was a bucket of ice water over their heads. One of them rose to question Meyerson.

"Let me understand this," he said with a quizzical look on his face and his fingers resting lightly on his temple. "GM bought EDS for $2.5 billion, but we're going to work for you?"

"That's right," Meyerson said. "All of you, as well as everyone else in GM's computer operations, work for EDS — and for me — as of today."

The man paused.

"That means we're all going to be under your compensation system and work under EDS's philosophy?"

"Right again," Meyerson said.

"And this is going to be a separate company with the EDS name, but owned by GM?"

Meyerson nodded once more.

The man stopped, unwilling to absorb what he was hearing. Finally he sat down. "Bulllll . . . shit," he exclaimed under his breath, loud enough for Meyerson to hear. Amid some mumbling, Meyerson heard: "Wait until Reuss hears about this." The man was in charge of computing under Lloyd Reuss, vice president and group executive for the Chevrolet-Pontiac-GM Canada manufacturing group.

In fact, the majority of data processing managers in the audience belonged to separate GM fiefdoms. They had pledged their allegiance to the rulers of groups or divisions such as Reuss.

The careers of everyone in the audience had, at one time or another, been sponsored by various GM vice presidents. Lloyd Reuss's data processing manager, for example, owed his career at GM — and his loyalty — to Lloyd Reuss. His security and future, he believed, were tied to Lloyd Reuss. Hence he and the others were utterly panicked and unhappy at the prospect of being forcibly transferred to EDS.

"Let me ask you something," said another manager, rising to his feet. "Has EDS had any experience with computer-aided design or computer-aided manufacturing?"

"Not much," Meyerson said.

"Well, how do you expect to take over CAD/CAM operations when you don't know anything about them?"

Riedlinger watched quietly while Meyerson attempted to field the hostile questions alone. One by one, for five hours, the GM managers stood up to hurl invective at Meyerson and at EDS. Meyerson remained as calm as possible, explaining again and again why a GM-EDS partnership was positive. To Riedlinger, Meyerson looked as though he was trying to play Superman and to deflect bullets off his chest.

Of course, there were aspects of the industry, such as manufacturing, that EDS intended to learn more about, Meyerson explained, but that lack of knowledge didn't preclude the need for a coordinated computing strategy under one umbrella.

Riedlinger felt tremendously uncomfortable as he watched Meyerson on the podium. They had encountered hostility in the line of duty before, but he had never had to deal with so much of it in the very first moments. In the past they had been able to persuade data processing workers at client companies that EDS's system held out great advantages. If they refused to be convinced, Riedlinger could replace them later on. Obviously, that wasn't going to be an option here. GM was so huge, and they were surrounded by enemies. There they were, two guys from EDS in a roomful of resentful GM managers. And their putative sponsors, Roger Smith and Alan Smith, seemingly had left them to twist in the wind.

"Look," Meyerson said. "It's true that EDS is a much smaller company than GM. Over the past twenty-two years, we've formed associations with numerous large organizations for the purpose of developing an overall computing strategy, which GM, at the moment, doesn't have. GM can become a much more efficient organization by approaching computing from a top-down basis. Your chairman has spoken of the need to . . ."

Meyerson pressed on with his speech, though he looked into the eyes of the GM managers and saw that they weren't buying his sales pitch. They were unloved children who had been put up for adoption. The transfer to EDS was the ultimate in surprise and culture shock.

As soon as this meeting ends, Riedlinger thought, they're all going to run back to their groups and figure out ways to stop EDS. Early in Riedlinger's career someone at EDS explained to him: "Our policy is, if someone doesn't tell us what to do, we'll tell them."

We'll tell them, Riedlinger thought, but it'll be a hell of a bloody war making them obey.

Al Mair stood by the window in the "color room" of GM's design center waiting for President Ronald Reagan's helicopter to land. As head of the technical staffs, Mair was given the job of presenting GM's supersecret Saturn project to the President for inspection. Saturn was a futuristic project to build a new small car with a totally new and revised manufacturing and marketing system.

Mair should have been excited by the occasion, but all he could feel was betrayal and annoyance at the invasion of his offices and laboratories by EDS. Yesterday, one of his data processing managers told him that EDS planned to take all GM data processing workers and transfer them to EDS. Why hadn't Roger Smith at least explained this?

From Sloan's brilliant concept of decentralized management, GM had turned into a huge central bureaucracy with a few nonautomotive men pulling all the levers. Now the heir to this system of numbers-oriented management — who, Mair guessed, probably understood very little about computing — had gone out and spent billions on a computer-services company without a word of consultation with GM's top scientists and engineers. What was GM coming to?

"Al, do you have a moment?"

Standing next to him was Alan Smith, who was waiting for the President to arrive with the chairman and the rest of GM's top executives. He looked upset.

"Please be sure that all of your group accepts and treats the EDS people properly," Smith said. Although Smith didn't say exactly what he had heard, it was clear that the rancor caused by EDS's landing in Detroit had reached his ears.

"Alan, we always treat everyone properly. But why don't you tell the vice presidents yourself. They're all right here, let me assemble them for you," Mair replied. He wasn't quite sure what Alan Smith had in mind, and he was upset. He called over Bob Frosch, Bob Eaton, Tom Matthews, and Irv Rybicki, who were standing nearby. Alan Smith and Roger Smith had turned EDS people loose in the technical center without consulting him, and now they wanted to know why EDS hadn't received a cordial welcome. At sixty-three years of age, Mair was only two years away from GM's mandatory retirement age, close enough to let Alan Smith know how he resented the way EDS had been thrust upon him. Smith repeated his short admonition for the GM technical vice presidents who worked in Al Mair's group.

A few days later, Meyerson and Riedlinger paid Al Mair a visit. He was among the first twenty-three GM top executives with whom the EDS executives scheduled appointments in their first weeks in Detroit.

Meyerson explained his plan to consolidate all of GM's computing activities and the efficiency Roger Smith wanted to gain by associating with EDS. Of course, the association meant bringing all of the research lab's computers, including a sophisticated Cray supercomputer and all computer personnel, into EDS.

"It sounds as if you've been told that we don't know what we're doing," Mair said to Meyerson. Mair agreed that GM wasn't as skilled in data processing as it should be. But it bothered him that, once again, outside experts rather than GM executives were being given the power to make changes. "Do you realize that GM builds 40,000 cars and trucks every day using the computer expertise this group supplies? I'm not sure you even know what materials a car is made from, let alone how it is built. Scientific and engineering computing is far different from the kind of computing you're used to."

In principle, Mair embraced the idea that GM should lead the world in computing, he told Meyerson, but there had to be a plan and it had to be organized in a reasonable, orderly manner. Assembly lines require much greater accuracy and reliability than Medicare claims offices, Mair told Meyerson.

Meyerson was accustomed to dealing with excuses and obstruction. No matter. He would simply report the roadblock to Roger Smith, who would take care of it with a phone call.

As Meyerson and Riedlinger proceeded with their visits to top GM executives through July and August of 1984, they quickly learned how much institutional resistance existed at the world's biggest car company. Roger Smith hadn't been kidding about GM's frozen management and the bureaucrats' hatred of anything that threatened the safe, warm nest. By comparison, Al Mair's reception was more pleasant than most. At General Motors Acceptance Corporation, GM's car-financing subsidiary and a major user of computers, GMAC president Bob Murphy treated the EDS executives coolly, ignoring them for the first few minutes they sat in his office. When Meyerson finally asked a few questions about GMAC's computer systems and said he thought EDS might be able to speed response time, Murphy told him curtly that GMAC didn't need EDS's help.

Meyerson called Alan Smith after the meeting. Don't worry, Smith said; I'll take care of it.

Next they visited Alex Cunningham, executive vice president in charge of North American car operations, the main source of GM's revenue. A powerful, rotund native of Bulgaria who wore his long hair combed straight back on his head, Cunningham glared at the two men.

Meyerson tried to break the ice by mentioning something inconsequential about a recent vacation. Cunningham didn't respond. Meyerson commented on a memento from Cunningham's days as an RAF fighter pilot. Nothing.

As Meyerson finally launched his standard "EDS is here to help" oration, Cunningham raised a hand to stop him. "It will be a cold day in hell before I'm going to help pad the pockets of a bunch of rich Texans."

So much for the mad Bulgarian, Meyerson thought.

Riedlinger took notes during these sessions. Cunningham's comment about "rich Texans" wasn't the first snide remark he had heard referring to GM's spending to buy the EDS stock. Apparently, the details of the stock holdings of top EDS executives and managers were widely disseminated within GM, prompting a great deal of anger and jealousy over GM's multibillion-dollar payments and promissory notes for EDS shares and the unvested EDS incentive shares. GM executives themselves weren't exactly underpaid by the standards of U.S. industry, but they weren't earning anywhere near the fortunes that had been locked in by top EDS people. As for GM data processing managers, many of them were $50,000-a-year workers who regarded themselves as every bit as skilled as their millionaire counterparts at EDS.

As Meyerson and Riedlinger pondered their gloomy feelings and the dim prospects of quickly winning the hearts and minds of GM executives, they were abruptly surprised and heartened by Don Atwood's upbeat reception. Atwood, vice president and group executive in charge of GM's Truck and Bus Group, welcomed the EDS men with open arms. GM, under Atwood's direction, was finishing the retooling of a van-assembly plant in Baltimore and shortly afterward was to open three new pickup-truck lines in Ft. Wayne, Indiana, Pontiac, Michigan, and Oshawa, Canada.

"We're putting in the most advanced automation equipment we've ever used in these plants. It's all run by computers and we need lots of help with the computer systems. You can save my life," Atwood told the men.

It was the first time anyone in GM operations had acknowledged EDS's expertise in anything. It was the first time anyone appeared eager and grateful for EDS's help. Although their problems were far from solved, Meyerson and Riedlinger were relieved to have found an ally. As a result of Atwood's cooperation, Meyerson decided to send the ablest of EDS managers on the GM account to the Truck and Bus plants in Atwood's group.

EDS was still deep in the jungle, but at least the troops had begun marching forward.

The reports of opposition at GM reached Ross Perot instantly. He never was shy about directly calling EDS managers, even junior managers, personally to find out how they were doing. EDSers, even the greenest recruits, knew better than to speak to the boss with anything less than extreme candor.

Neither Perot nor his attorney, Tom Luce, was unduly concerned. Together they had finished shepherding the educational-reform bills through the Texas legislature and now could turn their full attention to GM. To them, it looked as though EDS troops were encountering typical resistance from the locals, albeit on a very much larger scale than they were used to. EDS nearly always encountered such resistance — until the chief executive lowered the boom, which Roger Smith undoubtedly would do if and when he was needed.

"Don't worry," Smith assured Perot and Meyerson, "Rome wasn't built in a day." Smith had warned them about GM's bureaucratic torpor and dislike of change. He was confident, he told Perot, that everything was going to fall into place.

While Meyerson and Riedlinger were defending EDS's beachhead in Detroit, EDS and GM negotiators in Dallas, assisted by their investment bankers and lawyers, continued to hack through the details of the merger agreement. All that had been signed so far was the memorandum of understanding. Nothing was official and GM couldn't pay for the EDS shares until the agreement was finished. Once that was done, approval by shareholders was necessary. Every day without an agreement meant a great deal of lost interest payments for EDS shareholders, so the negotiators tried to work fast.

In some respects EDS clearly was to be a GM subsidiary; in others, it was to remain a separate entity. The legal and financial problems were complicated and esoteric. Creating GM Class E shares posed obstacles at the Securities and Exchange Commission and the New York Stock Exchange. The SEC haggled with GM over how EDS's profits were to be accounted for. The Big Board had to be convinced to bend its rule prohibiting multiple classes of stock; and the exchange tentatively approved listing of Class E shares.

Outstanding tax issues also loomed, which could mean a swing of several million dollars in either direction for Ross Perot's bank account. The contingent notes guaranteeing the $125 a share value of GM Class E shares after seven years posed a tax puzzle for GM's and Perot's lawyers. Depending on how the IRS interpreted the value of the notes, Perot might be taxed at the capital-gains rate or at the much higher rate for ordinary income. GM understandably wasn't willing to indemnify Perot completely against the higher tax bill. Perot needed an expert's expert on taxation.

He asked Marty Ginsburg, a professor of tax law at Georgetown University and an eminent Washington tax guru, to render his opinion. Ginsburg and Perot had met in New York in 1971 during the Dupont Walston affair. (Ginsburg also had done tax work for GM relating to the building of GM's New York headquarters.) The two had grown quite fond of one another. When Ginsburg visited Dallas he stayed in the Perots' guest house and ate breakfast with the family. He never needed an alarm clock at the Perot's; Ross used the intercom to call "Y'up, Marty?" each morning.

On June 19 Bill Gayden flew to Washington on an EDS jet to pick up Ginsburg and briefed him on the problem on the return flight to Dallas. By the time they reached Perot's office, Ginsburg had formulated a response.

(Several weeks later, Elmer Johnson, GM's general counsel, hired Jack Levin, a former law partner and tax specialist at Kirkland and Ellis in Chicago, to represent GM's interest. Ginsburg and Levin conferred in early August. When they had finished, the tax experts reached a conclusion that had a salutary, multimillion-dollar effect on Perot's tax liability and also satisfied GM.)

"Marty, I insist that you send me your bill for this," Perot said. He knew Ginsburg earned far less as an academician than he would in full-time private practice.

"Don't worry about it, Ross," Ginsburg said. "It's on me."

"Well, at least let me make a contribution in your name to a university," Perot said.

"Sure, Ross, we'll talk about it sometime," Ginsburg said, fending him off. When Ginsburg once had needed help, Perot had done him a great personal favor a few years earlier, something deeply touching that he refused to discuss with anyone. He couldn't accept money from Perot.

A few weeks later by telephone, Perot jokingly threatened to endow a chair in Ginsburg's name at Oral Roberts University. Ginsburg relented, agreeing instead to let Perot spend $1 million to endow a chair in Ginsburg's name at Georgetown University law school.

*   *   *

After EDS's first month in Detroit, it was obvious that the 240 EDS workers assigned to GM under Ken Riedlinger's command weren't nearly enough to tackle the job at hand. Only about two dozen of the 240 were top EDS managers; the rest were lower-level technicians and workers. Another 750 reinforcements were on the way, but most of EDS's 13,000 workers already were committed to EDS's other clients.

Perot was adamant that EDS's existing clients weren't going to be sacrificed for the sake of GM, so Meyerson decided that only about 1,000 EDSers could be spared for the GM account. The rest were to be hired from the outside or absorbed from GM. Approximately 10,000 GM computer experts and data processors were slated for transfer to EDS after the merger agreement was signed.

EDS had to hire thousands more systems engineers, programmers, technicians, and trainees right away. A coast-to-coast recruiting campaign touched most U.S. college campuses and every city where large concentrations of computer experts were employed. EDS no longer could afford the luxury of sifting highly motivated students and gung-ho ex-military types from the applicant pool; a demonstrated ability to deal with computers and systems — and a clean record — were sufficient.

Riedlinger attempted to discern a clear picture of GM's computing systems in order to begin drawing up a master plan. But lower-level GM data processing workers, in many cases, behaved in the same recalcitrant manner as the executives. When Riedlinger made appointments to interview computer managers, they often didn't show up for meetings or left messages referring Riedlinger to assistants who didn't have the information he was seeking. GM managers he was finally able to pin down tended to answer questions in monosyllables, volunteered little, and handed him stacks of reports to read instead of explaining how systems worked.

The computer workers were afraid and resentful. Like their supervisors, they believed GM had sold their birthright to EDS. As GM white-collar workers, they were entitled to automatic cost-of-living increases, automatic annual salary increases, and one of the most generous benefits packages in U.S. industry. As soon as they transferred to EDS, they feared, their health and pension benefits would be reduced, cost-of-living allowances dropped, and compensation increases tied to performance.

They were right. Only the most senior EDS executives were wealthy. The average EDS worker didn't enjoy nearly as lavish a compensation package as his counterpart at GM. EDS pensions weren't as generous.

Health insurance wasn't as comprehensive. It wasn't so much due to stinginess as it was to Ross Perot's ideas about incentives. EDS didn't reward average workers, it rewarded the stars.

Riedlinger attempted to comprehend the mentality and attitudes of GM workers, whose ineffable hatred of EDS was at a level he had never encountered. He read *On a Clear Day You Can See General Motors* and *My Years at General Motors,* by Alfred Sloan, and distributed copies to EDS managers.

Dealing with resistance from GM and the long hours was mentally and physically exhausting. Riedlinger and other EDS managers were working twenty-hour days, living and eating for weeks at the Troy Hilton. At the same time, they were trying to coordinate moving their families from Dallas and other cities to Detroit. A few weeks after the merger, while Judy Riedlinger searched for a house to buy in Bloomfield Hills, the couple rented a small apartment on Fourteen Mile Road in Troy. They felt like transients living from suitcases, and the hostility from people at GM made them feel suspected and unwanted, strangers in a strange land.

One day after work, Riedlinger came out to the parking lot and found the tires on his car slashed. It wasn't the first incident. Threatening letters had been arriving at his office bearing the salutation: "Dear Nazi Riedlinger . . ." Unordered pizzas were delivered.

As he stood in the parking lot, annoyed by the petty harassment, a part of Ken Riedlinger sympathized with the wounded sensibilities of GM computer workers. He knew exactly what they were afraid of. He had delivered countless speeches telling GM workers they had nothing to fear from EDS and, indeed, should expect bigger and better professional opportunities in data processing. But he knew as well — because he had been through it himself — that a career at EDS was much more demanding and took its toll on personal and family life. There were broken promises, financial disappointments — the $50,000 bonus, for example. Reward at EDS was supposed to be based on performance, but he had seen plenty of exceptions. Was EDS a cult? He always laughed when people said that. But he supposed it was, in a way — a cult devoted to excellence. He loved belonging to the best of the best, but now he believed it had a dark side, too.

Riedlinger could see how EDS's unsettling influence on GM's data processing workers was a powerful stimulant for the United Auto Workers, which for years had tried with little success to unionize GM white-collar workers. More than 300 data processing workers jammed a Warren, Michigan, UAW hall in early November to hear a pitch from the union. EDS was just the opening the union needed to launch a new organizing campaign.

The union activity worried Perot and Meyerson, too. Unions and organizing efforts were unknown at EDS. Perot always said he had nothing against unions, but he didn't believe they were necessary when everyone in the workplace treated one another with understanding and respect.

Riedlinger wondered if Roger Smith or John Gutfreund or Ross Perot, in their scariest nightmares, could have imagined an EDS and GM "alliance" turning out like this.

As a lifelong fan of the Chicago Cubs, Steve McClellan could hardly contain his joy. In September 1984, it was looking as though his beloved Cubs might finally win a National League pennant, the first since 1945. In the American League, the Detroit Tigers had led since opening day and appeared poised for a championship series. Ken Riedlinger told McClellan that he was arranging series tickets and to count on seats at Tiger Stadium when the Cubs and Tigers clashed in Detroit. A replay of the 1945 series. Fantastic!

For McClellan the World Series would be an exciting backdrop to his primary mission in Detroit. He was responsible for checking the progress of the GM and EDS merger on behalf of Salomon Brothers' clients and potential investors in GM Class E stock.

McClellan had been impressed with the way Bob Scully and Jerry Rosenfeld, Salomon Brothers' investment bankers, had pulled the GM deal off. The creation of the GM Class E stock had been a stroke of pure genius. It gave the EDS people an incentive to stay with the company and make it more profitable than ever. In some ways Class E stock also solved many of McClellan's ambivalent feelings about the change in EDS's ownership. On the one hand, McClellan expected to be rewarded, in the form of a year-end bonus, from Salomon Brothers' $7 million investment-banking fee. After all, he had suggested EDS as a target and had supplied crucial intimate knowledge about the company for GM. On the other hand, McClellan wasn't happy at all with the idea of no longer being able to follow and recommend EDS stock for Salomon Brothers' clients.

Now, with the creation of GM Class E stock, he would have his bonus and the company would stay independent to boot. Investors would be able to buy Class E shares. McClellan's long experience at EDS was going to prove very valuable for clients as he monitored the merger's progress.

Later that month the hapless Cubs booted away the National League pennant. Salomon Brothers spent $240 for two tickets so McClellan could take a client to see the Cubs play the San Diego Padres in Chicago. But the Padres took the series.

By the time McClellan arrived in Detroit, the Tigers and Padres were squared off for the championship. But baseball was no longer on his mind. He was anxious to find out how quickly Riedlinger and the EDS managers were taking over GM's computing operations. The answer would reveal how much EDS was able to charge GM for its services and how quickly the impact would show up in EDS revenue and profit. He was thinking about the pending issue of Class E shares and how much they would be worth.

McClellan was aghast at what he found. By the looks of things, Riedlinger and his team were having a miserable time. Revenue was the least of EDS's worries. EDS was a transplanted organ fighting to prevent rejection by the host. Although the EDS men didn't tell him they were discouraged, he saw they were worn and tired, as though they had been squeezed through a wringer. McClellan had seen them tackle tough jobs before. EDS people always went hell-bent-for-leather, he thought, running every marathon like a sprint. They were tough, but he had never seen them so badly beaten up.

At a meeting with one of EDS's senior managers, McClellan made the mistake of asking how it felt to be part of GM.

"I don't work for General Motors," the EDS man growled at him. "I work for EDS."

The irritations will subside eventually, Perot thought, reaching for his telephone. For what seemed like the hundredth time in the space of a few weeks, Ross Perot asked his secretary, Sally Bell, to connect him with Roger Smith.

He had just had another go-round with GM treasurer Courtney Jones. First GM had the audacity to publicly release EDS's earnings despite the fact that the prerogative was clearly reserved for him as chairman of EDS. He ran EDS, and therefore he announced EDS's financial results to shareholders. The next irritation was about Class E stock. Ad-hoc trading had sprung up in GM Class E shares weeks before they were issued. So-called when issued trading was made possible by specialists who issued a kind of promissory note to deliver the shares when the company issued them. However, the trading price was a blind guess based on available, but possibly incomplete, information. To Perot, who knew plenty about Wall Street shell games, the practice looked sleazy. After deploring "when issued" trading to GM directors, Perot called John Gutfreund at Salomon Brothers and John Shad, chairman of the SEC, to try to have it stopped. He didn't want exchange specialists and other speculators touting securities that hadn't been issued because unwary investors might be hurt. Only the market insiders had a foolproof chance to make money.

"This is a sucker's game and it hits right to the core of our credibility," Perot told Gutfreund and Shad. "You're taking a pretty girl and turning her into a streetwalker. I don't want anyone peddling Class E shares before all the information is available."

GM treasurer Courtney Jones intervened and asked Perot to call Roger Smith. Smith then told Perot: "I'm having trouble getting the facts on this one."

Exasperated, Perot called the New York Stock Exchange to lodge a complaint. He was more than a bit surprised by what exchange officials told him:

"We only permitted the trading because Salomon Brothers asked us to allow it on behalf of GM."

Roger Smith and Courtney Jones have decided to establish a market for Class E stock no matter what I say, Perot thought.

The controversy simmered as Jones specified the letters "GME" as the stock symbol for GM Class E shares. Perot had, politely but firmly, asserted that "EDS" be used as the symbol.

"Courtney, we've got a brand name here, so why not advertise it?" Perot said. "Besides, we want investors to think EDS, with a price–earnings multiple of twenty when they buy the stock — not GM, with a price–earnings multiple of seven. Right?" Perot had the distinct impression that this relatively minor issue was a matter of principle for GM's treasurer's office. In effect, GM asserted the position: "This is GM stock and it will have a GM stock symbol. Period." It violated his understanding with Smith, but there was little he could do without provoking a major confrontation.

Smith's approaches to conflict resolution didn't make Perot happy. Obviously, Smith was trying to appease his executives and Perot simultaneously. In the meantime, all he said was: Don't worry, Ross, we'll take care of it. You know how difficult these things are in an organization this size.

As a matter of fact, Ross Perot didn't see why such issues should be difficult at all. They had ironclad agreements in black and white, including the definitive merger agreement that became official on October

18, 1984, the date of shareholder approval. He had separate clarifications with Smith that they had written out and sent over the fax machine. And they had been over all of this verbally dozens of times: EDS was going to remain an independent company and Ross Perot was going to continue to run it as he always had.

Was it too much for Courtney Jones and the rest of GM simply to accept the facts, as Roger Smith laid them out?

Perot was hearing plenty from Mort Meyerson, Ken Riedlinger, and other EDSers about resistance from GM on the operating level. He was less worried about that. In military terms, the EDSers in Detroit were the first wave of assault troops pinned down on the beach by hostile fire. Sooner or later they would move out of their foxholes and begin conquering territory.

Perot expected to encounter jealousy at GM over the generous compensation for top EDS officers. For that reason he insisted that Roger Smith agree to allow him the final say on compensation matters at EDS. Now it was Smith's duty to make sure everyone at GM knew he had supported the compensation agreements. A few weeks before the merger became final, Tom Walter, EDS's chief financial officer, forwarded a request to Greg Lau, GM's assistant treasurer in charge of compensation, to set aside 20 million GM Class E shares for stock incentives for key executives. Details were spelled out in the proxy and approved by shareholders: for the next ten years, EDS could grant up to 20 million Class E shares to key executives. Lest anyone miss the significance, the proxy specifically stated that the new stock incentive plan "will have terms similar to and substantially as favorable to participants as the existing EDS plans . . ." In other words, as long as EDS prospers, the rich will keep getting richer.

Perot also forwarded to Lau a copy of a previous agreement made with Mort Meyerson a year earlier, before GM came on the scene, promising to pay Meyerson one percent of EDS's net profits as his salary. In 1984 Meyerson's salary was $712,000 under the formula. Subsequent to the merger, Meyerson's salary could easily triple or quadruple as revenue and profit soared. Meyerson had been uncomfortable with the increase, which seemed inappropriately high. He told Perot the one-percent formula obviously wasn't equitable any longer, and they agreed to work on an alternative.

Perot forwarded all the compensation plans to the GM treasurer's office. It was a busy time. They could work on the details later.

*   *   *

Every year, a couple of weeks before Christmas, General Motors throws a bash for the media. For one evening each year, in the interest of the holiday spirit, GM relaxes its normally tight lipped, reserved relations between itself and the working press.

GM's yuletide press party has become a hoary Detroit custom, a reminder of happier times when GM's preeminence in the industry was beyond question, when writers had fewer reasons to point at GM's weaknesses or expose its warts. In those days, GM execs and automotive reporters regularly tossed down martinis together and gossiped good-heartedly, sealing their relationship at Christmas. In fact, many of GM's press and public relations people were recruited from the ranks of the Detroit-based automotive press.

The Detroit Press Club, traditional site of the party, is an ugly, low-slung, seedy building in the heart of downtown. A herd of mostly older veterans still huddles at the bar, swapping news tidbits and war stories. Reporting's younger generation, eschewing Lucky Strikes and Jim Beam, generally relaxes at suburban watering spots such as the Midtown Cafe in Birmingham, Sparky's in Grosse Pointe, or the Franklin Racquet Club on Northwestern Highway.

On the evening of GM's 1984 Christmas party, journalists young and old descended on the club, reporters from the wire services and national magazines, and TV personalities. The GM public relations people glad-handed the press and introduced GM executives, who, as usual, bestowed holiday wishes and scampered home as quickly as possible. GM execs normally were uncomfortable dealing with gangs of questioning reporters.

The reporters in such a setting were grateful for the few minutes of free chat and the hospitality of drinks and hors d'oeuvres. They also stayed alert for stray tidbits of news fallen from alcohol-loosened lips.

On this particular evening, reporters peppered the GM execs with questions about the quality gap between GM and Japanese cars, poor performance of the highly touted industrial robots in GM plants, and horrendous morale in the ranks. Roger Smith was particularly juicy prey. The reporters hectored him mercilessly about rumors of problems with EDS, about a "lulu" of a news story that he had tantalized them with months earlier. He didn't want to talk about any of it; he shouldn't have mentioned the lulu in the first place. Every reporter in Detroit wanted to find out about the lulu first.

If there was one cool and relaxed GM executive at the party it was Elmer W. Johnson, the company's vice president and general counsel.

Few journalists in the room had heard of Johnson and no one was rushing up to pry secrets from him. Johnson stood to the side of the press-club bar, a Scotch in hand, looking a little lonely. In a city that deified "car guys," Johnson had barely begun to comprehend the arcane and complex alchemy of designing and building automobiles and selling them to the public. A lawyer, he was much more comfortable conversing about the governance of large corporations, a field in which he had specialized as managing partner of Kirkland and Ellis, the nation's biggest law firm.

Less than two years earlier, Roger Smith had asked Johnson to be GM's general counsel, a job most corporate attorneys considered the pinnacle of their field of law. Johnson declined. He was earning a couple of million dollars a year at Kirkland and was happily ensconced in a $900,000 Lake Shore Drive condo in Chicago, piloting the huge law firm and serving on the board of his beloved Chicago Symphony.

Johnson's law practice had provided plenty of professional stimulation from the corporate arena. Dozens of chief executives and boards of directors retained him to render legal advice in moments of crisis. Over the years, he had helped Westinghouse Electric untangle potential liabilities in connection with ruinous uranium contracts. He had guided Firestone Tire and Rubber's internal corruption investigation, which put a vice president behind bars. He had persuaded Archie McCardell to allow himself to be fired as International Harvester chief executive, a creative and tricky solution that saved McCardell a huge income tax liability and diplomatically paved the way to bring in a more effective chief executive.

Quietly and behind the scenes, Elmer Johnson had become a one-man kitchen cabinet for top management and directors. His personality and demeanor helped him immensely in the role. He spoke softly and, as often as not, wore a winsome smile. Johnson was a tall, slender, bespectacled man, whose gestures and language rarely telegraphed threat. He wasn't shy about bestowing a compliment or passing along a kind word, habits that had helped relax and reassure his clients at Kirkland and Ellis despite their legal difficulties.

Of course, over the years Elmer Johnson also had proven himself to be a tough negotiator when the occasion called for it. He was ambitious as well, it was true; no shrinking violet could rise to the helm in a place like Kirkland and Ellis.

Roger Smith had been given Elmer Johnson's name by former Dupont chairman Irving Shapiro. Shapiro suggested that Smith might be able to attract a man of Johnson's stature, who didn't lack for pay or professional challenge, by offering him the chance to participate in top management, to play in a game he had previously only coached. (Shapiro himself had begun his career as an attorney before rising to Dupont's top management post.)

Smith wasn't deterred by Johnson's first refusal.

"Well, I've found my man, Elmer," Smith told him on their second meeting, as they sat down for lunch on the eightieth floor of the Standard Oil Building in Chicago.

"That's great, Roger. Who is it?"

"You," Smith said.

Johnson demurred once more, explaining that he had just accepted a job a few months earlier as special counsel to Ameritech, the Chicago-based telephone company. Johnson's appointment at Ameritech had caused a minor controversy in legal circles. Not long before the appointment, Kirkland and Ellis had hired a sizable staff of lawyers in Washington with an eye toward developing a relationship with newly deregulated AT&T. But since Kirkland couldn't represent AT&T and its spinoff, Ameritech, without risking a conflict of interest, several of Kirkland's Washington lawyers working on AT&T were fired so that Johnson could accept the Ameritech job. To now leave Ameritech for GM might stir up resentments again.

"Don't say no. Just listen," Smith said. "I'm going to make your life interesting. I don't want a lawyer, I want a businessman who is going to have a broad impact on this company. You'll start as vice president in charge of the legal department and I'll change your job every couple of years."

When Smith waxed creative his enthusiasm was infectiously persuasive. Johnson knew that few men had ever been hired from outside GM at the vice president level. But Smith told him the sky was the limit with respect to his potential impact at GM — even the office of chief executive wasn't beyond his grasp.

Chairman of General Motors! What did a lawyer like him know about cars and trucks? Not much, he thought. But what had he known about telephones or tractors? Johnson's strength, he believed, lay in organizational capability, in defining and controlling the currents and structures of the powers that govern large companies; in other words, the use of rational principles to bring out the best results from economic groups. A few years earlier, Johnson had devoted himself to a crash study course in economics, philosophy, and politics in order to plug what he thought were gaps in his knowledge. He had been eager to develop an intellectual approach to improving the strength of U.S. corporations.

The job of GM vice president provided the perfect laboratory to test his ideas, but should he accept it? Was a place like GM really open to change? Did an outsider have a chance? And what about the chance to one day run GM? Could he turn his back on a chance like that?

Johnson consulted his friends, among them Jim Gustafson, his mentor and a professor of philosophy at the University of Chicago. Gustafson had guided Johnson's reading in the early 1970s and Johnson reciprocated by supporting his teacher while he wrote *Philosophy from a Theocentric Perspective*.

Take the job, Gustafson had told him. But Gustafson warned Johnson about setting his heart on running GM one day. Smith may have held that carrot in front of many people, he told his friend.

Seeing GM plain was a bit of a shock to Johnson. He had worked with large bureaucratic companies before, but he hadn't expected to be so thoroughly underwhelmed by so many of the top GM executives and managers he met. Through politics and loyalty, as well as a bare minimum of competence, GM had raised an uninspiring cadre of leaders at a time when it needed gifted direction. One of Johnson's first jobs at GM included supervising press and public relations. Smith had warned him about the resistance to change, but he found out that resistance reached all the way to the top: when he suggested Smith find a new vice president of public relations, the GM chairman refused. Jack McNulty, the vice president of PR, was a close confidant of Smith's. McNulty just wasn't effective, Johnson opined. But Smith vetoed the idea; he and McNulty were close, and he never fired people who were loyal to him, Johnson learned.

So Johnson backed off, determined to learn more about GM, bide his time, and build credibility more slowly until he amassed the power for bold action. Few reporters at GM's Christmas party would have guessed that Johnson planned to make himself a force in GM's fourteenth-floor executive suite, let alone a potential future chairman.

The handicappers betting on a dark-horse future GM chairman that frosty December evening were having more fun speculating about a short, crew-cut man from Texas with as little experience building cars as Elmer Johnson.

THIRTEEN

The Innovative Mind of Roger Smith

B
Y early 1985, Roger Smith had emerged in popular thought as one of corporate America's premier innovators. Lee Iacocca had saved Chrysler, and Smith was doing the same, in his own way, for GM. Unlike Iacocca, Smith lacked star quality and charisma. He lacked the chemistry of leadership, the best-selling autobiography. Instead, he relied on vision and GM's storied financial power to propel GM forward.

Smith was willing to smash idols in order to make his vision of the future come true. GM's joint venture with Toyota to build small cars at an old GM plant in Fremont, California, was a risky, heretical, nontraditional way for GM to learn about the Japanese manufacturing system. He spent billions in GM's plants to plunge into flexible automation and robotics with the goal of boosting productivity and quality. Instead of reconciling GM's struggles with hourly workers once and for all, Smith aimed to leap beyond them with technology and ideas about management borrowed from the Japanese.

In January of 1985, five months after President Reagan had been given a sneak preview, GM publicly unveiled its most ambitious innovation, Saturn. Until then, Saturn had been a rumor outside GM. Detroit had seen similar all-out campaigns from GM before with the Corvair in the 1960s, a car that gave GM a black eye because of questions about its safety, and the Vega, a 1970s import-fighter too heavy and unreliable to make any inroads in the marketplace.

In Smith's mind Saturn was far more than a new car. In fact, the Saturn car itself was almost beside the point. Saturn was a way of reinventing GM inside GM. If Saturn succeeded in forging improved relations with workers, GM might sweep away confining work rules in the factory and pay workers according to productivity instead of automatic hourly wage scales. The GM chairman then would have accomplished a feat that had eluded his predecessors on the fourteenth floor since the 1937 sit-down strike in Flint: Saturn aimed to join hourly workers with designers, engineers, and marketers as equals in status and working conditions, to produce the world's best vehicles. From the outset, representatives from the UAW and GM executives sat at the same table to plan Saturn — a significant departure from the practices of a company that still operated separate washrooms and cafeterias for hourly and salaried workers in the plants.

This was the innovative mind of Roger Smith. Reaching for revolutionary solutions to intractable problems. Daring to question ideas and concepts never before questioned at GM. Putting his reputation, and his company's fortune, on the line.

U.S. business groups and the media responded enthusiastically to Smith's vision. It can be safely said that from 1983 through 1985 there were few awards for executive or businessman of the year that Roger Smith either didn't win or was too busy to accept. *The New York Times Magazine* featured him on its cover and in a glowing article recited the changes he had brought to GM. Every journalistic broadside touched on the same points: his background as an accountant; the early stumbles; frustration with GM's molasseslike bureaucracy; his desire to ignite a corporationwide fire for change; his unprepossessing looks and squeaky nasal voice; but, crowning it all, the genius of his vision.

Ross Perot, often described as Smith's partner in the vision, was pleased to add his voice and prestige to the image makers. GM was a big, ungainly company that Perot had vowed to help Roger reshape through EDS. Cary Reich, author of the *New York Times* profile, interviewed Perot about the campaign to change GM.

"If you want to get an elephant to move, then you have to know where the sensitive spots are," Perot told him. "Roger knows where they are. In fact, he knows how to get that elephant to dance."

In a subtle way, Perot's jest belied his growing awareness of GM's bureaucratic torpor, reported daily to him by EDS managers. Perot's statement was a kinder variant of what a former GM director said about the company, quoted in the same article: that GM over the years had grown "fat, dumb and happy."

For anyone but Ross Perot, lampooning GM as a dancing elephant might have been a dangerous and possibly fatal breach of GM's taboo against public self-criticism. Perot didn't worry. This was the role he and Smith had agreed upon, after all, to make the elephant dance. By GM standards his talk was seditious. Certainly no one at GM before him had ever dared voice such opinions in the open without risking serious career damage. But the GM chairman had said many times that he welcomed Perot's colorful outspokenness. In fact, he appeared to enjoy it.

Seats were reserved for Ross and Margot Perot, not far from Roger and Barbara Smith, at the Saturn celebration dinner at the Westin Hotel in Detroit on February 1, 1985. Perot had suggested the idea of a gala evening to Smith in order to recognize and to honor the top union and company managers and executives who had worked on the project. In a break with GM's corporate traditions, Perot suggested that UAW members and their spouses and the spouses of the Saturn team members also be invited. To symbolize the camaraderie of the Saturn plant floor, Perot urged Smith to do away with the head table and seat everyone on the floor together. It wasn't the first time GM and UAW executives had dined together, but it probably was the first time their wives had met.

Thinking over a request by Smith that he make a presentation at the dinner, Perot came up with what he thought was a brilliant idea: he would distribute copies of a favorite book, *Leadership Secrets of Attila the Hun.* Written by Wess Roberts, a Salt Lake City psychologist, the book treated organizational leadership — a trait woefully lacking at GM, he thought — in an original, readable way. The book theorizes about how Attila might have led his tribe; it is sprinkled with aphorisms of Attila's leadership philosophy. For example: "A chieftain neither dresses nor arms himself at the expense of his Huns. His dress and weaponry may be of subtle distinction as is accepted by custom. Yet, it must never be offensive in cost, adornment, or in ignoble superiority over those he leads, lest they will scorn him." This was Roberts's way of cautioning business executives against exaggerating the splendor of their cars, dress, corporate jets, and dining rooms. Perot thought GM execs were way too concerned with the perks of office, and this was a way to deliver a gentle, inoffensive — but instructive — dig.

Perot, who regularly ate in the EDS cafeteria, frequently traveled on commercial airlines, and carried his own suitcases, identified with Attila. He loved the book and often handed copies to people at EDS.

Perot called Riedlinger in Detroit. "Roger asked me to think of a memento from EDS to distribute at the dinner. I'm going to send you a few hundred copies of *Leadership Secrets of Attila the Hun* and I want you to see that every person at the Saturn dinner has a copy."

Because Roger Smith's staff was organizing the dinner, Riedlinger called the chairman's office to find out how to make sure the books would be distributed. He was asked if he could first send over a copy. No problem, Riedlinger replied.

A few hours later, Riedlinger heard from a GM staffer at fourteenth-floor headquarters. "Mr. Riedlinger, I'm sorry, but this isn't thought to be appropriate material to be handing out at the Saturn dinner."

Perot isn't going to like this, Riedlinger thought. The dinner was Perot's idea in the first place. Smith never would have thought of it. Now Roger's people had taken over and refused to hand out a perfectly inoffensive book. He didn't relish the thought of telling Perot that the fourteenth floor had banned *Attila* from the dinner.

"Well, hell, don't worry about it," Perot finally told Riedlinger. "I'll take care of it."

Perot got no further with Roger Smith's staffers than Riedlinger had. GM didn't like *Attila,* and that was that. Perot knew that he was subtly teasing GM with the book, but in his mind it wasn't malicious or in poor taste. Certainly the incident wasn't serious enough to fight about. But for Perot, the eeriest part of GM's refusal was the fact that a highly paid staff of a $100 billion corporation had time to deliberate over distribution of an eighty-six-page paperback at a banquet.

On the evening of the dinner, Smith was charming and effusively complimentary to the people who worked on Saturn. He distributed the obligatory plaques. Ross Perot presented Smith with a gold watch with an eagle on it. The evening was a lovefest with the auto-workers union. The room was jammed with UAW members, who genuinely were caught up in the spirit of the event. UAW vice president Don Ephlin, often the target of internal union criticism for cooperating with GM, lauded the GM chairman for the courage to pursue his vision, and Smith responded by inviting Ephlin to join him one day in driving the first Saturn car off the line.

When it was Perot's turn to speak, Smith introduced him as the man who, through EDS, was going to help make Saturn a "paperless" corporation and rid Smith's in-box of hated paperwork.

"Say good-bye to the Xerox machines," Smith told the audience. "Say good-bye to all those pieces of paper you don't want and don't give a damn about."

Smith also ribbed Perot good-naturedly about his junior status as a new GM board member, which required him to sit near the end of the table in GM's huge boardroom.

Stepping to the podium, Perot seized the moment to draw attention, ever so subtly, to the significance of the new relationship between salaried and hourly GM workers represented by Saturn. In the Saturn plant the UAW agreed that their members would accept straight weekly salary at 80 percent of normal wage levels and additional payments tied to productivity. It would be the first GM plant without time clocks. In return, GM promised a no-layoff policy. Implied was a greater sense of responsibility and sharing — and an end to the underlying enmity between the people who organized the work and the people whose hands and tools actually built the product.

"I hope that by the time I get to the middle of that table in the boardroom, Roger, if I ever make it and if I don't get thrown off, there will be no such words in our vocabulary as *management* and *labor*," Perot said. Was this a reference to the friction between EDS and GM? If so, Smith wasn't going for the bait. Or was Perot telling Smith he had his eye on his job? Perot was smiling, but was he miffed about *Attila*?

Perot talked about EDS and the close relationship between EDS workers: "We were close and informal as we are tonight. We knew one another, cared about one another." The loudest applause came from the union members in the audience. "I can't wait to see you put Saturn cars on ships and send them overseas." More applause. "You'll have revolutionized the way we work. It will be the thrill of your business careers."

This was a Perot stump talk. The future greatness of U.S. industry lay in the ability to adapt, to change, and to beat foreign competition. He was playing to a very appreciative audience, a fact GM's chairman didn't fail to notice.

"One of the high points of my life and career has been meeting Ross Perot," Smith told the audience when Perot sat down.

The GM executives in the audience, including Al Mair, Alex Cunningham, and Alan Smith, knew that buried beneath Perot's and Smith's cordiality was a real and growing tension between EDS and GM.

*　　*　　*

The enormous expense of Roger Smith's multibillion-dollar vision was intended to be spread over several years. The installments began mushrooming during the spring of 1985. GM's capital costs were estimated at $9 billion for 1985, compared with $6 billion a year earlier. Wall Street analysts studying GM's financial condition weren't overjoyed as they began adding up the cost of EDS, high-tech automation, and a host of capital improvements at car plants. At the very least, GM was going to pay a big penalty in near-term profitability. But as long as the investments paid off further in the future, they reasoned, the outlays weren't bad news.

At the $600 million Detroit-Hamtramck plant, built for the assembly of new-model Cadillac Sevilles and Eldorados, Oldsmobile Toronados, and Buick Rivieras, almost 2,000 programmable computerized devices were ordered for the assembly line, compared with 1,200 devices at GM's next most modern plant. Nearly 400 workers trained in the plant for a year before it opened, at a cost of $40,000 to $50,000 salary per worker, plus training expenses.

At every opportunity Smith was forced to defend the outlays. Automotive reviewers claimed buyers didn't care how cars are made, only about quality and appearance. Smith retorted that it had become fashionable to talk about the shortsightedness of U.S. industry; well, GM was investing in the future. Smith wasn't concerned so much about Wall Street's demand for quarter-to-quarter earnings increases as he was about being number one in the twenty-first century. Indeed, his spending binge wasn't over. For several years Smith had had his eye on Hughes Aircraft, the mammoth aerospace company based near Los Angeles. He had received advance notice from Irving Shapiro, the former Dupont chairman and a trustee of the Hughes Medical Institute, that Hughes was to be sold.

Years earlier Howard Hughes had donated Hughes Aircraft to the medical institute bearing his name rather than sell it to comply with the wishes of the Department of Defense. The IRS, however, wasn't satisfied with the arrangement, under which most of Hughes's profits were plowed back into its operations untaxed, while the institute received a relatively small annual dividend. Finally the IRS demanded that Hughes be sold, and the medical institute hired the Morgan Stanley investment-banking house and its head of investment banking, Bob Greenhill, to conduct an auction.

Smith was absolutely dazzled by Hughes's array of space-age technologies, much as he had been dazzled by EDS's computer expertise. This was the "lulu" he'd been talking about to reporters, a $4 billion or $5 billion purchase that would vault GM into the top ranks of defense contracting, satellite research, and exotic technologies such as lasers and optical imaging. He had to have it. Boeing, Rockwell International, General Electric, Ford, and several others also were interested in the blue-chip maker of missiles, radar, and satellites. (Ironically, Hughes Aircraft hadn't built airplanes for years.) Smith, through Salomon Brothers and outside consultants, let it be known that GM intended to win the auction. Under Morgan Stanley's auction rules, each bidder declared one best and final bid. Greenhill believed the one-bid rule would force the most eager bidder to make a preemptively high offer.

GM's finance committee and the directors, including Ross Perot, approved Smith's preliminary pursuit of Hughes Aircraft. To several directors, Hughes looked like an attractive way for GM to diversify away from the mature car and truck business and into defense and high technology, which had better prospects for growth. Moreover, Smith argued persuasively that Hughes possessed scientific and electronic skills that would be useful to automotive designers. He told directors about holographic or so-called heads-up displays for jet-fighter pilots that might be adapted to cars. He rhapsodized about Hughes laser systems that one day might notify drivers when an unseen object strayed into their path.

Ross Perot listened to Smith's reasoning. From what he had seen in his first year inside GM, executives and managers at the operating level were having enough trouble absorbing EDS without throwing another acquisition into their lap. Besides, GM needed to pay much more attention to improving its current lines of automobiles than to developing space-age gadgets for them. Since the merger, he had received a torrent of mail from unhappy GM customers who claimed their cars didn't work properly and GM couldn't fix them. Perot called some of the letter writers and talked to GM dealers in Dallas. He asked people from EDS to check. His research confirmed that GM was having terrible problems with poor-quality cars being released for shipment and, in particular, design and manufacturing errors that resulted in many bad transmissions and engines.

Moreover, Meyerson's and Riedlinger's experience in the GM organization showed that GM managers weren't anxious to learn from strange technologies or alien cultures. Perot knew that the rocket scientists from California were a breed as different from Detroit automotive engineers as both were different from EDS's gung-ho systems engineers. Hughes Aircraft was bound to be just another giant and expensive distraction from the task of making great cars, Perot thought, one more way to spend money rather than to roll up our sleeves and clean up the mess.

Although Perot wasn't crazy about Hughes in early 1985, his concerns hadn't crystallized into active opposition, and certainly not if it meant a confrontation with Smith. The other directors seemed willing to pursue Hughes, so he'd go along for the time being.

In early 1985 EDS managers for the second time prepared a list of recommended stock incentive grants to be awarded to EDS workers for 1984. Tom Walter had sent the first list to the GM treasurer's office in New York, but nothing happened.

By historical standards the awards were generous; not outlandish, the managers thought, but reflective of the enormous personal discomforts many EDS families had gone through during the jolting moves from Dallas to Detroit and to other GM installations around the country. EDS workers had been breaking their backs, in hostile conditions similar to what Meyerson and Riedlinger were experiencing, to make the merger work.

Twenty million Class E shares, about ten years' worth of awards, had been legally set aside for key EDS workers under the merger agreement. But weeks went by with no response after Mort Meyerson sent the suggested awards to the GM treasurer's office. Meyerson called Perot in March to tell him EDS managers were beginning to wonder why the stock awards weren't confirmed.

Perot had been calling Smith more and more frequently about operating conflicts between EDS managers and GM executives. During one of these calls, he mentioned that compensation questions hadn't been decided either. It was a problem. The morale of EDS was at stake, Perot told Smith; moreover, Perot had made a personal commitment to Meyerson and others that their people were going to be taken care of.

Was it necessary to promise Meyerson one percent of EDS's profits? Smith wanted to know. It seemed excessive.

Meyerson doesn't expect that, Perot told Smith. Our salary agreement predates the merger, he said. Mort agrees the numbers don't make sense now. But we've got to establish some salary for him, something reasonable that takes into account how vital he is to us.

"Roger, I've made these commitments to Mort and to my people, and if I've got to reach into my own pocket, I'll do it. But I want you to know I expect GM to honor its commitments," Perot said.

Well, Ross, I'll look into this and we'll let you know, Smith told him.

When Perot called Roger Smith again a few weeks later to ask for a decision, Smith invited him to Detroit. An icy chill still entombed the city when Perot, Bill Gayden, and Tom Walter arrived for the meeting. GM's executive dining room was closed, so Smith ordered sandwiches for the group. He was very cordial, but he set straight to the task at hand, withdrawing EDS's list of proposed stock awards from a file drawer. He ran his finger down the list, asking why several individuals were receiving the number of shares proposed. He didn't disagree. He didn't agree. Smith seemed interested in the details of the plan, not the principles that lay behind it. The meeting broke up quickly.

"I'll have to check back with Greg Lau and let you know," Smith said. "We'll be back in touch soon." Lau was the assistant treasurer in charge of GM's compensation plans.

Perot, Gayden, and Walter discussed the GM chairman's reaction on the flight back to Dallas: it looked as though Smith didn't want to award the shares because they represented too much compensation, yet he didn't know how to say no. Walter was astonished that Smith was prepared to engender bad feeling by delaying and dissembling; if he didn't like it, why not just say no?

EDS's compensation plan directly contradicted Smith's perception of status and propriety at GM. He may have been known as an innovative and creative thinker, but he possessed a strong traditional streak as well. EDS workers who dealt with GM's New York treasurer's office had heard gossip and relayed it to Dallas: Smith and other top GM executives were furious that already wealthy EDS executives stood to earn more than GM counterparts by virtue of the lavish stock incentives awards. Perot wasn't the problem. He earned $68,000 a year and didn't qualify for the incentives. But Meyerson's annual salary, $712,000 the year before, plus stock and bonuses, put him in the same league as Smith, and Smith didn't like it.

"Look, Tom," Perot finally said to Tom Walter a few weeks after the meeting with Smith. "Just pay Mort through January according to his old formula. As for the stock plan, we'll get this thing straightened out somehow."

We'll get things straightened out. Increasingly, that was Perot's response to EDS's battles with GM.

In his thirty-year career as a lawyer representing public corporations and specializing in securities law, Elmer Johnson had learned the value of thinking defensively. Time after time, huge and supposedly sophisticated public corporations had called on him and on Kirkland and Ellis, his law firm, to defend them against legal actions by shareholders angry about poor management, faulty disclosure of material information, and, on occasion, malfeasance and gross criminality. Shareholders, through their lawyers, attacked the companies he had represented, saying: You in management and on the board should have known about the problems and done something.

In a way, they were right. Corporate law generally protects the officers and directors of publicly held companies from shareholder litigation as long as they can prove they made a loyal, good-faith effort to review major decisions and keep an eye on the store. It's called the Business Judgment Rule. Decisions might have been incredibly dumb or ineffective, but they are rarely illegal in the eyes of the law. What is important in court is being able to prove that you thought about the issue and acted in a way you thought was good for the company.

When officers and directors fail to think about obvious problems or fail to act forcefully, the Elmer Johnsons of the world have a much tougher job. Defending against skillfully executed shareholder actions was tough work and could be incredibly embarrassing to the corporation. The shareholders didn't win very often. When they did, management's reputation often was permanently stained.

Elmer Johnson had been around long enough to know a potential lawsuit when he saw one. And he saw a big one at GM when he looked at the Class E stock shares issued to the public and to the members of EDS's management as payment in the merger. Under the provisions of the merger agreement, GM had agreed to give EDS an exclusive contract for all its computer business and agreed to be charged standard commercial prices for the work. It looked like a terrific deal for the Class E shareholders: fed by GM's billions in computer outlays, EDS revenue and profit could only soar, fueling the price of Class E stock. But was the arrangement beneficial for holders of GM's common stock? True, GM owned 100 percent of EDS and, thus, benefited from EDS profits. GM also owned a great deal of Class E stock, which tracked EDS's profitability; thus GM benefited from higher Class E stock prices.

However, holders of GM common stock might argue convincingly that GM's management had signed a sweetheart deal with Ross Perot instead of buying the most cost-efficient computer services. Might not holders of GM common stock argue that GM's profits were being funneled into the pockets of Class E holders to the detriment of common-stock holders?

There was no way to prevent lawsuits — GM currently was party to about 25,000 of them — but there were ways to get ready for them if they appeared. That foresight, Elmer Johnson believed, was a general counsel's highest calling.

Early in 1985 Johnson invited Ira Millstein, a senior partner of Weil, Gotshal and Manges, to lunch with him and GM's associate general counsel, Paul Zalecki, in New York. Millstein had attracted Johnson's attention with his vigorous — and ultimately successful — defense in a shareholder lawsuit against GM directors over alleged brake defects in GM's X-body line of midsize cars such as the Chevrolet Citation. In the face of Millstein's defense, the lawsuit was thrown out of court inside of six months. Millstein's law firm, coincidentally a tenant in the GM Building in New York, owned a sterling reputation for legal work on behalf of corporate managements and boards of directors.

At lunch, the three lawyers discussed ways to ensure that all shareholders, Class E and common, were treated fairly and equally. An important issue for Johnson, although he had heard of the disagreements over compensation and other matters, was so-called transfer pricing — a classic problem in a company whose divisions buy from one another. How should EDS's prices be determined so that both classes of shareholders were treated fairly? Could the lawyers perhaps devise a formula to determine fair prices?

With a method of ensuring fair treatment, the lawyers might head off conflict and protect themselves against future legal action. (The lawyers knew that their task was sure to be further complicated when GM bought Hughes Aircraft, since Roger Smith and Salomon Brothers already were talking about issuing a third class of GM common stock to pay for the acquisition.)

Johnson, Millstein, and Zalecki concluded at lunch that GM's board probably needed a special committee of directors whose job it would be to review GM's relationship with EDS. Millstein agreed to study the matter, put his thoughts and recommendations on paper, and report back to GM.

Two decades earlier, when government had been more interested in stopping business from becoming too strong, Millstein specialized in antitrust work. But as antitrust enforcement waned and businesses began worrying about weakness rather than strength, Millstein turned increasingly to the field of corporate governance, which in practice meant acting as outside counsel to top management and directors. As his experience grew richer, he also taught corporate governance at Yale, Harvard, and Columbia.

A lifelong New Yorker, Millstein remembered Perot from the days of Dupont Walston. Perot had been the Dallas Cowboy, galloping up to New York to make Dupont a showcase brokerage, to show people in the securities business that they didn't know what they were doing. At one point during Perot's problems at Dupont, rival Wall Street securities executives seemed to Perot to be conspiring to freeze Dupont out of lucrative syndications and underwritings and to steal his top-producing brokers. Perot was furious. Dupont consulted Millstein about legal action, but ultimately he decided against it.

The corporate boardroom, like Wall Street, was a club, a damned exclusive one, with rules written and unwritten. Elmer Johnson didn't have to explain to Millstein the obvious tensions between a man like Ross Perot and GM executives. Millstein immediately detected the undercurrents of what was going on between Perot and GM. Perot didn't bother himself much about club rules, Millstein knew. It was a problem, one bound to cause trouble at a place like GM.

Shortly after the GM deal had closed, Perot had received a telephone call from a friend in Dallas who knew he was interested in historical memorabilia. Ross, the friend said, you won't believe what's for sale. One of the four original copies of the Magna Carta. Signed by King John of England in 1215, the document was a model for the cause of democratic government and individual liberty.

This was the ultimate historical document, the Dead Sea Scroll of western democracy. What a magnificent treasure to own! For Perot, this was equal to a lover of fine painting being offered the Mona Lisa.

Perot called on Tom Luce, who deepened his understanding of the Magna Carta's significance by reading Churchill's *History of the English-Speaking Peoples*. The lawyer then consulted with Decherd Turner, a library curator of the University of Texas. They advised Perot to go for it. The two men flew to Great Britain with Perot's authorization to pay $1.5 million if the document was authentic.

Turner confirmed that the copy was authentic, and Luce turned over Perot's check. With the Magna Carta pressed in a glassed picture frame and wrapped in brown paper, Luce left for home. On landing in Dallas, he was asked by a customs agent if he had anything to declare.

"Oh, just the Magna Carta," was his deadpan reply.

"Okay, sir, thank you very much," said the agent, winking at him.

(The historic piece of parchment was displayed at the Bicentennial celebration of the U.S. Constitution and later put on permanent exhibition at the National Archives.)

During the Magna Carta acquisition, Perot kept Luce informed about his and EDS's mounting frustration that GM wasn't living up to the merger agreement. Luce wasn't the type of lawyer who favored immediate confrontation. He was convinced that a solution existed, but because he hadn't had much direct contact with people from GM, he needed to understand their perception of the conflict.

Luce called Elmer Johnson, GM's top lawyer and, by now, a group vice president in charge of operating staffs. Johnson clearly held authority over GM's legal staff and was a rising, though largely unnoticed, power in the corporate hierarchy.

"Tom, I've been concerned ever since the merger about the potential legal problems posed by multiple classes of common stock. We may be very vulnerable to challenges by holders of GM common who think we're unfairly favoring GM Class E holders. Or, vice versa, Perot and other Class E holders might think we're favoring holders of regular GM common," Johnson said. "I've asked Ira Millstein at Weil Gotshal to look into some ideas, but I think we're going to recommend to Roger a special committee of outside, non-GM directors to oversee the GM and EDS relationship. It will deal with Hughes Class H stock as well."

This seems like an eminently sensible approach, Luce thought. By having outside directors, in effect, pass on any conflicts between GM and EDS, neither side will be able to put its own self-interest into the argument. They'll be able to decide what's right based on the merger agreement. It's a reasonable compromise, and it just may work. If it doesn't, Luce thought, we're still covered. The merger contract looks airtight. Besides, Ross has the facsimile memos containing Roger's personal guarantees.

Luce had been surprised (and pleased) to read the fax memos, reconfirming everything EDS wanted. He hadn't a clue how Perot had managed to convince Smith to put it all down like that in writing. If the misunderstandings didn't go away soon, it would be most helpful to have the documents.

FOURTEEN

From Vision to Reality

WITHIN months of EDS's arrival in Detroit, a few hundred GM data processing workers, incensed by their forced transfer to EDS, petitioned the United Auto Workers union for affiliation. EDS hadn't found permanent quarters in Detroit, had barely unpacked its bags, and an organizing effort was under way.

Horrified at the prospect of a union inside EDS (it had never happened in EDS's twenty-two-year history), Ken Riedlinger set out to find the toughest and most skillful anti-union counsel in the country to blunt the organizers.

Within a few weeks, several law firms with nationwide reputations for dueling with organized labor sent experts to Detroit to help EDS plot strategy for the defeat of the UAW. The first step, the lawyers advised, was a letter from Riedlinger to GM's 7,000 data processors announcing EDS's intention to resist the union. The tersely worded message accused a band of malcontents of stirring up trouble.

The letter, composed by the lawyers and sent out over Riedlinger's signature, only fanned the flames of ill feeling and suspicion against EDS. GM executives and managers, who resented the merger for numerous reasons, added another grievance to the list: EDS was insensitive, upsetting the company's delicate relationship with the UAW.

In early January, in an attempt to soothe the raw feelings, Riedlinger mailed a second letter to all GM data processors transferring to EDS, suggesting that everyone try a fresh start based on mutual respect and understanding. He apologized for conveying an attitude that might have been interpreted as arrogant or uncaring.

Riedlinger wasn't backing down from the fight against the union, just softening his rhetoric. He had never meant to sound so strident. His theory was to stay low-key and quell rumors and gossip. He wanted GM workers to understand that they had nothing to fear from EDS. Quite the contrary: EDS could offer them professional opportunities they had never had before. He had been telling GM managers not to worry about EDS's dress codes; they only applied in locations where EDS workers needed to be unobtrusive. Obviously, if GM data processors were getting along well where they worked, they were to dress as they usually did. EDS didn't tolerate any kind of drug use or drinking during working hours, but Riedlinger told people he didn't intend to enforce rules against cohabitation. He had more important things to do than check where everyone slept at night.

As was often the case with large contracts, EDS decided not to enforce the requirement that new workers from GM sign an employment contract and ethics code promising to abide by the rules and refrain from competing with the company for three years after leaving.

Because of his more liberal approach, Riedlinger was concerned that Perot and Meyerson would banish him for going soft. He tried to persuade Meyerson to sign a memo showing he agreed with the concept of dropping employment agreements for GM workers. The memo might protect him later if Perot got angry. Meyerson tore it up.

Riedlinger felt increasingly bitter and unappreciated. Perot and Meyerson didn't have to wrestle with Smith and the other GM executives on a daily basis as he did, he thought. In his view, Perot was hiding out in Dallas and Mort wasn't spending more than a couple of days a week in Detroit. Their anger at his anti-union letter didn't really surprise him. Perot and Meyerson couldn't fathom the GM workers' paranoia and hatred of EDS and of their own management for sending them to EDS. Perot and Meyerson didn't understand the tenuous labor situation in the auto industry. Hundreds of thousands of UAW workers were needed every day for the assembly of GM cars and trucks. The last thing GM wanted was Ross Perot's and EDS's anti-union philosophy to spark a labor war.

(In fact, Perot and Meyerson met with new GM data processors, fifty at a time, until they had talked to more than a thousand of them, in an attempt to explain the EDS philosophy and to soothe their feelings.)

Despite his difficulties with GM and his feeling that his bosses at EDS didn't understand him, Riedlinger was doggedly set on making the merger work. This was the biggest data processing job in the world, the biggest job of his life. Meyerson and Perot were incredibly naive, he thought; they could never understand the scale or complexity of a place like GM until they lived inside the beast. They only knew how to second-guess him and make unreasonable demands, causing him further troubles with GM. Over the past ten years he had worn the mantle of Attila, because toughness and tenacity were expected of him. Now Riedlinger's doubts were growing. The hard-driving routine he had honed made him increasingly uncomfortable. He felt the discomfort each day as a new batch of hate mail arrived at his office from GM workers. The tire slashings didn't let up. GM workers *should* be apprehensive, he thought. But if they'll quit beating on me, maybe I can help them find a way to get along under the EDS umbrella.

Mired in their own merger problems, Perot and Meyerson weren't completely aware of the impact the conflicts were having on Riedlinger. Later, when he would have a chance to reflect on what happened to Riedlinger during this period in Detroit, Perot would conclude that he and Meyerson had made a mistake in selecting him for the job. In this case, Riedlinger's tenacity wasn't serving him — or EDS — well.

For its part, GM clearly had underestimated — or hadn't thought through — the difficulty of persuading its computer people to transfer to EDS. Roger Smith first suggested that GM workers move to EDS but remain covered by GM pay scales and benefits. Perot promptly vetoed the idea. Nothing would destroy EDS's esprit faster than having two classes of workers with two tiers of compensation. So Smith agreed in January to placate GM's disgruntled data processing workers with money. Those who gave up more lavish GM benefits to transfer to EDS were compensated with a one-time award of up to $15,000 worth of Class E stock. In return, they promised to forgo all transfer-related lawsuits against GM and EDS.

Older GM workers close to retirement who didn't want to lose their GM pensions were permitted to go on inactive layoff for two years and then retire with full benefits. Workers with enough seniority were entitled to a sweetened severance package from GM if they chose; about 600 of the 7,000 data processors took it.

The incipient labor revolt was settled by compromise. In bygone days

EDS well might have fired the uncooperative workers. In extreme cases Ross Perot was willing to sever relations with a client who didn't live up to the agreements. Neither of those options was possible this time, for EDS's client also was its owner.

For the first time in his career Mort Meyerson felt as if he were trapped in a maze without an escape. The GM relationship was floundering before it began. EDS executives charged with making it work, Ken Riedlinger and the others, were killing themselves working night and day. They hadn't been bred or trained for the schizophrenic nature of EDS's role as supplier, computer consultant, and independent subsidiary of GM. They had never encountered such an inherently conflicted arrangement and, quite frankly, neither had Meyerson.

In the good old days, EDS managers who ran into roadblocks with their clients turned to Dallas headquarters for succor and counsel. EDS executives gave their managers a lot of responsibility; they expected them to perform swiftly and to deliver results. Meyerson and the higher-ups in Dallas acted as buffers and release valves. They absorbed heat from the client, evaluating what was legitimate complaint and what were the cries of internal data processing managers about to lose their turf. Meyerson's job was to be a higher authority, to back local EDS managers so that they were able to fulfill the contract with as little interference as possible.

At GM, Meyerson suddenly discovered that he lacked the power he needed to back Riedlinger and the EDS team. Smith's early promise to name him a vice president of GM simply evaporated. Riedlinger and the other EDS managers sensed his diminished power and it made them nervous. Meyerson detected the mounting tension in their voices and in their behavior. It wasn't just Riedlinger. During a video conference in February 1985, EDS vice president Kenn Hill, a former helicopter pilot who had been wounded in Vietnam, exploded at Meyerson when the EDS president told him more help wasn't available to send to Detroit. Hill rarely, if ever, raised his voice.

Meyerson, the institutional safety valve, wasn't able to help. The situation wasn't healthy. He had to find some way to make GM more receptive, if for no other reason than to protect EDS managers like Riedlinger and Hill from self-destructing out of sheer frustration.

Meyerson's attempts at breaking the logjam at GM using personal diplomacy weren't promising. He faced undisguised resentment in most of the business meetings with GM division executives. As might be expected, the GM executives believed that EDS was poaching on their turf.

At Perot's urging, Smith called several meetings to order executives to be more cooperative. Nothing seemed to help.

The GM executives undoubtedly were embarrassed when EDS pointed out that they were wasting millions on inefficient purchasing. Riedlinger had found an IBM 3081 processor that was being rented for $68,890 a month; over twenty-two months it cost GM $1.5 million, and yet GM could have bought the machine outright for $1.24 million. Another IBM 3081 processor was costing $166,640 a month in lease payments: GM had spent $3.5 million on a machine whose original price was $3.1 million, and it still was worth $1.6 million. Not only were these contracts wasteful, but Meyerson was receiving reports that some were sweetheart deals with ex-GM employees and friends of current employees.

Then there were the drugs. Meyerson received a steady stream of reports from EDS managers about cocaine and marijuana use at GM computer installations. A GM data center in Ohio was reputed to be a particular trouble spot. He didn't know the facts, but the situation demanded investigation. GM's vital storehouse of information was too sensitive to leave in the hands of irresponsible or venal people. He ordered an investigation by EDS's private security agents. GM, meanwhile, refused to turn over personnel records indicating which workers might have drug problems. Meyerson had no intention of firing or harassing workers if they were getting treatment, but he also didn't intend to promote them to positions of responsibility without knowing whether they presented a danger.

When he wasn't stamping out brushfires, Meyerson searched for ways to keep the tenor of EDS's relationship with GM positive. He suggested ways to economize. He showed how EDS was able to integrate existing computer systems and establish new ones. Most GM executives and managers, except for a few like Don Atwood at the Truck and Bus Group, resisted EDS at every turn, pointing out EDS's relative inexperience in scientific and engineering computing.

The expansive use of computer technology and the integration of existing systems — Roger Smith's dream — called for far greater spending than previously by most GM divisions. In order to draw a detailed blueprint for fulfilling the dream, EDS managers first needed to know what equipment was owned and how much it cost.

GM's comptrollers resisted this invasion of their bailiwicks. No supplier or consultant had ever been given a breakdown of GM's costs.

GM rarely signed long-term fixed-price contracts, which were specified in the merger agreement. GM's way was to shop among several sources, find the best deal, and retain the option to renegotiate the price on a regular basis. Because of its size, GM exercised considerable clout over supplier profit margins. Indeed, GM held life-and-death power over some of its suppliers.

As the GM finance men read the situation, Smith had paid $2.5 billion to make EDS an in-house computer consultant and supplier, with the promise of guaranteed long-term contracts. It completely undercut finance's power to control costs. EDS virtually dictated contract terms. The higher outlays for EDS computer software systems promised lower divisional operating profits, which certainly was going to reflect badly on their financial targets and their year-end bonuses. EDS claimed the newer, expensive systems improved overall productivity and saved money; and, in any case, EDS profits resulted in value gains through the GM Class E stock that GM owned, an idea GM comptrollers didn't accept.

There was something terribly wrong here, the finance men began to say amongst themselves. After all, we bought EDS, not the other way around. We should be getting preferential — not premium — prices. How dare EDS dictate to us what we're going to spend on computers? What's to prevent them from ripping us off? They were astonished that Smith, with his supposed financial acumen, had been lured into a sucker's deal by Perot's Texas Rangers. Hadn't Roger thought this through? Didn't it occur to him how it was going to play out in real life?

At first Meyerson believed that a few telephone calls from Smith to division vice presidents would be enough to stifle the grumbling. Smith had promised Perot in writing to bring everyone on board. As a newcomer to large corporations, Meyerson didn't entirely grasp the concept of malicious obedience. No one dared disobey the chief executive's direct orders, yet any GM executive worth his salt knew how to subvert orders with red tape or how to slow them into oblivion by literal, but inappropriate, following of directions.

Smith was only Smith; he was one person. GM, on the other hand, was a vast empire, with plants spread near and far. If a single accountant in GM's Van Nuys, California, Camaro plant decided to impede EDS's progress in installing automation systems, Smith wasn't going to hear about it, and there certainly wasn't much he could do anyway.

"It's like ordering soldiers not to smoke in line," Smith once explained apologetically to Meyerson. "You know that as soon as you turn around they're going to light up."

It was tough at first for Meyerson to grasp that Roger Smith didn't have the power to push a button and make something happen in his own company. At EDS there had always been disagreement and fighting. But when a decision was reached, everyone marched in one direction. No one dared disobey Perot or Meyerson if they dispensed an order.

The peculiarities of Detroit's automotive culture and GM's massive size made Meyerson feel like a fish out of water. For the first time in his business career he wondered whether his Jewish religious identity might be complicating attempts to deal with GM. He had met few Jews since coming to GM, and he had heard that the automotive industry didn't employ many. In fact, he didn't see as many minorities in positions of real power as he saw in Dallas or New York; there were, it seemed to him, few blacks, few Hispanics, few women. Ninety-five percent of the people he dealt with at GM were like Smith, middle-aged white men from the Midwest.

Since he had arrived in Detroit, no one from GM had invited Meyerson to dinner or to their homes. That seemed odd. He and Perot entertained scores of clients, including many from GM, at their homes in Dallas. No one at GM seemed much interested in the fact that he was thousands of miles from his home, wife, and children and might appreciate a little warmth and hospitality.

He was more appalled that no one at GM seemed interested in extending personal courtesies and perquisites to help him carry out his work more easily. Meyerson assumed that a company that leased or passed out thousands of new cars to white-collar workers (whether or not they traveled as part of their jobs) might be able to provide a car for him so that he could go from Newark Airport to Armonk, New York, to negotiate a volume discount on IBM computer equipment. Every GM executive he had met had access to a car and a heated garage where an attendant filled the gas tank daily and buffed the car to a sparkling shine. Yet, incredibly, Meyerson was informed by an assistant in the office of GM treasurer Courtney Jones that there wasn't a car available for him.

Meyerson reported the details of his cool reception to Perot. EDS's founder was angry. He was aware, of course, that Meyerson hadn't wanted the deal with GM after the blowup with Smith but was breaking his neck to make the merger work out of loyalty.

When Perot mentioned Meyerson's social ostracism to Smith, the GM chairman explained that he shouldn't take it personally because GM executives rarely entertained one another. (In other words, Perot thought, you treat one another coldly as a matter of course.) As for providing a car for Meyerson in New York, Smith told Perot he'd see what he could do. Nothing happened.

Out of the blue, Smith invited Meyerson a few weeks later to dinner at Bloomfield Hills Country Club. The evening was pleasant, but Meyerson assumed Roger was simply attempting to placate Perot, a triumph of form over substance, Meyerson thought glumly.

At his first GM board meeting in the summer of 1984, Ross Perot announced to directors that he intended to be an advocate for GM's customers, shareholders, dealers, and workers. He was assigned to the board's public policy subcommittee, a relatively unimportant board committee, compared to the powerful executive and finance committees. He resented his assignment. Again, he didn't make an issue of it with Smith. In his opinion, he should have been placed where important strategic and financial decisions were made. First of all, his stake in GM amounted to more than 11 million Class E shares, or about 0.8 percent of the voting power. No one else on GM's board had remotely as large a financial interest as he did in the corporation's success. Smith himself had managed to amass a paltry 26,574 GM common shares in his thirty-six-year career.

At several public gatherings following the merger, the news media asked Perot whether he one day hoped to take over as GM chairman, a plausible question since at age fifty-five he was five years younger than Smith, who was scheduled to retire in 1990 at age sixty-five.

No, Perot answered again and again, he and his family liked their lives just fine in Dallas. Besides, he couldn't think of a better way to spend the rest of his life than working as a GM director and through EDS to help GM make the world's best cars at the lowest prices. Only by producing the best cars were the hundreds of thousands of American working men and women assured of future employment. Perot was a bit embarrassed by the questions and told Smith so.

Smith just laughed and claimed he didn't mind: "These [GM] people need to be shaken up a bit."

What did Perot know about cars that qualified him to "help" GM? Automotive journalists asked him the question, probing his presumption about being able to cure Detroit's ills. Not much, he answered. He knew the basics of business; they were the same in a Pittsburgh car dealer's showroom as in a Texarkana corral: if you don't produce the best product at the lowest cost, you'll soon be losing jobs to those who do.

His words to GM directors were more than rhetoric. What he had learned so far suggested to him that Smith and GM — and, therefore, American working people — needed plenty of help to become competitive. He loved Smith's creativity. Smith was no mere accountant; he looked for the unobvious answers, a trait he had always prized in Mort. But creativity wasn't enough. GM's far-flung, logy bulk troubled Perot. Every corner of GM was a well-defended feudal fiefdom, divided by turf struggles between and among GM divisions. Bureaucratic inertia frustrated Smith, too. He vowed to stop it, but nothing worked. He felt like Harry Truman, who had joked about the panel of buttons on his desk that weren't connected to anything.

Smith showed some signs of willingness to let Perot help. In early 1985 he asked Perot to evaluate a small company. Comau Productivity Systems (CPS) was a U.S. subsidiary of Fiat, the Italian carmaker, that specialized in automation projects for automotive assembly lines. Lloyd Reuss, then vice president and group executive in charge of the Chevrolet-Pontiac-GM Canada car group (CPC) wanted to invest in CPS.

Ken Riedlinger set up a dinner for Perot and the Comau executives at Oakland Hills Country Club in Birmingham, a suburb north of Detroit. Since EDS was increasingly supplying the computers and people for GM's automation projects, Riedlinger tagged along to the dinner.

Perot's interviewing style was informal. He "visited" for a few minutes and then invited the Comau executives to explain, without charts or esoteric language, the nature of their business and the benefit to GM. As Riedlinger listened, he kept his eye on his boss, watching as Perot grew increasingly annoyed at the presentation by the Comau people. The facial signs and body language were subtle, but Riedlinger had worked for Perot long enough to recognize them. The people from Comau explained that they intended to use GM's capital investment in their company to hire engineers. Comau's technology didn't sound like anything special to Perot, who admittedly had only limited knowledge of industrial automation. Neither EDS executive was able to understand why Reuss and CPC wanted to invest in Comau. Why not hire Comau and have it work on automation with EDS? That way automation expertise resided in EDS, as envisioned by the merger.

One of the Comau executives boasted to Perot of his company's worldwide experience, including an automation project in Russia. Riedlinger cringed. Did this guy imagine that Perot the superpatriot was going to be impressed by the fact that Comau had helped the Russians?

The next day Perot called Smith to tell him that he thought investing in

Comau was a terrible idea. Smith thanked Perot warmly for taking the time to give him an assessment.

The next time Perot heard of Comau was on the day GM announced the acquisition of a 20 percent stake.

For Meyerson, the ides of March 1985 was an appropriate time to inform GM's chairman of how seriously conditions were deteriorating between the two companies. The incident that prompted the meeting with Smith was relatively insignificant, but it ate at Meyerson. During a chance meeting with an acquaintance in California, he heard that a high-ranking official of GM's Delco Electronics subsidiary was bad-mouthing EDS to a GM supplier.

"If you expect us to kill ourselves to fulfill your vision, then our teammates must pursue the same vision," he told Smith. "This is like working with the KGB. We don't know who our friends are and who our enemies are. Roger, I can't do this job unless we can agree on some fundamental changes," Meyerson told him, peering out over the frozen March cityscape of northern Detroit visible from Roger's fourteenth-floor suite.

Smith listened with complete composure. There had been no repeat of the tantrum, and Meyerson decided, in order to be as effective as possible, to try and put the episode far from his memory.

Meyerson told Smith that he was fed up with GM managers actively subverting the agreement, with the abuse, the lack of personal courtesies, the negative attitudes.

"After nine months on the job, there's still no feeling of camaraderie among EDS and GM data processing people. There's very little team-work," Meyerson said. "The lower-level people apparently are getting their signals from the executive ranks, most of whom oppose the deal and actively subvert it. That translates to constant negative attitudes as you go down the organizational ladder.

"EDS people are abused and belittled wherever they go. Riedlinger, Jeff Heller, and others are getting threatening and obscene telephone calls at their homes. They're being harassed by people, obviously from GM, who have smashed car windows, slashed tires, and ordered all kinds of unwanted merchandise. We've had to hire security people to watch Riedlinger's house."

The UAW's organizing effort got a big boost when someone at GM sent a magnetic tape with all the names and addresses of GM data processing workers to the union, Meyerson told Smith.

On the business side, Meyerson explained, GM's use of computers was shortsighted and wasteful and had to be corrected. GM had given away ownership and marketing rights to computer software systems it had paid to have developed, which meant that EDS couldn't resell them. The ability to resell systems had been a fundamental principle of the merger and one of EDS's main opportunities for growth.

Instead of being grateful when EDS managed to reverse an unfavorable $7 million software pact with IBM, GM purchasing and operating managers complained of interference.

"I'm convinced the resistance we're getting is partially connected to all kinds of sweetheart deals I hear rumors about between GM and ex-GMers running leasing companies," Meyerson said. "Every time we try to do something about it, we find we're treading on protected area and it turns into a b.s. political fight.

"Roger, our people are getting worn out. No one has said a word of praise about the $120 million EDS saved GM by consolidating purchases of equipment and software or about the great work our people have done in the Baltimore van plant."

He brought up Smith's efforts to trim capital outlays for computer systems and data centers. EDS wanted GM to apportion $6 billion of its $36 billion in capital outlays over the next five years for data centers, telecommunications equipment, new computers, satellites.

"There's no way for EDS to win. We're in competition with the operating groups for capital dollars," he told Smith. "We cannot and will not fight with our customers."

Smith attempted to alleviate Meyerson's concerns. It was too much to expect, he said, given the circumstances, for everyone to welcome EDS immediately with open arms. Change came slowly at GM. He and EDS must be patient.

The GM chairman cleared his throat. A big reason for GM's hostility to EDS, Smith told Meyerson, might be connected to Riedlinger. He was alienating GM managers with steamroller tactics. The anti-union letter he sent was a disaster. He was getting into fights everywhere he went.

Meyerson wasn't sure. He had seen Riedlinger in action. On balance, Riedlinger's aggressiveness was a greater tool than a handicap, he believed. Meyerson had attempted to control Riedlinger's aggressiveness over the last decade with varying degrees of success. When Riedlinger was on one of his highs, very few people were able to match his energy or his inventiveness. When he was low, in one of his black tempers, he needed to be reined in or slapped down. Perot had wanted to fire him a couple of times, despite all his achievements, because he had been too abrupt or grating with EDS colleagues. Meyerson always smoothed things over.

Meyerson defended Riedlinger because he saw how valuable he was when his emotions were in check. If people didn't make mistakes now and then, they weren't taking the kinds of business risks they should be taking. Riedlinger's mistakes were mistakes born of zeal. Most of EDS's top executives, including himself, at one point or another had made blunders that might have ended their careers at other companies. Each one later was able to succeed in the long run because the triumphs were bigger and more numerous than the failures.

He would warn Riedlinger to cool it.

Bonus day always was an exciting, nerve-wracking event at Salomon Brothers, and this year Steve McClellan was particularly keyed up. A year earlier McClellan, a research analyst, had begun channeling his intimate and detailed knowledge of EDS to Salomon's investment-banking partners. The close personal contacts at a company were the most valuable assets he or any researcher possessed, and EDS unquestionably was his favorite company, his pet. Being asked to work with Salomon's investment-banking team to sell EDS to GM was the pinnacle of McClellan's career. Research analysts don't always get opportunities to play near center stage. Salomon's bankers, Bob Scully and Jerry Rosenfeld, said they had needed him to pitch EDS to GM. He was skeptical at first, perhaps a bit wary of aiding in the sale of a company that clearly thrived on independence. But, by God, it had worked! EDS was sold with the agreement to preserve its independence and to issue its own class of stock.

Now came time to divvy up the rewards. As at most Wall Street firms, success at Salomon wasn't measured by titles or perks, but by money. Unquestionably, the GM-EDS merger was a highlight of the firm's very profitable year and was ballyhooed as such in the 1984 annual report. Somewhat reserved by nature, McClellan took Scully aside in December to ask him to make sure the partners who passed on bonuses realized what a key role he had played. Salomon was no different from any other company; particularly among the bankers, office politics played a part in deciding who was permitted near the feeding trough and how richly he ate. The researchers normally were seen as supporting actors; how often they were right about stocks was important, but they rarely were rewarded like the bankers. Scully promised he would remind the right people about McClellan's special contribution.

Salomon had earned a $7.5 million investment-banking fee for the EDS merger. Moreover, Salomon gained the considerable prestige of having handled a major financial transaction for GM, which brought with it the probability of future GM business. Customarily, year-end bonuses reflected, in part, key participation in high-fee transactions. Naturally, Scully and Rosenfeld deserved the lion's share of the spoils, McClellan reasoned. They stood directly beside Roger Smith and Courtney Jones during the action. They were the stars; he was cast in a supporting role, albeit a very important one. He hadn't any doubt that without the insights — his insights — gathered during a decade of meetings with Ross Perot, Mort Meyerson, and the others at EDS, there would not have been a deal. Without him, Roger Smith might never have considered EDS's unusual corporate culture and esprit. Indeed, the EDS idea might never have been proposed. McClellan had conferred directly with F. Alan Smith, GM's top finance man, spinning out the details of EDS's contracts and business methods, knowledge of which neither Scully nor Rosenfeld possessed.

From what McClellan gleaned from his colleagues at the firm, he expected to earn at least 1 percent of Salomon's fee as a bonus; 10 percent wasn't unheard-of. Last year he had earned $200,000, including his year-end bonus. This year, his bonus from GM-EDS was bound to push him to $300,000.

Bonuses sometimes compose as much as two-thirds of a person's annual salary. All of the firm's several thousand employees, from lowliest secretaries to senior partners, were cycled into their supervisors' offices at three-minute intervals on bonus day. No matter what you thought you were worth in a particular year, you didn't really know until the moment of truth in the boss's office. Later on, when the checks were passed out, everyone rushed downstairs to the banks with large lump-sum payments in order not to lose so much as a day's interest, which for the bankers might amount to several hundred dollars. The Chase Manhattan branch in Salomon's lobby reserved a special window on payout day for Salomon workers, and most banks in the financial district stayed open an extra hour.

"Please be in Mr. Salomon's office at 10:15," the voice on the telephone told McClellan. At the appointed hour McClellan walked in. Waiting for him were Bob Salomon, a senior partner and head of research, as well as a member of the founding family. With him was Ed Olsen, McClellan's supervisor.

"We're very happy with your work," Salomon said. He added a few more of what McClellan regarded as obligatory platitudes. "And your compensation this year is $200,000, the same as last year."

He was, quite literally, speechless. The next few moments passed very slowly. He regained his voice:

"You do realize what part I had in the EDS merger?" he asked, trying not to sound hurt.

"We're aware of that factor, but as research goes, so go the research analysts," Salomon said. They blamed his bonus on the overall limitations on bonuses in the research department. He shouldn't consider this a personal slight, they said.

Later that day he saw Scully.

"They didn't pay me," he told him bitterly. Scully insisted he had made the right people aware of McClellan's contribution.

So that's the way it was. Salomon expected him to join the team when it suited the investment bankers, but the firm wasn't willing to pay him. He felt humiliated; they had made him feel like one of them, which had quieted his skepticism about the selling of EDS. And then, after using what he had to contribute, they refused to pay him what he assumed was his share.

Eight years at Salomon and still an outsider.

The needle on the gauge measuring Roger Smith's patience with Ken Riedlinger was moving out of the green and into the red zone. The answers Riedlinger heard from Smith about the Mickey Mouse problems EDS had encountered changed from "we'll take care of that" and "Rome wasn't built in a day" to an ominous-sounding "you guys just aren't patient enough."

Meyerson, meanwhile, informed Riedlinger in an irritated fashion that Roger and others at GM weren't happy about Riedlinger's hard-driving manner.

It's true I'm pushing you, Meyerson told him, but you have to be careful how you push Roger and the others. In addition to everything else, he's already quite unhappy about your salary, which he regards as way too rich.

Riedlinger didn't appreciate Meyerson's criticism. Riedlinger had been put in charge of the world's biggest data processing contract and he was embarrassed at having to stroke a bunch of petty egos. As executive in charge, he didn't appreciate having to find out why, for instance, GM wouldn't fix broken air conditioners for EDS. But his own EDS managers pushed the problems up to him when GM didn't resolve them, so he had no choice.

Meyerson, meanwhile, wasn't always available to back him and was showing increasing annoyance at having to listen to his tales of defeat. As much as possible, Riedlinger tried peaceful, nonthreatening negotiations with F. Alan Smith, GM's executive vice president of finance, Jack Edman, vice president of finance working for Alan Smith, and sometimes with Roger Smith himself — only to hear now that the GM execs had been complaining about him to Meyerson all along. The walls seemed to be closing in. Every imbroglio traveled in a great circular route and kept landing on Riedlinger's doorstep. The hostility against him kept growing.

"You look pretty smug, like a guy betting his job. You might be out on the street looking for a job tomorrow," Smith had said out loud to him at a GM capital budget meeting.

"I bet my job every day," Riedlinger replied, full of bravado. He made a mental note to stay out of Smith's way for a while.

Later that day, Riedlinger unexpectedly received a phone call from Perot, who somehow heard about his statement to Smith. Perot complimented him for standing up to the GM chairman. "Whatever happens, you'll always have a job with me," Perot told him. Perot's telephone call buoyed Riedlinger and temporarily erased any apprehension he had about his next confrontation.

Riedlinger's deteriorating relationship with Meyerson bothered him far more than Smith's tart remarks. He had harbored ambivalent feelings about his boss since 1975 when he first signed on to help Mort sell Medicare contracts. He loved working for him because Mort was smart and always at the center of the action. When they were winning new contracts and EDS was making money he had been elated. But he hated the way Mort asserted control by making him wear a pager, by ordering him on assignments out of town on short notice, by constantly reminding him of his place as a subordinate.

Riedlinger also hadn't forgotten the $50,000 bonus for going to New Jersey that he believed Meyerson reneged on.

(Perhaps because of his highly stressed state, Riedlinger chose to overlook that Meyerson, on July 16, 1984, less than three weeks after his new assignment began at GM, raised his annual base salary to $200,000 a year from $140,000. On October 14, 1984, Meyerson gave Riedlinger a stock bonus worth $462,000; and the next month he raised his annual salary another $14,862 a year. Still, Riedlinger was angry about the cash bonus he felt he deserved.)

On operating matters, he and Meyerson always talked pretty straight to each other and generally agreed about what was needed to get the job done. Now the daily communication was becoming strained. He tried to make Mort understand that hundreds and thousands of new EDS data processing workers in Detroit literally had no place to sit down because GM managers were preventing EDS from using existing office space. He had closed an indoor garage and turned it into offices. When he approached Mort about leasing additional space, the EDS president hit the roof. He accused Riedlinger of erecting a Taj Mahal in Detroit and trying to create his own little empire. Riedlinger shot back that it was impractical to run all these decisions through Dallas; he needed the flexibility to make decisions such as how much office space to lease on his own.

Riedlinger suspected the reason so many local decisions were routed through Meyerson and other EDS executives in Dallas was the same reason EDS wasn't committing the resources he needed to do the job: Perot and Meyerson were fighting hard to maintain EDS's independence from GM. EDS's work at GM constituted three times the dollar amount of all EDS's other billings. GM and Detroit were a giant magnet, drawing the strength and soul of EDS away from Dallas. Every triumph by GM, every compromise of EDS's principles, brought closer the day GM finally and completely took over.

On Monday, April 29, 1985, EDS held its second board meeting as a GM subsidiary. As agreed in the merger contract, the board meeting was held in Dallas.

Despite the merger's terrible start, no one was giving up hope. Mort Meyerson was determined to do as much as possible to make the relationship work. He was frustrated, but he remained convinced that a logical formula existed somehow, somewhere, that encompassed the needs of both organizations.

The EDS board consisted of Roger Smith and the GM executive-committee members and Ross Perot and his top officers, including Ken Riedlinger. Perot had been careful to specify that his directors outnumber the GM directors by one. That way, GM was theoretically outvoted on any policy difference that cropped up between him and Smith.

When the EDS officers gathered for a rehearsal on Sunday, the day before the board meeting, Meyerson seemed particularly testy. He scolded Riedlinger for failing to prepare the capital budget requests earlier. Riedlinger spent Sunday night doing so. He expected the next day to be long and tense.

The board meeting on Monday contained a polite but spirited debate between Smith and the GM officers on one side and Perot, Meyerson, and the EDS officers on the other. The GM troops didn't understand why fixed-price data processing contracts were going to be so expensive. Isn't that why we bought EDS, to make computing less expensive?

Perot and Meyerson tried to disabuse them gently of that notion. GM said it wanted a twenty-first-century company, and that cost a lot of money; the provisions of the merger called for EDS and GM to conclude contracts that established spending levels. The meeting droned on for four hours. It was a genteel replay, on the board level, of events since Day One.

To Riedlinger, it looked as if Roger Smith and GM president Jim McDonald and the other GM officers were bored silly and couldn't wait to get out of the room. When it was his turn to speak, he recounted the projections that he and Meyerson had formulated calling for hiring several thousand new systems engineers to work on GM's computer systems.

Suddenly the GM chairman turned to him.

"I just hope you're not hiring lots of people who we're going to have to fire someday," Smith said. The comment wasn't nasty, just cautionary.

Riedlinger answered the GM chairman sharply. As was his habit when challenged, Riedlinger's tone shifted to combative.

"We'll be hiring 10,000 systems engineer trainees. This is how many people we need, and I don't think it will be done with fewer," he said to Smith.

Fortunately Smith didn't blow up, though he well might have if his mood had been different. Meyerson watched in shock. He wondered if Riedlinger was losing control of himself, speaking that way to Roger Smith in a public meeting, especially when he had been warned that Smith had his eye on him.

Suddenly, Meyerson stood up: "EDS will negotiate the contracts with GM operating divisions before the next board meeting." He paused dramatically. "We have the people and resources to do that, rest assured."

The short declaration had defused the tension. An air of relief settled over the room. The meeting adjourned, and the GM officers headed straight for the airport to catch their airplanes to Detroit. The dozen EDS executives who had attended the meeting stayed in the boardroom, laughing and joking with one another. To Riedlinger, it seemed as if a mood of giddy celebration had seized them. The GM officers were satisfied with Meyerson's pronouncement. The contracts were going to be negotiated on EDS's terms, they must think. The conflict was over; Meyerson had said so.

Riedlinger didn't join in the festivities. Meyerson might think that he would get those contracts signed, but it wasn't going to happen. No matter what Smith said, the operating divisions weren't going to go along on EDS's terms. He finally realized that Smith didn't really have the power to make GM do what he decreed. He felt slightly queasy, for he realized he was headed back to Detroit the next day, again saddled with Mort's impossible expectation of signing all the contracts within ninety days.

"What's your problem? Why are you so quiet, Riedlinger?" Meyerson said to him. The other EDS officers stopped talking.

"Oh, nothing. I'm just grooving," he said. Meyerson, his antennae at work, detected Riedlinger's thoughts, which were anything but acquiescent.

"No, I want to know what the problem is," Meyerson said.

He's goading you, Riedlinger said to himself. Don't react.

All right, Riedlinger thought, if he wants to know, I'll tell him. But he isn't going to like it.

"The problem is that the contracts with GM aren't going to get signed in ninety days. It doesn't matter what you say. It doesn't matter what Roger says," Riedlinger said. "We don't know what GM's costs are, within half a billion dollars. We don't have people to negotiate contracts. Our customers don't want the contracts. The whole thing is impossible."

There was a pause.

"I guess that means you don't want to do this job anymore," Meyerson responded. The other EDS officers looked on.

"No, I'm going to get it done, Mort. I'm going to make this camel fly," Riedlinger said.

"Tell me how. Tell me exactly what you're going to do," Meyerson said.

"I don't know, Mort. You just told Roger we would do this in ninety days. I don't have the slightest idea how we are going to do it," he said.

Again Riedlinger felt as if Meyerson was pushing him, always pushing. He blurted out: "You've led EDS into this swamp, now you figure out how to get us out."

An angry Meyerson declared: "The meeting's adjourned. Riedlinger, I want to see you in my office."

The confrontation between the two men, now removed from the boardroom, turned heated. Kenn Hill had been waiting to speak to

Meyerson about something else; as soon as he heard the two men begin having words, he excused himself.

As Meyerson remembered the discussion, there was no name-calling or profanity between them, but it was a tough discussion that turned painful when he told Riedlinger that if he couldn't do the job at GM, he would find someone else who could.

The anger they inflicted on one another after so many years of kinship wasn't what finally broke Riedlinger's spirit. It was this: Meyerson again accused him of building an empire in Detroit, a Taj Mahal with himself as the rajah.

"You've lost your marbles, Mort," Riedlinger said, rising from his chair. He couldn't stand having his motives questioned. All he wanted was for EDS to succeed. This was far more extreme than any of their previous arguments. In fact, he had never in his life dared say anything like that to Meyerson. Oddly enough, he felt free, exhilarated.

"Ken, this isn't a productive meeting. I know you're frustrated, but you've made a fundamental mistake by showing everyone at EDS you're frustrated. I'm going to ignore what you just said. If you still want this job, then call me in the morning. If I don't hear from you by 9:00 A.M. I intend to go to Detroit and replace you," Meyerson said. (Riedlinger maintains that Meyerson never told him his job depended on the call.)

Riedlinger didn't look at Meyerson as he stormed out of the office. For the first time in years he was his own man. He had done the right thing by telling Mort off. He drove to Love Field where an EDS Learjet was waiting. Before boarding he telephoned home.

"Judy, I just quit." He told her what he had blurted out to Meyerson. By tomorrow, he told her, he and Meyerson would probably patch things up. He wasn't really sure whether he had quit or not, but he felt wonderful having stood up to Meyerson.

"You did what?" she said. Judy Riedlinger was shocked. Watching Ken and the rest of EDS fight their way through the GM meatgrinder for the last ten months hadn't been easy. Meyerson, she noted bitterly, hadn't done much to encourage or reward Ken. To see her husband succeed at something he cared about was important to her. More important, though, was building a life together.

"Come home," she said. "We'll celebrate."

By nine the next morning, when Meyerson hadn't heard from Riedlinger, he went to see Perot to tell him what had happened. Riedlinger, meanwhile, notified his secretary that he was taking Tuesday off. He hadn't slept in forty-eight hours. He had no intention of calling Meyerson. In his view, Meyerson had rebuked him viciously, impugned his loyalty. He was tired of hearing Meyerson's scoldings. He and Judy played tennis, hung pictures, and ordered a pizza for dinner. He assumed he would go back to work and things would blow over. Perot called to talk about the blowup with Mort. Things would work out somehow, Perot said. He told Riedlinger to stay at home until he could talk to Mort.

That evening a friend from EDS called Riedlinger's home.

"I'm sorry, Ken," the friend said.

"Sorry about what?" Riedlinger asked.

"You didn't hear? You're out. Meyerson replaced you today."

FIFTEEN

───── ═══ ══

Buying Hughes Aircraft

Just as the public acclaim for Roger Smith reached a crescendo, cracks in the foundation began to appear. No single disappointment or event sparked the doubts about the course the GM chairman was steering for the automaker. Rather, it was a confluence of developments, suggesting serious miscalculation and previously unrecognized delusion in GM's throne room.

A single poor quarterly earnings report rarely changes Wall Street's fundamental view of a blue-chip company like GM. Hence, the 34 percent profit drop announced in late April 1985 didn't set off alarm bells. Analysts had encouraged major GM shareholders to expect better. The results, Smith explained, were entirely consistent with extensive spending to modernize plants, buy new equipment, and acquire EDS.

Far less easy to explain away was GM's eroding share of the North American car and truck market, which management tried to blame on a short strike the previous year that caused the loss of a quarter of a million vehicles' worth of production. In a year-to-year comparison, GM's market share dropped a couple of percentage points to about 43 percent of the market, which doesn't sound like a major tragedy until one considers that a single percentage point of the U.S. car and truck market represented about 150,000 vehicles and perhaps up to $1.5 billion of lost revenue. In Detroit, blood is spilled to capture a tenth of a percent of market share.

GM's most devastating setback came in the luxury car market segment, which traditionally commands the highest profit margins and, in absolute terms, accounts for a disproportionately large part of corporate profit. Weak Cadillac sales cast a dark shadow over GM's entire line of cars. Since Sloan's day, GM marketing psychology portrayed Cadillac as the apotheosis of all the corporation's efforts. Buyers were supposed to climb the marketing ladder from Chevrolet through Olds, Pontiac, and Buick, always dreaming of the day they reached the Cadillac pinnacle. If the pinnacle was no longer a worthwhile goal, buyers might decide to stay off the ladder.

What caused the evaporation of sales? To vastly oversimplify the problem, GM's cars remained expensive in price and mediocre in quality and design at a time when the competition was becoming very good. GM cars weren't horrible, they simply didn't meet new, higher standards set by the imports. Thousands of design problems plagued GM engines and transmissions. Styling was awkward and unimaginative. The cars looked too much alike. To cite only one striking but characteristic example, GM announced in April 1985 that almost a million Cadillac V-8 engines produced between 1983 and 1985 were susceptible to leaks of coolant into the compartment holding the engine oil. To its credit, GM expanded the warranty on the engines, but it took more than two years of dithering to pinpoint the problem and announce the recall. For a while dealers, using faulty information from GM, were blaming car owners for not changing the oil promptly, one more reason why great numbers of Cadillac owners switched to Mercedes, Lincoln, and luxury Japanese models.

To complicate matters, GM didn't seem eager to satisfy the swollen ranks of unhappy customers. In 1983, to settle complaints filed with the Federal Trade Commission, GM washed its hands of its worst warranty claims by turning over arbitration of customer disputes to the Better Business Bureau. The Better Business Bureau quickly was swamped with more than a quarter of a million claims nationwide. In some cities, angry owners of GM cars were greeted by constant busy signals when they tried to phone in their complaints.

Incredibly, in the drive to automate plants, computerize operations, and capture new technologies, GM had forgotten the basic tenet of the car business or, for that matter, any business: satisfy the customer. GM cars, once the choice of the well-heeled, no longer stacked up against foreign and domestic competitors in design, cost, or quality. And customers in 1985 were finding this out in droves and choosing alternatives. It was as if all the separate service complaints of the past few years, the styling errors, the pricing blunders, and the insensitive responses to customer complaints had reached a critical mass in the marketplace and now constituted a new resolve among the car buyers to avoid GM. The company's virtual franchise to supply half the nation's cars was slipping away fast.

In the face of shrinking demand for its cars and trucks, GM chose a risky short-term recovery tactic in the spring of 1985. Rather than slow down the factories until product ills were cured, GM decided to speed production and flood the market. By simultaneously offering big rebates and incentives, GM hoped to wrest back its lost share through sheer force of financial muscle. After all, with a much bigger cash war chest than Ford or Chrysler, GM had less to lose in a discounting war with its domestic rivals. The risk, of course, was that customers might turn up their noses anyway and force a production shutdown and massive layoffs. The deep discounts required to clear lots of unwanted vehicles cut deeply into corporate profit without a recovery of market share.

Overproduction followed by financial incentives to stimulate sales was a strategy sure to alienate the 25,000 or so GM dealers nationwide. The dizzying roller-coaster of off-again, on-again incentives made financial planning difficult for dealers, eroding the goodwill and loyalty already seriously depressed by the shocking slide in GM product quality.

"Steve, how can we present Riedlinger's . . . departure . . . to the security analysts in a way that won't raise concern about the relationship with GM?" Meyerson asked McClellan. Meyerson had told McClellan that Riedlinger had burnt himself out at GM and had to be replaced. Technically, that was true. McClellan believed Meyerson because he had seen how frazzled they all had been the previous autumn. The explanation side-stepped the issue of the hostility between the two organizations. Not even McClellan could know about it.

EDS security analysts meeting at the Hilton Hotel near Dallas–Ft. Worth Airport hadn't any idea yet that Ken Riedlinger had been replaced by Kenn Hill and Bob Sharpe almost two weeks earlier. They had less of a clue about what difficulties Meyerson and Perot and the rest of the EDS officers were having making Smith and GM live up to the merger agreement.

Carefully choosing his words, Meyerson explained to McClellan that

Riedlinger's role in leading the troops had required him to be hatchet man. GM wasn't familiar with EDS's culture, he said with a bit of understatement, and Riedlinger's job was to assert the differences. That had made him persona non grata with GM.

"What's going to happen to him?" McClellan asked.

"We'll bring him back to Dallas to cool off," Meyerson said.

"If Ken's departure isn't indicative of anything, I'd spread the word just as you portrayed it to me," McClellan said. He and the other analysts were assured that the friction portrayed between EDS and GM in a few newspaper and magazine articles was a thing of the past. EDS revenue from GM was only headed higher. Despite everything, Meyerson still was optimistic.

McClellan returned from the Dallas security analysts meeting — still not overly concerned about Riedlinger's departure or the clash of cultures — and wrote an upbeat report to investors on GM Class E shares, predicting a 21 percent compounded profit growth for several years. Like most analysts, McClellan had praised the acquisition to investors and didn't want to believe things were going sour.

Back in New York, McClellan accepted an invitation to breakfast with Merrill Lynch's head of research at the Vista International Hotel in lower Manhattan. Because there really are few secrets on Wall Street, he figured Merrill Lynch probably had heard about how he had been shafted by Salomon Brothers on bonus day. He wasn't looking particularly for a chance to jump ship, but Merrill's offer sounded good. Very good. The brokerage wanted to nearly double McClellan's salary and bonus immediately.

A week later McClellan appeared as the "special guest" on *Wall Street Week,* the Friday night show on PBS, fulfilling a long-standing invitation. Brokerages love the publicity they get when their analysts appear on the show.

On Monday following his appearance, McClellan again was summoned to Bob Salomon's office, this time to receive congratulations. He had handled himself with aplomb, Salomon said. Rukeyser could be a merciless inquisitor; he had skewered research analysts and self-promoting wizards before.

"You were great, Steve," Salomon said. "You really made the firm look good."

Talk is cheap, you bastards, McClellan thought with barely suppressed exultation.

"Thanks very much. I'm resigning."

*　　*　　*

GM's worries on the automotive front didn't divert Smith's determination to win the Hughes Aircraft auction a whit. Morgan Stanley investment bankers leaked word in May: Ford and Boeing each were preparing offers of about $5 billion. The deadline for final bids was June 4. Salomon Brothers' bidding strategy for GM correctly assumed that Smith and GM were prepared to pay whatever was necessary to win Hughes. Thus, Salomon bankers needed to secure GM the opportunity to make a preemptively high offer after the so-called final bids were tendered. (Technically, the auction rules precluded last-minute changes.)

A few hours after Hughes Medical Institute trustees sat down to review bids on June 4, Morgan Stanley by telephone requested "clarification" of GM's $5 billion-plus offer, which consisted of $2.5 million cash and shares of a new class of common stock. In its bid, GM proposed forming a new subsidiary consisting of Hughes Aircraft and parts of Delco Electronics and issuing 50 million shares of a new GM Class H stock, representing the subsidiary, to the medical institute. Since the value of the new GM stock wasn't entirely predictable, Boeing's $5 billion offer initially appeared to be the highest and, therefore, winning bid . . . unless, of course, GM was willing to sweeten the cash portion of its offer to compensate for uncertainty over the value of the stock.

Reached in Salzburg, Austria, where he was attending a meeting of GM's European advisers, Smith agreed to kick in another $200 million cash and improve the price guarantees on the GM Class H stock to be issued to the medical institute.

Done, said Morgan Stanley bankers. Roger Smith's "lulu" was home. Somewhere within Hughes, somewhere among the 73,000 engineers and scientists, lay another vital element of Smith's high-tech dream for GM's future.

True enough, Ross Perot had voted with the rest of the directors to allow Smith to pursue Hughes. Yet he couldn't shake the concerns that gnawed at him about the expense of buying Hughes and the growing questions about Smith's strategic vision.

The early warning signals of deep trouble in GM's core automotive operations, the eroding market share, and lower profitability all troubled Perot. He wasn't one to panic at a single short-term profit slide, but he didn't ignore telltale signals either, especially if they heralded more serious trouble ahead. GM's 1985 second-quarter profit, announced in late July, was down 28 percent, the second consecutive substantial drop and the second straight time GM surprised the investment community with a lower-than-expected quarterly profit. On the day second-quarter profits were announced, investors punished GM stock with a spirited selloff that knocked $1.50 off the share price. The selloff in and of itself didn't disturb Perot. Once more he was hearing a warning that the corporation was losing its way. As a director and owner of 11 million GM Class E shares, he could ill afford to ignore mounting evidence that Smith was throwing money at GM's problems with little hope of return.

"I'd like a full and detailed report on Hughes," Perot told Smith. He intended to check the company personally to see if the acquisition made as much sense as Smith claimed. Smith had won Hughes and he had his heart set on buying it; he shouldn't mind if Perot gave the company a once-over before GM wrote the check. GM treasurer Courtney Jones assigned an assistant in his office to send Perot the information he requested.

By August, after reviewing mounds of information, Perot was more than uneasy about spending $5 billion on Hughes. He was worried.

From the figures compiled by the GM treasurer's office, not only was Hughes not particularly profitable, but a dangerously high percentage of its profit derived from a handful of government defense contracts. Having been heavily dependent on government contracts in EDS's early days, Perot knew how vulnerable government expenditures were to changing political winds. Hughes also had been having troubles with quality control in one of its missile factories.

To make matters worse, everything Perot heard emanating from Washington suggested increased budgetary pressures and reduced defense outlays in the future. The Russians were making conciliatory noises. He worried that Hughes might suffer a revenue and profit slump, especially if Reagan and Gorbachev cooked up another arms agreement.

According to Smith's explanations to Perot and the GM directors, the most important reason for buying Hughes was to capture its technology, not its profitability. As in the EDS acquisition, he was buying brainpower. Hughes was a leader in satellite systems, in communications, and in arcane sciences such as laser physics and holography. Smith wanted Hughes scientists to help GM incorporate advanced processes used in jet fighters and missiles.

Rocket scientists thought and worked in terms of "systems," a trend Smith had been briefed about and that intrigued him. Systems engineering, he learned, hadn't yet been applied much to automotive engineering. Engineers shouldn't design a mere brake, Smith was told by his experts, they must design "braking systems" that meshed harmoniously with other vehicle systems and advanced production processes.

Perot didn't know much about such abstract concepts, and he was certain Smith didn't either. Perot believed GM should face up to less ethereal issues, such as making pieces of sheet metal fit together properly, designing internal-combustion engines that didn't leak oil and coolant, dealing fairly with customer complaints, and learning how to react more quickly and responsively to automotive styling trends. GM was in the throes of organizational malaise; it wasn't the time for more shopping. Smith was buying one of the world's great collections of scientists at a time when GM wasn't solving mundane, straightforward engineering and business problems.

Hoping to head off conflict with Perot on the Hughes acquisition, GM late in the summer of 1985 sent a large group of executives to Dallas to present the case in favor of the purchase. Included were Elmer Johnson, GM's top lawyer, Don Atwood, GM executive vice president, and Stan O'Neal, the assistant treasurer from GM's office in New York assigned to provide financial information on Hughes.

Atwood, a highly regarded electrical engineer, presented GM's case for pursuing Hughes's technologies. He explained the importance of "systems" engineering and of Hughes's advanced electronics capabilities. The car was headed for a fantastic transformation, he said, just as the camera had evolved from a mechanical instrument into an electromechanical instrument.

O'Neal tried to present slides explaining the financial aspects of the Hughes purchase, but Perot didn't want to watch a slide show. He had been over the figures already. This was a sales pitch, not a hardheaded analysis of the pluses and minuses.

"Now put all the slides and papers away. Even the prettiest lady in the world has a wart somewhere," Perot told the GM men. "I want to hear about the warts."

O'Neal answered a few of Perot's questions, attempting once more to start his slide presentation. Perot again stopped him. He asked about the potential danger of shrinking defense budgets. Atwood responded that Hughes was heavily oriented to research contracts, so-called black (secret) defense work that was less vulnerable to cutbacks. GM knew what it was doing, he assured Perot.

Despite Atwood's answer, Perot believed many of Hughes's research contracts were involved with Star Wars and nuclear weapons programs and were quite vulnerable indeed. Again Perot pointed out that Hughes's overall profit appeared to be too dependent on a small proportion of contracts, the loss of any of which might prove disastrous to the company's finances.

"Stan, could you break down which Hughes contracts account for the biggest proportion of profits?" Perot asked.

O'Neal responded that he would find out.

The meeting far from quenched Perot's skepticism.

"You've eliminated some of my concerns," Perot said diplomatically. "Hughes unquestionably possesses great technological capabilities. However, I'm still concerned that lower defense spending is going to hurt Hughes. This isn't the time we should be paying the very top dollar."

Listening to Perot's statement, Elmer Johnson believed that the EDS founder respected Hughes's technological assets. Yet, on balance, he and the GM executives had failed to convince Perot of the acquisition's wisdom. Consequently, the probability had grown that Perot was going to assert his opposition to Hughes.

Smith wasn't likely to cherish opposition, Johnson knew, no matter how much the GM chairman valued Perot's counsel.

Elmer Johnson flipped through the pages of Ira Millstein's report. As expected, the Weil Gotshal senior partner had sketched for Johnson the legal rationale for forming a special committee of GM directors to oversee and supervise the relationship among the different classes of GM shareholders. What was good for the owners of GM common stock, the report warned, wasn't necessarily good for the owners of GM E or GM H stock.

A year ago Johnson had theorized about the possible usefulness of an oversight committee as a means of dealing with potential conflict. EDS's inability to forge long-term contracts with GM operating divisions and the struggle over compensation plans now were very real. The time had come to brief Roger Smith about Millstein's report, which suggested formation of such a committee. Then he would tell Perot through his attorney, Tom Luce.

As a practical man who believed in compromise, Luce was quite amenable to the creation of an impartial body whose job was to see that GM lived up to the contract with EDS.

Luce's client, on the other hand, was underwhelmed.

"Tom, you don't need a committee of elders to read and reread our deal with GM to figure out what needs to be done," Perot said. A committee, he said, only meant more reports, more meetings, more telephone calls — and no action.

Perot wasn't well versed in the ways of large corporations. He had never served on any corporate boards nor had he joined business organizations like the Conference Board or the Business Roundtable. Otherwise, he might have viewed the oversight committee more as a defensive legal maneuver than as an elaborate (but unnecessary) forum for conflict resolution.

"A fairness committee is just another way for GM to avoid doing the right thing," Perot told Luce.

Luce thought Perot was too negative about a move that looked to him like a genuine diplomatic initiative by GM and Elmer Johnson. But in a decade of tending to Perot's legal affairs, he had learned never to underestimate his client's instincts.

Perot didn't know that he wasn't the only GM director with deep doubts about Hughes. At least one other, a director with far less appetite for outspokenness than Perot, one who possessed a special expertise in this matter but was wary of openly challenging Roger Smith, also believed the $5 billion expenditure for Hughes was a mistake.

Unlike Perot, this director didn't hold a meeting to voice his reservations. It wasn't his way, it wasn't the corporate way, to question one of the chairman's pet projects in front of other GM officers. He dared not say anything publicly. To do so, he believed, was to end his effectiveness as a director. He belonged to a team; and there was no sense in riling the chairman if he was in the minority.

To this director, the defense business hardly looked like a promising opportunity for GM's capital. Like Perot, he questioned GM's capabilities to transfer Hughes's technologies to cars and trucks. If GM truly wanted engineers with a better orientation to the "systems approach," wasn't it cheaper and simpler to hire engineers who possessed that skill? After all, it didn't take a genius to see that $5 billion bought an awful lot of engineering talent.

Was there a way to influence Smith, the director asked himself, to stop the chairman from a strategic blunder without provoking an embarrassing scene?

Perhaps a carefully worded, confidential letter might influence him. Maybe it could raise doubts about Hughes ever so slightly and, combined with other measured doubting voices, convince him to reconsider. He wrote a letter that was polite, he thought, well-meaning, and deadly, deadly serious.

The next time they met, Smith thanked him — very cordially, the director thought — for his ideas. He understood and appreciated the director's reservations.

But in the matter of Hughes Aircraft, Smith wasn't swayed a bit by the worries of Ross Perot, a concerned director, or anyone else.

SIXTEEN

Losing It

Eds's management conference in Laguna Niguel, California, during the week of August 3, 1985, was a hiatus of good feeling amid the day-to-day fighting with GM. Three hundred and fifty of EDS's top managers and their spouses crowded into the glittering new Ritz-Carlton overlooking the Pacific for a few days of business meetings interspersed with dining, socializing, sports, and a trip to Sea World, which EDS rented one evening for its private use.

By this time quite a few managers attending the conference were, in fact, ex-GM data processors who had reluctantly given up GM benefits and affiliation, made the transition to EDS, and resolved to accept their new lives. The Laguna Niguel meeting, with its camaraderie and good cheer, demonstrated that EDS shock troops also knew how to throw a party. The GM spouses in particular were thrilled to be invited to a management conference; it had rarely happened to them previously at GM. Mort Meyerson, who acted as host, invited spouses to attend the business meetings, not just the recreational events.

The atmosphere of the conference was merry, and there was little talk of fighting with GM operating divisions that were resisting EDS. After lunch one day, the lights were dimmed and a huge screen was filled with a gag videotape broadcast of EDS officers running along the water's edge to the musical theme from *Chariots of Fire*. Ken Riedlinger, now exiled from EDS, Jeff Heller, and several other top EDS officers were shown dressed in running shorts and carrying briefcases, splashing through the surf. The hilarity of the videotape infected everyone, especially the newcomers from GM: by being invited to share an inside joke, they were, in a sense, initiated into the small, tight group of people who cared deeply for one another. At the end of the conference, everyone signed two huge posters that were presented as gifts to Meyerson and Perot. They were emblazoned with the motto of the conference: "We're All One Great Team." In small measure, at least, the tide had turned on the daily operational frictions between people from EDS and those from GM.

Beneath the good feeling, however, was a giant unresolved worry for EDS. Roger Smith still hadn't approved or disapproved the proposed awards of stock under EDS's stock incentive plan. The keystone of EDS's compensation system, the incentive shares were to have been awarded late in 1984. Because of the merger, the award was to have been made in early 1985. Now it was summer and there was still no action. Although the merger agreement assured Perot and Meyerson the freedom to award the number of shares they thought proper, only GM was legally permitted to issue shares, and so actual power to issue EDS's incentive shares resided with GM and Greg Lau, the assistant treasurer in charge of GM's compensation plans.

For the last eight months, EDS had heard nothing about the stock awards, save the one meeting in Roger Smith's office attended by Perot, Bill Gayden, and Tom Walter. Smith called now and then to ask questions about EDS's proposal but made no commitments. Since the meeting, Perot had mentioned to Smith several times, by telephone and at board meetings, that the compensation plan wasn't moving forward. The delay began to annoy him. In the first place, Perot personally had requested EDS managers to work hard to make the merger succeed, and he had moved many people to Detroit, all with the understanding that they would be rewarded for their efforts. His credibility was on the line. Smith was standing in the way of his keeping his word to the troops. Second, the failure of the compensation package to move forward was, in Perot's opinion, another significant breach of the merger agreement, in addition to GM operating divisions' failure to sign firm contracts with EDS.

What seemed like inaction to Perot was, in fact, GM's grindingly slow deliberation in preparation for turning the plan down. Lau dissected the proposal in New York. Memos passed back and forth to Detroit. But all the bureaucratic activity boiled down to one essential truth: Smith didn't like EDS's proposal to issue about 7 million Class E incentive shares to several thousand top people. It violated GM's most fundamental hierarchical rule, because it made EDS managers far wealthier than many higher-ranking officers at GM, especially Roger Smith.

That Smith previously had agreed to allow Perot to compensate EDS managers as he wished, that 20 million incentive shares were set aside in the proxy and approved by shareholders at the time of the merger, was of little consequence. The GM chairman wouldn't allow so much wealth to be distributed.

In August Smith told Perot. He tried to remain firm but conciliatory while dismantling EDS's stock incentive plan.

"Viewed purely from a compensation viewpoint the [EDS stock incentive] program might well be considered, in retrospect, as excessive — having gone far beyond any reasonable expectancy at the time of inception. While this reflects, to some degree, a measure of the success achieved by the efforts of the executives in the normal course of business, much of the increase in the value of the stock was also made possible by the GM-EDS merger," Smith said.

Besides, he said, the top EDS people already were incredibly wealthy. By GM's calculations, Mort Meyerson's Class E shares were worth more than $100 million, assuming they were all held and worth a minimum of $125 a share, as promised in the agreement. Bill Gayden's incentive shares would be worth $45 million, Ken Riedlinger's, $25 million, Les Alberthal's, $25 million.

"Obviously these numbers are far in excess of what any competitive compensation studies would indicate, and, in fact, are in excess of what any of our top GM executives (including myself) can expect," Smith told Perot. By his reckoning, the latest EDS incentive plan was going to cost another $300 million. In other words: You folks are already quite rich — richer than me! — and GM made you that way.

Another bone sticking in Smith's throat was Meyerson's salary, which had been raised to $851,000, more than his own or anyone's salary at GM, excluding year-end bonuses. (Strangely, Smith's letter didn't mention Perot's long-standing agreement to pay Meyerson an annual salary equal to one percent of EDS's net profit. The agreement had been submitted to GM for review at the time of the merger. No one challenged it, so Perot hadn't any reason to believe there was a problem. Perot and Smith later agreed that Meyerson's salary was to be set by GM, but no one at GM had done so. When months dragged by without

Meyerson receiving salary, Perot ordered it paid under the existing formula.)

In a letter to Perot, Smith suggested substitution of a new incentive plan, patterned on GM's own. Instead of issuing incentive shares, which are "sold" to the employee at a nominal price such as 5 or 10 cents a share, he proposed issuing incentive stock options, which require the outlay of the full price of the shares at the time of the award. Thus, if shares are selling for $40 at the time the options are exercised under GM's plan, and they rise in price to $60 when the shares are bought, the executive pays $40 for shares that are worth $60. In essence, the executive has been awarded $20. Income taxes are deferred until the shares are sold.

Under the EDS plan adopted in the mid-1970s, the executive pays a few pennies for shares that are worth $40. But in order to pay the immediate tax bill on shares with a value of nearly $40, it was always assumed that half the shares would be sold to pay income tax. In order to award an executive a $50,000 stock bonus, EDS actually awarded $100,000 worth of stock, assuming that nearly half the shares must be sold immediately to pay taxes. For that reason, all of EDS's stock awards looked twice as valuable as they really were (under the old tax rates).

EDS had solid reasons for preferring its own system. Under Smith's stock-option proposal, if the value of the stock dropped — even for reasons unconnected to the company's performance — an executive might suddenly be in the position of holding incentive stock that was worth less than he paid for it. If he had borrowed money to buy the stock, he might have been caught in a terrible cash squeeze.

Perot and Meyerson believed that incentive stock was a vital aspect of EDS's corporate character. Much more than salary or bonuses, incentive stock gave key players the best reason possible for protecting EDS's profit margins. Incentive stock was the reason so many top executives had stayed with the company. Sure, EDS executives and managers were rich. Perot acknowledged it; they had built EDS into a powerhouse and made EDS shareholders wealthy. True, only the top few hundred out of 14,000 in EDS made it to the elite category of wealth, but the rest of the work force owned stock also and was energized daily by the chance to one day join the top group.

"Roger, I think you're making a huge mistake by stopping our stock options," Perot said in a telephone conversation in late August. "First of all, you're breaking a fundamental agreement you made with me and with my organization. You're causing a great deal of bad feeling and it's not going to help the relationship between GM and EDS. But if you're determined to do this, then I think you ought to come to Dallas and explain your thinking to everyone.''

Smith agreed to come to Dallas on September 3, 1985, the day after Labor Day, to brief Perot and the EDS officers about his intention to substitute his stock plan for theirs.

Hearing that Smith was coming, Meyerson geared up for action immediately, making sure Bill Gayden, Tom Walter, and the other officers saw a copy of a letter Smith sent to Perot turning down the plan. He wanted them well prepared to speak up at the meeting if necessary.

On August 29, Walter, who was fishing for silver salmon and char with his son at a remote spot 450 miles southwest of Anchorage, Alaska, was astonished by the approach of a seaplane. The pilot handed him a Federal Express envelope. Inside was a copy of Smith's letter. After reading it he knew he was returning home to a showdown.

On Labor Day afternoon, Meyerson assembled the officers at EDS headquarters to make sure everyone understood the significance of Smith's letter and to solicit ideas and arguments with which to counter Smith's position the next day.

A few days before his departure, Smith mentioned to a few people on the fourteenth floor of GM headquarters that he was flying to Dallas ''to stop those people at EDS from throwing away $300 million.'' Within minutes, the tom-toms were beating. Word of Smith's comments had spread among enough people to be picked up by an EDS manager, who immediately called Dallas to warn Perot that Smith was on the warpath.

By the time the GM jet was in the air with Smith aboard, every EDS officer had heard a version of the GM chairman's remarks. Each one was expecting a vigorous confrontation.

Smith first met with Perot and Meyerson alone in Perot's office. He outlined what he planned to say to the EDS officers. It wasn't a genteel presentation. He called them greedy and accused them of being motivated only by personal wealth.

"Roger, you can't say you're going to do one thing and then do something else," Meyerson said.

"Things have changed," Smith said.

"What's changed?" Meyerson asked.

"A lot of wealth has come EDS's way as a result of all the GM business," Smith said.

"That was a given! Look how well the stock is performing. Our people are doing extraordinary work, given the conditions.''

"The numbers are just too big," Smith insisted.

"EDS compensation is minuscule compared to what we've accomplished," Meyerson shot back angrily.

Perot, who had been watching, jumped in to extinguish the sparks: "Let's talk about this like adults. We should hold off on some of this until we get started downstairs."

The large meeting with Smith, in EDS's fifth-floor conference room, with all the officers in attendance, began peacefully. Perot was there, as was Meyerson. But it was Tom Walter, EDS's mild-mannered chief financial officer, who was designated to respond directly to Smith's letter.

Of EDS's inner circle, Walter was perhaps the most courtly and gentle, and certainly one of the best liked. He was a handsome man who was chosen to deal with security analysts because of his knowledge, sincerity, and personal charm.

Rising to his feet, Walter reviewed Smith's case against EDS stock incentives. He then made a point of his own: the financial assumptions underlying Smith's objections to the EDS stock program were faulty.

"You see," he said to Smith, while the others listened, "your numbers aren't correct." He wanted to explain that the huge amounts of stock that GM assumed were parceled out to EDS executives weren't as big as they looked. The largest numbers presented in Smith's letter assumed that every share of EDS stock still was held; in fact, many of the shares had been sold years before to pay taxes. At the very most, the true values of the stock payouts were about half as big as they looked.

Walter didn't get a chance to finish his point.

People in the room later would remember Smith's angry explosion as being wondrous and terrifying at the same time: wondrous for the extreme colors and sounds it brought to the room, terrifying because none of them had ever seen someone lose his temper so completely in a business meeting. In fact, the majority of EDS officers in the room had never seen Smith in person at all, except in videoconferences or at large cheerleading sessions.

"Don't tell me my numbers aren't correct," Smith sputtered. His already ruddy expression flushed a furious scarlet. His voice rose almost to choking, and he slammed his briefing book on the table.

Inadvertently, Walter had delivered the most humiliating insult possible to a GM financial executive. Smith might have endured accusations of being a poor marketer or manager. Telling a GM finance man he had "bad numbers" was invitation to a brawl.

"I didn't come down here to be insulted," Smith shouted. By this time flecks of saliva had formed at the corners of his mouth. The EDS officers stared in disbelief as the chairman of the world's biggest and most powerful company lost it.

After ranting for several minutes, Smith slammed shut his folder of papers. "I rest my case," he declared with finality.

Perot, seeing that Smith was about to walk out of the meeting, moved to the GM chairman's side.

"Now, Roger, I don't think we need to get to this point. I'm sure there's a way to work this all out," he said in his most soothing voice. It took a few moments, but Perot was able to calm him down. Mollified, Smith returned to his seat.

Walter then calmly returned to explain EDS's position on stock incentives, careful not to imply that Smith or GM was dealing with the issue from a position of ignorance. The meeting continued as if nothing had happened.

While Walter spoke, Perot glanced across the room at Meyerson. At last he grasped the totality of what Mort had seen and tried to explain in the spring of 1984 when Smith went berserk during negotiations in Alan Smith's office. Meyerson hadn't wanted to do a deal with GM based on what he had seen. He had tried to warn Perot about Smith, but he wasn't able to convey the depth of his concern.

After the meeting concluded, Perot took Meyerson aside.

"Now I know what you were talking about," Perot said. "Your instincts were right about Roger. If I had seen something like this, if I had understood what you were talking about, I wouldn't have gone through with the deal."

Perot drove Smith back to the GM jet at Love Field.

"It's extremely unfortunate that this happened," Perot told the GM chairman.

Smith's tantrum only deepened Perot's concerns about being able to conduct business with GM in the EDS style. Smith obviously grasped the EDS incentive system quite well — he simply refused to grant Perot and Meyerson a free hand to administer it. And when challenged, he relied on a violent temper to quell opposition. It played poorly with the EDS officers, who were particularly offended that Smith had vented his anger on polite, soft-spoken Tom Walter.

"You know your people, Ross," Smith said as they headed west on the LBJ Freeway. "Do you think any of them are going to leave EDS because of . . . what happened today?" He sounded worried. Without its people, EDS wasn't much of an asset.

"I think if you insist on enforcing your own ideas about compensation, then you better do something to make them more palatable," Perot said.

The GM chairman agreed to shorten the vesting period on incentive shares already held by EDS officers to two and a half years from ten years. EDS's new incentive plan, which Smith forced the company to accept, was reduced substantially: the number of incentive shares was cut by more than 50 percent, and the number of people covered was reduced to several hundred from several thousand. A few weeks later, Mort Meyerson, Tom Walter, and some other top EDS officers, as a protest, decided to forgo their incentive stock and spread their several hundred thousand shares, worth a few million dollars, over the rest of the people in the plan.

As much as it angered him, Perot hadn't any alternative but to accept the crumbs Smith threw. According to their agreement he was independent, yet the power to issue incentive shares rested solely in the GM board, which Smith controlled absolutely.

Roger Smith's gamble to recapture GM's lost share of the North American car and truck market failed utterly in 1985.

By flooding the market with vehicles, and attracting customers to them with low-interest loans, GM hoped to restore to itself at least a shadow of its former dominance. Dominance and the perception of customer loyalty are vital to GM's image in the marketplace. To some extent, people choose GM cars out of inertia. If enough of the herd begins to run in a different direction, those who buy GM only from a sense of belonging to the pack will defect. The disaster at GM's Cadillac division illustrated another significant problem: GM's loss of young, affluent, educated buyers.

By the fall of 1985, Ford and Chrysler resolved to match and beat GM's low-interest-loan incentives, which served to neutralize GM's advantages based on financing strength. In turn, GM's bullish production of cars and trucks landed on dealer lots and largely stayed there. With GM dealer lots clogged with unsold cars and the cost of incentives running high, the third-quarter financial picture for GM North American operations looked dim.

For GM to lose money on cars in America wasn't unprecedented. GM and the other major carmakers lost billions during the recession of the early 1980s. But the industry now was in the midst of an economic boom; the U.S. automotive market was humming. This was a time for making money.

Security analysts again were surprised and disheartened as GM's net income in the third quarter of 1985 came in far below expectations and included an operating loss from North American car and truck operations. Much of the reason for the poor results, Smith explained, was the 40 percent increase in capital outlays for EDS and high-tech tools and equipment. Not to worry, GM assured financial advisers and shareholders; there will be a payoff for the spending down the road. The 1986 Cadillac Eldorado and Seville models will propel Cadillac back on the right track.

To Ross Perot, GM clearly couldn't afford to spend $5 billion or more on Hughes Aircraft at a time when its automotive business was weak. Smith's posturing about timely expenditures of capital funds didn't mask the severe market crisis for GM products.

There must be a way to stop the Hughes deal before it was too late, Perot thought.

"Elmer, it's Tom Luce."

The EDS lawyer didn't relish having to make this telephone call.

"I guess you heard what happened," Luce said. Elmer Johnson, GM's general counsel, had indeed known that Smith was going to meet with the EDS officers in Dallas to lay down the law about stock incentives.

Luce described Smith's histrionics and their impact to Johnson. Luce had predicted a blowup in the making when the two lawyers talked a few months earlier. Perot believed GM wasn't living up to the deal and Luce wanted to let Johnson know it.

"I was afraid something like this was going to happen," Luce said.

"Tom, it looks as if the oversight committee is going to be presented to the board within the next couple of weeks," Johnson said. "This may be our best hope of putting some of the issues before an impartial jury of directors. The committee probably is going to consist of the members of the audit committee, all of whom are non-GM directors. They'll be the most independent of Roger's influence and the most objective. I hope that will be palatable to Ross."

Luce hoped so, too. He, Perot, and others at EDS had doubts about just how independent the outside GM directors were. A look at GM's finances and the Hughes acquisition didn't suggest that GM's board had rigorously challenged Smith's strategy of spending its way back to preeminence.

"Let's stay in touch," Luce said.

*   *   *

In the year since GM and EDS had merged, a great deal of Perot's complaints had flowed over the desk and through the telephone of GM treasurer Courtney Jones.

When Class E shares began trading before their issue date, Perot complained to Courtney Jones. When Mort didn't get a car to use, Perot vented his indignation at Jones. As one of the architects of the merger and as a GM financial executive whom the top EDS officers knew well, Jones was presumed by Perot to have the power and responsibility for fulfilling the deal's promises and provisions.

On one occasion, after severely hectoring the GM treasurer, Perot was taken aside by a member of the GM executive committee.

"You know, it's not Courtney who's putting up these roadblocks," said the GM executive. "It's Roger. The heat you've been giving Courtney is falling on the wrong person."

So that's how it worked, Perot thought. Roger does the dirty work and it's up to Courtney to fend me off. Now he felt sympathy for the GM treasurer; the EDS group had truly enjoyed meeting with him during the negotiations, and they wondered why he had become so troublesome afterward. Now Perot knew the answer. Another of Smith's deceptions.

At October's GM board meeting, Perot asked for a chance to speak. A week earlier it had been announced that Courtney Jones was leaving GM to assume the post of chief financial officer of Merrill Lynch. A headhunter had approached the youthful treasurer; the opportunity was too good to pass up.

"In recognition of the years of dedicated service of Courtney Jones and the pivotal role he played in the partnership of GM and EDS, I move that the GM board commend him," Perot said.

No one seconded. The directors glanced nervously at Smith.

"We don't commend people who leave General Motors," Smith said icily.

Newly relieved of his duties as senior vice president of EDS in charge of the GM account, Ken Riedlinger in the late spring of 1985 spent a great deal of time with his wife, Judy, resting, emotionally recuperating, and playing tennis at the Square Lake Racquet Club in Bloomfield Township. Technically he still was an EDS executive and received a paycheck; but he had no duties.

At the end of May, the couple drove to a tennis camp and then to Santa Monica, California, where they checked into the Pritikin Longevity Center. Perot had suggested it. Several EDS executives, including

Meyerson and Riedlinger, had spent time at Pritikin in the past, recuperating from ill health and the rigors of air travel and fast food.

On the morning of June 4, Riedlinger opened a newspaper and learned that GM had won the auction for Hughes Aircraft. Reading the story gave him a wistful pang. Whatever bitterness remained from his last volcanic meeting with Meyerson was submerged beneath a sudden desire to be accepted back at EDS. Until then he hadn't thought much about what he was going to do next; he assumed he would return to EDS, or perhaps he might work for one of Perot's personal business interests. Hughes was the answer, it was perfect! He could coordinate data processing between Hughes and EDS.

Riedlinger sat down and composed a long telegram to Meyerson begging for another chance in EDS and selling his skills for a job at Hughes. The telegram, with a copy for Perot, cost $400. A few days later, when Meyerson failed to call, he telephoned Dallas. "I'll think about it," Meyerson said unenthusiastically.

In July, the Riedlingers left on a long-planned-for vacation to the Wimbledon tennis championships where, from a front-row seat arranged by the head of EDS in England, they saw Boris Becker win the men's title. On the day of their return Riedlinger called Meyerson again. This time the EDS president was definite:

"I've given the job at Hughes to someone else," Meyerson told him. He had toyed with the idea of finding a job for Riedlinger but decided against it. Meyerson felt there was resentment against Riedlinger at GM and at EDS. With the incredible amount of his attention and energy demanded in Detroit, Meyerson had no strength left to worry about Riedlinger. "I don't think you and I are ever going to work together again," he said wearily.

Riedlinger's pride precluded him from begging again.

"Fine," he said. "Good-bye."

Next he dialed Perot. He had told Riedlinger just a few months earlier, after Riedlinger stood up to Smith, that he would always have a job for him. After explaining what Meyerson had told him, Riedlinger told Perot that he was ready to begin looking for a job. If Perot was to keep his promise, now was the time to do so.

"That's fine, Ken," Perot said. "Take six months if you need." Perot didn't offer him a job. The conversation between the two men drifted to the types of positions Riedlinger might seek. Riedlinger's EDS employment agreement precluded any direct competition with EDS for three years. They talked about large companies, like Ford or Chrysler, and small companies; obviously, he wasn't going to consider any job that directly competed with EDS, such as head of data services for an automaker. They discussed the idea of him starting a new business. He was disappointed that Perot didn't want him but was resigned to it.

Riedlinger interviewed at Ford and Chrysler. He and Judy liked the Detroit area. Despite his difficulties, he had enjoyed the power and scale of the auto industry. And, he concluded, somewhere in the back of his mind was a spark of revenge that kindled a desire to join one of GM's competitors.

Allan Gilmour, Ford's executive vice president of finance, hired Riedlinger with the understanding that he would carry out several special projects before being assigned to a permanent job — outside of Ford's data processing area, as promised in his EDS employment contract.

Ford specified only one condition before hiring Riedlinger. The company wanted to interview Perot about Riedlinger to make sure there were no problems he was hiding.

Perot highly recommended Riedlinger to Ford.

A few days before the October 7 date on which Riedlinger was scheduled to start at Ford, a routine press release was written announcing the event. Riedlinger was described as Ford's new "executive director of special systems projects." The word "systems" in the job title was unfortunate. Several news organizations erroneously speculated that the word meant Riedlinger was going to be working on Ford's computer systems, which would have been a breach of his EDS employment contract and his understanding with Perot.

When Perot read the newspapers he was furious. He telephoned Riedlinger, who failed to convince him it was all a giant misunderstanding. Then Perot called Ford press relations specialist Mary Joseph to verify Riedlinger's claim that the job had nothing to do with data processing.

Roger Smith also was angry. He feared that Ford, guided by Riedlinger, might try to steal EDS's best managers and executives.

What Riedlinger regarded as EDS paranoia, the all-encompassing need to dominate and control his life, had spilled into his new job. In a few days, the anger died down. Riedlinger apologized to Ford executives for the flap. He was embarrassed, he told them, and he promised to prevent anything like it from happening again.

A week or so later, Riedlinger sent an announcement to relatives and a handful of friends at EDS letting them know, in case they hadn't seen the newspapers, that he had moved to Ford. This time he knew better than to try to explain his job description.

Incredibly, a blistering letter arrived in his office a few days later. It was from EDS in Dallas. Somehow Perot had gotten hold of a copy of his announcement and wrongly concluded that Riedlinger was using the message to lure people from EDS to Ford. EDS attorney Claude Chappelear called Riedlinger and implied that legal action might follow.

He had had enough: ''I know where the skeletons are at EDS, Claude, and I have the maps to find them. Think about that before you start threatening me with legal action,'' he told Chappelear. He didn't hear from the lawyer again.

Then he sat down to write Perot. It was a short note, which he felt motivated to write by the pain that choked him. The hurt of being rejected by Perot far outweighed any regret over the millions of dollars in stock incentives he lost through his departure from EDS.

''I didn't double-cross you,'' he wrote. ''I never was recruiting for Ford. Your misinterpretation of my motives was what caused me to leave EDS in the first place. Any doubts I had about doing the right thing are now gone.''

SEVENTEEN

The Peace Treaty

I n early September, two weeks after Smith's showdown in Dallas,
GM engaged McKinsey and Company management consultants
to try their hand at negotiating a peaceful operating arrangement with
EDS.

John Stewart, a New York–based McKinsey partner who had helped
reorganize GM a few years earlier, met with Meyerson, Alan Smith, and
GM executive vice president Alex Cunningham to discuss emergency
formation of a GM-EDS "working group." Stewart's memo to GM
suggested that the group, by mid-December, recommend "a series of
actions which will resolve the difficulties that now exist between GM and
EDS." McKinsey was knowledgeable about GM's inner workings,
having masterminded several projects, including GM's sweeping reorganization of North American automotive operations.

Until a solution was found, EDS continued to bill GM divisions for
work performed without reaching an overall agreement on pricing or
contract terms. But agreements on work to be done were slow in coming.
And sometimes EDS received the amounts it charged, sometimes not.

Hiring McKinsey was a classic exercise in dithering by the GM brass,
Perot told Tom Luce. When Smith and the others are mired in a crisis, the
first thing they do is hire a consultant. Then, they'll have a lot of meetings

to define the crisis. Afterward, they'll appoint a committee to talk about the crisis.

If you see a snake, Perot always said, just kill it — that's the EDS way. Don't appoint a committee on snakes. GM doesn't have to hire expensive herpetologists, Perot thought; all Roger's got to do is decide to live by the merger agreement.

Luce called GM general counsel Elmer Johnson to suggest they talk. At Elmer's suggestion, Luce flew to Detroit on October 22, 1985. Luce, Johnson, and two GM associate general counsels, Gene Hartwig and Paul Zalecki, went out for a dinner conference at the venerable Detroit Club, one of the city's last stuffy eating clubs for corporate chieftains and old-money plutocrats.

"Look, Elmer, I'm going to be open with you and tell you where my client is coming from," Luce said. He and Johnson had met face to face only once before, during the series of GM executive dinners at Perot's home. Luce correctly deduced that Johnson, as something of a newcomer at GM, retained an outsider's mentality. He didn't speak in the same cliches or reflect the same mindset as the other GM executives; he didn't talk about the GM way of doing things. For that reason, Luce was particularly hopeful that Johnson might provide an outsider's perspective and analysis.

"First of all, you're not dealing with some crazy cowboy," Luce told Johnson. "Ross Perot is very careful about what he does. He doesn't jump into deals blindly. He knew exactly what he was agreeing to, and now you're dealing with a guy who thinks he's been screwed by GM and by Roger Smith."

Luce enumerated the agreements about EDS's independence, about Perot's right to compensate his executives, about EDS's mission ultimately to take over all of GM's computer operations and bill GM on the basis of fixed-price, long-term contracts at standard commercial prices, about the so-called alliance between the companies to make GM and EDS number one in their industries.

Johnson listened intently. He told Luce how much he admired Perot and then asked him about their relationship. Luce explained their history, starting with Dupont Walston a decade earlier.

"Elmer, I assume you're aware of the personal memos between Roger and Ross that cover all the points of the merger in detail. . . ," Luce said.

"No, I'm not," Johnson said, leaning forward.

"You mean Roger never mentioned the memos to you?" Luce said, incredulous.

When Luce explained the fax correspondences, Johnson hid his surprise. The last thing any lawyer wants to discover is secret written agreements between a client and a potential adversary. How could Smith have done this without at least informing GM's legal department?

"Could you send me a copy of those memos, Tom?" Johnson asked. "And I'd like you please to send a copy to Ira Millstein by Federal Express. He'll be at his home in Westchester this weekend. Let's not wait until Monday."

Luce left Detroit a bit relieved. He had come half expecting a stone wall and was gratified by Johnson's patience and concern. Here is someone who understands where Ross Perot is coming from and will approach our problems by looking at facts, Luce thought. He won't try to roll over us by saying: "This is the way we do things at GM." Elmer Johnson comes from outside the cocoon. If anyone can break the logjam, he might be the one.

For the past six weeks, Perot had been piecing together the snippets he had heard from people at various levels at GM. "Don't try to argue with Roger." "He'll mow down anyone who stands in his way." "The GM system requires you to prove your loyalty by eating dirt. It starts with Roger and trickles all the way down the system." Management by intimidation. Perot was seeing it in action. Mort had warned him. People at GM were telling him.

He sat down to compose his letter to Roger Smith. At the top of the paper he wrote CONFIDENTIAL; he hoped Smith's assistants wouldn't read what he was going to write. Someone needed to speak to the man in plain, unvarnished English, outside the boardroom, and far from the public eye.

October 23, 1985

DEAR ROGER,

In order to resolve my concerns about the Hughes transaction we need to address two areas. . . .

Perot first asked for a full independent briefing by outside investment bankers and lawyers, not by the kind of GM team that had come to Dallas to persuade him to go along with the deal. He wrote:

Specifically, I do not want a Hughes sales presentation.
. . . The next step is to openly address and solve the problems

between us. Failure to do so will allow the same problems to adversely impact Hughes. The only issue is the success of GM. Our compatibility is not the issue. In the interest of GM you are going to have to stop treating me as a problem and accept me as a large stockholder, an active board member, an experienced businessman.

You need to recognize that I am one of the few people who can and will disagree with you. An increasing number of people are asking me to tell you something that they feel you need to know; are concerned that you won't want to hear; [and] that they are afraid to tell you. I will tell you anything that can build and strengthen GM, whether you want to hear it or not.

For instance, most senior GM executives have said they don't believe Hughes is going to help GM become competitive.

In our relationship I will support you when I believe you are right. I will tell you candidly when I think you are wrong. If you continue your present autocratic style, I will be your adversary on critical issues. I will argue with you privately. If necessary I will argue with you publicly before the board and the shareholders.

You and others at GM may think that I will simply get frustrated and go away if you continue to make life unpleasant enough. You need to understand that I cannot leave because of my obligations to EDS's customers, EDS's people, the Class E shareholders [and because of] my responsibilities as a GM director.

My agenda has one item on it — to see GM succeed. I have no interest in a line management role in GM. I don't expect that all of my ideas will be accepted. I do insist that they be heard and thoughtfully considered. I will be constructive in all of my efforts to see that GM succeeds, and I will expect the same from others.

Perot itemized what he regarded as points of contention between himself and Smith. He accused Smith of appearing bored and intolerant during a business meeting in Detroit in early October. Smith had grown angry when an executive implied that GM didn't have a corporate strategy and, thus, people in the company were confused.

You need to understand that your style intimidates people. Losing your temper hurts GM. Your tendency to try to run over anyone who disagrees with you hurts your effectiveness within GM.

You need to be aware that people are afraid of you. This stifles candid, upward communication in GM.

You need to know that GMers at all levels use terms like "ruthless" and "bully" in describing you. There is a widespread feeling throughout GM that you don't care about people. . . .

The business issues can be resolved if we approach them openly, candidly and in good faith. UAW-style confrontation, misinformation and misleading statements are unacceptable to me from this point forward, as a GM director.

Perot cited the early trading of Class E shares and broken promises about compensation as examples of what he would no longer tolerate.

The foundations for a future relationship are honesty, openness and candor — or simply put, mutual trust and respect. From this point forward, actions count — words don't. We must focus all of our energies on helping GM win.

Roger, my goal is to successfully resolve these problems. I have tried to define them as a first step. This is not a personal issue between us. The issue is the success of GM. I am committed to doing my part to see that we win, and I know that you are, too. I suggest that you and I visit about these issues. Let me know when you want to meet.

SINCERELY,

ROSS

Two weeks later, after Luce and Johnson's meeting at the Detroit Club and Perot's letter, the GM board was scheduled at its regular monthly meeting to vote final approval of the Hughes Aircraft acquisition.

Without the independent briefing he had requested and any new insights that might have come from it, Ross Perot decided to oppose the transaction. He considered all the arguments in favor presented to him by Don Atwood and the GM financial department, and he was certain, from the facts he had seen, that GM didn't need Hughes, especially at a premium price of $5.2 billion in cash and stock.

His opposition was sure to cause a stir.

"Ross, this isn't going to help us get EDS's long-term contracts signed," Luce told his client. It was a polite way of reminding him that Smith, for all his faults, still was EDS's main sponsor, and a vote against Hughes was likely to alienate him. Elmer Johnson had told Luce that as far as he knew, no one had voted against anything in a GM board meeting since the Depression. And they both knew Perot's single dissenting vote wasn't going to make any difference anyway.

From Perot's expression Luce knew immediately he had said the wrong thing.

"That's a hell of a note when your own lawyer advises you against acting as an independent director," Perot said.

Perot chose to bypass Luce's oblique warning about crossing Smith. He intended Hughes to be an issue of principle, a "gut issue." Perot was convinced that GM was making a disastrous mistake, and he wanted the record to show he had opposed it. Afterward, he would hold a press conference in New York and distribute copies of his GM boardroom speech to the press. He had lost a lot of personal regard for Smith since the blowup in Dallas; publicizing the speech might put some pressure on the GM chairman to clean up his act and put GM's house in order.

On Friday, November 1, 1985, Tom Luce and Mort Meyerson flew to New York. They had decided, in light of the pending vote on Hughes two days hence and the deteriorating relations between Perot and Smith, to spend some time with Elmer Johnson and Ira Millstein finding a way to put the GM-EDS relationship back on the right track.

Luce and Meyerson dropped their bags at EDS's apartment on Sixth Avenue and 55th Street in Manhattan.

For the next two days, the pair shuttled back and forth from the EDS apartment to the General Motors Building. The law firm of Weil Gotshal, Ira Millstein's law firm, occupies several floors of the GM Building. The tableau from Millstein's corner office on the thirty-second floor was a heartstopper. Spread below Millstein's picture window was a chunk of the world's finest real estate: the verdant southeast corner of Central Park, with its ballfields and the skating rink, the Plaza Hotel, Bergdorf-Goodman's, and the Gulf + Western building. The rolling hills of northern New Jersey lay in the distance. Next to Millstein's private corner office was his conference room, its walls papered with presidential citations. A long table, stocked with piles of fresh yellow legal pads and cups of sharp yellow pencils, spanned the room.

Recollections of what happened during the two days that Millstein and Johnson conferred with Meyerson and Luce differ on some significant points. However, at the conclusion of the discussions, the four men initialed a written agreement — a "peace treaty" between GM and EDS — that was submitted for approval to GM's executive committee as the basis of a compromise.

Luce and Meyerson recall long conversations with Millstein and Johnson in which the GM attorneys acknowledged that Roger Smith's effectiveness in dealing with EDS had been seriously compromised. The facsimile memos between Smith and Perot were a major reason. It was all there in black and white: Smith had agreed to certain things and wasn't fulfilling them. Another reason, Luce recalls the GM lawyers acknowledging, was Smith's violent tantrum in front of the EDS officers, which had damaged his credibility and caused a great deal of personal friction with Perot. For these reasons, the GM lawyers suggested a general strategy to search for a *modus vivendi* removing Smith and Perot from the conflict.

Luce and Meyerson agreed to discuss this negotiating tack. But as the four men explored possible ways to take Smith and Perot "out of the loop," Meyerson began to suspect that GM's true agenda, in fact, might be finding a way to remove Perot from GM entirely. The feeling was reinforced when Millstein and Johnson suggested the possibility of separating EDS's telecommunications business from the rest of the company and allowing Perot and Meyerson (if he wanted to) to buy it. In return, Perot had to agree to remove himself from active participation in the rest of EDS.

"You don't understand," Meyerson explained to them. "EDS is indivisible. It doesn't contain little units you can move around like blocks."

Well, then, the GM lawyers suggested to Meyerson, perhaps you might convince Perot to take a less active role, to do the things he's always wanted to do but never had time for, to fade more into the background. He's got fabulous wealth, they said, and he's accomplished everything he wants to accomplish. We get along well with you, Mort. If you helped Perot agree to fade out, perhaps you would be able to move into a more active role, take over his seat on the GM board.

It was unmistakable. They were proposing that Meyerson betray Perot, help them push him aside. Afterward he would be rewarded with the helm of EDS and a seat on the GM board.

"I don't think it's right," Meyerson said, stifling his indignation as much as possible. Luce also was shocked by the suggestion, but said nothing.

(Ira Millstein and Elmer Johnson maintain they never offered Meyerson the helm of EDS or a seat on the GM board and never suggested Perot should step down from active management.)

Yet the four men did agree on a way to remove Perot and Smith from the field of fire. Their discussions concluded late Sunday. The peace treaty between GM and EDS was typed and prepared for submission the next morning to the GM executive committee, Roger Smith and his five ranking officers. Without Smith's agreement the document would be meaningless.

The treaty called for appointment of a committee consisting of Perot and Don Atwood "to study and recommend to the board of directors what steps, including specific target dates, GM should take to insure that it produces world-class quality cars at the lowest competitive cost." Alex Mair, the group executive in charge of technical staffs who had been an oracle years earlier of GM's competitive problems, was designated "chief support person" for the Perot-Atwood committee. Mair, who was scheduled to retire six months later in the spring of 1986, agreed to stay on if the committee needed his help.

In the treaty's second major provision, EDS senior vice president Les Alberthal was placed in charge of EDS's accounts at GM — the business Riedlinger had run — and instructed to channel progress reports to Jim McDonald, GM's president. McDonald, scheduled for retirement the following summer, also was named the final authority in any operating disputes between the two organizations.

The treaty also called for pursuing several "initiatives having high priority in [Mort Meyerson's] mind and for which he asked the support of Roger Smith and James McDonald. . . ." (The initiatives subsequently were approved unanimously by the executive committee.) They included instructing McKinsey to keep working on a definition of EDS's computer strategy for GM. Another initiative specified dates by which contracts and pricing agreements were to be signed: GM would sign one-year fixed-price contracts no later than December 15, 1985, a month hence. Long-term, fixed-price contracts were to be signed a few months later, "in early spring."

As a compromise to the lingering bitterness over EDS's truncated compensation plan, Meyerson agreed that all future stock incentives, whether awarded in GM or EDS or the soon-to-be-established GM Hughes Electronics unit, be paid in the shares of all three units, "the purpose being to promote a better spirit of cooperation and teamwork among the employees of all three entities."

As the dry leaves skittered across Fifth Avenue and the harvest moon beamed down over Manhattan, Meyerson and Luce exited GM's white stone monolith, the initialed agreements in their briefcases. They hailed a cab to Perot's hotel.

Perot wasn't impressed.

"Ross, we think this is worth a try," Luce said. His lawyerly confidence in written agreements was speaking. At bottom Luce didn't believe in war, which no one wins; he believed in compromise.

"OK," he said. "You fellas think it's worth trying, we'll give it a run. But I'm telling you, this is something they're agreeing to in order to get past this board meeting. They don't know what to do about me or about EDS, and they'll sign just about anything at this point."

Luce had found out long ago that the only thing that impressed Ross Perot was results. Process meant very little to him. To GM, process was everything. The meetings, committees, flowcharts, lines of authority, matrices, treaties — GM felt secure amid procedures. In the current predicament, however, agreeing to a procedural solution might bring them past the crisis, Luce thought, and give time a chance to heal some wounds.

"Have you decided what to do about Hughes?" Luce asked.

In Perot's hand was a copy of the speech he had written for the board meeting. Following the meeting it was to be duplicated and handed to the major news organizations.

"Ross, I don't think this is the time to go public. We've just signed a peace treaty. How's it going to look if we set off a hand grenade on the Hughes acquisition? We might as well not have talked to them at all about compromise," Meyerson said. Luce agreed.

When Perot set his mind to do something, the only people at EDS who had a chance of convincing him not to proceed were Meyerson and Luce. This time Perot acquiesced to the advice of the two men, reluctantly agreeing to keep his opposition to Hughes quiet for the time being.

"There's something else you should know, Ross," Mort said. "Elmer and Ira sounded me out about helping them get rid of you and taking over EDS myself." Meyerson didn't have to tell him that he and Luce had ignored their feeler.

"These guys must be incredibly stupid if they think they can pull something like that," Perot said. "Well, don't worry about this. It just proves what level of people we're dealing with here."

The next morning Perot and Meyerson agreed to meet for breakfast before the GM board meeting. As Meyerson was crossing 55th Street he bumped into GM president Jim McDonald, who was headed for the GM Building. They shook hands. McDonald, a proud, straight-shooting manufacturing engineer from Bay City, Michigan, was known throughout GM for his dynamic speaking and communications skills. It was whispered inside GM that he had very little respect for Smith or many of his strategies. But McDonald was too much a loyal "team player" to make his views known outside the fourteenth floor.

"Do you think the problems between Ross and Roger are going to be solved?" McDonald asked. After the Dallas meeting, the reverberations had been felt by the executive committee, raising the fear that what previously had been seen as a border skirmish between the two men and the two organizations might lead at any moment to nuclear showdown.

"Can't say," Meyerson replied. "My guess is he'll vote his conscience on Hughes, but not go public."

The twenty-fifth floor of the GM Building contains the GM treasurer's office and very little else besides some offices and a grand ornate boardroom, which is used only a dozen times a year. Perot always marveled at the elaborate paneling and joked with Meyerson about the teak forests that must have been felled to construct it. To Perot, the boardroom's decor bespoke GM's bloated self-importance, its concern with trappings over substance.

The morning of the GM board meeting is usually reserved for board committee meetings. If there is any spirited discussion or dissent over an item to be decided by directors, it normally occurs in the committees. By the time an item of business reaches the full GM board for approval, it is more a formality or a news item than a question still to be debated.

On Elmer Johnson's recommendation, the executive committee approved the peace treaty reached the previous day. While the committee was meeting, Perot gave a copy of his Hughes speech for the board meeting to Johnson and Millstein to review. Inasmuch as he had decided not to distribute the speech to the newspapers, Perot was prepared to listen to the GM lawyers' suggestions for ways to drive home his points without unnecessarily starting a war.

Johnson and Millstein immediately suggested that Perot get rid of a request in the speech to meet privately with non-GM directors. Perot had wanted to discuss with the directors his perception of GM's ills in greater detail — without Smith listening. (He had asked Smith to arrange such a meeting a few weeks earlier but was turned down.) Johnson and Millstein believed a private meeting with outside directors would be interpreted by Smith as subversive. Perot agreed to delete it from his speech.

As the full board began deliberation of the Hughes acquisition later that day, Perot asked Smith for permission to speak. He walked to the splendid wooden pulpit and laid his papers in front of him. He put on his reading glasses.

"I request that my comments be recorded verbatim and made part of the permanent records of GM," he said. Perot's request was mildly provocative since it implied that someone later might try to disavow what he said. (In a previous version of the speech he asked that his remarks be read into the board minutes. Johnson and Millstein suggested instead that Perot's speech be kept elsewhere in GM's "permanent record." That way, an outside attorney who someday asked GM to produce the minutes of the meeting for a legal action wouldn't know that Perot had delivered a speech attacking a decision of the board.)

> Fourteen months ago I told the members of the GM board that the only reason we at EDS decided to sell our company to GM was to become involved in the challenge of building the best cars in the world at competitive prices. At the time of the acquisition we were told that we would work together as partners to accomplish this goal. Over a thousand members of the EDS team volunteered to go anywhere in the world, and did. All of us looked forward with great enthusiasm to spending the rest of our business careers helping GM win. The stakes were enormous: 788,000 jobs at GM. Over three million jobs indirectly created by GM. An important segment of the U.S. economy and tax base.
>
> As a GM director and large stockholder, I have had a special interest in the success of this effort. First, I needed to understand the car business. During the past fourteen months I have talked with several thousand former GMers who joined EDS. We visited in small groups where I could listen and learn. I have visited with hundreds of GM employees in middle management through top management — either individually or in small groups where I could listen. Over 200 of these managers and executives have had dinner and spent the evening in my home teaching me about GM — in an environment where I could listen and learn. I have read and studied any written material I could obtain to learn more about our competitors. I have been particularly interested in our most successful competitors, and their techniques.
>
> In addition, the EDSers working for GM all over the world provide me with a continuing education of what is really happening at the working level. At my first board meeting I told you that as a director I would be an advocate for the stockholders, the car buyers,

the car dealers and the employees. I have spent a great deal of time visiting with and listening to these groups. I have personally responded to customer complaints directed to me. I have spoken to the car dealers at their national convention, visited their showrooms and visited with them individually and in small groups. I have carefully read the letters from stockholders, answering their telephone calls and tried to learn from them.

GM is large and complex. I would prefer to have continued this process for a longer period of time before making any comments to the board. The Hughes transaction requires me to speak today:

The driving force behind the Hughes transaction is a desire to acquire additional advanced technology for GM. I ask my fellow board members to keep in mind that I have spent my entire business career in advanced technology companies. Most of my time will be spent today talking about GM, and what we must do to make it competitive, because the Hughes acquisition must be considered in that context.

He paused for a moment to grab everyone's attention.

General Motors . . . should . . . not . . . acquire . . . Hughes.

There are a number of reasons why I consider this to be a poor business transaction. First, let's examine it from GM's point of view.

Then Perot sketched the gory details of GM's recent loss of automotive market share and quality leadership, despite its preponderance of resources, financial and engineering. He included facts most directors probably didn't regard as news, yet he wanted to buttress his case solidly and make them understand he had done ample homework before spouting off.

Perot was careful during his speech to compliment GM executives Jim McDonald, Alex Cunningham, and Don Atwood, who were in the room, calling them "the finest executives in our industry." Saying this also had been suggested by the GM lawyers.

But he never mentioned Smith. If the omission wasn't intentional, it was highly revealing.

"Our core problem is that the GM system is too centralized. Very little responsibility and authority is given to experienced talented executives and managers. GM is procedures oriented, not results oriented. Too much time is spent in nonproductive meetings. Matters that would take minutes or hours to be resolved in a normal business environment take weeks, months, or may never reach decisions at GM," he said. "Senior management is too isolated from the people."

The "GM system," he said, isn't related to "the rules of the business, profit, competition, or the international marketplace."

Intentionally or not, the next arrow was aimed directly at Smith's high-tech strategy, which, ironically, had brought Ross Perot and EDS into GM. GM had spent billions on high-tech machinery for its plants and still was producing low-quality cars and trucks. Perot cited Jim Harbour, a widely respected automotive consultant, who observed that Japanese plants achieved high quality with very old equipment, relying instead on clever management to eliminate waste and defects.

In a visit to a Cadillac dealers conference, Perot told the directors, he was dismayed to hear how upset they had become about Cadillac's poor quality.

"I then asked, 'Why aren't these problems being solved?' The answer was: 'GM doesn't give people the responsibility and authority to get things done — and the GM system avoids individual accountability.' "

Perot said he had asked the dealers, as seriously as he knew how, what he could do to help. A dealer blurted out to Perot to help him get a Honda franchise. Immediately. Hondas need a tenth as many repairs as Cadillacs, the man said.

None of GM's problems was irreversible, Perot said. Jaguar had made a big turnaround recently with very little expenditure of capital. And Jaguar's chief executive had once worked for a GM subsidiary.

"I doubt seriously if [he] could have accomplished this dramatic recovery working inside the GM system," he said.

Another carmaker, Toyota, rose from the brink of bankruptcy in 1951 to number-three automaker in the world. Its capital spending was a fraction of GM's, but Toyota employees worked as a team, and managers listened to suggestions from the lowliest worker on the assembly line. Lest anyone try to dismiss Toyota as an inappropriate comparison, said Perot, the company now was building assembly capacity in the United States and managing once-unruly GM workers in Fremont, California!

In Perot's opinion, GM's $5 billion Saturn project was another exercise in capital spending excess. Honda invested $600 million in a U.S. plant employing 3,000 workers to make 300,000 cars a year. Saturn's $5 billion would employ 6,000 workers building 400,000 to 500,000 cars a year, he told the board. Indeed, the directors knew a great deal about

Saturn — they had approved the Saturn budget — but it was unlikely they'd ever seen the numbers compared that way.

"The point I'm trying to make is that we can become so preoccupied with using capital . . . [and] our front-end investment will be so large that it alone will make it difficult for GM to be competitive. The experiences of our successful competitors demonstrate that people — plus the intelligent application of capital — are the keys," he said.

Obviously, GM could ill afford to waste capital on Hughes, he said, piling on the arguments he had presented to Elmer Johnson and Don Atwood and the GM financial department earlier in the year in Dallas.

By pestering the GM finance department, Perot discovered that only two of Hughes's 5,000 contracts (mostly to the U.S. Department of Defense) accounted for 30 percent of profits; only 10 contracts accounted for a whopping 65 percent of profits. Hughes was very vulnerable to loss of a single important contract. To this he added another bombshell, not generally known outside of GM's finance department: "Hughes' earnings are now down from forecasts made at the time the GM board reviewed this prospect. This came as a surprise. If Hughes can't forecast its short-term earnings, why should we have confidence in its ability to forecast long-term earnings?"

GM directors must reconsider and vote again, he urged. The gauntlet was thrown down. The directors who had been hearing bits and pieces, whispers of Smith's behind-the-scenes tussles with Ross Perot, now heard and saw for themselves the depth of his opposition.

He wasn't through speaking, however. Perot saved his last rhetorical flourish for the board itself. He had been astonished during the last eighteen months of meetings, he said, how little discussion and questioning he had heard from the board.

As stewards for one of the world's largest corporations, whose future success can dramatically impact the lives of several million people and the economy of the United States, I urge each of my fellow board members to think about the following ideas: We need to become more active in understanding what is really happening inside GM. If GM is to change, it must start at the top, and we are the top. We the members of the board are the shareholders' voice, serving as their elected representatives. We must change the format of board meetings from passive sessions with little two-way communication to active participatory sessions that allow us to discuss real issues and resolve real problems.

As board members, we must send a clear signal to the corporation that the shareholders are not simply a nuisance to be dealt with at the annual meeting, and avoided whenever possible.

Perot raised the volume of voice ever so slightly:

They own this company.
We must make it clear that the management serves at the pleasure of the shareholders, and must not act as owners simply because our shareholders are widely dispersed, and there is no concentration of ownership. Corporate America has a peculiar process that we must recognize. The managers of mature corporations with no concentration of owners have gotten themselves into the position of effectively selecting the board members who will represent the stockholders. In this environment, the directors must be particularly sensitive to the stockholders, our owners.

Finally Perot conceded what, by that time, they knew: Hughes wasn't the real question for him. It was the future of GM.

I am concerned that our corporate wealth gives us a sense of false security. We must generate a sense of urgency while we are strong. We can be the finest car company in the world. We must become the finest car company in the world. The directors of GM must provide the vision and leadership to move boldly toward that goal. Thank you.

It was a safe bet that nothing quite like Perot's critique had been heard inside the walls of GM's boardroom. His broadside was full of revolutionary fervor, delivered with all the passion Perot could inject. He was suggesting no less than abandonment of Smith's capital-spending strategy and a return to basics. He wasn't asking to be GM's chairman, but he was asking for his thoughts and ideas to be accepted as new guiding principles for GM's chairman.

GM directors, however, weren't likely revolutionaries. The other GM executives on the board — McDonald, Atwood, and Cunningham — were as committed to the GM system as Smith was. The system had become a majority of one. The outsiders, by and large, came from large U.S. companies, too; some enjoyed virtual autocracy in their own companies; they had heard these criticisms of GM and corporate America before.

Smith had no intention of rebutting Perot's comments. He politely thanked him and asked if anyone had any questions.

Perot didn't truly expect the GM board to table the Hughes acquisition — it would have been unrealistic only weeks before the closing — but he did hope for more than he got:

A wall of vague, uncomprehending, slightly shocked stares and silence. No one made a comment. No one asked a question.

Roger Smith thanked Perot and moved on to the next order of business.

EIGHTEEN

Losing Patience

U NTIL the General Motors board of directors meeting in November
1985, antipathy between GM and Perot remained hidden from
public view. Because of a legal technicality related to Perot's
vote against the Hughes transaction, the veil would be abruptly lifted.

The proxy disclosure statement that GM was legally required to send
to all shareholders explaining the reasons for the $5.2 billion Hughes
transaction contained 88 pages of densely worded legalese followed by
158 pages of appendices packed with numbers. Among the hundreds of
thousands of numbers and facts presented in the weighty document was
a seemingly unremarkable four-word clause, which appeared to be
included as an afterthought. The clause stated that the GM board
approval of the Hughes acquisition was carried out "with one director
dissenting."

Inclusion of the clause was no afterthought but the subject of some
intense hand-wringing by GM lawyers. Arguably, GM might have left
the clause out, since Perot's dissent didn't change the outcome of the
vote. Smith preferred telling the shareholders as little as legally required
about the inner workings of the board. In the past he had sometimes
shown that he regarded shareholders as a nuisance; for example, he had
tried unsuccessfully to cook up a separate annual meeting for gadflies and

troublemakers in 1982; and he spoke to Wall Street security analysts only sporadically.

Wall Street wouldn't need any guidance to understand the significance of the four-word clause or that it signaled rare open dissent inside the GM boardroom. Putting two and two together and linking dissent to Perot also wouldn't require the services of a Sherlock Holmes.

Elmer Johnson argued that disclosure of the dissenting vote should be included in the proxy. In thirty years as an SEC lawyer he had learned what penalties awaited corporations that failed to disclose relevant information to shareholders. If the Hughes acquisition ever resulted in a shareholder lawsuit, he wanted to be on solid ground in defending the board's actions; he wanted to be able to demonstrate that shareholders knew there was a dissenting vote against Hughes and approved it anyway. Always better to overdisclose, Johnson liked to say, than underdisclose.

Within days of the proxy's release, newspaper stories about the Hughes acquisition appeared, referring to the mysterious disclosure of ''one director dissenting.'' A few enterprising telephone calls to EDS headquarters elicited confirmation from Ross Perot of the dissenting director's identity.

While Wall Street and the financial press wondered how serious the rift between Perot and GM was, Johnson and Tom Luce, two eminently skilled and reasonable lawyers, met through December and January to work out a master pricing agreement between EDS and GM that temporarily relieved some of the pressure on the relationship.

Ira Millstein, Bob Messineo, and others working with the oversight committee stood at the Weil Gotshal chalkboard and attempted to devise an arithmetic formula that was fair to both sides. If EDS made too big a profit, GM shareholders might legitimately feel exploited. However, GM, as a shareholder in EDS, also shared in EDS profits, so its financial interests in the matter weren't completely clear.

Struggle as they might, no one's math was good enough to devise a formula that satisfied everyone.

Luce and Johnson did manage to agree on a temporary arrangement under which all work was to be billed on a cost-plus basis; EDS charged its costs plus 9½ percent. In the meantime, negotiations continued toward the signing of fixed-price, long-term contracts, the mainstay of EDS's performance ethic.

The cost plus 9½ percent contracts raised another issue. GM, quite naturally, wanted detailed, independent accounting of EDS's costs during the cost-plus phase, which meant a regular and thorough audit by GM controllers.

This spelled trouble. Perot would no sooner permit GM auditors to comb through EDS's books than he would invite Willie Sutton to inventory his silverware drawer. Overnight, Luce saw that another explosive issue between the two companies now was on the table.

"You realize, of course, that the agreement specifies that EDS is entitled to its own independent auditor," Luce said. Johnson indeed realized it, but he also believed in the tenets of good corporate governance, which called for central accounting and double-checking.

At this stage the two lawyers were acting as surrogates for their employers but also trying to keep the relationship on a reasonably even keel by exercising independent judgment. Each understood the perspective of the other; they spoke amicably; and neither was handicapped by the bad personal chemistry that had poisoned the air between Smith and Perot since late the previous summer.

As the pricing negotiations ground slowly forward, Luce came to believe that Johnson was the strongest voice of reason at GM. He invited his counterpart to Dallas as his guest for a charity dinner in February that was being held to honor Perot. It would be an opportunity to get to know one another better and perhaps iron out wrinkles in the relationship between Perot and Smith.

Johnson flew down to Dallas a day before the dinner to speak to Luce's partners about the process of building a law firm. The two men flew together to Austin later in the day to see a $15 million collection of rare books that Perot had donated to the University of Texas. Johnson had majored in English at Yale; to hold first editions of Shakespeare, Milton, and Chaucer in his hands was unbelievably thrilling. That evening, Perot threw a bash at his home for a select group of guests who arrived in town early for the dinner. Songwriter Sammy Cahn played the piano and talked about tunes he had written for Frank Sinatra.

The Winston Churchill Foundation had decided a year earlier to bestow its award on Perot. The organization was devoted to sending outstanding scholars from the United States to study at Churchill College, Cambridge. The scholars who had received money from the foundation were distinguished; eight Churchill scholars had won Nobel Prizes. Only Margaret Thatcher and Averell Harriman had previously been honored with the foundation's award.

The main ballroom of the Loew's Anatole Hotel in Dallas was decked out in magnificent fashion on the evening of February 18, 1986. Prince

Charles was to present the award to Perot. Lady Diana, for undisclosed reasons that supermarket tabloids claimed were connected to marital problems, chose not to come along. Nancy Reagan represented the U.S. government. The evening featured regal entertainment, including the Dallas Symphony Orchestra, the Naval Academy glee club, the Marine Drum and Bugle Corps, and a surprise appearance by opera diva Leontyne Price.

Roger and Barbara Smith attended, as well as Marlene and Mort Meyerson. So did Elmer and Connie Johnson, who sat with Tom and Pam Luce. Merrill Lynch analyst Steve McClellan was there, seated at a table donated by his brokerage. Over medallions of veal with sun-dried tomatoes, hundreds of guests, each of whose seat represented a donation of $1,000 or more, listened to orchestra music, patriotic songs, and, of course, lots of speeches.

The Prince of Wales, who had seen his share of glittering ceremonies, confessed to being dazzled by the Texas-sized spectacle. He lauded Perot's accomplishments, the hostage rescue, and the founding of EDS. Someone obviously had told the Prince of Wales what Perot was most proud of: his ability to create jobs and his trust and respect for the people who worked for him. At the appointed moment, he hung the Churchill medal around Perot's neck.

Perot's speech focused on Sir Winston's accomplishments and the great speeches he had delivered, particularly during World War II. What captivated Perot was the British prime minister's ability to rally a nation. He stirred the dinner audience, reciting in his distinctive twang the phrases memorized by every British schoolchild.

The people who sat with Roger Smith at the GM table noticed that Perot fixed his gaze in their direction when he recited the speech Churchill gave at the Harrow School in the fall of 1941:

"Never give in, never give in, never, never, never, never."

Since his first days at GM, Elmer Johnson had been unimpressed with the corporation's public relations skill. He had been given the responsibility of supervising public relations. If deteriorating relations with Perot resulted in a public donnybrook — as they nearly had over Hughes — GM was sure to need speedy PR help from the outside, Johnson knew.

Ira Millstein suggested that Johnson meet Gershon Kekst.

In the world of corporate takeovers, raiders, poison pills, and junk bonds, Gershon Kekst was arguably the foremost professional shaper of public opinion, specializing in the affairs of Wall Street. What Kekst provided wasn't exactly press relations, not exactly public relations, not exactly shareholder relations. It was, in the words of Washington image makers, spin management. Companies, encouraged by their lawyers, hired Kekst and Company to improve their image when they launched hostile takeovers; others hired him to help defend against hostile takeovers. By selectively sorting and releasing information to reporters, a technique far too sophisticated for most in-house public relations people, Kekst associates endeavored to place white hats on their clients, to shape the story to their clients' advantage. Gershon Kekst had represented Boone Pickens, and he had represented companies attacking Boone Pickens. He translated the parlance of Wall Street traders and counseled chief executives on what words to use, what points to make, what denunciations to deliver. During Pickens's assault on Gulf Oil, Kekst attempted to convince reporters that Boone had a history of deserting shareholders. Kekst succeeded in persuading many Gulf shareholders not to trust Pickens. Pickens failed in a proxy contest to close his pincers on Gulf.

By the time Elmer Johnson hired Kekst, the Manhattan public relations man numbered dozens of Fortune 500 companies among his clients. Many of these clients weren't in any immediate trouble but kept Kekst on retainer just in case.

Kekst listened to a history of the turmoil between Perot and GM. He had seen similar-looking situations grow into full-scale disasters at other corporations. Corporate managements tended to wait too long, hoping dissident shareholders like Perot eventually would listen to reason or go away. The simplest and most effective survival tactic was to get rid of the irritant as soon as possible.

Kekst advised Millstein and Johnson: Get rid of Perot now — while you still can.

The 5,000 or so GM hourly workers assigned to the Hamtramck, Michigan, car-assembly plant were praying for Roger Smith's twenty-first-century vision to come true more fervently than anyone.

The Hamtramck plant, nicknamed Poletown, employed more high-tech robotics and computer-driven equipment than any automobile plant in the world.

Far from displacing workers, high-tech meant jobs for thousands of workers who previously had been laid off from GM in the face of foreign competition. Poletown was the living representation of what Roger had been preaching. It was GM's chance to leapfrog the competition.

As the day drew near in early 1985 to introduce the new 1986 luxury car models built at Poletown, GM engineers were having a devil of a time de-bugging the hundreds of advanced machines and laser-guided devices. No sooner did the robots in the body shop weld sheet metal properly than the new modular painting robots commenced spraying one another. The lasers worked well one day and conked out the next. Much of the time the workers just waited, read newspapers, and eyed the machines nervously. The engineers and managers responsible for the factory felt the pressure, too; the stressed-out plant manager took early retirement.

If GM had tried to introduce one or two glitzy automation projects instead of dozens and dozens, the Poletown plant might have opened smoothly. GM's software and engineering expertise, under extreme deadline pressure, just wasn't sufficient for the job.

Poletown's manufacturing snafus foreshadowed another bit of very bad news: the cars GM managed to build at the plant were bombing in the marketplace. GM had downsized the Cadillac Sevilles and Eldorados, Oldsmobile Toronados, and Buick Rivieras to increase fuel efficiency at a time when buyers wanted more size and power. Once again the new designs failed to excite buyers, and worse still, they closely resembled other, less-expensive GM models.

GM wasn't alone. High-tech delays had plagued Ford and Chrysler as well. But this was little comfort to Perot, who was reading and hearing from people at EDS about the growing mess at Poletown. His pleas to GM directors a few months earlier to forget about Hughes and concentrate on GM's basic businesses had fallen on deaf ears. GM's 1985 profit was down from a year earlier and so was profit in the first quarter of 1986. Smith had told managers to cut discretionary spending and yanked the company's management retreat at the Greenbrier resort in West Virginia back to Detroit.

Perot's concern about GM's operating glitches were to be addressed by the two-man committee, consisting of Perot and Atwood with help from Al Mair, set up in the framework of the peace treaty. The committee was charged to come up with methods of building world-class cars at competitive prices. Perot had been skeptical of GM's sincerity from the outset, and his skepticism was borne out by events. He called Atwood a number of times and couldn't get him to commit himself to a meeting. Obviously, the idea of forming a committee was GM's way of stalling opposition to Hughes and preventing a press conference. Now that the Hughes deal was approved, Perot surmised, GM was dropping the plan to involve him. (Jim McDonald asked Al Mair if he would be willing to extend his career past normal retirement to help the Atwood-Perot committee; Mair agreed but didn't hear another word.)

At EDS's first-quarter board meeting in Dallas, Perot hoped Roger might say something to dispel the rapidly spreading public notion that GM was being soundly thrashed in the market by foreign and domestic competitors. Instead, Smith handed Perot a list of "auditing concerns," detailing instances in which EDS, apparently at Perot's direction, had refused to allow GM auditors to go over EDS's books.

Perot was stunned. How could Smith concern himself with such trivia in the midst of a disastrous reception of GM's cars? As the bad news about GM operations mounted, Perot grew more certain that GM's captain was badly off course and stubbornly uninterested in navigational advice.

With Perot and Smith supposedly kept out of the line of fire by the treaty, Mort Meyerson desperately searched for some common ground for agreement with GM executives Alex Cunningham and Alan Smith.

The discussions went nowhere. Each conversation rapidly turned into an argument. Every argument with GM, Meyerson discovered, had a circularity that kept coming back to lavish EDS compensation, EDS's need to understand and be patient with GM's institutional torpor, charges of unreasonably high prices for EDS services, and accusations of slow response by EDS to GM's requests.

The rumors of the impasse over pricing of EDS services had spread to Wall Street, causing widespread sale of GM Class E shares. Security analysts were alarmed at the falling price of the stock, which had been trading in the high forties and now was dipping below thirty-nine. A few turned bearish. Chuck Taylor, a Prudential-Bache analyst, called EDS investment relations in early February 1986 to say that he had heard that GM and EDS weren't able to agree on pricing and contract terms. If that was so, the earnings outlook for GM Class E was clouded. Peter Anastos, who supervised the Alliance Capital mutual fund's 2.7 million share stake in GM Class E stock, called EDS shareholder relations, shaken and upset by the stock price decline. If he didn't get a better feel for contract negotiations with GM, Anastos said, he was going to recommend sale of the shares.

Since he was getting nowhere with Alan Smith and Cunningham, Meyerson decided to try GM president Jim McDonald. McDonald, who was designated to arbitrate Meyerson's still unpaid salary, struck Meyerson as a sympathetic, avuncular sort of man who might offer useful suggestions to break the impasse. He seemed willing at least to talk.

Meyerson traced the history of GM's agreement with EDS, bringing McDonald up-to-date on the skirmishes, including the latest auditing disputes, through early 1986. He dragged out all the documents and briefing booklets for the GM president to prove what had been said and what had been promised. Meyerson also briefed McDonald on Wall Street's nervousness.

"GM made certain representations to Wall Street in writing about what EDS expected to earn and what kind of profit margins it was going to have. If you've changed your mind about that, you've got to say so," Meyerson said. He didn't have to explain to McDonald his belief that GM, by failing to live up to the terms of the merger agreement, was leaving itself open to charges of securities fraud.

"Tom Walter and I are receiving a steady stream of phone calls from analysts wanting to know if earnings are going to be consistent with our disclosures," he said. "Until last month I had been very confident that ultimately things would work out."

McDonald stroked his chin, considering what Meyerson had just presented to him. Smith hadn't consulted McDonald about buying EDS. After umpteen meetings with Meyerson in his office, it wasn't apparent to him what he could do.

Meyerson felt like a beaver who had built a dam of arguments and explanations a dozen times — and watched as high water washed it away again and again. The peace treaty had turned out to be a sham. He had been over the agreements with Johnson, with Roger Smith, with Alan Smith, with Alex Cunningham, with scores of GM managers, and now with Jim McDonald. There had to be a way; he wasn't giving up yet.

On a blustery day in mid March, after meeting McDonald in Detroit and again making no progress, Meyerson drove to City Airport in Detroit to board the EDS Learjet for the flight back to Dallas. He felt extremely weary but undefeated. As the jet climbed, Meyerson pulled out a yellow legal pad. He sat alone in the aircraft's cabin, facing toward the back of the plane with his legs propped on the rear seat.

As he scratched down some thoughts outlining yet another possible means of breaking the impasse, his mind wandered over the hundreds of methods and compromises he had already suggested to GM and that had all turned to dust.

Meyerson put the pad and pen down and turned off the overhead light. A strange sensation came over him. As he sat in the darkened cabin, he intuitively knew there was nothing more for him to do. It was over. There wasn't going to be a compromise, there wasn't going to be a solution. As often as he had butted his head into the wall, it wasn't going to fall. GM was capable of swamping him in meetings and memos and telephone calls and conferences and peace treaties until the end of time. Now it seemed so clear: Roger Smith hadn't any intention of fulfilling what he and Perot agreed upon, and there wasn't a damn thing they could do about it.

The utter frustration of the past two years singed his insides. His eyes were burning. He had only felt this way once before as an adult, when he and Perot had reached the end of the line on Wall Street at Dupont Walston. As the tears rolled down his cheeks, he stuffed the yellow legal pad back into his briefcase.

The Learjet hurtled through the darkness toward Dallas.

The next morning Meyerson walked into his office and asked Sherry Martino, his secretary, to come in. He dictated a short note to Perot, resigning from EDS, and asked her to type it.

Envelope in hand, he walked down the hall to Perot's office.

"Ross, I'm sorry I have to do this. I've got to resign," Meyerson said. "We're not dealing with honorable men. I've failed and I'm tired of running into the wall and not getting anywhere. It's obvious I'm not the one to get the job done."

Perot's first reaction was surprise, quickly followed by anger at GM. Because of GM's refusal to live up to the deal, he thought, EDS was going to lose Mort. First Riedlinger had been driven beyond what he could do by the GM system. Now Mort. Two of EDS's best men, men who had dedicated their entire professional lives to EDS and to Perot, had done everything humanly possible to make the merger work. And they had self-destructed in doing so.

Perot, who had ventured into the heart of the Iranian revolution to rescue EDS people in trouble, felt just as responsible for Meyerson's fate as he had for his captured executives. He blamed GM, just as he had blamed the Iranian government, for what had happened.

"Mort, you can't mean this," Perot said.

"I'm sorry, Ross, I'm unwilling ever to go to Detroit again," Meyerson said. "It's clear GM isn't going to keep its part of the bargain, and I'm not going to participate in the dismemberment of EDS. I've put too much of my life into it.

"You should select a new president of EDS, and I'll help that person in any way I can," Meyerson said. Les Alberthal was the best man for the job, he told Perot.

Alberthal was a good, solid, loyal — if unspectacular — EDS executive who had served in a variety of managerial posts all over the country and endured the demands of working for Perot and Meyerson. (Meyerson once transferred Alberthal from EDS's office in San Francisco back to Dallas and then transferred him to an EDS office in Topeka, Kansas, before he could unpack the trunks from California.)

Both men felt glum, so Meyerson tried to lighten the mood a bit: "Well, at least this solves the hassle over my salary."

Though Meyerson's mind was made up to have nothing more to do with GM, Perot wanted to stop him from jumping ship entirely.

"Mort, don't resign," Perot said. "Why not stay on as chairman. You can be in charge of acquisitions to build up EDS's non-GM accounts." He hated to lose Meyerson's creative touch, the serendipitous, sometimes almost whimsical, way he viewed business problems.

"I'll think about it," Meyerson said. He did and decided to stay temporarily, but in the background, as vice chairman.

On April 28, 1986, EDS held its second briefing for Wall Street security analysts since becoming a part of GM at the Amfac Hotel near Dallas–Ft. Worth Airport.

Steve McClellan, now nearly a year in his new job at Merrill Lynch, was optimistic and growing more so about EDS's progress. The ripple of controversy surrounding Ross Perot's vote against the Hughes Aircraft acquisition and the flap about pricing hadn't troubled him unduly. He had seen Perot stubbornly keep his own counsel numerous times in the past, and Roger Smith repeatedly said he found the trait refreshing.

As McClellan walked into the auditorium with the other analysts, he noticed Marlene Meyerson, Mort's wife, and Jean Walter, Tom's wife, seated in the audience.

That's strange, he thought. EDS wives showed up at management meetings out of town. They never before had come to presentations for security analysts at home.

"Hi, Marlene," McClellan said. "What's up?"

"Well, I get to see Mort so little with all the trips back and forth to Detroit, this is a chance to be together," she joked. Although this was an emotional moment for her and her husband, she gave no hint to McClellan of what he and the others were to learn a few moments later, that Mort was relinquishing the presidency to Les Alberthal and taking over as vice chairman. Tom Walter, who had grown frustrated in the effort to formulate a compensation system acceptable to GM, relinquished his post as chief financial officer. Walter, the analysts were told, would help Meyerson with acquisitions.

The subterfuge masking Meyerson's Waterloo at GM worked perfectly.

McClellan didn't suspect for a moment that EDS's creative chief operating executive was really stepping aside because he no longer could deal with GM. In Merrill Lynch's research report to investors published a few days after the meeting, McClellan brushed lightly over Meyerson's departure, saying it "added some uncertainty" to EDS's prospects.

McClellan and the other analysts instead focused on what they judged to be a very positive development, the announcement of the compromise master pricing agreement negotiated by Tom Luce and Elmer Johnson. Under this compromise, EDS agreed to bill GM on a cost plus 12 to 14 percent profit basis for 35 percent of its revenue from GM. For another 10 to 15 percent of the GM revenues, billing would be on the basis of negotiated long-term fixed-price contracts. The final 50 percent would be on a cost-sharing, overrun-sharing arrangement with a guarantee of at least a 9½ percent profit margin.

The master pricing compromise replaced the long-term, fixed-price contracts EDS was promised in the merger agreement. The compromise was something both lawyers believed the two sides could live with. All that remained was for the individual GM contracting groups, 128 in all, to sign individual agreements with EDS.

The pricing issue between EDS and GM seemingly resolved, McClellan boosted his investment rating on Class E shares to the second-highest possible.

Meyerson's decision to step aside as EDS president was the last straw for Perot.

He intended to give Roger Smith one more chance to return to their original idea of a true alliance between GM and an independent EDS.

He told Smith at the GM board meeting on May 5, 1986, in New York that he was through compromising his principles in the name of harmony. When he returned to Dallas, he summarized what he had told Smith and mailed the letter to him.

May 7, 1986

DEAR ROGER,

The purpose of this letter is to confirm our understanding of May 5.

1. I will run EDS in accordance with the intent and the spirit that we agreed to in our verbal conversations, memoranda written during negotiations, and the agreement of purchase. Basically, this means

I will run EDS, just as I ran it before GM acquired EDS. Specifically, I will be responsible for the compensation of EDS people.

2. I agree to keep you informed in advance on all major issues. In the event that you and I cannot agree, we will go to the Board. Each of us will present our position and let the Board decide.

3. You agree to contact me directly on any EDS issues that concern you. No intermediaries will be used in the future. No ultimatums will be given to anyone at EDS.

4. There must be no confusion within GM that Les Alberthal and the entire EDS team works for me. Les and Kenn Hill will coordinate EDS's activities relating to GM through Don Atwood. Don will be our principal customer contact for all GM and Hughes data processing business. EDS will remain where it is on the GM organization chart.

5. I will not attempt to create a compensation program for EDS that looks like GM. Some things that I do may look unorthodox to GM but they have worked to build a strong EDS team and produce results.

We have never lost a key person. We will continue to create incentives to focus our people on EDS's and the shareholders' objectives — significant dependable profit growth. We have purposely created programs that are difficult to compare with [the programs of] other companies in our industry. We have never had a stockholder complaint about the way we compensate our people.

A substantial number of EDSers have become wealthy as a result of their contributions. This opportunity motivates every EDSer. It is fundamentally important that this opportunity not be lost in the future. We have kept our best people by compensating them in ways that say to them: "You are different — you are special — you are the greatest — we appreciate everything you do." We must continue to do this in the future. We have always compensated our people immediately for outstanding contributions, and must continue to do this in the future and without the burden of a long, slow approval process.

6. Salaries for the vast numbers of EDSers are determined at the project level, and driven by the project's required contribution to profit. This is what we have always done. It works. We will continue to do it.

7. We pay bonuses throughout the year at the working level for

outstanding ideas and exceptional work, primarily to individuals not included in the bonus pool. This is all covered by project budgets, driven by profit contribution and does not disrupt EDS's profitability.

8. I will make the final determination on salaries for officers and brief you before informing the officers.

9. I will determine Les' salary. His base salary will not exceed $450,000. Leaving decisions about officer compensation to me is essential, if we are to solve the problems we have had with the people of EDS.

10. If Mort and Tom make exceptional contributions to the growth of EDS in the future, I will pay them bonuses and award them additional shares within the framework outlined in this letter. I want to make sure you understand this because it is important not to turn our two most gifted people into second-class citizens.

11. By November 1 of each year I will brief you on our profit forecast for the coming year and our bonus accrual plan. Once we agree, this will become the basis for our budgets and bonus accrual.

12. Each November I will review the bonus accrual formula with you that I have created for the coming year. After you sign off on it, I will make all the final decisions about how the bonuses are distributed, and will not send a list of bonuses for individuals to anyone in GM to approve. [Perot then outlined EDS's profit projection for 1986.]

13. We don't pay bonuses unless our profit goals are reached. If we fail to reach our profit goals, the money accrued for bonuses will be diverted to profits and no bonuses will be paid until after the profit goals are reached. For example, if we can only reach our profit goals by applying part of the bonus accrual, I would pay only the remainder in bonuses.

[Perot discussed the Hughes bonus plan, rejecting Roger's suggestion that EDS adopt it. He outlined the number of incentive shares and stock options he wanted to grant.]

18. GM's compensation people will not be involved in EDS's compensation in any way, unless I request their assistance.

19. The only other area I can think of where we might have a future problem is capital expenditures. My sense is that this is working well, and that the financial people at GM are being routinely and satisfactorily updated. I am going to talk with our people about this, to make sure the flow of information is timely and complete.

20. Alan [Smith] and I will continue to be the link regarding all matters relating to the financial side of the business, including tax

problems, audits, etc. This is working smoothly. It works best when Alan mentions a problem to me, I discuss it with my people, and they decide to ask for advice or assistance, where necessary. I will see that each matter is taken care of.

Roger, if the arrangement is satisfactory with you, please countersign this letter and it will become the basis for our working together to beat the Germans, Japanese, IBM and anyone else that shows up.

This arrangement will put EDS back on track, and completely focused on what we have to do to support GM and build EDS.

SINCERELY,

ROSS PEROT

ROGER B. SMITH
(to countersign)

As he had predicted, the previous November's peace treaty wasn't worth a damn. By now agreeing to consult Smith on major compensation decisions, Perot felt he already was stretching beyond the terms of the merger. Suggesting that GM directors solve any impasse was a concession as well, designed to put Smith's mind at ease. If this was what it took, Perot was willing. Smith's signature prevented GM from going back on yet another agreement.

The day Perot mailed the letter to Smith, he received a letter from the GM chairman. In it, Smith explained a formula under which he planned to pay Les Alberthal.

Perot couldn't believe it. The dispute over Meyerson's salary had contributed to his departure as president. Now Smith wanted to tinker with Alberthal's pay! He had told Smith at the board meeting a couple of days ago how important it was not to meddle with Alberthal's salary and that he, Perot, intended to handle it personally.

The spookiest part of Smith's letter wasn't the contents. The letter was typed on plain stationery and had no markings of having been typed by a GM secretary. Perot had never seen a letter from Smith that didn't bear his masthead as GM chairman. Was Smith trying to finesse Perot in some way outside of corporate channels? Had he retreated to his den at home? Maybe he was afraid of leaving written records of what he said.

A second letter from Smith, also typed on plain stationery, arrived a week later. It was written in a weirdly cheery tone and spoke about how positively relations were proceeding. Smith explained how Perot's ideas about compensation must reflect approval of GM shareholders and directors. (Smith referred to a GM shareholders lawsuit, filed in the 1940s, that forced Alfred Sloan and other GM officers to return part of their bonus money to GM. In Sloan's *My Years at General Motors* there is a long passage explaining GM's bonus system that fails to mention the lawsuit.) Finally, Smith expressed the hope that Perot had read his note on Les Alberthal's salary.

Smith wasn't listening, Perot thought, or he had simply decided to ignore what Perot had to say. He called Sally Bell into his office to dictate a letter.

May 19, 1986

DEAR ROGER:

This letter is in response to your letters of May 7 and May 14.

These letters ignore my letter of May 7, and our visit immediately after the [EDS] board meeting on May 5.

The purpose of my letter May 7 was to put our conversation in writing and to eliminate any possible future misunderstandings between us. The primary purpose of this letter, once we reached an understanding, was to allow me to run EDS as you assured me I could, at the time of purchase. The reason I am making such an issue of EDS's independence is because we are reaching a point of no return in EDS's relationship with GM. At the time of the acquisition the people of EDS were ready to go anywhere in the world to make this alliance work. Today, as a result of GM's efforts to GM-ize EDS, and the changes affecting Mort and Tom, the feelings of our people are very negative toward GM.

I used up most of my residual good will with the EDS people, plus Mort's and Tom's, to get everybody settled down to keep a positive face on the change at the [April 28] analysts' meeting.

Roger, you are going to see EDS disintegrate if GM continues to try to micromanage EDS.

The idea of having the GM compensation staff fiddle with Les' salary, bonus accruals, or having a detailed budget review from GM is completely inconsistent with everything we agreed to, at the time of the purchase.

Roger, it is obvious that you would like to ignore my letter of May 7. If you don't want to have a written understanding between us, then this leaves us looking to our options again, which I discussed with you in our last meeting.

1. The only worthwhile option is to work together in good faith. All of our experience demonstrates that we must have a written agreement to do that. Any matters we cannot resolve will be taken to the GM board.

2. As I told you, I am no longer willing to bend and compromise from our original agreement because it is so damaging to EDS. Therefore, in the absence of any clear understanding between us, I will run EDS and when we disagree, we are going to have whatever size fight is necessary, between us, with the board, or in full public view to get the matter resolved.

3. Your other option is to try to terminate me, in order to get rid of a nuisance. I want to make sure that you and every member of the GM board understand the magnitude and length of the fight that would result from such action. It would last for years and would be terribly disruptive to GM, EDS and all concerned. I don't want anybody to have any question about my resolve or willingness to do this, if you force me to. I have too many years and too much invested in EDS to see it destroyed.

4. The final resolution, if you want to get rid of me, is to handle the matter on a businesslike basis and buy me out. In my judgment, this would be a serious mistake for GM, but if that is what you want to do, it does reduce the issue to business terms.

We aren't going to resolve this by ignoring the big issues and focusing on one or two minor issues. We must deal with this matter head on, and resolve it.

Please study my letter of May 7. I believe it is a very sound way to work together. I will keep you fully informed, in advance. If we are unable to agree on an issue, we will take the matter to the board for resolution.

Let me know what you want to do. In the interest of preserving EDS's unique qualities and rebuilding a positive relationship between the two organizations, we should get this matter resolved quickly.

We are wasting energy fighting among ourselves at a time when we ought to be spending all of our energy building better cars, and selling EDS's services.

Sincerely,

Ross

A few days later Elmer Johnson called. The GM group vice president and general counsel had discussed Perot's letter of May 7 with Smith. Smith had some problems with Perot's terms, Johnson said. He wanted to discuss the matter on May 28 with Tom Luce and Perot in Dallas.

On the twenty-eighth Tom Luce and Elmer Johnson met for dinner at the Crescent Club in Dallas. As always, Johnson was genial and sympathetic. The bad news he brought was that Smith wasn't going to accept Perot's declaration of independence.

The dinner began without Perot, who joined the two lawyers later. When he arrived, Perot greeted Johnson warmly. To make conversation, the GM lawyer asked: "What sort of a day has it been for you, Ross?" Johnson enjoyed Perot and the breadth of the stage on which he acted. Personally he sympathized with many of Perot's ideas and felt an ideological kinship to the man, even though he was ethically and contractually committed to defending Smith's and GM's interests.

"Today I was arranging for Margaret Thatcher's son to be housed safely," Perot said. The United States recently had carried out an air raid on Libya with Great Britain's help. Because of the British aid, death threats had been sent to the British prime minister's son, who was living temporarily in Dallas. When Perot heard, he volunteered to let him stay with the Perots, who had plenty of security. Perot also had entertained the vice premier of the People's Republic of China that day.

Johnson chuckled. "It sure beats what I did today," he said. He had been in Indianapolis giving a speech at GM's Allison Gas Turbine division.

At this point, Perot's and Johnson's versions of what was discussed diverge significantly.

Johnson's salient recollection of the discussion was his gentle probing of Perot's willingness to be bought out by GM, a possibility discussed by Perot and Smith earlier in the month and then mentioned by Perot in the May 19 letter. Perot had raised the theoretical possibility but stated that, in his opinion, it would be a mistake.

Johnson, however, viewed the mention of a buyout as an opening to rid GM of Perot, an eventuality he had been considering since the previous autumn. As Johnson remembers the discussion, Perot was willing to entertain the notion of a GM buyout of his GM Class E stock at $48 a share. But Perot insisted on holding on to the contingent notes, which guaranteed a $62.50 minimum price per share in 1991.

"No deal, Ross," Johnson recalls telling Perot and Luce. "If we say good-bye, it will be forever." It made no sense to GM's chief lawyer to spend money to buy Perot's stock if GM remained linked to him in some way.

Perot and Luce maintain that they never discussed buyout terms in May. Perot's recollection, supported by Tom Luce, was that the GM general counsel simply explained why "sound corporate governance principles" prevented GM from giving Perot the autonomy he wanted.

Despite their differences, the dinner ended on a friendly note.

Johnson returned to Detroit, aware that he had accomplished little to head off a fresh outbreak of hostility.

NINETEEN

Perot's Summer Press Offensive

IN the spring of 1986, GM's slump in the automotive market had not yet been treated in a comprehensive way by the popular press, and it looked like a ripe front-page opportunity for the *Wall Street Journal*'s Detroit bureau. The story was filled with implications for the automobile industry as well as the national economy. GM's profits were weak in the middle of robust sales and profits by the industry at large. Reports emanating from GM plants and suppliers indicated that Roger Smith's high-tech dream was turning into a nightmare.

As proposed by the Detroit bureau, the story would explore the reasons for GM's fall from the pedestal of most profitable, most efficient of the Big Three. Since other publications for the past few years had been busily celebrating Roger's genius, this story would be a trailblazer, definitely ahead of the news.

The newspaper's editors in New York liked the idea. They flashed a green light to Detroit.

Among the GM officials, industry analysts, and sources from rival automakers interviewed for the GM story, Ross Perot was an obvious potential source of opinion and information. Most GM directors regularly declined inquiries from the press. Perot was different. He returned legitimate telephone calls from just about anyone, including reporters.

The telephone call from the *Journal* in early May was interesting to him, for it coincided neatly with Perot's tactical decision to turn the heat up on Roger Smith publicly as a means of forcing him to abide by the merger agreement. Prior to May, Perot hadn't directly criticized GM or Smith within journalistic earshot. Now, because he was angry about the events leading to the departure of Meyerson and Walter from the leadership of EDS, he was determined to go public — albeit in a carefully controlled manner.

The *Journal* reporter who asked Perot's opinions about the reasons behind GM's weak performance was startled to find himself suddenly being grilled by the EDS chairman.

"What do you think are the reasons that GM is in a fix?" Perot asked.

Perot wasn't waxing rhetorical or trying to flatter the reporter. He truly wanted to know. The reporter didn't know much about Perot and thought this unusual. Most top executives, if they will speak to reporters at all, don't bother concealing their contempt for questions that require them to justify their actions. They rarely submit to interviews unless their public relations advisers convince them that it is unavoidable.

Taken aback momentarily by Perot's questions, the reporter explained what he had discovered so far about GM's capital expenditures, cost and quality problems, inefficient parts operations, and the organizational inefficiencies that GM managers were complaining about.

Perot listened.

"Why don't you come down here to Dallas. We'll visit and we can talk about GM and your story," Perot said.

The next week Perot held forth in his office for several hours, describing to the reporter what GM was doing wrong and what he would do "to clean the place up." Perot spoke openly about his relations with Roger Smith and the frustrations of making the EDS merger work. Unlike most corporate chief executives, he didn't invite a public relations specialist to sit in on the conversation. Perot spiced his opinions with two years' worth of unexpurgated anecdotes from the belly of the beast, private experiences that hadn't been published anywhere.

Almost from the first moments, Perot conveyed the impression of a man who had tried to work quietly and forcefully within GM corporate channels — and had just about given up. He was the picture of a disgruntled outside director; with his 11.5 million GM Class E shares he also was an unhappy major shareholder. In fact, he was GM's biggest stockholder and at odds with management. The reporter knew what this meant: conditions clearly obtained for a very nasty corporate fight.

The reporter grew excited hearing about what was sure to be a hot story. Without a doubt, Perot and GM were on some sort of collision course. The fallout was certain to be at least as significant as the original story idea about GM's decline. And in some ways they were related; the problems that plagued GM were the very ones that prevented Perot and Smith from reaching an accommodation.

Perot insisted that his initial interview with the *Wall Street Journal* be conducted as a "backgrounder" only. The newspaper wasn't permitted to quote him directly (except for quotes he approved) or attribute information to him. Sensitive information about GM had to be independently confirmed before it could be used.

If GM perceived that he was on the attack, Perot explained, he wasn't going to be as effective as he would be if he helped journalists write insightful stories prodding GM to reform its ways. His only aim, he insisted, was to make Smith "do the right thing" for both companies. Perot's tactic of pressuring Smith and GM through the press was going to work only if he could do it in a gradual, measured way.

This posed a ticklish problem for the newspaper and the reporter. Good journalists normally have no business filtering reality from their stories. It is their duty to dig up important stories and tell them well. If Perot had become an irritant inside GM, it was a story that demanded to be told.

The reporter also was concerned about being "used" by Perot, the way journalists are used in Washington to settle scores with political enemies. Perot was being allowed to take semi-anonymous pot shots at GM — for his noble purpose, of course — and maybe to settle some of his own accounts with Smith.

Applying pressure through the press was a risky tactic that might blow up any minute. Smith could decide to fire Perot. Perot could assemble a group of investors for a hostile takeover of GM. A journalist had to be careful not to get so close to a story that he became a participant, or that he lost his perspective and moved too slowly to stay ahead of competing newspapers.

But if the *Wall Street Journal* didn't acquiesce to Perot's ground rules, he clearly wasn't about to proceed with the interview. He might decide to give the story to a rival newspaper. No one at the *Wall Street Journal* wanted to read the story first in the *New York Times*.

After consultations with the newspaper's bureau chief in Detroit and senior editors in New York, the reporter decided to agree to Perot's ground rules — provided Perot promised not to permit competing publications to print quotes and anecdotes the *Wall Street Journal* had agreed to keep on a background basis. With the ground rules understood, Perot agreed to reveal for the newspaper how and why his ambitions for the

GM-EDS "alliance" had failed to come about as set forth in the agreement two years earlier.

An interview was scheduled for May 21, 1986, in Perot's office in Dallas. The evening before, the TV docudrama of *On Wings of Eagles,* the best-selling book about the rescue of EDS executives in Iran, was broadcast nationwide. The next morning, the Iranian cabbie driving two *Wall Street Journal* reporters to EDS headquarters in Dallas became suddenly angry when he learned his passengers' destination. As they drove through the heavy security gate surrounding the building and past the stately green lawns that had once been a golf course, the cabbie offered a couple of unsolicited opinions, namely that the TV show had been a pack of lies and that Ross Perot was a despicable man.

A few moments later in Perot's office, Perot was laughing at the reporters' story about the cabbie.

"You don't see him going back to Iran, do you? He's staying over here and enjoying this country," Perot said. While the TV show had broadened Perot's public exposure, he worried that it had exposed him and his family to additional hostility from Iranian radicals. It also had exposed him to some good-natured ribbing that morning at EDS headquarters. People were telling him that TV actor Richard Crenna had been far too handsome to portray Perot accurately.

"I'm short, ugly, and have a Southern accent, and he wasn't any of that. I asked them who should have played me," he said. "They told me Mickey Rooney."

His down-to-earth, self-deprecating charm, so effective with journalists accustomed to condescension from chief executives, was intact. He was one of the world's richest men. His exploits were popularized on TV. He had counseled presidents and board chairmen. Still, he could chuckle engagingly enough about his enemies. He presented himself as just an ordinary fellow who got rich almost by accident. The reporters grasped immediately that these attractive personal qualities were sure to lend Perot considerable credibility and power in making his case against the GM ruling class — represented as it was by a squeaky-voiced accountant who spoke in disjointed, unfinished sentences and who had been disingenuous with the press.

"OK," Perot said to the reporters, sitting down in his rocking chair, "here's a quote you can use: GM is the largest, wealthiest carmaker in the world. It has more resources, human and financial, than any company in the world. It has everything it takes to make the best and most competitive cars in the world. Yet GM has failed to tap the full potential of its people. When you tap that, they'll build the finest cars in the world, and at a competitive price.''

Measured on a scale of journalistic explosiveness, his quote wasn't exactly an A-bomb.

Perot was just warming up. In terms similar to those he had delivered to GM directors during the Hughes board meeting, Perot proceeded to blast GM's sluggish, ossified style of doing business, leveling particular blame at GM's management for divisiveness between managers and workers.

''If you could wish for one thing,'' he said, ''it would be to heal the old rift between the people who make the cars and the people who are responsible for the business. Treat one another as equals. We've got to be much better listeners to the people who are doing the work. I love two-way communication, but I'll settle for one way as long as it's from the bottom up. From the top down only is no good.''

Perot ridiculed GM for ''using capital as a bulldozer,'' while failing to address the competitive realities of the marketplace. When auto executives ask for government to restore a level playing field, he said, they mean a return to the years immediately after World War II when ''we had no effective competition. That made us soft. That's what the level playing field means to people at GM. A field on which you own the bats, the balls, both teams, the dugouts, the lights, and the stadium.''

To a skeptical journalist, Perot's statements sounded like hopelessly simplistic, naive bleating. His locutions stated the need for revolutionary action, but in the real world no one starts a revolution at GM, much less an outsider from Texas with precious little experience in the car business. It was fine to talk about forging a warm, cuddly team to beat back Japanese competition. But surely Roger Smith wished and worked for the same thing every day. The fact that GM's biggest shareholder suddenly realized the company had problems was interesting but hardly a bell-ringer of a story.

Then began the off-the-record portion of Perot's interview (later released by Perot for publication), which he launched with the following preamble:

''Until we nuke the GM system, we'll never tap the full potential of our people.''

As the rules of attribution changed, Perot's message switched abruptly from a polite desire for orderly change to the rumblings of war. No longer was Perot merely critical of GM's performance. He was angry, and the focus of his anger was Roger Smith and the GM board.

In theory, he said, the directors were required to act as the shareholders' representatives, a counterbalance to measure the performance of Smith and top management. It was the board's job to straighten out GM, Perot said, not his as an individual director.

"The board is like a pet rock, just sitting there. It's a joke," he said.

The chairman picks the directors. Is the board a rubber stamp for Roger? Hell, no. We'd have to upgrade it to be a rubber stamp. They get $30,000 a year, a hot meal at every meeting, and a free car every three months. They should go out and buy GM cars like everyone else, ones that haven't been specially fixed up, and then they'd learn a lot about GM's problems. What does it prove to be driving a new car every ninety days?

Perot, of course, had bought his Oldsmobile, declining the perquisite that allows GM directors to test-drive new cars. Once in a while, dressed in casual clothes in order not to be recognized, he visited GM dealerships, pretending to be a customer. The undercover visits taught him a great deal about GM cars and the people who sold them. He was learning that Chevrolets and Buicks weren't held in as high esteem as when he was a young man, and that GM dealers also were selling Japanese and European brands because, as independent businessmen, they needed to offer products that customers wanted.

The subject of the interview turned to Smith. Perot had carefully analyzed the GM chairman's personality in the two years since making the deal and had come to the conclusion that basically he was a smart and well-intentioned — but timid — bookkeeper, obsessed with the perks and the honor of his office, mired in trivia, and afraid to confront GM's true problems head-on. Smith knew what the problems were. He was perceptive and analytical and had demonstrated excellent financial ability; but his reluctance to take strong action — except insofar as he spent large sums of capital — was manifest in his failure to keep his word on the EDS deal. And, in Perot's opinion, Smith used the power of his office to bully subordinates, stockholders, in fact anyone who disagreed with him. To Perot, these traits were more than personality flaws, they were the keys to preventing GM from building a competitive organization.

Roger loves the old system. He talks a good game [about change]. I'm the only guy who can talk straight to Roger. We've got a guy running GM who doesn't understand cars and doesn't understand people. He's very smart. But he hates the guys on the factory floor.

My dream is to see terms like "labor," "management," "bonus-eligible" eradicated tomorrow. I'd close all the executive dining rooms in the place. I don't know why we can't do it. When GM people first came down here, we went down to the EDS cafeteria and stood in line and ate with the other people. They were surprised. They said, "The food is really good here." I said, "If you ate in your cafeterias, you'd have good food, too."

He criticized Roger for spending far too much time, given the desperate condition of GM's core business, on the Business Roundtable, testifying in favor of tax reform, and worrying about the situation in South Africa. (Smith had failed to appear at a scheduled meeting with security analysts earlier in the year because he was delayed during a trip to South Africa.)

He's gotten a lot of good press. That's fine. But the problem is that he believes every word of it. When he started screwing around with EDS compensation I said, "You come here and tell everyone." He did. He was in a meeting with real people. They told him just what they thought. He lost control, totally lost control; quivering lips, turning blue, and said: "How dare you talk like that to the chairman of GM?"

I saw the head guy of one of the world's largest corporations totally lose control. At that point he lost me forever. If I had any thought he was this way, I wouldn't have sold EDS. If I had any thought I was dealing with a chief executive officer who doesn't tell the truth and is emotionally unstable, I wouldn't have sold. He can't run the place. There were twenty top EDS guys [at the compensation meeting]. Now they say, "When all else fails you get the chairman's temper tantrum." You're talking about the same guy who's got to gain the confidence of 750,000 workers to build great cars. Roger can't do it.

I've got to have a guy running GM who's dealing with facts. He is the basic problem. You're looking at the cancer. Roger is worrying himself to death about what I'll say. He's heard I'll write a book. He's afraid. Roger is image. Now you are down to the core of my tactics. He knows that if I ever go public with some of this stuff . . .

Perot pulled back. There was more he wasn't telling. A question remained: Were Perot's criticisms, revealed in the measured, discreet way he demanded that the *Wall Street Journal* report them, powerful enough to turn Smith into the kind of chief executive Perot wanted him to be?

Or was Perot masking some personal ambitions, and recruiting the press to help him?

"My dream is to get Roger to concentrate on his numbers and leave him as chairman until he retires," Perot said.

> I don't want to be chairman of GM, there are too many good people who know the car business. If we look back in ten or fifteen years, I will have never had a title, never had a job, just a board seat, but maybe I can sit here in Dallas and get this guy to do what needs to be done.
>
> My real motive is saving jobs. People won't believe that, so let's just say I own 11.5 million shares, and I want to protect my investment. I'll spend the rest of my career doing it.

One of the reporters wondered: What is Smith's reaction going to be? Wouldn't Smith react badly to the pressure tactics?

"After I wrote the letter last fall calling Roger a bully, he called me back. Butter wouldn't melt in his mouth fast enough," Perot said. "How shall I say this?" (He looked momentarily quizzical.) "Roger seems to respond best to harsh treatment. When I've had my hard conversations with him is when he's been the nicest."

What, the reporter asked, about the possibility that Smith will try to get rid of you somehow?

Perot laughed. He's already tried, Perot said. Members of the board's nominating committee discussed simply not nominating him for reelection to the board. All GM directors serve one-year terms, and, therefore, are kept on very short strings by the GM chairman, who effectively handpicks who he wants on the board.

"It's sicker than hell. Roger creeps around. He tried to get me off the board in January. I called him. I said, 'You need to know that I know you are trying to get me off the board. Don't even think about it. Don't even try. Tell those old farts that if they love pain forever, try it,' " he said.

Perot alluded to several attempts by GM auditors to check EDS's books. Auditing, in his view, just was a means for GM to impose authority over EDS and Perot. Perot had forbidden GM auditors from entering the building.

"I just keep this for when they come down here," he laughed, reaching into the drawer behind him. He pulled out a bright red Orkin Pest Control hat and put it on. His grin stretched across his face. "I've got Orkin stationery, too."

He was trying to keep things semi-humorous, but preventing GM auditors from entering EDS buildings was a dangerous act of belligerence. Smith wasn't likely to put up with it for long, the reporters surmised.

Wasn't it possible that Smith might physically impose GM's authority? the reporter wondered. Couldn't he issue new keys to EDS facilities or simply order GM security people to let the auditors in?

The question was unthinkable, outlandish. But Perot already had pondered similar dark thoughts.

Don't forget one thing, Perot said. EDS controls all of GM's computers, all its telephones, almost all its information that's stored in computer files. EDS people are loyal to me.

He didn't elaborate, but the implication was pretty clear. If Smith attempted *anschluss,* he'd be trying it with someone who had the power to turn off GM's telephones and computers. Perot wasn't worried about events proceeding in that direction.

"Basically I have to persevere. I still look for some change from Roger. But the only change I see so far is in reaction to pain. We all feel pain. Roger feels it quick. Take away the pain and you take away the change," he said.

But would Smith read Perot's criticisms and change, the journalists wondered, or would he read them and start working on a way to get rid of Perot?

"I realize I'm asking for something a little unrealistic. A guy who is fifty-eight years old and looks you in the eye and lies to you consistently isn't likely to change. But I've got to try.

"Roger is stuck with me," Perot said. "He has touched the tar baby."

The subterfuge of assigning Mort Meyerson to work on acquisitions as EDS's vice chairman initially fooled Wall Street, the press, and lower-level workers inside EDS.

It didn't fool Meyerson.

He had been excised from the body of his company as surely as if he'd quit or been fired. In May and June of 1986, he actually attempted, as his job had been described, to explore some fields in which to expand EDS. He showed up in his office at EDS as if nothing had happened. He scheduled meetings in New York.

Meyerson's heart wasn't in his new assignment, and he didn't know what to do about it.

In July, Mort and Marlene Meyerson and three other couples from Dallas flew to Europe for a three-week holiday. The Meyersons loved classical music and enjoyed hiking; Mort had suggested they all go to the Salzburg Music Festival and explore the Austrian Alps.

Night after night the Meyersons attended dazzling opera, symphony, and chamber music performances. During the day, they gloried in Austria's picture-book villages and soaring, snow-capped peaks.

At the end of a day in early August he had spent wandering along mountain paths, Meyerson was mildly surprised to receive a long-distance telephone call at his small country hotel from Richard Pascale. Pascale, a business professor at Stanford University, was working as a consultant for AT&T's top strategic planners, who were looking for advice on future business strategies. Two years earlier, just before GM had come along, EDS had failed to win a megacontract with AT&T. But EDS had landed several smaller contracts, and Meyerson was familiar with the communications giant. Pascale and Meyerson were acquainted with one another, so Mort was happy to share some opinions about the future of computing and telecommunications and some ideas about where AT&T might fit in.

The next day Meyerson decided to hike alone. The short chat on the telephone with Pascale rekindled some old thoughts and feelings about EDS that he had never been able to put completely to rest. As he climbed higher, straining his muscles against the path, he found himself thinking about his failure to find a way to forge a working relationship between GM and EDS that allowed EDS to carry out its labors independently — the only way EDS could truly be effective for the automaker. Intellectually, he had had a tough time accepting that no rational way existed to make the relationship work. He just hadn't found it. The rift wasn't his fault, yet it was, at least partly, his failure.

He had worked the problem up and down, backwards and sideways, and he still couldn't find a way out of the paradox: those aspects of GM that made EDS so necessary for GM's future — its obsessive preoccupation with control, for example — were the same aspects that prevented GM from giving EDS the free hand it needed. Meyerson sat down on a rock and contemplated the tiny chalets and ribbons of blue in the valley below him.

Something Pascale had said the previous day about AT&T stuck in his mind. Like GM, AT&T had to learn how to operate in fiercely competitive markets after years as a regulated utility. He thought for a moment, and the thought crystallized into an idea. That was it! That was the way to cure GM's need to control EDS while giving AT&T strategic direction, all in one fell swoop. The idea was childishly simple, really, but it would restore EDS's independence and put him and Perot back in firm control of the company. GM might well consider his idea, because it had the additional benefit of making a lot of money for GM and curing a merger headed for the ash heap.

He thought the scheme over again and again. It was beautifully logical. It made sense for everyone involved.

As Meyerson headed down the mountain back to the hotel, his step was brisk, he felt lighthearted for the first time in months.

He couldn't wait to tell Perot.

On July 22, 1986, the *Wall Street Journal* published a Page One story about GM under the flashline "Groping Giant." With a smiling drawing of Roger Smith was the grim anecdotal and financial evidence of GM's six-year slide during his chairmanship.

The story detailed how GM had started in 1980 with a recession-related loss and a 48 percent share of the U.S. market, and in 1986 dropped to a fast-eroding 43 percent of the market and lower profit margins than Ford or Chrysler. The story itemized, in depressing detail, GM's inefficient parts-manufacturing subsidiaries, unimaginative styling and design, and big-ticket expenditures that hadn't yet paid off.

Perot's comments appeared in the main story twice. He spoke of the need to tap the full potential of GM's people and the mistake of throwing money at problems. In a separate accompanying sidebar to the main article, Perot sharpened his lecture. To make his words less stinging to GM, he addressed his criticisms to include GM's rivals, Ford and Chrysler, as well.

"It takes five years to develop a car in this country," he said. "Heck, we won World War II in four years. We are spending billions to develop new cars. This isn't a moon shot. It's just a car." He dumped on auto executives who constantly blamed the lack of a "level playing field." Perot told them to stop substituting glitzy high-tech programs for fundamental management improvements.

The *Wall Street Journal*'s story was the first to question seriously Smith's heretofore unquestioned strategy. More important, the story flagged Perot as an in-house critic — and one accessible to reporters. Journalists now were sure to zero in for his colorful comments every time they wrote a story about GM.

The newspaper gave Smith his due. He gamely put the best face possible on a bad situation.

While conceding that he and Perot "don't see eye to eye on everything, . . . we get along fine," he said in the article. "He's just trying to encourage us along the lines of what we want to do. I don't think he criticizes us. He doesn't call up and say, gee, you're doing a lousy job somewhere."

Within days, competing business publications were cranking up stories of their own about GM and its outspoken director. *Fortune,* not quite sure that things at GM were as bleak as the *Wall Street Journal* had painted them, published Smith's apologia on August 18 under the headline "Roger Smith Takes On GM's Critics." In it, Smith blamed GM's market slide mainly on two UAW strikes. He praised EDS and described Perot as "a very impatient guy like all of us are."

"You've got to examine the word 'critical,' " Smith explained in *Fortune.* " 'Critical' can mean a lot of things to a lot of people. Ross in my mind has never ever been what I call 'critical-critical.' I mean he's trying to help. He's being 'helpful-critical.' "

As Smith tried to calm the waters, *Business Week's* Detroit bureau was getting set to roil them further.

The day the Meyersons returned to Dallas, Mort headed straight for EDS headquarters to tell Perot about his idea, conceived while sitting on a tree stump high in the Austrian Alps.

"Ross, it works like this," Meyerson said. "GM sells 25 percent of EDS to AT&T. At the same time, GM sells 50 percent of EDS back to public shareholders and keeps 25 percent of EDS for itself. That way, GM still has a big stake in EDS's operations inside GM, but Roger doesn't stay involved as the authority over EDS.

"AT&T will have the same involvement and the same stake as GM. AT&T needs a lot of help dealing in the competitive world. It's been a regulated utility. EDS can help and teach AT&T to deal with customers who need computing expertise. Basically, it's another megacontract for EDS.

"Best of all, EDS will be independent again. GM and AT&T will own big pieces of EDS, but neither GM nor AT&T will own a big enough stake to dominate us or try to change the way we do things," Meyerson said.

Perot listened intently. "The big question is whether Roger will go for it," he said. Notwithstanding the publicly traded GM Class E shares, the decision to divest EDS belonged to the GM management alone.

"GM can't lose. Roger can't lose," Meyerson pointed out. "With $3 billion a year in GM business, EDS has become so valuable in the last two years that the money he gets from the stake he sells to AT&T and the money he gets from the stake he spins off to the public will more than cover the original acquisition expense. In essence he'll be getting 25 percent of EDS for free."

This was what Perot loved about Meyerson. Now and then he came up with completely original, completely off-the-wall solutions to what had appeared to be intractable stalemates. Perot would never have thought of this in a million years.

"Mort, I love it," Perot said. "Talk to Roger and see what he says. He's a deal guy. He's going to grasp the financial advantages for GM immediately. He may go for it. See what he says. If he likes it, go ahead."

So in late August 1986, Meyerson flew to Detroit to explain the idea of selling 25 percent of EDS to AT&T and 50 percent back to the public.

Smith was polite and cordial, as if nothing untoward had ever happened between the two men or the two companies. Meyerson wasn't surprised that the financially minded Smith grasped immediately the potential benefits for GM — in terms of money and operations.

"Go ahead and try the concept on AT&T," Smith said. "You don't have to get into the details yet. First see if they like it."

"Do you want me to brief the GM financial staff?" If Meyerson had learned nothing else during the last two years, he had learned that deals don't get made at GM without active involvement of the financial staff.

Surprisingly, Smith said no. "You're better off by yourself," he said. "The financial staff will just slow you down at this point."

Meyerson flew back to Dallas elated. The next day he scheduled a meeting with Pascale, the AT&T consultant, and he asked EDS president Les Alberthal to sit in. Pascale was shocked. When he had solicited Meyerson's opinions on how to improve AT&T's competitiveness, he hadn't expected anything like this.

A week later Meyerson received word from James Olson, AT&T chief executive, asking for a meeting.

The fireworks Perot started in the newspapers and magazines made an immediate impact on the GM work force during the summer of 1986.

GM hourly workers, of course, were delighted with Perot's advice to heal old wounds, his critique of management, and especially his sentiments about "feeding the troops before feeding the officers," that is, giving the hourly workers decent profit-sharing checks before passing out fat bonuses to executives.

GM executives and white-collar workers, however, were a bit hurt and baffled. Perot was aiming zingers at their chairman, a leader widely celebrated as one of the leading lights of U.S. business. By responding to Perot's barbs in a conciliatory fashion, Smith appeared as a schoolyard milquetoast trying to avoid a fistfight. What power did Perot have over Smith and GM that they didn't know about? Why didn't Smith silence Perot as he would any other subordinate who dared go public with criticisms?

GM executives also were suspicious about Perot's motives. Perot talked a good game about alliances and the need to save workers' jobs. Sure, he had done things in the past that gave him credibility. But perhaps helping GM wasn't his true aim; maybe knocking off Smith and becoming chairman was. Perhaps he had borrowed a page from Boone Pickens's textbook or Carl Icahn's and now wanted to take over GM by luring Smith into a showdown he would be sure to lose. Little was unimaginable anymore in corporate America.

At the GM board meeting in August, the directors attended the preview of the company's 1987-model new cars and trucks at the GM proving grounds in Milford, Michigan, just west of Detroit. When the drive and demonstration were over, Ross Perot boarded a helicopter with Bill Hoglund, vice president and group executive in charge of the Buick-Oldsmobile-Cadillac group.

Hoglund, an engaging, youthful figure who had worked in finance and as head of Pontiac, was quite popular in GM because he treated people kindly and showed respect for their ideas. As it was for so many in GM's management ranks, for Hoglund his job was practically a family tradition: his father had been a GM executive in Europe, his brother was a GM executive in the locomotive division, and Hoglund's children worked for GM. A band of GM insiders regularly touted him as future chief executive material.

Perot knew that Hoglund was popular and liked him. Through Hoglund, Perot hoped to learn from executives below the top level, executives who had read the newspapers and knew he was acting as self-appointed ombudsman, what specific things he might be able to do as a director to wrench GM away from inefficiency.

As the helicopter flew toward Willow Run Airport and Perot's waiting jet, Hoglund asked Perot about the conflict with Smith.

"I'm just trying to get Roger to do the right thing," Perot said.

"It looks to a lot of people like you want to be chairman," Hoglund said.

"I don't want to be chairman and that's never been my purpose. There is no scenario in which I become chairman," Perot insisted. The helicopter landed at Willow Run. The two men continued their discussion in a hangar. "I just want to get this place cleaned up. Look, I can talk to Roger straight, in a way that you and others inside GM can't. I'd like you to speak to Reuss [Lloyd Reuss, head of Chevrolet-Pontiac-GM Canada group] and Stempel [Bob Stempel, head of Buick-Oldsmobile-Cadillac group] and some of the others and tell me exactly what I can do to be helpful — with specifics."

Hoglund agreed to talk with some of his peers and get in touch with Perot.

Hoglund maintains that he also warned Perot that going public with criticisms of GM was counterproductive and wasn't appreciated by GM managers and executives. Perot says Hoglund never delivered any such warning.

TWENTY

The AT&T Option

S INCE the previous April, when Mort Meyerson and he stepped aside from active management of EDS, Tom Walter had been taking it easy.

The longtime EDS chief financial officer had been Meyerson's right-hand man. Now, with Meyerson off center stage, he took more time off, as he had originally planned after his chemotherapy a few years earlier. As tough as it was not to be a part of EDS, Walter and Mort believed that Les Alberthal, the new EDS president, deserved a chance to operate the company on his own, without a couple of ex–big shots hanging around to second-guess him. Walter turned the chief financial officer's job over to Davis Hamlin and helped Meyerson look for ways to expand EDS's business.

Not yet aware that Roger Smith had given Meyerson the go-ahead to begin exploring the possible sale of EDS to AT&T, Walter was fishing near Lake City, Colorado, on Labor Day weekend 1986. Meyerson telephoned Walter's fishing camp and asked Walter to meet him in New York right away to begin talks with AT&T executives. An EDS jet picked Walter up at the Gunnison, Colorado, airport and flew him to Dallas, where his wife was waiting with a business suit. The jet then flew to Hilton Head, South Carolina, to pick up Stuart Reeves, another senior EDS officer.

The first Tuesday morning in September 1986, the three EDS executives met in Roger Smith's office on the twenty-fifth floor of the GM Building in New York to outline their negotiating strategy in greater detail before going to the AT&T Building on Madison Avenue. AT&T's business was an even bigger potential bonanza for EDS than GM's, representing billings of up to $5 billion annually. Added to EDS's $3 billion in revenue (including the GM account), EDS stood to become an $8 billion company if Meyerson's plan worked.

Smith was encouraging. He had spoken to AT&T chairman Olson, who turned the talks over to John Segall, AT&T's strategic planner, and Bob Kavner, AT&T's chief financial officer. The GM and AT&T chief executives agreed that the two sides should begin talking right away.

Smith invited the EDS men into the GM executive dining room for lunch to finish their discussion. As in the fourteenth-floor executive dining room in Detroit, Roger Smith tightly controlled the list of people permitted to enter the room. Walter glanced around at the plushly decorated room, noticing how the other GM executives had their eyes on the group. Remembering how quickly word had spread a year earlier about Smith's trip to Dallas "to straighten out" EDS on compensation, he wondered if they had heard that something was brewing between GM and AT&T.

AT&T, perhaps the world's premier telecommunications company, was trying very hard to break into computers with the Unix line of microcomputers. It had bought part of Olivetti, the Italian business-machine company, to help accomplish that goal.

Diversification into computers brought AT&T into direct competition with IBM. As the world's premier maker of computers, IBM possessed expert marketing skills and had ambitions of its own to diversify in the field of information processing; in fact, IBM had begun to encroach on AT&T's turf by buying a telephone company and developing telecommunications expertise. The technologies of computing, data, and communication were merging at lightning speed. As they did, the lines blurred between the business of computing and the business of communication, opening new fields of opportunity for companies with the size and financial strength of IBM, AT&T, and EDS. Meyerson and Walter persuaded AT&T's Kavner and Segall that EDS could be a powerful force in the battle against IBM by helping AT&T learn marketing and customer-service skills they had never needed as a regulated utility.

Kavner and Segall were attracted to Meyerson's logic. Standing at an easel, Segall used a black marker to record the points the men made in their conversation. Meyerson and Walter were pleased that the chemistry between the two sides seemed good; perhaps this marriage would go more smoothly than the stormy alliance with GM.

Day by day through September the talks gained momentum. AT&T hired various consultants to investigate particular corporate issues. Unraveling the GM Class E shares wasn't going to be a simple task, legally or financially. A compensation consultant was engaged to make sure a stock incentive plan was possible that made AT&T happy and that worked according to the principles established by Perot and Meyerson at EDS. No one wanted another dogfight over compensation like the one EDS had had with Smith.

As positive and upbeat as they were, the talks were operating, in one sense, in a highly artificial atmosphere. Smith, not EDS, ultimately held the legal and financial power to decide whether to sell EDS to AT&T. Smith gave the EDS men the go-ahead to negotiate, but they weren't — and never could be — his true proxies on a negotiating team for a multibillion-dollar transaction. The EDS men didn't think like GM. They didn't reason as Smith reasoned. And their primary interest — to be free again, and to set EDS free — diverged wildly from whatever Smith hoped to gain by selling EDS.

For Smith, the biggest attraction in selling EDS probably was the chance to jettison Perot. He had never bargained for the headaches he had suffered at the hands of this independence-minded billionaire. Sure, he said that he enjoyed Perot's go-get-'em attitude, that he thought EDS's spirit would be a valuable tonic for GM, and on a certain level he had been telling the truth. But the relationship just wasn't turning out the way he had planned. How was he to know that when Perot had talked about helping GM, he meant changing it? Not cosmetically, but from the roots. How was he to have predicted Perot's audacity, his impatience? Imagine someone selling his company for a couple of billion dollars to GM and then not letting GM auditors in the door! And now this: criticizing GM publicly in the press, the ultimate sin.

The October 8, 1986, issue of *Business Week* appeared on newsstands on the first Friday of the month. A rather angry-looking Ross Perot was pictured on the cover under the banner headline "Ross Perot's Crusade." Next to his picture was a quote from the article: "Revitalizing General Motors is like teaching an elephant to tap dance. You find the sensitive spots and start poking."

Perot had found a sensitive spot all right, Roger Smith's ego, and he was poking unmercifully.

The story inside the magazine was little more than a rehash of GM's problems as an automaker, a story now making the rounds of major publications. The important difference from the *Wall Street Journal* article in July was that Perot had sharpened his rhetoric, permitting *Business Week* to use some of his juicier quotes. It was *Business Week*'s cover, with its focus on Perot ridiculing GM as pirouetting pachyderm, that devastated Smith.

(Ironically, the GM chairman failed to recall that Perot had used a similar phrase once before — in a way that was complimentary to the GM chairman. A year and a half earlier, in the flattering *New York Times Magazine* profile of Smith, Perot had likened GM to an elephant. "If you want to get an elephant to move, then you have to know where the sensitive spots are. Roger knows where they are," Perot had said. "In fact, he knows how to get that elephant to dance." GM had no cause to be indignant, Perot said with mock innocence when the *Business Week* story came out; the tap-dancing elephant metaphor is old hat.)

As reporters and analysts called GM from all over the country to find out more about the outbreak of hostilities first hinted at in the *Wall Street Journal* and now amplified in *Business Week,* Smith and the GM public relations department frantically tried to obscure the increasingly obvious conclusion that might be drawn from the flying insults, namely that GM was in the midst of a bizarre struggle for power.

Every journalist who asked was told by a GM public relations representative that Smith and Perot continued to enjoy harmonious relations. Smith publicly backed up the fiction whenever reporters asked him about Perot. Privately, Smith was hurt and angry. How dare Perot picture GM as a tap-dancing elephant! The truth of the matter was that Perot was making him and GM look quite foolish, and he hadn't the slightest idea what to do about it apart from hoping the talks with AT&T might bear fruit.

The courtship of EDS and AT&T rapidly was turning into a full-scale love affair. Meyerson and Walter explained the several specific and immediate ways that EDS would be able to help AT&T by smoothly melding into AT&T's operations. Kavner and Segall were enthusiastic about the idea of carrying out a preliminary study to narrow down specific projects and goals, a study like the one EDS had done for GM prior to the merger.

The four men met for breakfast in mid October at the Tarrytown, New York, Hilton. Kavner and Segall clearly were excited about the fast-evolving talks with EDS. Kavner, in fact, told the EDS men that buying all of EDS from GM might be the best idea of all. If 25 percent of EDS was good, he said, 100 percent would be better still.

Meyerson's and Walter's sails deflated simultaneously. Selling all of EDS to AT&T would be as big a mistake as selling it all to GM had been. Meyerson didn't want to trade one giant bureaucratic master for another. Kavner and Segall had forgotten (or didn't care) about the importance of EDS's independence, which was Meyerson's principal focus and the original reason for suggesting the deal to Smith.

After the meeting, Meyerson telephoned Smith in Detroit to brief the GM chairman about what had happened, as he had during the entire negotiations. He reported that the talks were going well; in fact, too well: AT&T wanted to buy all of EDS.

Perhaps that's the way to go, Smith said. Meyerson was startled to hear that Smith was ready to get rid of EDS altogether if the price and conditions were right. Unbeknownst to the negotiators, Smith already had met with AT&T chairman Olson at Metropolitan Airport in Detroit, and they had discussed a possible sale. Smith felt that the time was now ripe to brief GM's top legal and financial executives, whose participation was vital to carrying out the final phase of negotiations.

Jim Evans, as a GM director and head of the audit committee, had been monitoring the auditing impasse between GM and Perot over the internal auditing of EDS since the previous spring. The merger agreement specified that EDS hire its own auditors. Perot had anticipated the problem and insisted on the provision; and the fax memos between the two chief executives, which Evans wasn't aware existed, reaffirmed the principle.

The GM organization, however, was thoroughly committed to the tradition of carrying out scrupulous internal audits of every one of its thirty-six operating divisions. The audits were performed according to specific tests and procedures, all specified in fat procedure manuals. No office and no plant was exempt. Moreover, the pricing compromise reached over the summer, which spelled out how to pay EDS for goods and services, specified that GM be allowed to check EDS's costs for work done at GM.

But each time GM controllers tried to inspect the books in Dallas, Perot said no. He had nothing to hide, he told them. He simply didn't want

EDS workers diverted from their work because they had to provide lists for GM, fill out forms for GM controllers, and conform to cumbersome GM bureaucratic procedures — precisely the procedures Perot wished to stamp out elsewhere at GM.

To Perot, the controversy over internal auditing was nothing less than a battle for the soul of his company. The myriad bookkeeping routines that EDS didn't perform in its own business — and had never performed — were what made it lean and efficient. To Perot, a GM audit was more than just another way to exert symbolic authority over EDS; it planted the seeds of GM culture inside the walls of his company. He wasn't going to allow Smith to "GM-ize" EDS. Smith's promise more than two years ago, to have anyone "shot on sight" for trying to impose GM's culture on EDS, was etched into Perot's mind.

Evans kept an office at Union Pacific Corporation headquarters in New York, where he had been chairman before his retirement. Perot called him at his office in early November to discuss a way around the problem. Legally, he told Perot, the GM audit committee was required to certify to shareholders that everything in GM was checked, double-checked, and counted. As chairman of the committee, Evans was responsible.

In that case, Perot said, I'll personally pay for Peat Marwick and Mitchell (a major accounting firm) to conduct an internal audit of EDS, in addition to the normal year-end audit. Just so long as the GM controllers stay away.

Evans and the GM controllers' staff thought Perot's solution might work.

On October 22, 1986, GM's top legal and financial executives convened at the Regency Hotel in New York to be briefed by Meyerson, Tom Walter, and Tom Luce on the status of the AT&T talks. Until that moment, EDS had been negotiating on its own behalf and that of GM, its owner. The GM side of the talks had proceeded in line with Meyerson's logic, born on an Austrian mountainside, of the way the deal should be structured.

With the GM financial staff taking over as negotiators, a new logic was about to replace Meyerson's. Leon Krain, GM treasurer, Don Atwood, executive vice president responsible for Hughes, and Elmer Johnson, GM's top legal strategist, wanted to know specifically what had been said in the negotiations and what issues were on the table. As the highest-ranking officer present, Atwood became the new *de facto* leader of GM's negotiating team.

The next morning the entire GM and EDS group, accompanied by Salomon Brothers investment banker Bob Scully, met with AT&T at the latter's headquarters. With AT&T thinking it might want to buy all of EDS, a major conceptual problem presented itself. A great portion of EDS's value lay in the $3 billion or so worth of guaranteed data processing business EDS was contracted to do for GM; but GM still wasn't necessarily prepared to guarantee the entire data processing contract to EDS.

In that case, the AT&T executives responded, EDS was worth a lot less than they had thought.

Meyerson watched his idea crumble in the hands of the GM negotiators. The 25 percent, 25 percent, 50 percent equity split that would have liberated EDS vanished before his eyes. He attempted to revive the compromise, shuttling from the GM side of the table to the AT&T side of the table.

At one point, Meyerson delivered a short speech emphasizing the importance of fully integrated systems and a companywide computing strategy. For this reason, he said, it was a good idea for GM and AT&T to give one supplier, namely EDS, an exclusive in-house contract. Meyerson's point, however, directly contradicted an opinion Atwood had expressed moments earlier in the meeting rejecting exclusive supplier contracts.

At a break in the talks, Atwood summoned Meyerson toward him.

As Meyerson approached, Atwood exploded, shouting that he knew more about computer systems than anyone in the room. He dressed Meyerson down like an errant schoolboy. By disagreeing with Atwood he had committed a cardinal GM sin: contradicting a superior officer in front of outsiders.

"Don't you ever cross me in a meeting," Atwood yelled.

Meyerson was shocked by the outburst, and embarrassed that Atwood had done it in front of everyone. He was furious, but he kept silent. This was Atwood's way — the GM way — of asserting his authority. It ended, once and for all, Meyerson's efforts to cobble together an agreement with AT&T.

The AT&T team, accompanied by Morgan Stanley investment bankers, returned to the big conference room. Without a guarantee of the data processing contracts at GM, they announced, AT&T wasn't prepared to pay a premium price for EDS.

It struck Meyerson and Walter that Kavner and AT&T had badly misjudged their negotiating position. AT&T, it seemed to them, had erroneously believed that Smith was so desperate to get rid of EDS that he would be willing to do so at a rock-bottom price.

AT&T, in fact, wasn't prepared to offer a price at all; and GM wasn't willing to ask for one. Atwood, the ranking GM executive, wasn't acting as though he was in favor of selling EDS at all; he had his own ideas about how to integrate EDS and Hughes into the GM organization.

The AT&T negotiations, born of so much hope, were nearly dead.

The way to solve the impasse — the only real way — was to clean house at GM. The way to do it was to remove Smith and his hand-picked board of directors and bring in new management and directors. The new board might include iconoclasts such as Larry Tisch, chairman of CBS, and Fred Smith, the founder of Federal Express. They wouldn't be committed to "the GM system" or anything like it. New management would abide by the EDS merger agreement and create an entire organization of tigers.

Perot spoke about the need for new directors, but he had never intended to try to put in his own slate, which would have necessitated a proxy contest. Luce and Meyerson had talked about a coup, only half jokingly, many times before. They asked each other all the obvious questions. Would a takeover of GM work? Could anyone raise the minimum of $30 billion it would take to buy all the shares? Were enough solid people available to replace the management of an organization that huge? Did Perot and EDS have the stomach for a big, nasty fight?

The EDS men concluded that a takeover of GM was theoretically possible. But they also concluded something else: EDS well might be killed in the process. The vast majority of EDS's clients — banks, insurance companies, small manufacturers, credit unions, Medicare providers — didn't want a Wall Street confrontation between EDS and GM. They wanted hassle-free, predictable data processing services every day. Mere controversy was scary enough. What if, during a proxy contest for control of GM, GM barred their access to information stored in EDS's data centers? EDS customers denied access to their information — for a day or even a few hours — would never hire EDS again. No one else would either. For that reason, the idea of fighting for control of GM always was a nonstarter, in the opinion of Meyerson and Luce.

As Meyerson, Luce, and Walter sat in the living room of the EDS apartment in Manhattan on the evening of November 4, 1986, it was obvious that the AT&T talks were about to dissolve.

In a positive development, the auditing fight had been cleared up just a few days earlier. Citing the need for a goodwill gesture, Perot had uncharacteristically relented. Perot called Jim Evans; Evans insisted to Perot that it was important to let GM auditors — not just the independent auditors Perot had offered to pay for — look at EDS's books.

"Is this personally important to you for GM auditors to be allowed into EDS?" Perot asked Evans.

It is, Evans told him.

"OK, then. The auditors can come in."

Perot didn't enjoy giving in. Letting GM auditors into EDS was against every business principle he believed in — but if that was all it was going to take to make peace, perhaps he could live with it somehow. Besides, if Mort and Tom could somehow save the AT&T deal, the audit might never come about.

A few days after Evans's telephone call, when Perot heard from Meyerson that meddling by Atwood and the GM finance team was killing the AT&T deal, he once more grew frustrated and angry. Perot had started to hope that EDS might become an independent company again. Things had been proceeding fairly smoothly until Smith had injected Don Atwood, Leon Krain, and Elmer Johnson into the talks. True, AT&T also had gotten grabby, but Mort and Tom could have handled that.

Tom Luce, sitting dejectedly with his compatriots in the EDS apartment, knew only one alternative remained.

"I'm going to approach Elmer about a buyout," Luce told Meyerson and Walter. "We've tried everything. Nothing works. It's the only way out short of war, and I think we've agreed a war means calling the bombers in on our own people. Things can't continue the way they are. But first I'm going to have to see what GM's reaction is, because I'm not going to bring up the idea of a buyout to Ross unless I know it has some chance of succeeding."

Meyerson and Walter, depressed about the collapse of the negotiations, didn't say very much; they didn't disagree with Luce.

The next morning, the negotiations between AT&T and GM about the possible sale of EDS finally ended. As everyone gathered papers into their briefcases and prepared to depart, Luce walked over to Elmer Johnson.

"I think we better talk about where things are going," Luce said. He didn't need to explain to Johnson that he meant "things" as they related to Perot and Smith. "Do you have plans for lunch?"

The two men walked from AT&T to the oak-paneled Edwardian Room at the Plaza Hotel.

"The first thing I've got to tell you, Elmer, is that what I'm about to say I haven't discussed with Ross. I'm coming to you because I see this is the only way out," Luce said.

"Now that the AT&T option is gone, I think a buyout of Ross by GM is the only way to settle this," Luce said. "It's not a great solution, but it's the best thing for him and it's best for Roger and GM."

Johnson didn't hesitate. "I think it's something we can do. I'll certainly take it to Roger," he said.

"Now remember, Elmer, Ross doesn't know anything about this, and I'm not going to take it to him as an idea in principle. You'll have to get Roger signed off on it before I take it to Ross. It isn't his style to back away from a tough situation like we've been having, so if I put the idea to him in principle, he's not likely to let me pursue it," Luce said.

They discussed the advantage of pursuing a buyout immediately. The tax-reform package passed by Congress was scheduled to take effect January 1. That left two months for Perot to sell his stake and receive more favorable tax treatment under the old tax law. If buyout talks dragged on past January 1, it could cost him millions of dollars and perhaps make the price too steep for GM.

A buyout of Ross Perot's stock had to pass the GM board of directors. However, the GM board was scheduled to meet only one more time in 1986, during the first week of December, so the two men only had about three weeks to hammer out an agreement before the last board meeting in 1986.

"What's it going to take, do you think, from Perot's standpoint?" Elmer said.

"I think you're going to have to buy out all his shares at the market price, plus retire the contingent notes at a mutually acceptable formula," Luce said. "I think GM is going to have to buy out Meyerson, Walter, Gayden, and the few people personally close to Perot."

"That shouldn't be a problem," Johnson said.

"What is GM going to need?" Luce asked.

"An anti-takeover agreement," Johnson said. "Something that stays in force until Roger's retirement in 1990. We'd want provisions to end the criticism and make sure the buyout is completely amicable."

"That shouldn't be a problem," Luce said. "But, remember, I can't make any promises. This is me talking, not Perot. He may decide he doesn't like the idea. I'm prepared to advise him to do it, but he doesn't have to listen to me."

Johnson thought it extraordinary — and slightly hard to believe — that

Perot's lawyer had the authority to broach the subject of a buyout of his stake in GM without Perot's approval. Luce had always told him that Perot gave him a great deal of latitude. But could he be really telling the truth? Johnson wondered. He had never had any reason to question Luce. Maybe sending Luce with this story was Perot's way of saving face, of avoiding the humiliation of asking GM to buy him out, of avoiding having to concede he had crossed swords with Roger Smith and backed down.

The two lawyers shook hands, and Luce headed back to the hotel to tell Meyerson and Walter what he had just set in motion.

TWENTY-ONE

Ready for Departure

R oss Perot's public inquisition of GM, so humiliating to Roger Smith and so destabilizing to his authority, was lent a certain poignancy by GM's grim financial performance in late 1986.

In the midst of one of the most robust automotive markets in U.S. history, GM reported a third-quarter 1986 operating loss. Only a big tax credit and profits from EDS, Hughes, and the General Motors Acceptance Corporation finance company prevented a net loss for the quarter.

Wall Street was understandably disturbed by GM's dismal showing. Ford and Chrysler, back from death's door, were proportionately more profitable than GM. For five years Smith had been spending and modernizing and had very little to show for his investments in the way of earning power. By the analysts' reckoning, too much expensive plant capacity was chasing too few car and truck sales. Muted warnings were broadcast to portfolio managers and investors to beware a possible cut in GM's sacred cash dividend.

The analysts, therefore, were somewhat heartened on November 6, 1986, when GM announced plans to close all or part of eleven North American factories and put nearly 30,000 employees, or 5 percent of its staff, permanently out of work. Among the assembly plants targeted for shutdown were the Clark Street Cadillac assembly plant in downtown

Detroit, the Camaro and Firebird plant in Norwood, Ohio, and a truck and bus plant in Pontiac. Bad news for GM workers was good short-term news for Wall Street. The price of GM stock rallied on word of the shutdowns.

The GM plant closings, though they affected several plants that already had been targeted for shutdown and many workers who had been warned well in advance that their jobs were in jeopardy, represented the tactics of disinvestment and retreat that Perot deplored for the nation. He had sold EDS so GM could become an enterprise that created jobs, not eliminated them. It disgusted him to think that the same GM financial-control experts who were wasting time on procedures to check EDS's books were presiding over the shutdown of GM plants. True, GM now was able to claim hundreds of millions of dollars'worth of write-offs as a result of the closings. The write-offs boosted profits, but they didn't bring GM any closer to the goal of whipping the competition.

By late October, Perot was explaining his views, in very strident terms, to just about any journalist who called his Dallas office. However, he required interviewers to agree to omit most of his provocative quotes from their stories. He was afraid too much heat would precipitate a crisis that might cause Smith to dig in his heels.

Ward's Auto World, a magazine produced by *Ward's Automotive Reports,* a highly respected trade publication based in Detroit, was interested in the mushrooming corporate battle between Smith and Perot. *Ward's* generally tended to focus on the nuts and bolts of the car business, but *Auto World* was expanding coverage in a more lively, colorful fashion. When Jon Lowell, a reporter for *Auto World,* called Perot, he was amazed to hear the unvarnished version of what already had been published in the national press. In his uncensored interview, Perot again was calling for an end to "the GM system."

"I'd get rid of the fourteenth floor. I'd get rid of the executive dining rooms. I would urge the senior executives to locate their offices where real people are doing real work," Perot told him. Perot assured him he hadn't any designs on Smith's job, but he was determined to change the way GM operated, including the way GM paid top executives.

"We need to change the rules of compensation," Perot said. "Let's say you're fifty years old and suddenly you can't get your $1 million bonus by being a good [corporate] politician. The only way you can get it is by building the best cars in the world and beating the competition. That will reprogram your sense of priorities pretty fast."

Lowell could hardly believe his ears. This wasn't simply a tough critique of GM based on its undeniably weak operating record. It was a direct attack on everything GM held sacred: hierarchy, authority, and the seventy-year-old executive bonus system. Perot wasn't talking reform, he was talking revolution.

As usual, Perot instructed Lowell to leave out the more extreme remarks from the interview in order to prevent Smith "from going berserk," which he would likely do if he read Perot's attack on the fourteenth floor.

Lowell, a bright former *Newsweek* correspondent and head of corporate public relations for Burroughs Corporation, thereupon informed Perot that he had taped their conversation. He told Perot he wanted to put everything from their interview in his story including, as journalists love to call sensational material, "the good stuff."

Perot was surprised to have been taped without warning, but said he needed a few days to think about it.

With time running out before copy deadline for the November issue of *Ward's Auto World,* Lowell took Smith aside at a party for Joe Callahan, retiring editor of *Automotive Industries* magazine, at the Detroit Athletic Club. That morning, in a separate interview with the GM chief, Lowell had told Smith about Perot's inflammatory comments and asked for his response. Smith professed astonishment and promised he was going to call Perot to verify what Lowell was reporting. Of course, Perot's views weren't any surprise to Smith, but the GM chairman immediately realized from Lowell's questions that Perot had begun going public in the most extreme fashion, and *Ward's* was prepared to publish what he had said.

At Callahan's party, Smith told Lowell he had talked to Perot and that *Ward's* was making a big fuss out of not much at all. Sure, he and Perot had differences, he told Lowell. That didn't mean Perot was the enemy. He was being critical in a helpful way. Ross was doing everything possible to help GM. He wanted the same things everyone at GM wanted.

Lowell was too shrewd to buy Smith's story. It was obvious he was trying desperately to minimize the public clash with GM's biggest single stockholder.

Over the din of the noisy cocktail party, *Ward's* editor Dave Smith explained to Roger Smith why the magazine wasn't going to hold back the Perot story or change it into something milder. Lowell, meanwhile, was talking to Perot by telephone in one of the club's private rooms. Perot told Lowell he would agree to release his comments for publication in *Ward's Auto World* provided he could see a copy of the story in advance. *Ward's* hadn't done this before, and reputable publications rarely permit it. But time was about up before the copy deadline for November, and the Perot story was dynamite. Lowell and Smith agreed to fax Perot a copy.

The draft of Lowell's story returned from Dallas substantially unchanged. Because of the time constraint, *Ward's* was forced to stick with its original cover for November; it was too late to put Perot's picture on the cover and too late to give the story prominent display. Instead the editors put a "tease" — a few words touting the story — on the cover.

Ironically, *Ward's* November issue pictured some rather flattering sketches of GM cars of the future, with the boast that GM was turning away from "boring" design.

The telephone rang at Bill Hoglund's home in Birmingham, Michigan, one day in the fall of 1986 as the controversy reached its peak.

"Bill, this is Ross Perot." Since their helicopter ride in August, Perot had been waiting to hear from Hoglund. Approaching Hoglund had never been more than a long shot, but Perot thought it was one worth trying.

"Have you spoken to anyone else there about what I might be able to do?" Perot asked him.

Perot wanted to know if Hoglund or other GM executives wished him to tell Roger about specific things that needed improvement. As he had told Hoglund during their helicopter ride, he believed he was able to speak to Smith in a straightforward way that GM executives could not.

Hoglund told Perot that morale in his organization, the Buick-Olds-Cadillac group, was suffering as a result of the bad publicity Smith was getting, and there was some speculation by analysts that soft sales of GM cars might be tied to Perot's tirades. As a lifelong GMer and an executive on the fast track, Hoglund had no interest in joining Perot's restructuring campaign.

"Ross, I don't think anyone wants to speak with you about anything at this point," said Hoglund. "The public bashing of GM and Roger isn't helping any of us."

Perot's impression was that Hoglund, like many at GM, was frightened by what was happening to his mighty company. But he was more frightened of what might happen to him personally if he dared ally himself with Perot or challenged the chairman directly.

The rest of the conversation didn't last long.

Two days after his luncheon discussion with Elmer Johnson in New York about a possible buyout, Tom Luce received a telephone call at his office in Dallas.

"Roger is amenable," Johnson said. True to his prediction, Johnson reported that the GM chairman had been most eager to buy out Perot.

"The provisions we talked about are all right. The price will have to wait until last, though," Johnson said.

"Elmer, that won't do," replied Luce.

"Trust me," Elmer said. "We can get it done in the framework we discussed."

Johnson might not have believed that Perot still didn't know about the buyout talks, but it was true; Luce hadn't told him. Perot's lawyer was embarking on one of the trickiest and most challenging gambits of his legal career. He didn't want to risk looking like a fool by broaching the subject with Perot before he was sure that GM was going to put a price on the table. Yet Luce clearly was stretching his authority by, in effect, negotiating for his client without permission.

Inherent in the buyout Luce was pursuing with GM was the belief that he now had no better solution to offer Perot. They had tried everything: compromise, peace treaties. He had wanted to be able to offer a legal solution, perhaps a shareholders' lawsuit that forced GM to live up to the merger agreement. But litigation, Luce believed, led to the same dead end as any open hostility with GM: a long, bitter fight in which EDS's non-GM clients would be frightened away, resulting in injury — perhaps fatal injury — to EDS.

Perot wouldn't allow harm to come to EDS, even if he was forced to leave GM to prevent it. Luce was sure of that.

Once Johnson signaled that Smith was amenable to a buyout, Luce decided it was time to tell Perot, even if the price wasn't settled.

"Ross, I want you to understand that I've done what I'm about to tell you because I truly believe that this is the best course for you and for EDS. It doesn't justify GM's actions. I wish things had turned out differently," Luce said.

It was the toughest moment of Luce's career. They were seated in Perot's office. The expansive, lush lawns in front of EDS headquarters building hadn't begun to turn brown yet, as they would inevitably with the onset of the dry Texas winter.

In minute detail, Luce recounted how he had asked Johnson to the luncheon meeting immediately after the AT&T negotiations disintegrated. He told Perot about the conditions for the buyout and about how he had disclosed the plan to Meyerson and Walter, neither of whom disagreed with it.

He watched for Perot's reaction. Had Perot exploded in anger, it would not have come as a surprise. When Luce finished, there was a pause.

"They'll never do it," Perot said.

Luce momentarily thought he hadn't heard Perot correctly.

"They'll never do it," he said again. "They'll never even put it on paper. This is such a dumb idea. Those guys at GM will never admit they had to spend all this money just to get rid of me."

"Ross, I'm telling you they're going to do it. Elmer said that Roger is amenable," Luce said. Over the weekend he had tried to guess how Perot was going to react to a buyout. This wasn't one of his guesses.

"GM won't put it in writing," Perot insisted. "I'm not going to waste time with this. You get them to put it in writing and then we'll talk about it."

The meeting was over.

Perot had been in enough fights in his life to know when a showdown of some kind was imminent.

On November 11, Tom Luce brought him a draft of a buyout agreement. Immediately Perot noticed there was a blank instead of a price.

"Tom, these guys are indulging in games," he said. "I'm not going to talk about this without a price."

Before deciding whether EDS would launch a proxy fight to unseat GM's management or start a lawsuit alleging securities violations by GM, Perot had to know how his troops felt about possible all-out war with GM.

The week before Thanksgiving, EDS's two dozen or so top officers (minus those EDS officers who had come from GM since the merger) were summoned to Dallas. They included Les Alberthal, the president of EDS, Kenn Hill, head of the GM account, and several others who had worked for EDS in senior positions for many years.

Perot briefed everyone candidly. And the officers, of course, had been reading the newspapers. If war was declared against GM, Perot told them, everyone in the room had to understand what was at stake. The future of EDS. Their jobs. Their financial security in the form of millions of dollars' worth of unvested Class E stock held by GM. He intended to win the fight, but they must know the risks.

A passionate debate ensued. Several officers believed that it was premature to escalate the conflict. Progress had been made with GM. True, they didn't have the fixed-price contracts, but those would come in time.

What about our non-GM customers? another officer asked. They're going to panic. We've already lost a couple of potential contracts because the companies don't want to sign with us until the GM hostility goes away.

The EDS executives were no longer the same young gung-ho tigers of a decade earlier. Their families were growing; their children were reaching college age. Many of them believed they had uprooted their homes and families for the last time when GM bought EDS. Their EDS stock had been turned into cash by GM, and most of them were as close to complete financial security as they had ever dreamed of being. In some respects, life inside GM had changed them.

Perot was heartened that an outspoken minority of EDS officers was ready to chuck everything and fight.

But a minority wasn't enough. All-out battle against GM management, whether on the legal or shareholder front, would need solidarity in the ranks. Perot realized from the comments of his officers that they weren't willing to follow him into battle again.

The reactions of the EDS officers didn't really shock or disappoint Perot. They had done everything he asked. They had tried like hell to make the merger with GM work the way he had wanted it to. They had been loyal, but now they were weary and shackled with golden handcuffs.

Perot, Smith, and the EDS directors convened at EDS offices outside Washington on November 18 for the regular quarterly board meeting. Elmer Johnson flew in from Detroit to meet Tom Luce. While the board met, the two lawyers talked.

Luce told Johnson he couldn't negotiate terms of a buyout without a price. Johnson said Smith didn't want to talk about money unless it was clear an agreement could be reached. Tentatively, they discussed what an agreement might look like should they be able to reach financial terms.

Johnson suggested that all the money Perot would be paid for his stock be kept in escrow for a period of time to keep Perot silent about the true circumstances of his exit from GM. The proposal was evidence of Smith's and Johnson's worry about criticism from Perot.

Perot would never agree to it, Luce told him.

"Besides, we can't get anywhere without a price for the stock, Elmer," Luce reminded him.

"If you agree to provisions preventing criticism by Perot, I'll fly back to Detroit with Roger and I'll get him to agree to a price," Johnson said.

"Not so fast," Luce said. "I haven't shown anything in writing to

Ross. I'll recommend it to him, but he hasn't authorized me to negotiate without a price."

Johnson also wanted a five-year agreement from Perot precluding him from competing in the computer business.

"No way, Elmer," Luce said. "First of all, Ross wants to have a place for his people to go if things don't work out for them at EDS. Second, you can't expect a guy like Ross to retire from business. You can't take a whole set of skills and say to a person like Ross that he can't do those things. What if the government comes to him, like Texas did on the education issue, and asks his help to reorganize a department like the Pentagon? He's not going to take a billion dollars and go live on an island."

They agreed on an eighteen-month noncompete clause covering nonprofit work, and a thirty-six month clause covering competition of any kind. He would be free to hire anyone from EDS after June 1, 1988.

The next day Johnson sent a draft of the agreement by fax to Luce in Dallas.

Luce brought the copy to Perot, who still refused to believe GM was prepared to spend hundreds of millions of dollars to silence him.

"It doesn't have the price," Perot said, pointing to the blank. "Just keep on working until it's all in writing, including the price." Whether he liked it or not, Perot slowly was being forced to accept the inevitable. Luce called Johnson to tell him that Perot wasn't going to bite on anything until GM offered a price for his stock.

While Johnson assumed Perot and Luce only were acting as tough negotiators by demanding that a price be specified, something else also was happening. Perot was trying to come to terms with the fact that he soon might be leaving EDS. EDS had been, outside of his family, practically his whole life. It was important for him to believe, perhaps to hope, that GM wasn't going to pay what it would take to get his stock and make him go away. To believe this, it was also vital to believe that the GM directors — and if not the directors, the shareholders or the public or someone — were going to intervene and prevent Smith from banishing Perot.

Hence, it was important to Perot that a buyout be perceived as stupid for GM, establishing bold and clear-cut grounds for someone to stop Smith from carrying it out. He insisted on the right to start competing ventures and to hire people from EDS within eighteen months. Surely the directors would not allow Smith to agree to that! After all, if he started a new EDS, the old EDS would certainly diminish in value.

A scenario was evolving in Perot's mind. In this scenario, Smith would offer him a huge premium for his stock as part of an agreement that gave him as much latitude for future business plans as he wished. In the next sequence, the buyout terms would become known publicly. At that point, with Wall Street and the newspapers and GM employees howling about Smith's stupidity, Perot would turn the deal down! The spectacle of GM's self-serving management would stand revealed. The momentum to oust Smith and replace GM's management system with an effective incentive-based meritocracy would be unstoppable.

Media watchers who read between the lines may have deduced a few days before Thanksgiving 1986 that Roger Smith was wearying of Perot's jabs — particularly those aimed at GM executive perks.

"We are all trying to change the corporation," the exasperated GM chairman told a *Detroit Free Press* reporter. Smith complained that everyone thought incorrectly that Perot was the first to recognize GM's problems. And he implied that the press was being unfair: "Ross has an office that makes mine look like a shantytown. He has Remingtons; he has a Gilbert Stuart painting hanging on the wall. Nobody runs around saying 'Get rid of Ross's office.' "

(Perot laughed when someone reported what Smith had said. Smith had missed his point entirely. Perot paid for his office furnishings out of his own pocket. Smith's office was paid for by GM shareholders.)

The *Wall Street Journal* the same day published the story of GM's then-secret talks four weeks earlier to sell EDS to AT&T. The story noted GM's problems integrating EDS as well as the escalating tensions between Smith and Perot. GM, in somewhat disingenuous fashion, denied that EDS was for sale. Journalists who had a chance to ask Smith about the AT&T talks received similar denials.

Smith didn't want to tell the truth and risk destroying EDS morale or bringing its operations to a halt by allowing the world to know what a headache the $2.5 billion acquisition had become. In any case, he and Johnson already were pursuing Plan B, the buyout of Perot. As soon as the details of the buyout were set, Perot would be history.

Smith had been slow to grasp that Perot was challenging him to justify his own concept of the way a business should work. The longer Perot stayed, the bigger the danger to GM's form of government and to Smith's stewardship. As the press clamor grew louder, weeks had gone by in hundreds and thousands of GM workplaces with very little accomplished but new speculation and gossip. The article from *Ward's Auto World* was tacked to many GM office and plant bulletin boards. GM executives and managers, not to mention the GM board of directors, were puzzled about why Smith didn't react in some way. By failing to act decisively when Perot first challenged him, Smith inadvertently was sending a signal to the troops that he was weak and that he, indeed, might be in jeopardy of losing his job.

Thanksgiving weekend brought a flurry of activity in Detroit, Dallas, and New York.

Salomon Brothers investment bankers, who had been at GM's side since the idea of buying EDS was hatched three years earlier, were asked for a quick study double-checking for fairness the amount GM was preparing to offer Perot. The "fairness letter" was a legal requirement targeted to GM shareholders, some of whom could be expected to challenge the buyout in court no matter how much GM spent.

The Salomon opinion had to be ready by Monday, December 1, the date of the December board meeting, when GM directors would have their last chance under the old tax law to approve the buyout. EDS stock had been selling for an average of $33 a share during November. Smith was willing to pay Perot an additional $23.50 a share for each of the contingent notes, plus a $5.40 a share special payment covering possible adverse tax treatment. In effect, GM was offering Perot and the small group of EDS confederates $61.90 a share for their stock, which, in any case, GM had guaranteed to be worth $62.50 a share in 1991.

Did $61.90 a share represent a premium price over the stock's true value? GM, anxious to show that it had done nothing really special to get rid of Perot, argued that it didn't. The stock probably was going to reach that value in a few years anyway. If it didn't, Perot's contingent notes forced GM to pay the difference. GM was just paying it a couple of years early.

On Thanksgiving, when Perot finally saw the amount of money he was to receive, he refused to believe that the GM board was going to approve. GM had just announced the big operating loss and the planned shutdown of eleven plants. It now was fairly obvious that GM hourly workers weren't going to receive a profit-sharing bonus in 1986 as a result of the corporation's lackluster earnings. How could the board justify spending $742.8 million to buy in almost 12 million GM Class E shares?

Perot called Ken Langone, his old investment-banking friend, the man who had helped underwrite the first public offering of EDS stock in 1969. Perot reached Langone at a Thanksgiving gathering at the home of Langone's son on Long Island.

The buyout talks had been kept under very tight secrecy, but Langone wasn't shocked to hear that GM was trying to get rid of Perot.

"Ken, I don't want to do this deal," Perot told him. "GM should have better uses for its money than this. I just want to get the place cleaned up. And I'm very concerned about what's going to happen to the EDS people if I go."

As Perot waxed idealistic, Langone focused on the practical. Perot had come to GM without experience in the politics and infighting in giant corporations. Langone, on the other hand, had watched the corporate wars as a professional investor for thirty years. As much as he admired Perot, Langone could well imagine why Roger Smith was willing to spend any amount to erase him from the picture. No chief executive in his right mind was going to permit a dissident to take potshots at management indefinitely.

"I'm just worried about one thing, Ross: the perception by the public — after this deal is over — that you greenmailed GM," Langone said. From a financial perspective, the terms were excellent for Perot. He knew Perot wasn't a raider who pestered management with the aim of being paid off. But cynics might not believe it. Perot's scenario — for GM to offer the deal and him to turn it down — wasn't going to work; GM lawyers were too sharp to fall for it.

"You need some kind of mechanism in this deal that will keep you out of the greenmail category. Some mechanism that will show people the real reason all of this happened," Langone said.

Ira Millstein and Bob Messineo, the outside lawyers hired to advise the GM board's oversight committee, worked intensively with Elmer Johnson over the Thanksgiving weekend to prepare a formal presentation of the case for buying out Perot.

The paramount consideration was legality. The groundwork was laid; the buyout was going to happen. They needed to be able to prove later on that Smith and the directors had thought the buyout through carefully and made sure it was the best solution.

Roger Smith, in the meantime, already was canvassing several current and former GM directors to confer with them. Agreement wasn't unanimous among directors that a buyout was the best alternative. Some were outraged by Perot's tactics and wanted him fired. In their view, he had violated corporate governance standards. While the board had the power to fire Perot as EDS chief executive, it is doubtful they had the legal power to oust him from the board before the June 1987 annual meeting.

John Connor, a former GM director who had retired a year earlier, counseled Smith to remain calm and wait for Perot to "self-destruct." The majority, however, was willing to support the GM chairman to carry out what he — and Elmer Johnson — thought best. The status quo, letting Perot keep taking shots at GM, was unacceptable. No one spoke in his behalf.

Shuttling back and forth from Thanksgiving family get-togethers to their offices in the GM Building, Millstein and Messineo prepared a briefing book for each director outlining the history of the conflict between Perot and the corporation, including the failed peace treaty of a year earlier. It emphasized Perot's unwillingness to permit GM auditors into EDS, the disagreements over pricing, contracts, and compensation, and, finally, the furor and employee malaise caused by the public blasts at Smith.

Finally sensing some acquiescence from Perot, Tom Luce flashed the green light from Texas. In his judgment, Perot was readying himself to accept GM's offer. Under the lawyers' plan, the oversight committee was to meet Monday morning to approve the buyout. Their approval was scheduled for review and approval by the rest of the directors at the full GM board meeting in the afternoon. Press releases from Perot and the company, explaining the transaction in conciliatory language and wishing one another well, would be released after the board meeting.

Smith, Johnson, and the GM directors hoped that by nightfall on December 1 Ross Perot would be no more than a vaguely remembered chapter in GM's history.

Luce called Perot on Saturday, November 29, two days before the GM board meeting.

"The final draft of the agreement is ready for you to look at, Ross," Luce said. They went over the document as he had gone over it with Johnson, in lawyerly fashion, line by line.

When they finished, Perot still didn't look convinced.

"The board will never approve it. I won't consider it until the board approves it and Roger signs it," Perot told him. From anyone else the statement might have been chalked up as psychological denial, pure and simple. With Perot, there was no telling. He hadn't objected strenuously to any provisions of the buyout agreement. He also hadn't told Luce he planned to sign it. Luce remained confident, however, that Johnson's reading of the situation was correct; that is, Johnson wanted the agreement, and he and Ira Millstein could deliver the GM board. Eventually, Perot would have no choice.

On Sunday morning, November 30, a *Wall Street Journal* reporter placed a telephone call to Cliff Merriot, a senior GM spokesman, for his official comment on a story the newspaper was preparing for Monday morning. The story, based on tips from sources close to the negotiations, said GM was offering to buy out Perot for $750 million.

Merriot clearly was incredulous. He had heard no such thing, not even rumblings. No other reporters had called.

Skeptical as he was of the story, Merriot promised to call senior GM officials, check, and get back to the *Journal*.

An hour later Merriot called back: "There is just nothing to say."

Millstein and Johnson, having heard of the telephone call and realizing that GM directors now were likely to be in the awkward position of reading about the buyout in Monday's *Journal* before they were asked to deliberate it formally, decided to move up the meeting of the oversight committee to Sunday night. The lawyers also decided to invite all non-GM directors to attend the meeting.

GM booked a double suite at the Regency Hotel in Manhattan, and the lawyers began calling as many directors as possible early on Sunday, asking them to try to attend the meeting.

Millstein specifically had asked Smith and the other GM members of the board — Bob Stempel, Lloyd Reuss, Jim McDonald, Alan Smith, and Howard Kehrl — not to attend the meeting of the oversight committee on Sunday night. The action the board was about to take stemmed from conflict between EDS and the GM management; the board was on more secure legal ground, the lawyers believed, if GM management directors weren't in the position of passing judgment on their own actions.

Directors, lawyers, and various advisers began arriving at Suite 1028 of the Regency Hotel on Park Avenue a little before 7:00 P.M. on Sunday evening. Several of them had rushed back early from Thanksgiving weekend holidays to attend the meeting. Ed Pratt, the chief executive of Pfizer Corporation who claimed he had crossed swords years earlier with Perot over the Vietnam Memorial, tried unsuccessfully to make new travel arrangements from a remote family gathering in rural Walterboro, South Carolina. The evening's events were about to vindicate Pratt, who had tried to persuade Smith in early 1984 that bringing in Perot was dangerous.

John Gutfreund, Salomon Brothers chairman, arrived at the meeting from Bermuda a bit late, still wearing a sweater. When Gutfreund asked where to stash the tennis racquet he was carrying, everyone chuckled. It was practically the only humorous moment of the evening.

After the waiters removed the remnants of a hastily eaten dinner, Jim Evans, as head of the oversight committee, convened the meeting.

One by one, key participants in the EDS merger — all from the GM side — entered the room to explain how Perot had trampled the legal, accepted tenets of governance. Dick Troost, head of GM's internal auditing, told about Perot's refusal to allow an audit. Greg Lau, GM's compensation expert, told about Perot's refusal to accept the GM incentive plans. Leon Krain, GM treasurer, explained the finances of the buyout. Don Atwood talked about how EDS was functioning since reaching a pricing compromise and how it was likely to function under Les Alberthal when Perot and Meyerson were gone.

The fact that Perot finally had compromised with Smith about compensation and that he had told Jim Evans he would agree to allow an internal audit, albeit reluctantly, was dutifully mentioned and recorded. But the directors chose to view Perot's compromises as irrelevant to the task at hand: technically, the facts refuted the argument that Perot was being bought out because he had flouted principles of good corporate governance. As everyone in the room understood, the buyout was taking place to remove an irritant to management, not to accomplish an audit of EDS. Only one man could rule, and their man was Roger Smith.

Bob Scully, the investment banker who had helped structure the merger, presented Salomon Brothers' analysis of the price GM was paying for Perot's stock. GM, he noted, was paying the market price for the shares and a fair price for the contingent notes. (A value for the notes wasn't determinable since they were nontransferable and, thus, no market for them existed.)

From GM's point of view, it wasn't a straight outlay of cash. Certain tax advantages shaved almost $11 a share off the $61.90 cost. And GM would have the GM E shares in return. Overall, the impact of a $750 million outlay for the stock on GM profit was negligible.

Speaking on behalf of Salomon Brothers, which had brokered the now-doomed marriage, John Gutfreund warned everyone in the room about the public relations fallout they could expect from a buyout.

"The press is going to be bad. Shareholders are going to scream," Gutfreund said.

Dressed in his tennis sweater, he puffed on his ever-present cigar, an imperious presence carrying himself like a true Master of the Universe. "But from what I can see, the relationship is untenable. You're deciding whether to go with Roger or with Ross. The board appointed Roger. If you're deciding to stay with Roger, you have to get rid of the other. The only question is how. From a financial perspective, the deal isn't bad." The evidentiary reports establishing the basis for board action dragged on for several hours.

The second phase of the meeting was the directors' discussion of what to do.

Smith, who acquiesced to Millstein's wishes and did not attend the meeting, nevertheless had reported to directors by telephone that Perot was going to accept the buyout arrangement and "wanted to do what was best for GM."

A few directors at the meeting thought buying Perot out was wrong. The buyout particularly irked Murph Goldberger, the president of the California Institute of Technology.

"If Perot did what we've been hearing about for the past few hours, and we think that's wrong, then we ought to fire him," Goldberger said. "We should show some moral rigor. How can I go home and explain that we paid $750 million to get rid of Perot if we think he's done something wrong?"

Theoretically, the GM lawyers said, Smith indeed had the authority to remove Perot as EDS chief executive and throw him off the GM board. Johnson and Millstein explained why they believed that firing Perot was a potentially disastrous course of action. First of all, it promised lawsuits without end, the ghastly public relations image of GM beating up its biggest shareholder — and the possibility of sparking a proxy fight against management. In short, Perot was sure to retaliate with scorched-earth tactics that might cost everyone in the room their jobs and damage GM.

Buying back Perot's stake let directors sidestep the firestorm of recrimination from Perot. The yammering from disgruntled shareholders would be a problem, but a minor one compared to what was going to happen soon if Perot didn't leave.

"Both courses — firing and buyout — are within your rights," Elmer Johnson said. "Ira and I have stated why we think a buyout is preferable. One thing I think we can say about Ross is that he's a man of his word. If he agrees to go quietly, he'll do so. We think going quietly is far preferable for GM and well worth the money."

Evans called for a vote. The buyout passed the oversight committee unanimously. At one o'clock Monday morning, knots of lawyers and directors were still standing about in the Regency's tenth-floor double suite, discussing the consequences of the buyout. They had chosen their only viable option swiftly and without excessive emotion, exactly as GM's lawyers had hoped they would.

In a few hours the board and Roger Smith were scheduled to convene to vote final approval and bid Perot farewell.

TWENTY-TWO

Buyout Bombshell

As the GM directors conferred in Manhattan, Tom Luce, Tom Walter, and Mort Meyerson sat in the living room of Meyerson's home in Dallas on Sunday evening, November 30, 1986, reviewing the terms of the buyout contract.

At 10:00 P.M., the telephone rang. After receiving word from Elmer Johnson confirming passage of the buyout agreement by the oversight committee, Luce showed Walter and Meyerson where to sign.

By almost every standard measurement, Bill Gayden, Walter, and Meyerson were about to strike it rich. The buyout agreement instantly liquefied their GM Class E stakes, which were worth tens of millions of dollars under the contract's guarantees. They were cashing in their tickets at the winner's window. The men didn't feel like winners, though. The payments formalized their exit from EDS, a bitter process begun almost from the moment GM bought the company. Soberly, they leafed through the pages.

"That's it, then," Meyerson said. "It's over."

The only blank spot on the contract was the place for Perot's signature.

"I think he'll do it," Luce said. "I told GM he'd sign. But he keeps telling me he wants the board to approve it first and Roger to sign before he does."

Perot waited at his home that evening for someone at the GM board meeting to say or do something to stop the buyout. He didn't imagine that he had any secret admirers among the directors. Considering his demonstrated lack of regard for their independent judgment, that was surely out of the question. His only hope lay in one or more of the directors making a strong case against the expenditure of $742.8 million, an obscene amount of money to give up in light of GM's operating problems. Eventually the directors were going to have to deal with GM's downward spiral. A crisis was going to force them to wake up, as Chrysler and Ford had been forced to awaken. Might the $742.8 million payment to Perot, in the eyes of one conscientious director, be the last straw? Assuming a director opposed the buyout, it was going to take an uncharacteristic act of defiance against Smith to speak against it.

It was Perot's self-confident nature, as well as his optimism, that allowed him to hope for the impossible to happen as late as Sunday night.

By 9 o'clock Monday morning, December 1, most investment analysts and portfolio managers had read their *Wall Street Journal*s and were girded for a rough day of trading in GM Class E stock, GM common stock, and, perhaps, the whole market.

The *Journal* article told of GM's buyout offer to Perot, while specifying that he wasn't sure to accept. Offering to buy Perot's shares at a premium price implied much more trouble with the merger than GM previously had disclosed. Holders of GM Class E shares were entitled to ask themselves indignantly: Why should Ross Perot get a better price from GM for his shares than me? Indignation is a short step from anger and revenge, powerful feelings that could motivate portfolio managers to unload GM shares.

By mid-morning, GM directors, joined by Roger Smith and other members of the GM executive committee, were in session in the boardroom. It devolved to Johnson to call Luce and make sure Perot had signed the contract and that all the details were set. Smith wasn't about to announce the buyout and allow Perot an opening to wiggle out of.

"Tom, the board is ready. Is everything set?" Johnson asked.

"Elmer, Ross wants the board to approve it and Roger to sign it before he puts his name on it. I think he needs a little more time," Luce said. Perot absolutely didn't want to be the one to go first. What if he signed, and the board turned it down? It might look as if he had asked for the money and GM refused. Besides, he still wasn't absolutely sure he was going to accept GM's money, if it were offered.

"Nothing doing," Johnson said. "I'm not presenting this to the board on a hypothetical basis. Either he signs the papers now or nothing is going to happen."

Luce reported the development to Perot. Johnson had seen through the gambit; he understood all too well that Perot wasn't in this for money and, if given the chance, might use the awkward appearance of the buyout against Smith.

"Has he signed?" Johnson asked.

Luce told Johnson he hadn't, handing the phone to Perot. Perot insisted the board vote for it first, but he said he would sign it if the directors did. He still was convinced a director might stop the buyout.

"Tom," he told Luce, "one of those guys has got to stand up and say 'Guys, this is ludicrous.' "

But no one did. A few minutes later, Johnson called Luce to say the board had voted the buyout and Smith had signed it. Luce told Perot.

"You're kidding," Perot said, looking genuinely nonplussed. He had been waiting for the cavalry to arrive. Reluctantly, Perot signed the papers.

Johnson called Morgan Guaranty bank to release the money to be wired to Perot's bank account in Dallas. Luce called the bank. The money hadn't arrived. Ten minutes went by. Fifteen. Luce called Johnson in New York.

"What's going on? You said you wired the money," Luce said. "Our bank doesn't have it."

Incredibly, three-quarters of a billion dollars in the form of an electromagnetic impulse was floating unaccounted for somewhere between New York and Dallas.

After a few minutes of frantic checking, the glitch was corrected and the funds arrived at Perot's bank.

When arrival of the money was confirmed, Luce reported to Perot. "The directors approved the papers, Roger signed it, and the money is in your account," Luce said. Perot no longer was chief executive of EDS, his stock (as well as that of his associates) was transferred to GM, and Smith accepted his resignation from the board.

In a prepared statement for the press written by Jack McNulty, GM vice president of public relations, Smith lauded Perot's "entrepreneurial vision and ideas." Almost as an afterthought, the press release mentioned that GM directors approved the purchase of Perot's stock and notes, without mentioning the price.

Perot, in a reciprocal prepared statement also written by the GM public relations chief, was quoted as saying he was "pleased that the process of integrating EDS within General Motors has been completed."

Both statements lacked candor. Moreover, they fooled no one. McNulty had trotted out the operative euphemisms, so often used after corporate wars, which strained to convince that adversaries were parting on a friendly basis.

Had the statements been true, Elmer Johnson wouldn't have insisted on a provision in the agreement under which Perot and GM promised to refrain from criticizing one another, on pain of a $7.5 million penalty. GM went so far as to specify that in case insults started flying again, a three-man arbitration panel would be set up to judge what constituted a violation. GM had insisted on the anti-mudslinging provision after Luce told Johnson that Perot wasn't about to place the proceeds of the stock sale in escrow as a guarantee against criticism. Luce had tried to reassure Johnson that if Perot signed the agreement to remain silent, he meant to abide by it.

But with the money and stock having changed hands moments earlier, it looked as if Perot had his own ideas about how he wanted to present his position to the public. Perot knew that to read the GM press release was to conclude that he had greenmailed GM. Langone was right. He didn't, in fact, want the money and was willing to give it back. GM, on the other hand, desperately needed to conserve resources for its battle to become a competitive car company. It mattered more that GM shareholders and the public understand what was at stake than that he adhere to an agreement cooked up by lawyers.

Perot took the elevator down to EDS's first-floor cafeteria, where several dozen Dallas-based reporters and TV crews were waiting to interview him. He passed out copies of the following press release, given a few minutes earlier to the Dow Jones financial newswire:

At a time when General Motors is:
— closing 11 plants,
— putting over 30,000 people out of work,
— cutting back on capital expenditures,
— losing market share,
— and having problems with profitability,

I have just received $700 million from General Motors in exchange for my Class E stock and notes. I cannot accept this money without giving the GM directors another chance to consider this decision. This money will be held in escrow until December 15, in order to give the GM directors time to review this matter and the events that led to this decision.

If the GM directors conclude that this transaction of December 1 isn't in the best interests of GM and Class E shareholders, I will work with the GM directors to rescind the transaction.

Brilliant yellow sunlight bathed Manhattan just before noon on December 1, 1986, as Paul Zalecki, a top GM attorney, Bob Messineo, a young Weil Gotshal attorney, and Ira Millstein emerged from the GM building. Perot had the money. GM had Perot's stock. The nightmare was over, time for a celebratory lunch.

The three lawyers had just sat down at the City Athletic Club on Park Avenue and 56th Street when the maître d'hôtel summoned Millstein to the telephone. He excused himself. A few minutes later he returned from the cloakroom visibly upset.

"You're not going to believe this," he told the other two lawyers. The call was from GM headquarters, telling Millstein what the Dow Jones newswire had just carried from Perot's press conference.

The lawyers hurried back to GM, where the mood of relief had turned black. Millstein and Johnson were particularly furious. They had negotiated the agreement in good faith. Now, after accepting the money, Perot had delivered a parting shot to the groin.

Millstein immediately called Luce's office in Dallas to demand an explanation. He was told that Luce had gone home and couldn't be reached. (Luce had worked late into the night for several days in a row; he had gone home to shower and change as soon as the money was received. When he came back to EDS headquarters an hour or so later, he found out what had happened and explained to Elmer Johnson by telephone that he had had no idea what Perot had been planning.)

Johnson and Millstein huddled. The first thing the board must do, they agreed, was to reaffirm the buyout and release the reaffirmation to the Dow Jones financial wire, stamping out unequivocally any confusion over whether GM might rescind the transaction. As far as they were concerned, Perot could put the money in escrow for as long as he wanted; he was out of GM and wasn't coming back.

By noon, GM stock was off $3 a share amidst a wave of selling. GM Class E stock was skidding to a $4.50 a share loss for the day. As

Gutfreund had predicted the day before, investors were disappointed and angry.

With the GM reaffirmation of the buyout released to the news media in the early afternoon, a pitched rhetorical battle broke out between Perot and GM for the moral high ground in the transaction. Perot's first shot, the surprise announcement of his escrow plan, caught GM completely off guard. It was now obvious that Perot had no intention of fading quietly into the night, his pockets full of money. Stepping before a microphone in front of a crowd of reporters in EDS's cafeteria in Dallas, Perot ridiculed the buyout agreement he had just signed.

"Now don't ask any questions that will cost me too much money," he joked. If GM tried to enforce the $7.5 million gag clause, he told the reporters, he would happily write the check.

As Langone had anticipated, a reporter asked Perot if the $750 million he and his compatriots had been paid wasn't just another form of corporate greenmail.

No, he explained, it's really "hush-mail." GM didn't want to hear what he had to say, so they paid him $750 million to shut his mouth. He didn't like what happened, but GM had forced it. The explanation sounded odd, like saying "the devil made him do it." The skepticism from some reporters at the press conference was palpable. How could someone just make off with $750 million and say he wasn't happy? Perot obliged them with a Perot-style explanation.

"Is spending all this money the highest and best use of GM's capital? Individuals aren't important here. The issue is that both EDS and GM remain strong and viable. I want to give the directors a chance to do the right thing. It is incomprehensible to me that they would want to spend $750 million on this. I am hopeful that people will suddenly get a laserlike focus on what needs to be done and do it," Perot told the reporters.

So why did you take the money? a reporter asked.

It was the only way to get the buyout into the public arena, he answered.

Perot had dreamed of a firestorm of protest over the buyout from shareholders, GM employees, UAW officials, GM dealers. In this dream the uproar built until its crescendo was too much for GM directors to bear. They invited Perot back, returned his stock, took back the money. Then, in his fantasy, they tossed Smith out on his ear.

Initial soundings from Wall Street and the press in the first few days after the buyout tended to support his dream. John Neff, manager of the

Windsor mutual fund, which owned 3.8 million GM shares, called publicly for Perot's reinstatement. Marilyn Weinstein, an analyst for the College Retirement Equities Fund, which also owned 3.8 million GM shares, lamented the lack of consideration for shareholders' interests evidenced by Perot's ouster. Editorial cartoonists made great sport lampooning Roger Smith's "ransom" payment to escape Perot's clutches. *Automotive News,* Detroit's weekly bible of the industry, excoriated Smith and GM as "losers" for ousting Perot to silence criticism.

Most of the actual selling of GM common shares, however, was restricted to relatively small investors and for a short period of time. Only a few institutional managers were angry enough to dump their GM stock wholesale. A $750 million buyout didn't endanger GM's ability to pay the quarterly dividend, their primary concern. GM's share price had been stagnant for decades; according to hardheaded financial analysis, Perot's departure didn't appreciably worsen GM's prospects.

GM Class E stock, on the other hand, suffered a terrific beating from investors. Without Perot, EDS's potential for future revenue and profit growth was severely diminished.

Steve McClellan, the Merrill Lynch research analyst who had spent a career interpreting EDS for investors, tried to view Perot's departure as coldly and unemotionally as possible. Two years earlier he had thought GM's acquisition of EDS was going to differ somehow from other acquisitions because of the creation of the E stock and Smith's assurances of independence. In truth, the merger had evolved like so many others McClellan had seen, a short honeymoon followed by disillusionment and rancor and capped with golden handshakes. GM had stifled EDS's independence by buying it; now GM was beefing up its heavy-handed authority over EDS by pushing out Perot and Meyerson.

McClellan admired the business ethic that Perot and Meyerson had created at EDS. Would EDS still have a life force without Perot and Meyerson? McClellan called Les Alberthal, EDS's newly appointed chief executive, to hear about EDS's prospects in the post-Perot era. After chatting awhile with Alberthal, McClellan was persuaded that GM wasn't about to do anything further to jeopardize its $2.5 billion investment in EDS. Surprisingly, some top EDS executives were saying the company might now be better off without Perot. With Perot gone, Alberthal told McClellan, the bickering would die down. Many fixed-price contracts still weren't signed as specified in the merger contract; but now GM had to fulfill the obligation to sign them, Alberthal said. A nonpublic provision in the buyout agreement, insisted upon by Perot, called for GM to sign the contracts promised in the original merger. (GM scheduled a meeting for analysts in New York a day after the buyout to repeat the promise to sign the contracts.)

Believing that Alberthal's forecast was correct and swallowing his feelings, McClellan flashed a "buy" recommendation on GM Class E shares to Merrill Lynch clients. The buyout had a silver lining, he told them: negotiated peace.

Had Perot accepted his $700 million quietly and gone about his business, Elmer Johnson almost certainly would have been willing to deflect and subdue the questions about the circumstances of the EDS chief executive's departure.

A few hours after the board rejected Perot's escrow offer, Johnson granted interviews to selected members of the media on a deep background basis. Until then, GM had offered only a skimpy, misleading account of what had happened. Reporters were eager to know who had asked for the buyout, Smith or Perot. Johnson, in interviews, told of Perot's letter of the previous May, suggesting a possible buyout. Perot's letter to Roger saying he intended to run EDS his own way did mention a buyout as a possible solution, but recommended against it. Johnson left out the part about Perot's recommendation against a buyout, which made his letter look like a request to be paid off.

Speaking as a "source close to GM," Johnson also informed reporters that Perot's lawyer, Tom Luce, again had approached GM about a buyout in early November, citing pending changes in the tax law. Technically, Johnson was telling the truth, although he failed to mention that Smith jumped at the chance to buy Perot's stock.

Johnson's statements in the interviews put a new spin on Perot's actions. No longer did Perot appear to reporters as the untarnished hero. Johnson portrayed him as an opportunist, not an idealist. He had sold his company to GM and forgotten that it didn't belong to him anymore. GM graciously had encouraged Perot to stay on and employ his leadership skills in behalf of both companies. Instead, he had twisted and perverted that role into a grab for the chairman's power; not the formal title of chairman, but the behind-the-scenes power of someone who could call the shots to his liking, in contradiction of the accepted, time-honored rules of corporate governance. And when Perot's power grab didn't work, he came to GM with his hand out. Johnson ridiculed the escrow gambit, telling reporters Perot only developed a conscience about the highest and best use of GM capital "one second after he got the money."

The attacks had nothing to do with Johnson's personal view of Perot. Privately, he admired Perot and, in fact, agreed with many of his criticisms. He agreed GM was far too bloated, too bureaucratic, and too weighted down by mediocrity. As an outsider, he found GM's preoccupation with executive perks to be unhealthy at a time when so many improvements were needed. The executive bonus system and the profit-sharing plan for hourly workers should work according to the same marketplace rules: his thinking on the subject of executive bonuses was lifted straight from Perot's hymnal.

But Johnson believed in the survival of the corporation. He believed in the gradual, incremental progress within a corporate democracy with checks and balances, and he favored change within an intellectual framework. Revolution didn't attract him. GM had room for only one monarch. Smith might not have been Johnson's first choice to lead GM, but he was the board's choice as chief executive, and it was Johnson's duty as GM's top lawyer to protect GM from Perot.

Any sympathetic feelings Johnson harbored for Perot's ideas were overshadowed by his anger and sense of betrayal. Luce had promised him that Perot was a man of his word; if Perot signed the agreement, he would abide by it. Johnson, without understanding that no one — not even Luce — could completely predict or control Perot's actions, believed that Perot had gone back on an understanding.

Perot's last-minute turnabout surely didn't win Johnson any points with the directors or the executive committee. The affair had made him look a bit naive, and he wasn't without ambitions of his own. As a reward for guiding GM through this and other corporate crises, he hoped to rise higher in the corporation and extend his influence, perhaps one day to run GM — a possibility Roger Smith had mentioned when he hired him.

In the summer of 1986, about six months prior to the buyout, Perot had accepted an invitation to address the Economic Club of Detroit on December 8, 1986, at the club's regular Monday luncheon. Roger Smith, a director of the group, had agreed to introduce Perot.

The prestigious Economic Club had been host to U.S. presidents, royalty, Nobel Prize–winning economists, diplomats, and industrial titans. Perot was a speaker in this tradition, but now he was also in the headlines. In the storm of publicity during the week of December 1 over Perot's departure from GM — and when it became clear that Perot had no intention of canceling the speaking engagement — requests for tickets to his speech poured in from all over the country and the world. Overnight Perot and GM had become big news in Europe and Asia; foreign TV stations asked to send crews to film his speech.

Speaking before the Economic Club happened to fit neatly with Perot's strategy to keep the $750 million buyout in the public eye. He didn't harbor any strong hope of GM directors taking him up on the escrow offer, for they had shot it down immediately. But he still wanted to show everyone that the future of GM wasn't a personal issue — Ross versus Roger — it was a policy issue for the nation. If he could make people see that GM had been misguided, the resulting outcry might spark a change; it wasn't possible to predict how a situation like that might play out. All he could do was keep saying as loudly and clearly as possible that hundreds and thousands of American jobs and livelihoods were at risk at GM — and hope a reaction followed.

In an effort to maximize his public exposure in the days following the buyout, Perot agreed to appear on NBC's *Meet the Press,* ABC's *Business World,* and PBS's *MacNeil-Lehrer Report.* On Sunday morning, December 7, ABC correspondents Dan Cordtz and Sander Vanocur pressed Perot in a televised interview to tell them what he had in mind for GM now that he had been bought out. Did he have a plan, like MacArthur, to return?

Perot hinted there might be more to come (without specifying from whence) and offered the interviewers his populist message, which he felt was sure to play well before a large TV audience: Don't blame workers for U.S. industrial woes, he said, blame the leaders; workers can't make policy and they can't perform to their potential unless leaders find a way to tap it. No one needed help figuring out which leaders he was talking about.

The same day, in Washington, Smith was playing host to Ronald and Nancy Reagan at a GM-sponsored evening of music and entertainment at the Kennedy Center for the Performing Arts. A few hours before showtime, Jack McNulty, GM's vice president of public relations, went to Smith's room at the Ritz-Carlton to review plans for the evening, as well as the next day's script for the Economic Club lunch in Detroit.

"I've got a couple of zingers for you to use against Perot," McNulty said. "People around GM have been giving them to me, Roger."

GM was suffering a royal bashing at Perot's hands. The troops were dying for Smith to strike back, McNulty told him. He showed the GM chairman a list of some verbal jabs he had prepared for use at the Economic Club. One was an introduction calling Perot "the mouse that roared."

Smith scanned McNulty's list: "I'm not going to do it, Jack. I'll keep these in mind and if the occasion demands I'll use them, but I don't want to provoke the man."

After the performance at the Kennedy Center, Smith and McNulty flew back together to Detroit on the GM jet.

Monday, the morning of the Economic Club speech, was gray and drizzly in Detroit. Smith informed McNulty that he wanted to meet Perot's plane when it landed at city airport. The PR man volunteered to go along to deal with reporters if they showed up. Smith declined.

When Perot's plane landed, Smith went out to greet Perot. "Sorry we couldn't give you better weather, Ross," he said pleasantly.

Perot responded just as pleasantly, behaving just as obliviously as Smith to the events of the past two years. A car full of EDS managers was at the airport to greet him. He got into their car, while Smith rode back to town alone in the back of his black Cadillac limousine.

The original 900 or so reservations, a typical response for an Economic Club luncheon, swelled to more than 2,000 in response to the heated published exchanges between Perot and Smith in November. The Economic Club finally cut off lunch reservations for Perot's speech at 7,124: Cobo Hall kitchens simply weren't able to feed more people at one sitting. (President Reagan had drawn the second-biggest Economic Club crowd ever in 1982 when 6,800 showed up to hear his address.)

Smith dutifully played host at a preluncheon reception for dignitaries. The last months of fighting with Perot clearly had taken their toll on the GM chairman. He looked drawn, the pale skin on his face mottled with the crimson eruptions that always signaled when he was nervous or tense. But he forced a brave smile as he stood in line pumping the hands of Detroit notables. Nearby loomed a brawny GM security man, pressed into service to protect Smith in the unlikely event of a scuffle.

Perot handled the swarm of reporters with his usual ease, using mildly barbed answers and winks to telegraph his lingering anger over the events leading to his departure. But he avoided any naked threats. In the press conference before his speech he told the news people, "GM ought to have a car that can ice-skate," considering the money the company spent on research. He insisted that Smith and the directors had thrown $700 million "at a guy who didn't want it." He had been preparing formally to oppose GM's bonus system just before he was bought out, he told reporters, leaving them to wonder if GM executives might have engineered the buyout to protect their bonuses.

As usual, Perot was great copy and wonderful grist for the cartoonists.

His vocabulary, timing, and folksy humor were a public relations dream. By lunch, most of the reporters were laughing at his jokes, almost as if by arrangement. Only a few continued to express skepticism about whether someone who had just received more than $700 million from GM really had a right to feel regret about anything. One or two suspected that the show of anger against GM was all part of a giant ruse by Perot to hide a longtime desire for a payoff.

When the press conference and reception were over, Perot and Smith entered the huge Cobo Hall convention hall together. Before them, the mass of people and TV cameras gave the room the air of a giant political rally. Anyone who expected to see rhetorical fisticuffs from Perot and Smith was disappointed.

The GM chairman was the perfect host. He and Perot sat next to each other on the raised dais in front of the crowd, chatting as amiably as if they had just been introduced at a Kiwanis meeting. Obviously it was no place to argue. Every eye in the cavernous hall strained for a view of them.

When Smith stood to deliver the formal introduction, he overflowed with praise, describing his former ally — without a trace of irony — as "a remarkable human being," and likening him to Winston Churchill. His words seemed comically dishonest, given the open combativeness of the previous week.

In his turn at the podium, Perot sidestepped the chance to skewer Smith and the GM system. He delivered his stump speech instead, a patriotic ode to American ingenuity. Standing in the capital of auto country, on terrain he had left behind when he agreed to the buyout, he wanted the public to know that his agenda had been noble, his exit from the stage of American business only temporary; he wanted to convince people that no matter what anyone said, his fight with GM had always been — would always be — about winning and creating jobs, not about power or ego or money.

Perot didn't mention GM once. Instead he lamented, once more, the decline of American competitiveness. His hyperbole was grand, his speaking style polished. The audience, which contained not a few workers from EDS and GM, was rapt; it gave him a thundering ovation when he finished. Small wonder he had evoked the dedication that had made EDS a great company, small wonder the entire star-crossed episode had grown from Roger Smith's admiration of him.

It was one thing to ridicule GM executive bonuses, to accuse the generals of donning gold braid while the soldiers walked barefoot in the snow; it was quite another to offer a workable alternative for transforming the system. Yet he had offered the troops at GM — again and again during the previous two years — the opportunity to embrace EDS fully, to accept EDS's operating ethos and his ideas about organizing a team effort, competitive attitudes, and compensation geared to incentive and motivation.

If Perot ultimately failed at GM, it was his and EDS's failure to win the hearts and minds of auto country, represented by many of the people in the hall before him. Could he have succeeded in a role at GM with real authority and power? What would have happened if Roger Smith had said yes to EDS's compensation package and ordered his auditors to leave EDS alone? Would chaos have reigned if some executive perks were eliminated and worker and managerial bonuses were tied to the same formula?

What was sure was this: the working people, bureaucracy-bound managers and menial laborers alike, were enchanted by the simplicity of his style and the inspiration bound up in his message. Had a vote been held at the Economic Club on December 8, 1986, Perot would have been elected. Unfortunately, his biggest fans were the disenfranchised.

TWENTY-THREE

You Say Goodbye and I Say Hello

Having chosen exile from EDS and GM, Ross Perot was a wealthy but bitterly disappointed man during the closing days of 1986. As far as he was concerned, the company he had founded and poured himself into for twenty-four years was lost in action. EDS was gone, beyond the reach of any rescue team.

Clearly Perot had won the rhetorical skirmishes with GM during the final days. Those who had listened knew why he had taken the money and given up his stock. The only way to have fought GM was to have risked destroying EDS.

The swell of public opinion ran in his favor even on GM's home turf. A readers' poll in *Ward's Auto World* elicited a 96 percent positive response to the question of whether the car company should have listened to Perot's ideas. Letters to the editor of the *Detroit Free Press* ran 88 percent in his favor. The hometown *Automotive News* published an editorial calling GM a ''loser'' for feeling so threatened by Perot that it was compelled to spend megamillions of capital to banish him.

By an overwhelming margin, investors seemed to side with Perot, too. An important group of institutional managers, custodians of large holdings of GM stock by pension funds and mutual funds, were angry and demanded an explanation from GM management. To them, Perot appeared to be just the in-house critic GM had needed to improve its faltering performance. The institutions owned GM stock primarily for the purpose of receiving the historically safe quarterly cash dividend. Some appreciation in stock price would have been a welcome change. Instead, Perot's buyout caused a big selloff, costing the institutions hundreds of millions of dollars in paper losses. The investment managers wondered if more bad news was on the way, perhaps a cut in the dividend on GM common stock.

Holders of GM Class E shares were likewise hurt by the slide in share value; many were furious that GM did not extend the same favorable treatment for their stock that Perot had received.

Gershon Kekst, the New York public relations man who early in the conflict had urged Perot's ouster, now warned Smith and Johnson — as had John Gutfreund — that negative investor reaction to the buyout was not to be taken lightly. Kekst advised GM to move swiftly and decisively to explain the reasons for its actions. The worst thing GM could do would be to maintain haughty silence, for that would only confirm a picture of weakness and indecision at the top and, perhaps, a tendency to retreat from a fight.

It hadn't escaped Kekst's notice that T. Boone Pickens, Jr., the peripatetic takeover player from Amarillo, seized the occasion of the Perot buyout to lambast GM management publicly. Calling Perot "the best acquisition GM made in my lifetime," Pickens sounded very much as he did in 1983 when he attacked Gulf Oil Corporation, the industrial giant (and Kekst client) driven into a white knight merger with Standard Oil of California. It was only a matter of time, Kekst believed, before Pickens or Carl Icahn or some other takeover artist was tempted to hold up an apparently vulnerable GM management.

The storm Kekst predicted was not long in gathering. Two weeks after the buyout, the Council for Institutional Investors, a group whose forty member funds controlled several million GM and Class E shares, invited Smith and Perot each to explain their positions with respect to the buyout. Harrison J. Goldin, New York City comptroller and cochairman of the group, told reporters his group was displeased with GM. The Wisconsin Investment Board, another member of the council, reacted angrily to Wisconsin's $5 million paper loss in GM Class E shares; a spokesman declared that shareholders "will continue to be shorn like sheep," unless they acted more forthrightly. The council's meeting in Washington, D.C., was a golden chance for Roger Smith to reassure investors and restore lost credibility.

Incredibly, Smith flubbed his first opportunity to explain GM's position by failing to show up at the meeting as scheduled. For reasons that were never clearly explained, Goldin and the press received word that Smith was coming, while GM maintained that he never intended to appear.

On the day of the meeting, an unseasonably warm December 17 in the capital, sleek GM limousines pulled up in front of the National Trust for Historical Preservation on Massachusetts Avenue, depositing Don Atwood, Elmer Johnson, Les Alberthal, and GM treasurer Leon Krain.

As TV cameramen and reporters elbowed each other for a good spot near the curb to view the expected dramatic arrival of Perot's limousine, the once and future Texas businessman came striding down the street from the opposite direction and stood at the back of the crowd, looking for all the world like an out-of-town computer salesman on his way to a convention. It took a few comic moments for newsmen who didn't know Perot to realize the guy who had arrived on foot, without entourage or ceremony and carrying his own briefcase, was the one they were supposed to photograph and question.

When Goldin realized Smith wasn't going to appear at the meeting he hit the roof. A political animal reared in New York City's partisan wars, Goldin derived his prestige at that moment not from any ability to determine GM's competence in the Perot affair but from his power to command the presence of Perot and the chairman of the world's biggest industrial concern. Perot appeared pleased to be there, grateful for the chance to again make his case. But Smith, by his failure to show up, conveyed arrogance. He had sent only his hired hands.

"We have a right as major holders of GM stock to hear an explanation from the chairman. If we can't hear it from this chairman, then maybe some other chairman," Goldin declared ominously. During the break, Johnson called Smith to warn him Goldin was on the warpath; Smith quickly agreed to a private meeting as soon as it could be set up. The realization finally was sinking in. GM's public constituencies were demanding answers.

The meeting in Washington was the first of a series of meetings in early 1987 between GM executive delegations headed by Smith and institutional investors to explain GM's reasons for ousting Perot.

Smith argued that the buyout had served a legitimate business purpose, because the relationship with Perot had broken down and had to be terminated cleanly. If GM had paid a premium price for the stock, it was only a small one. Perot had flouted principles of good corporate governance, he said, refused to be audited, tried to institute ruinous compensation packages for his own executives. Perot sold his company to GM and then refused to act in accordance with rules instituted for the greater good for all shareholders, not just GM Class E shareholders and his circle of confederates.

GM also packaged its description of Perot's misdeeds into a letter to individual shareholders who wrote questioning the buyout. The letter stated that Perot had been seeking a buyout since early 1986 and that he had never shown any reservations about a buyout until a moment after it was approved by the board.

In December and January more than a dozen GM and GM Class E shareholders filed lawsuits challenging the buyout in various state and federal jurisdictions. By a strange twist of fate and the law, Perot was named a codefendant with GM in most of the actions, though his self-appointed role had been shareholder advocate.

As in the vast majority of cases of shareholder litigation against large corporations, the lawsuits against Perot and GM stood little likelihood of winning more than legal fees for plaintiffs' attorneys. Elmer Johnson and Ira Millstein had prepared scrupulously for legal action well in advance. By pointing to the impartial deliberations of the oversight committee, GM lawyers faced a relatively easy task of proving that the directors had decided honestly and faithfully on the best course for GM when they chose to buy out Perot. Whether it was the smartest way was problematic, but the lawyers could argue strongly that it was legal.

Despite Perot's rhetorical victory, the only vote that counted in the contest for corporate power belonged to Roger Smith and the lawyers.

The man who refused to leave the EDS prisoners in Iran had been forced to leave his people behind at GM.

A few of the senior officers of EDS threw a small going-away party for him in early 1987, presenting him with a telescope so he could keep an eye on them. He promised them there would always be a place for them if they got tired of GM. The buyout agreement would allow him to soon go back into business and hire them. Perot gave up his office and moved out of EDS headquarters. He took up new quarters a few blocks away in the Park Central neighborhood of North Dallas, with the telescope next to his window overlooking EDS headquarters.

He was biding his time. Perot had relatively little to do but fiddle with more than $2 billion worth of personal investments, which were managed by the company set up for that task, The Perot Group. The Perot Group had three divisions, petroleum investments, real estate investments, and cash and bonds. Perhaps anticipating the crash of late October, he was suspicious of the runaway bull market and wouldn't touch stocks.

Perot's investment ideas sometimes sprang from odd places. One evening a few weeks after the buyout, Perot was watching a public television show about Steven Jobs's project to build educational computers.

Like Perot, Jobs had been forced to leave the company he helped found, Apple Computer, in a corporate power play. Perot was so taken by Jobs's spirit and his determination to regroup and build an educational computer that he called him to let him know that he would be glad to help.

When Jobs called a month later to say he needed investment capital, Perot dispatched Mort Meyerson, Tom Walter, and Bill Gayden to Jobs's home near San Francisco to examine his operation. (Walter and Gayden were working for The Perot Group; Meyerson was working in his own investment company.)

Jobs invited the three ex-EDS executives to his offbeat home, which featured a Harley-Davidson motorcycle planted in the center of the living room as a piece of art.

The men were impressed with Next, Inc., Jobs's company. In early February 1987, Perot wrote a $20 million check to buy a 16 percent stake in Jobs's business. Next was precisely the kind of project that appealed to Perot. It was an advanced educational workstation that would be able to bring the wisdom of many teachers to colleges and universities across the land. In addition to a computer screen, the Next workstation would run audio and video. Carnegie Mellon University and Stanford University, anxious to develop the workstation for their students, also invested.

To Perot's delight, Jobs spoke of Next's commitment to manufacturing the workstations in the United States.

"If we aren't able to make what we invent we might as well start learning to speak Japanese," Mr. Jobs told the *Wall Street Journal*.

The uproar in markets and the press about GM's weaknesses flared for a few months following the buyout.

Public relations expert Gershon Kekst counseled Smith to have faith that the vituperation would run its course if GM took decisive action to improve its image. GM's business prospects, freed from Perot's interference, were a mixed bag at best. Still, the company desperately needed to show a more positive face to investors and the car-buying public.

Hence, GM threw a gala presentation for security analysts in the spring of 1987 heralding the newly tooled Linden, New Jersey, Chevrolet Corsica/Beretta assembly plant. During two days of meetings, Smith painted a rosy picture of GM's future profitability, describing a parade of new and exciting cars and trucks slated for introduction through 1990. He promised to use GM's financial strength to buy back from the public up to 20 percent of GM's common stock.

But the big bombshell from the meeting was Smith's promise to cut more than $10 billion from GM's costs in the coming years, a figure that sent analysts scurrying for pencils and calculators to total the potential impact on future profits. Smith's cost-cutting message reassured investors and resulted in several recommendations by analysts to buy and accumulate GM stock. The share value soared about $25 a share between the analysts meeting and the October 19 crash.

GM introduced several new and significant vehicles to the market in 1986 and 1987: the Corsica and Beretta; the Buick Regal, the first of a new line of midsize cars; and a new GMC and Chevrolet pickup truck. While praising improvements in the new vehicles, critics generally cautioned that GM still wasn't matching the best Japan had to offer.

A month or so after the analysts' meeting, Smith tapped Robert Stempel, an engineer with solid grounding in vehicle mechanical systems and with experience running Chevrolet and GM's European operations, to replace the retiring Jim McDonald as president. Because Stempel's engineering specialty was the automotive product itself — engines, suspensions, transmissions — rather than the manufacturing process, the promotion was viewed positively by automotive analysts as enhancing GM's chances of improving its market position, which had sunk to a disastrous 36 percent of the domestic market, a post–World War II low.

At the same time that he promoted Stempel, Smith promoted Elmer Johnson to executive vice president and nominated him to the GM board of directors, a step closer to the chairman's seat. The promotion added Johnson to a group of three men — Stempel, Lloyd Reuss, and Alan Smith — theoretically in line to succeed Smith as chief executive when he retired in 1990. At the 1987 GM annual meeting of shareholders, Smith announced a modification of the company's executive bonus system. The cash portion of the bonus was dropped in favor of stock, a move that appeared to tie managerial rewards closer to performance of the company.

Perhaps Ross Perot had managed to leave his mark on GM after all.

*   *   *

When he first joined GM, Elmer Johnson told Roger Smith that he did not intend to be an armchair philosopher.

By late 1987 GM's decline in the marketplace had not been halted. Johnson, who previously had been in charge of all personnel functions, pressed Smith to allow sweeping organizational changes. Convinced that GM was being slowed down by mediocre talent at the top, Johnson wanted Smith's authorization to fire about 20 percent of GM's top 500 executives, men earning $125,000 a year and more.

Smith wouldn't allow it. He was convinced he could turn GM around without that sort of tumult.

Johnson also opposed Roger Smith on Saturn. With far too much vehicle-making capacity in North America already, he believed the time wasn't right to be building a new plant in Tennessee. It was a risky tack to oppose Smith in front of the board of directors on what clearly was his pet project, but Johnson felt he didn't have to keep quiet to prove his loyalty. He had defended Smith against Perot despite some natural sympathies he had for Perot's point of view.

Others on the GM board had reservations about Saturn as well, but no one stood by Johnson's side when he challenged Smith on Saturn before the board of directors in late 1987. The directors, not surprisingly, supported the chairman.

In early 1988 GM was ready for another public relations pick-me-up. A $20 million three-way extravaganza at the Waldorf-Astoria during the first week in January for 14,000 invited guests focused on future car and truck products. Inside GM they called the exhibition ''Rogerama,'' a lavish recapitulation of the chairman's modernization program and an effort to repair GM's badly tarnished image. (In *Fortune* magazine's most-admired list, GM had dropped to 254 from 16 in two years.) The underlying message of the show was that GM was being unfairly vilified and wasn't getting credit for the investments and their inevitable payoff.

''Rogerama,'' ironically, turned out to be an opportunity for Bob Stempel to prove his mettle on center stage. A tall, commanding figure, Stempel handled himself with aplomb in the public spotlight. While Smith seemed flustered by some of the hostile questions he received at the show, Stempel answered them forthrightly and smoothly in a booming voice. He looked very much a logical successor to Smith.

Elmer Johnson, meanwhile, also had succession on his mind. He sought a greater mandate than he had been given, but after five years at GM he remained an outsider and an object of suspicion in a culture that felt alien to him.

Johnson needed Roger Smith's support and the backing of top executives around him to stay a powerful player in the inner circle. The bid to stop Saturn had hurt his standing with his peers. Like Perot, Johnson remained convinced that GM — despite the show at the Waldorf — was floundering. He believed he had the organizational talent to run GM. But in order to be a credible successor to Roger Smith — or, at the very least a member of the top team — he needed to demonstrate that he could wield power and authority.

To gain critical automotive experience, Johnson tried to convince Smith to let him run the gigantic Chevrolet-Pontiac-GM of Canada vehicle-making group. Either he was going to be allowed to make a difference, he told Smith, or he was going to leave.

And so, when his bid to run the Chevrolet-Pontiac-GM of Canada group died for lack of Roger Smith's interest, Elmer Johnson resigned from the corporation. His former law partners at Kirkland and Ellis in Chicago welcomed him home.

Mort Meyerson's stake in EDS had made him financially comfortable long before the merger with GM. But because of his participation in the Perot buyout on approximately the same terms as Perot, Meyerson realized a windfall of nearly $30 million for his GM Class E stock.

Money was not a big part of his agenda. At the age of forty-eight, Meyerson wanted another opportunity or venture as challenging as EDS had been. He was not sure how, he was not sure what it was. He approached the problem analytically, in the same manner he had approached EDS's business problems.

Until Meyerson found the answer, he accepted the unpaid job of coordinating efforts to attract the $12 billion federal "supercollider" scientific project to Texas. Annette Strauss, the mayor of Dallas, asked Meyerson to take charge of promoting Dallas as a center of international trade; he agreed.

Meyerson also worked to complete construction of Dallas's new symphony hall, to which Ross Perot had donated $10 million on condition it be called the Morton H. Meyerson Symphony Hall.

He relaxed a bit more than usual, rode his bicycle a lot, and spent time with his wife and two children at their home in Dallas and at their retreat in Santa Fe, New Mexico.

The February 1988 edition of *Fortune* magazine pictured Ross Perot on the cover next to a headline reading: "How I Would Turn Around GM."

More than a year after the buyout, Perot continued to speak out about the importance to the national economy of "cleaning up the mess" inside the world's biggest automaker. In a blunt 2,500-word manifesto, he called for the firing of all authoritarian managers, the scrapping of the cumbersome committee system, and the abolition of the lavish legacy of GM's glory. Close the fourteenth-floor headquarters in Detroit and the ornate boardroom in New York, he urged.

Executives, newly focused on beating Ford, Chrysler, and the Japanese, should fan out to the factories and engineering studios, where the real work was being done. The leaders should build a team with one mission: to manufacture the world's finest cars at the lowest price. All GM's outside directors should be replaced with directors who owned a significant personal stake in the company.

Perot's article never blamed Roger Smith for any of GM's problems or for the conflict that led to the buyout. In fact, he complimented Smith for his creativity. The last thing he wanted was to foster the impression that his beef with GM had been a personal feud. Revitalizing GM was the point, ensuring jobs and securing prosperity for the future.

Thoughts of EDS and how he had lost it were never far from his mind. He could see his old headquarters every day from his office window. And he was always receiving telephone calls and visits from men at EDS who once had worked for him. Some calls were purely friendship. Others were meant to let him know that nothing was the same for them since he and Meyerson had left. GM, to be sure, hadn't taken any drastic steps to dismantle EDS's operating procedures, they told him. Business was quite strong. The GM operating divisions had signed contracts to buy EDS services, along the lines of the compromise worked out two years earlier. But the excitement that Perot's inspiring leadership had provided was gone. Perot encouraged them to keep marching forward.

That spring, Perot received a telephone call out of the blue from Anthony Frank, the new Postmaster General. Frank knew of Perot and EDS's expertise and asked him if he would like to think about ideas to streamline the U.S. Postal Service. Perot laughed: if ever there was a bureaucracy bigger, more hidebound, and more in need of streamlining than GM, it was the Postal Service.

There was no use in being coy. Perot had had very little to do since the buyout. He didn't enjoy coming to the office each day looking for something to do. He needed action. Helping the Postal Service was just the sort of grand challenge that appealed to him. It was monumental, like reforming education in Texas.

At the same time, it occurred to Perot that a consulting job for the Postal Service also might provide the perfect opportunity to spring some of the younger EDS managers who had come to him and said they were bored, the managers he had left behind and who needed a way out of GM. Les Alberthal and the senior officers wouldn't be looking to leave EDS and he wasn't about to provoke Roger Smith by offering them jobs, even though he would soon be entitled to do so under the terms of the buyout contract.

Perot's understanding of the buyout agreement with GM was that eighteen months after the buyout he was free to start a data processing company on a nonprofit basis, as long as it remained nonprofit for eighteen months. That was his understanding when he signed the contract and that is what his lawyers told him he would be free to do. He further understood that he could hire anyone he wanted from EDS to work for his nonprofit company. Tom Luce had ensured this freedom, and Perot had discussed it with EDS's officers before he agreed to the buyout. He wanted them to know they would have an escape hatch if life at GM became unbearable.

Perot's wealth permitted him to capitalize a new company with ease, although it perforce would be tiny, certainly not the size or importance that would anger Roger Smith or former EDSers.

His new outfit might be small, Perot thought devilishly, but it would be the absolute best at what it did.

On June 1, 1988, exactly eighteen months to the day after he signed the papers selling his Class E shares to GM, Perot announced the formation of HWGA Partners, which stood for Here We Go Again, the parent of a new data-services company to be called Perot Systems Corporation.

Perot decided to stay away from active management. He hired a few dozen EDS managers to run Perot Systems and set aside a significant portion of stock for them as an incentive to make the new company perform in an outstanding fashion. He hadn't a clue how the contract with the Postal Service would work out, whether it would provide enough revenue to keep Perot Systems busy or whether there would be more contracts in the future.

But Perot knew that whatever happened to his new company, he again was swimming in the middle of a vigorous, competitive enterprise, and that excited him. If the past had been any lesson, life from now on promised to be anything but dull.

Postscript

O N June 19, 1988, three weeks after Ross Perot announced the formation of his new company, EDS asked the government's General Services Administration to void the $500,000 consulting contract Perot Systems had signed with the Postal Service. EDS claimed the contract wasn't bid properly.

After the government agency hearings and legal skirmishing in court, the GSA temporarily suspended the contract.

On September 27, 1988, EDS filed a lawsuit against Perot and Perot Systems, charging that Perot had violated his $700 million buyout agreement with GM. The suit charged that Perot Systems was competing illegally in the data-services field for a profit and was engaging in "predatory" hiring of EDS employees.

Perot denied the charges.

GM maintained that the lawsuit against Perot was filed according to the wishes of EDS's management, not those of GM's management or Roger Smith.

Angry because he believed GM was reneging on its agreement to let him start a new company, Perot filed a countersuit against GM and EDS in Texas state court, alleging antitrust violations. Perot Systems also announced it intended to bid for the Texas Medicaid contract held by EDS.

On December 19, 1988, the U.S. Postal Service announced that it was dropping its proposed contract with Perot Systems Corporation, citing procedural difficulties. Perot, meanwhile, disclosed that he was hiring more people and had signed several data processing contracts.

A trial date for EDS's lawsuit against Ross Perot was set for early April 1989 in Fairfax, Virginia, state court.

Bibliography

In addition to the books listed hereunder, this book was based on articles previously published in the *Wall Street Journal, New York Times, Dallas Times-Herald, Dallas Morning News, Business Week,* and *Fortune.*

Brooks, John. *The Go-Go Years.* New York: Weybright and Talley, 1973.

Cray, Ed. *Chrome Colossus.* New York: McGraw-Hill Book Co., 1980.

Drucker, Peter F. *Adventures of a Bystander.* New York: Harper & Row, 1978.

————. *Concept of the Corporation.* New York: The John Day Company, 1946; revised edition, 1972.

Follett, Ken. *On Wings of Eagles.* New York: William Morrow and Co., 1983.

Gustin, Lawrence R. *Billy Durant: Creator of General Motors.* Grand Rapids, Michigan: William B. Eerdmans Publishing Co., 1973.

Lee, Albert. *Call Me Roger.* Chicago: Contemporary Books, 1987.

Reich, Cary. *Financier.* New York: William Morrow and Co., 1983.

Sloan, Alfred P., Jr. *My Years with General Motors.* New York: Doubleday & Co., 1963.

Wright, J. Patrick. *On a Clear Day You Can See General Motors.* New York: Avon Books, 1979.

Yates, Brock. *The Decline and Fall of the Automobile Industry.* New York: Random House, 1983.

Index